L'Internationale
Post-War Avant-Gardes
Between 1957 and 1986

B. Moments

Arrays of Internationalism

Close

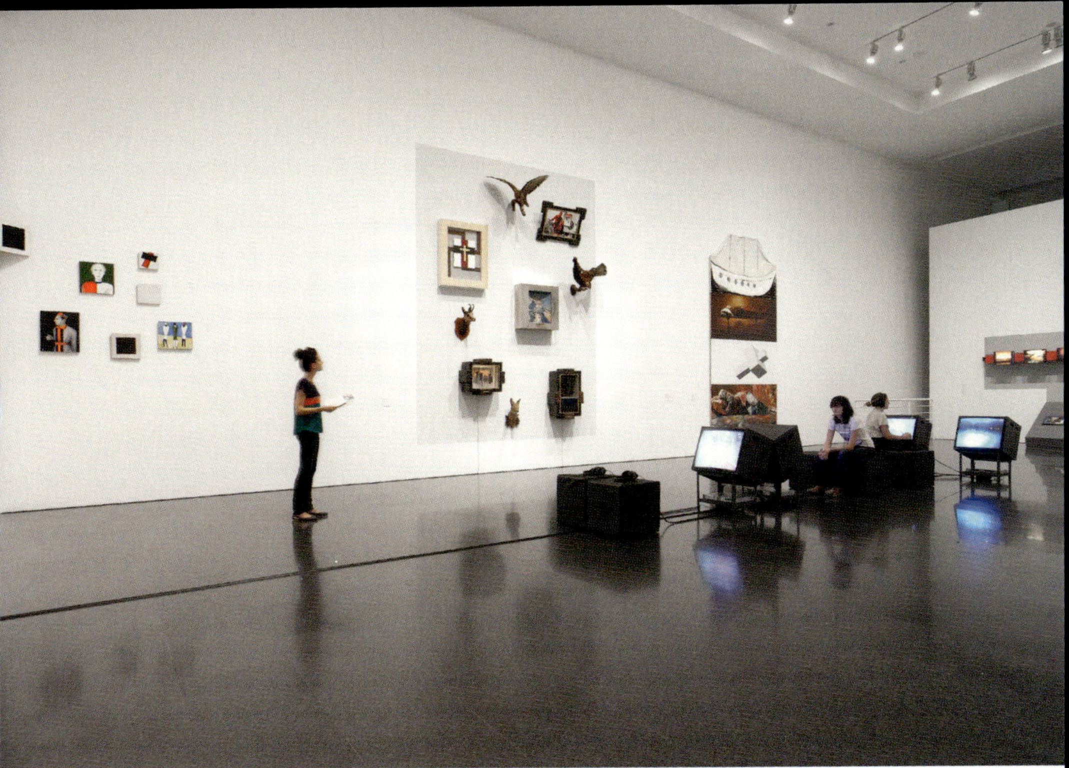

Museum of Parallell Narratives. In the Framework of L'Internationale exhibition, MACBA, 2011, Photo by Rafael Vargas

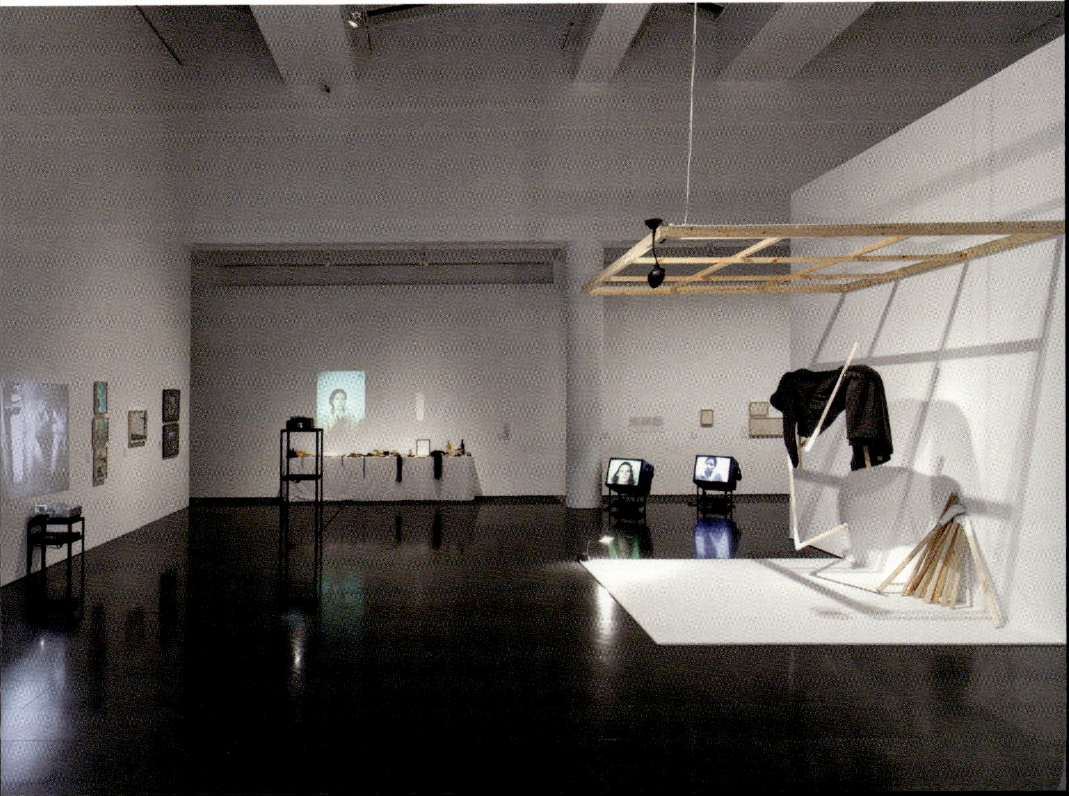

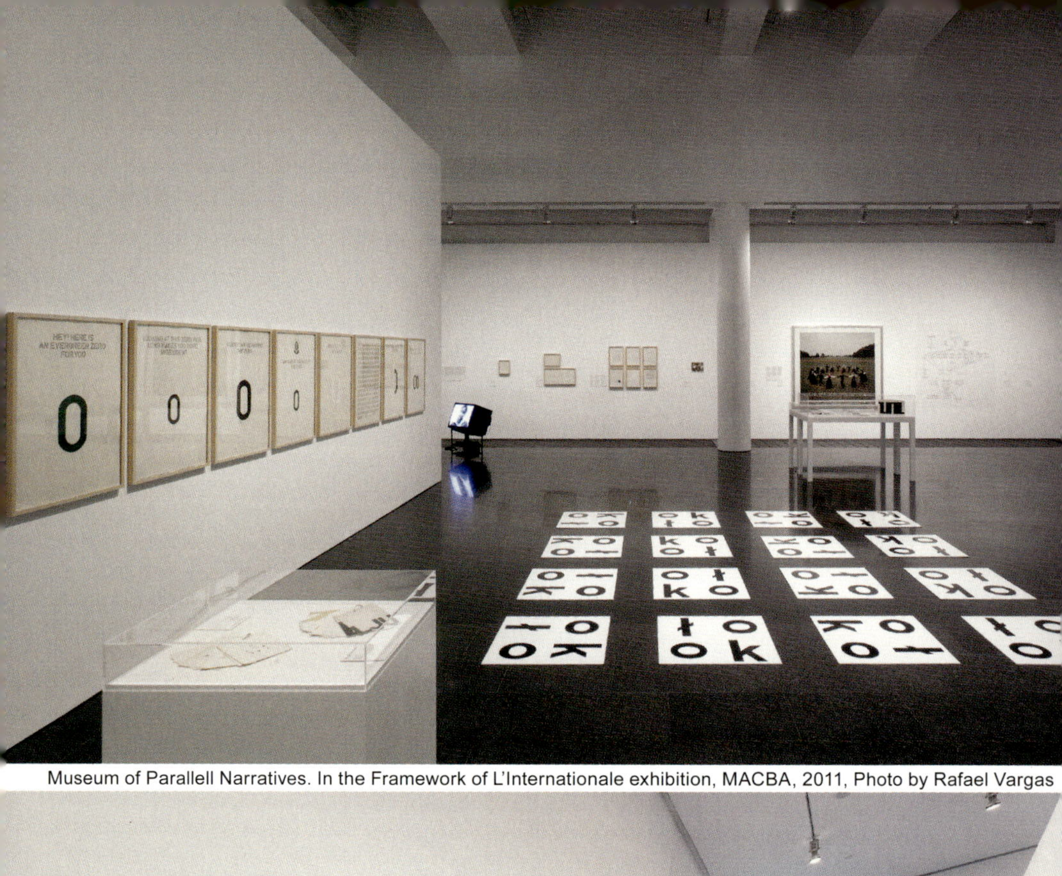

Museum of Parallell Narratives. In the Framework of L'Internationale exhibition, MACBA, 2011, Photo by Rafael Vargas

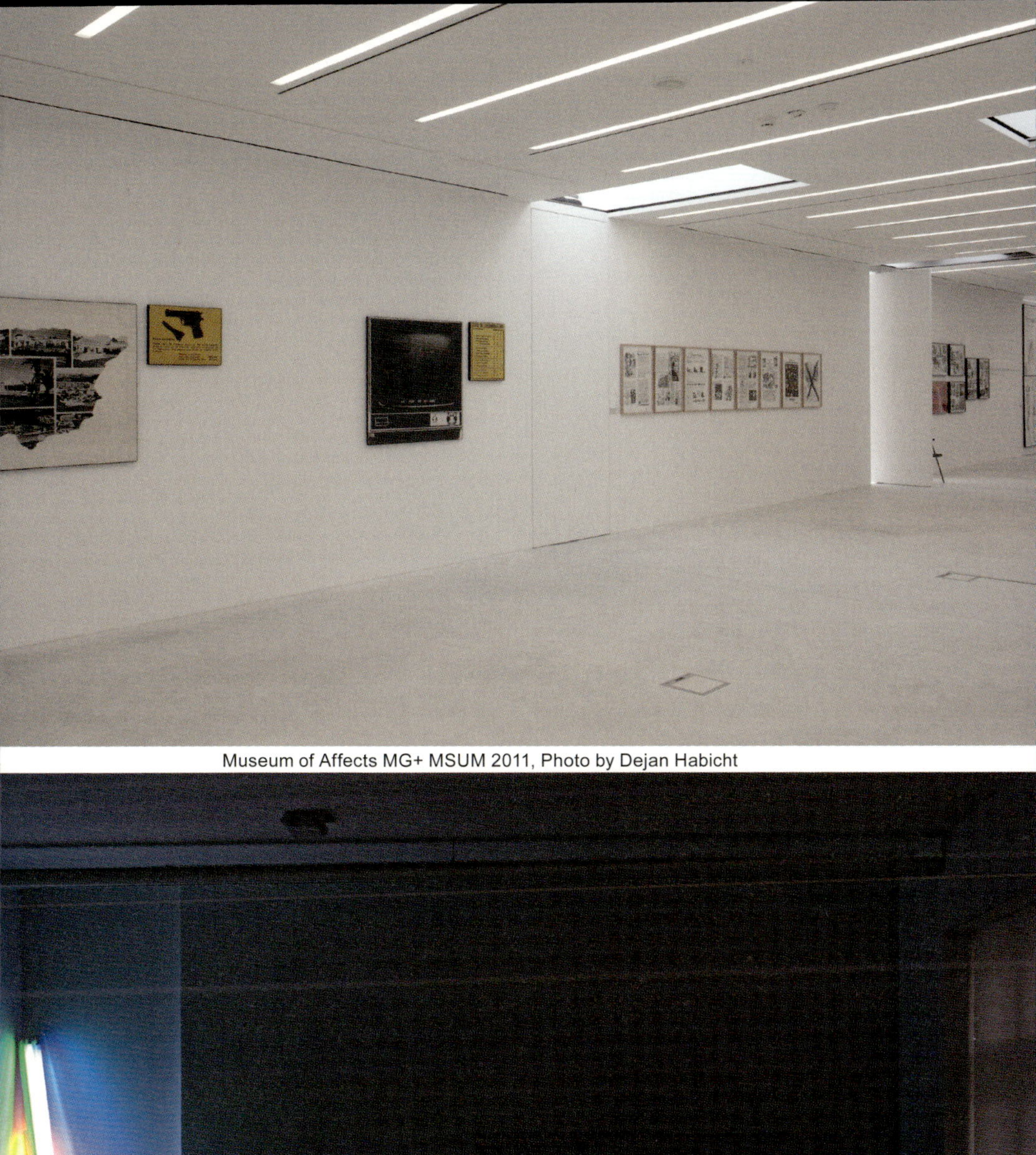

Museum of Affects MG+ MSUM 2011, Photo by Dejan Habicht

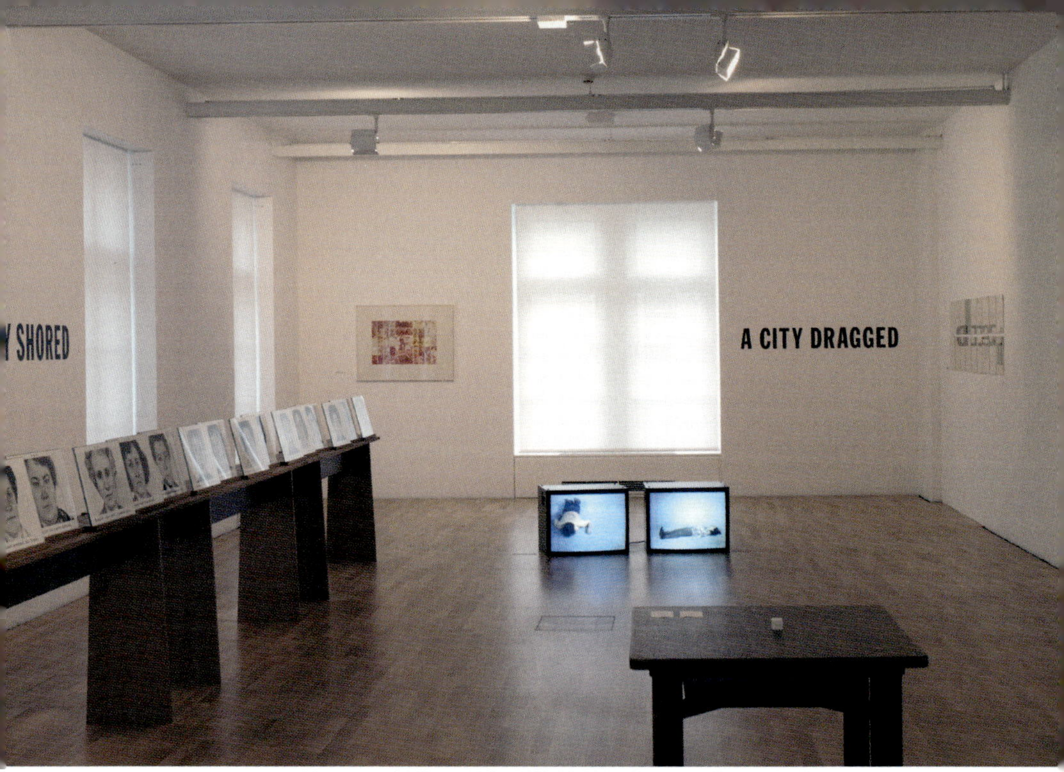

Museum of Affects MG+ MSUM 2011, Photo by Dejan Habicht

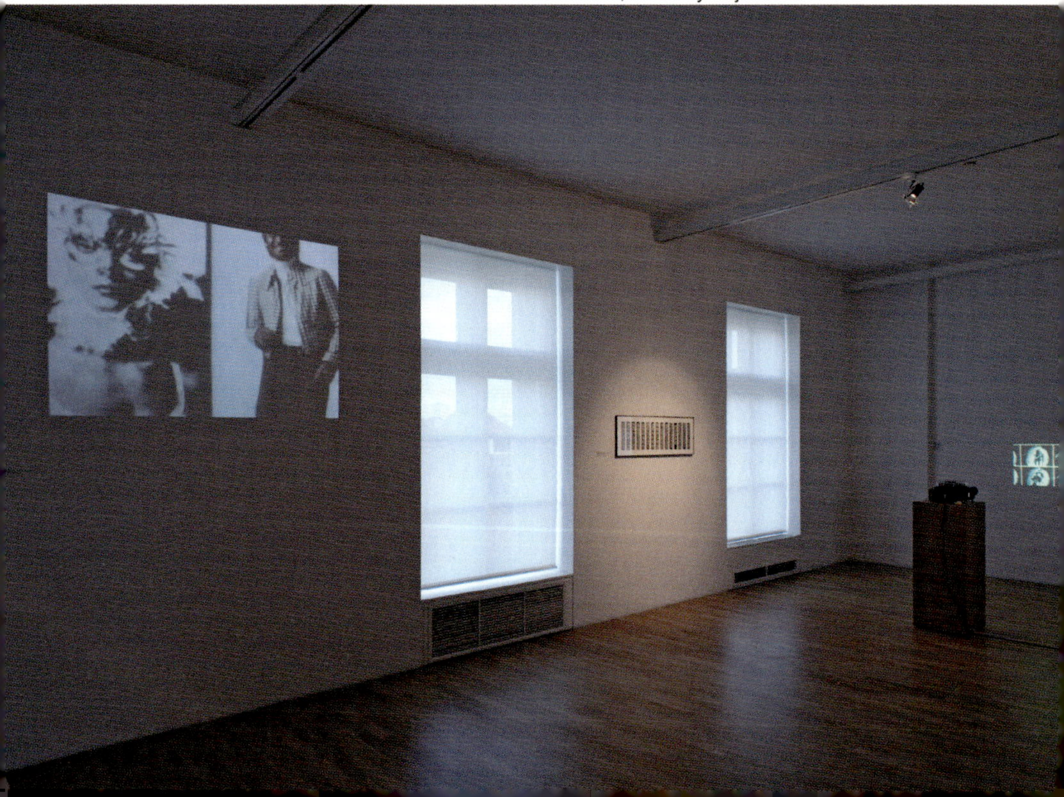

Museum of Parallel Narratives, Museu d'Art Contemporani de Barcelona (MACBA), Barcelona (2011)

The exhibition *Museum of Parallel Narratives* presents a selection of works from the Arteast 2000+ Collection of the Moderna galerija in Ljubljana, the first-ever collection of postwar avant-garde Eastern European art, and seeks to discover what sort of art system, if any, accompanied the production, presentation and musealization of these artworks. *Museum of Parallel Narratives* speaks of artists who worked on the edges of a well-ordered world and its art system, and, indeed, addresses its own position at the edge of an era that has seen an acceleration in the establishment of an art system in the space that can still be justifiably called "Eastern Europe". The exhibition is also connected with the principal idea behind the wide-ranging project, L'Internationale, of which it forms a part.

With all of these elements, the exhibition goes beyond the usual attempts to present Eastern European art, which in the main have sought only to offer a condensed version of the art of the region, without engaging with the complexities of its context. While providing a comprehensive overview of postwar avant-garde art in Eastern Europe, *Museum of Parallel Narratives* also sets itself the task of presenting new knowledge about the region. The exhibition draws attention to the fact that museum collections are tools for producing new knowledge and new working methods, and are not only a means for consolidating that which is already known. In this way, museums increasingly acquire, along with their representative function, a performative role as well.

Let us look first at the kind of art that is presented in the exhibition and then at how the micro-politics of this art influences the logic behind what the museum collection does. The exhibition presents sixty-two artists and eight artist groups representing most Eastern Europe countries: it includes more than a hundred works, mostly originating between 1961 and 1986, but also several more recent items. The represented period is in keeping with that of the long-term research program of L'Internationale, which addresses postwar avant-garde art between 1956 and 1986. This was a time when dictatorial regimes of various kinds

presided over a large part of the world, but it was also a period
marked by the postwar belief in a new modern era, one in which
advanced technologies played an increasingly dominant role, the
world was better connected by new transportation and communication systems, and the mass media was gaining power: a time
of both politically and economically isolated spaces and expanding globalization.

While it is true that the postwar avant-garde movements
presented here were opposed to the existing regimes, this opposition was not always expressed through an explicitly political
content. What made them political was the fact that they employed various gestures to create certain micro-political situations. In this regard, the works in the exhibition may be divided
into a number of separate groups.

The first group (Marina Abramović, Geta Brătescu, Ion
Grigorescu, Tibor Hajas, Sanja Iveković, KwieKulik, Jan
Mlčoch, Karel Miler, Petr Štembera, Ilja Šoškić, and Raša
Todosijević) presents body art and other forms of performance
art. In this kind of creative practice, the artists intensified the
experience of social isolation, marginalization, and vulnerabil-
ity. In their performance work these artists consciously relived
everything that characterized the grey, everyday life of socialism, thus making visible the lack of freedom in society and various forms of social pressure.

The second group (Sano Filko, Alex Mlynarčik, and Vlasta
Delimar and Željko Jerman) presents unique forms of happenings and rituals that were based on appropriating the socio-
political reality and its phenomena. These artists were not trying
to change the environment in which they lived; rather, they used
it as a kind of 'found society'. Such happenings represent, essentially, real-time excerpts from the found society, within which
the artists directly observed various relationships, including
themselves, trapped in different social contradictions.

In the third group (Josip Vaništa [Gorgona], Neue Slowenische Kunst groups [IRWIN, Laibach, Scipion Nasice Theatre],
the OHO Group, Walter de Maria and Andrei Monastyrsky) we
find group art actions in which the collective methods of the
work became the central theme of the art. In these works, the
micro-political situations, which acted as a counterweight to the
macro-political environment, become foregrounded. Through
these actions a method of group working was developed that

offered an alternative to the dominant ideology of collectivism. Here, too, belong various self-organized working methods that filled some of the gaps in the still-undeveloped art system.

While under socialism the authorities might tolerate the presentation of so-called unofficial art in marginal spaces such as youth clubs, student centers, artists' studios or private apartments, a much stricter attitude was taken toward events in the public space. As a result, all the actions in the public space that are presented in the fourth group (Braco Dimitrijević, Tomislav Gotovac, Jiří Kovanda, Milan Knižák, Paul Neagu, the OHO Movement [Naško Križnar, Milenko Matanović, David Nez, and Drago Dellabernardina] and Goran Trbuljak) instantly acquired a political, anti-institutional and anti-ideological marking. Many street actions of this kind, whether representing minimal departures from everyday routine or, indeed, provocations, helped passers-by to mentally shift the boundaries of what was permissible.

In the fifth group (Stanislav Droždž, Dimitrije Bašičević Mangelos, Josip Vaništa [Gorgona], Julije Knifer, Miklos Erdely, the OHO Movement [Marko Pogačnik, I. G. Plamen, Franci Zagorčnik], Nuša and Srečo Dragan, Vlado Martek, Jiří Valoh and Endre Tot) we find work in which the use of language and materiality present an opposing position to established modernist forms of art, and which were, in general, directed against the art establishment. By relocating the language of politics into an art context, these artists were usually trying to draw attention to the emptiness of that language. Through visual, concrete poetry and the use of the material aspect of paint, paper and film ribbon, they underscored the independence and non-ideological nature of things in themselves.

Socialist reality was dominated by the imaginary of a drab and mundane existence touched by signs of Western consumerism. In the sixth group (OM Production, Natalia LL, Tomislav Gotovac, Josef Robakowski, and Sanja Iveković and Dalibor Martinis) can be found works that are based on the use of photography, film and video in an investigation of the media image in the socialist socio-political context—a context with little inclination for glamour or spectacular media images. When mass-media images appeared in artworks, they served precisely as comments on the duality that was defined by an ideology of modesty, on the one hand, and unrealized desires for glamour, on the other.

In the decade before the fall of the communist regimes, art became more explicitly political; at the same time, it operated as an important lever of the civil society in its fight for democratic change. The seventh group (Borghesia, Ion Grigorescu, Marina Gržinić and Aina Šmid, Neue Slowenische Kunst [the groups IRWIN, Laibach, New Collectivism and the Scipion Nasice Theatre], Vitaly Komar and Alexander Melamid, Alexander Kosolapov, Mladen Stilinović, Kazimir Malevich of Belgrade, Ilya Kabakov and Vladimir Kupriyanov) takes as its theme various forms of totalitarianism (whether communist, Nazi or capitalist). The retro-avant-garde and Sots artists especially, but also certain representatives of the alternative culture of the 1980s, combine the imaginaries of different totalitarian societies so as to draw attention to the ever stronger and ever more obvious contradictions in socialist society.

The significance of the Arteast 2000+ Collection of the Moderna galerija in Ljubljana lies not only in the fact that it is one of the pioneering collections of Eastern European art, but also in the fact that it originated in the region itself. Thus it heralded a move toward the establishment of an art system in Eastern Europe. The label 'Eastern European art' became a relatively standard term only after the fall of the communist regimes. If, previously, the art of this region shared a similar political context, today, in post-communist times, the similarities and common interests derive from an urgent need to construct a well-functioning art system. One of the essential elements of any art system is the historicization and collecting of the art in a given region. For this reason, the establishment of the Arteast 2000+ Collection represents a watershed in the historicization of Eastern European art. In the formation of alternative, anti-hegemonic positions, the processes of historicization must include not only the history of art but also the history of the social conditions surrounding its production. In the time since the Arteast 2000+ Collection was first conceived, there has been a great deal of research on Eastern European art that now affords us a fairly complex view of the subject. But very little analysis has been devoted to the art system of the region. The *Museum of Parallel Narratives* exhibition offers both a comprehensive presentation—for the first time in ten years—of this pioneering collection of Eastern European art and a new understanding about the lack of a functioning art system in Eastern Europe and the current efforts to establish such a system.

But just as *Museum of Parallel Narratives* does not aim to provide an encyclopedic survey of Eastern European art, it also does not try to describe all the complexities of the problems surrounding an undeveloped art system. Instead, the exhibition focuses primarily on the role of museum collections in this system. The lack of a well-developed art system in Eastern Europe has had at least two important consequences: first, postwar avant-garde art was for the most part absent from Eastern European museums, nor was there any systematic historicization of this art; and second, a number of artists responded to this lack by assuming the role of curators and archivists themselves in order to, at least partially, fill the gaps in their local histories.

Among other things, *Museum of Parallel Narratives* asks how the history of art originates. In order for a work of art to become part of the history of art and its collection, a certain frame of reference must exist for which there must in turn be an art system with an ideological and capital-based framework. In Eastern Europe there was no such framework, at least not in any form that was comparable to the West. We know about certain artists and artworks today, not because we have seen them in museums or read about them in books, but largely because other artists have made reference to them. In this way a parallel history of Eastern European art came into existence. In order to describe how this narrative originated—let's call this narrative self-historicization—along with the artworks from the collection the exhibition presents individual projects by artists who devoted a large part of their creativity to precisely this practice of self-historicization. This term implies an informal system of historicization performed by artists who, lacking a suitable collective history, have been forced to seek their own historical and interpretive contexts. Because the local institutions that should have been systematizing postwar avant-garde art and its traditions either did not exist or were disdainful of such art, these artists were compelled to collect and archive documents associated with their own art, the art of other artists, broader artistic movements or the conditions of producing such art.

A number of significant Eastern European artists, such as Artpool (György Galántai, Júlia Klaniczay), Zofia Kulik, Július Koller and Lia Perjovschi and CAA, devoted a large part of their activities to creating archives that today serve as extremely valuable resources concerning the unofficial art in the various socialist countries as well as its conditions of production. Especially in the 1980s, artists felt a strong need to self-contextualise their own art production. This interest has undergone a resurgence in the past decade, with artists of different generations conceptualising their work as, among other things, a tool of historicization. For the *Museum of Parallel Narratives* exhibition, Alexander Dorner, the IRWIN group and Mladen Stilinović have developed special projects, categorized here as fictive histories. In these projects, the artists—who have often dealt with the processes of historicization in their work—draw particular attention to the ideology of art collections and, at the same time, to the communicative power of art. Their works present fictive mini-collections, as it were, in which connections that not so long ago would have been impossible between Eastern and Western artists are now realizable. These artists were given the task of selecting works from the Van Abbemuseum in Eindhoven and the Museum van Hedendaagse Kunst in Antwerp (M HKA) that belong to the trans-institutional organization L'Internationale. The three projects show us, among other things, that even when the individual works were created in relative isolation, they nevertheless shared a surprisingly extensive commonality with works from other spaces. We can only speculate what it would have been like if, at the time of their creation, it had been possible to see them together in a single museum collection. With these three new projects, the exhibition *Museum of Parallel Narratives*, which itself is one of the projects organized by L'Internationale, is already testing new possibilities for communication between various Eastern and Western collections.

In a special segment of the exhibition, alongside the artworks and their descriptions, are to be found diagrams of the artists relating to the musealization of Eastern European art. These primarily contain information about the presence of works by the individual artists in public and private collections—in the artists' own local spaces, in the West and elsewhere around the world—as represented over the different decades leading to the present; this information is based on questionnaires sent to the individual artists and provides an important report on the workings of the art system in the region. As was to be expected, the representation of individual artists in public and private collections was extremely low before the fall of the communist regimes. Beginning in the 1990s, however, interest in their work, as seen both in local and in foreign collections, grew considerably. Extensive growth could also be seen after 2000, the year the Moderna galerija in Ljubljana established its Eastern European collection. Such an examination of the growing presence of individual artists in art collections also helps us to understand the construction of the Eastern European narrative. Here, of course, the parallel historicization by the artists themselves and their projections for the future have particular significance. And all of this, taken together, forms the vision of a future museum collection based on the resonance between various narratives.

The exhibition *Museum of Parallel Narratives* was conceived around four different narratives: the Collection of Micro-political Situations (Moderna galerija collection), Artists' Diagrams (the non-existence of the art system), Self-histories (four artists' archives), and Fictive Histories (works from L'Internationale museums' collections).

Zdenka Badovinac, curator

U.F.O.– Gallery – Ganek Gallery[1]
Project – Manifesto

[1] Július Koller's archive from the Július Koller Society

U.F.O.-Gallery is the first gallery for Cosmo-humanist culture in the world. It is a communication media between heaven and earth. It is fictitious gallery, which employs attractive mountaineering peak Ganek of High Tatras with its oblique shelf called **"Galéria Ganku" (Ganek Gallery)** as a visual and physical symbol of Cosmo-humanist culture and communication with unknown civilisations of all kinds.

The aim of **U.F.O.-Gallery** is to mediate contact of alternative subjective participations, which is engaged in communication with unknown phenomena both on the Earth and in the Cosmos. The **U.F.O.-Gallery** is a conceptual gallery for alternatives of communication.

Draft of the **U.F.O.-Gallery** statute:
The **U.F.O.-Gallery** has no headquarters; it is constituted by members of committee and project participants; it is a selective

confrontation of called upon or accepted project members; the confrontation is lead by committee members (as well as acceptance of new members); the committee will inform the members about activities and will present the activity of the **U.F.O.-Gallery** in various ways and forms. The visual sign is a photographic picture of **Ganek Gallery** in the High Tatras.

The **U.F.O.-Gallery** Organisational and Consultancy Committee: J. Koller, I. Gazdík, P. Meluzin, P. Breier, M. Adamčiak
Secretary: I. Gazdík

Proposal membership enlargement: R. Matuštík (art critic), R. Sikora (academic painter), J. Meliš (academic sculptor), D. Tóth (academic painter), K. Viceník (research worker), M. Kern (academic painter)

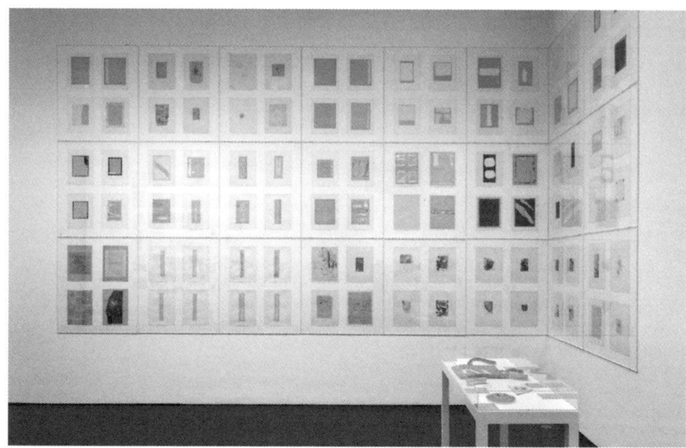

Museum of Parallell Narratives. In the Framework of L'Internationale exhibition, MACBA, 2011. Photo by Rafael Vargas

Artpool
Active Archive 1979–2003

The idea behind the Artpool project is to create an Active Archive built from specific artistic activities. This differs from traditional archival practices in that the Active Archive does not collect solely material existing "out there," the way it operates also generates the very material to be archived. By documenting the thoughts circulating within the worldwide network of free and autonomous art, this live archive is brought into being but still remains invisible to profit-oriented art.

The continuity of Artpool's activity is maintained through publications and the building of personal relationships. Artpool contributes to parallel projects and processes in creative and communicative ways and organises its own events related to its specific topics. The archive expands through calls for projects, co-operation and exchange as well as circulating information and enlarging the network.

The Active Archive is a living institution that can be interpreted as an organic and open artwork or an activist kind of art practice. Its field of operation is the whole world; it works with an exact aim and direction sensitively detecting changes and adjusting accordingly. In the annually renewing program, which after being defined keeps constructing itself through chance, only the essential concept is permanent.

In the course of time the documents accumulated in the Active Archive become subjects of art historical research. The interrelation of historical and art research methodologies improves one's ability, in a way never experienced before, to perceive problems and to venture into new, previously unknown, research methods.

The two main benefits of the Active Archive are that an art oriented toward visions of the future will not separate from its past, and that a dynamic approach to history will

replace a hermetic, futureless one. These two factors represent the basic principles and conditions of paradigm shift in the world of art.

György Galántai

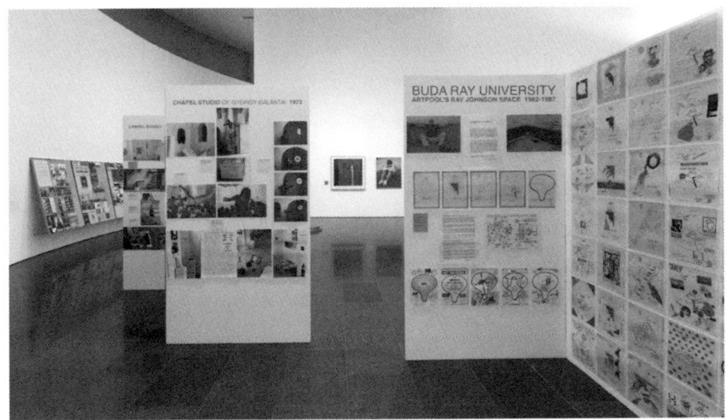

Museum of Parallell Narratives. In the Framework of L'Internationale exhibition, MACBA, 2011, photo by Rafael Vargas

From the KwieKulik Archive

Presentation for the "Interrupted Histories" at the Moderna Galerija in Ljubljana prepared by Zofia Kulik, January – February 2006

In cooperation with Agnieszka Szewczyk

I am no museum or gallery custodian. I am an artist. How can I separate my own work from the job of showing works of other artists? If this set of works, presented here now, were to be called "an archive," perhaps, it should be more objective and refrain from the recollections of many of my own achievements. On the other hand, if this set of works were to be called "a collection", then it could presumably be considered as a part of myself. It is like food which I have eaten to date.

The materials come from the KwieKulik archive—the archive of Przemysław Kwiek and Zofia Kulik.

Between 1971 and 1987 we were the so called "artistic couple"; we jointly signed all of our works. Yet, we had met earlier, in 1961, when we were both attending the evening classes of sculpture at the **House of Culture of the Youth**. Later, we studied at the **Academy of Fine Arts** in Warsaw, so we have studied sculpture for 10 years altogether. Having finished our studies we were expected—according to the then dominant ideology—to design tombstones, build monuments, decorate venues for rallies, meetings, manifestations... However, as early as 1967/68 Kwiek ceased to sculpt "normally". He started to transform his sculptures, recording each stage of this activity with a camera. A year later he even "added" a live model to a clay composition. What interested me was a projection as such. At the time I was living with the camera at my eye.

The materials presented here illustrate how far our interests and practice drifted away from what the "establishment / authorities/ state/ family" had expected from us. Indeed, we did make our living making tombstones and decorations and carving commemorative plaques, but we never called these jobs "art". Similarly, we were not satisfied with the label of "the alternative" or "the underground" artists; we always wanted our work to be treated seriously. We wanted professional institutions to be at our "service" in the same way they were at the "service" of traditional artists. Thus, we persistently tried to establish some kind of an independent organisation for "new media" in Poland.

The majority of materials presented here are artistic publications prepared by Polish artists either by hand or illegally; if they happened to be legal, they were usually made on the occasion of events managed by student organisations. Unfortunately, many of the materials in our archive, especially photographs and slides, but also audio-recordings, still require systematising before they could be presented to the public.

One can find several publications and official correspondence in these art-related materials, among which are:

1. Bulletin of PP PSP (The State Enterprise of the Visual Arts Ateliers) from 1973.

This enterprise was a monopolist "distributing" work among artists and taking care of the visual identification of the Communist regime. For us, however, it was an epitome of an instrument for derogating artists.

2. Several letters from 1979–1980 concerning the foundation of the Association of New Media.

3. Hand-written application to the Censorship Authority from 1979, requesting the possibility to photocopy several pages from "Western" publications.

We are showing only a few genuine documents; the absolute majority of them are computer-made reproductions.

Zofia Kulik

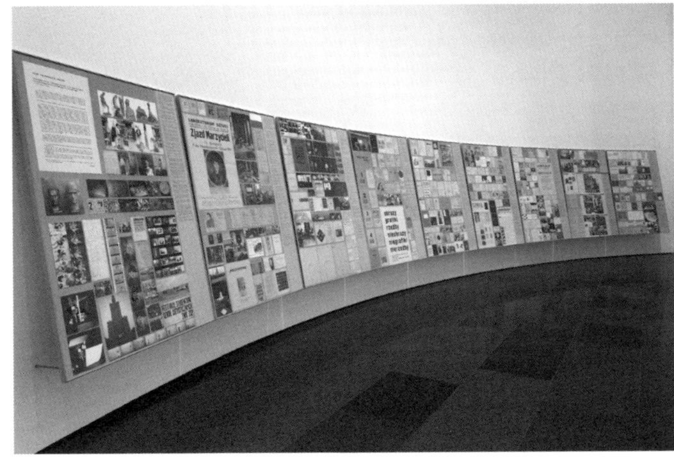

Museum of Parallell Narratives. In the Framework of L'Internationale exhibition, MACBA, 2011, photo by Rafael Vargas

CAA/CAA
Contemporary Art Archive/Centre for Art Analysis

Frame for contemporary art/culture

A database (international) focusing on art theory, cultural studies, critical theory

Comprehensive collection of works (multiples, replica, copy) slides, video tapes, CDs, catalogues, books, reviews, documentations of international, regional, national art and cultural events.

From one-to-one dialogues to group discussions, lectures, presentations, workshops, exhibitions or TV programs.

A **Contemporary Art Museum in files** – professional context for art production.

A **"Voice- activated installation"**

A **work in progress (The Archive)**

A **Platform** for a) critical attitudes and debates b) dialogue, communication, empowerment c) relations on issues reflecting the current debate in the art field and new cultural theories, about the social and political relevance of art, the autonomy and context of art **(The Center for Art Analysis).**

Active since 1985 under different names:

1985–1987: **In the context of nothing**. Interdisciplinary research (informal meetings and discussions in our flat with students, journalists, writers, people from theatre, art, music or science world); 1987–1991: **Experimental Studio** in the **Art Academy Bucharest**; 1991–today: **Open Studio** hosting interdisciplinary meetings with professionals from various fields. The studio as a public space; 1997–today: **In the general context of overproduction.** The international archive of contemporary art—thematic and chronologic selection, a capsule of knowledge; 1999–today: **Center for Art Analysis:** preserving a space for criticism and intellectual attitudes. **Detective:** permanent research from the perspective of an Eastern artist with international career. Being too late in the common history—a detective searching for sense, hidden and lost ideas, works and artist … from local, regional, international cultural/art histories; 2001–today, **Dizzydent** with critical attitude for a professional articulate context.

Initiated by Lia Perjovschi with the help of Dan Perjovschi and supported by artists, curators, art historians, institutions and NGOs from all over the world.

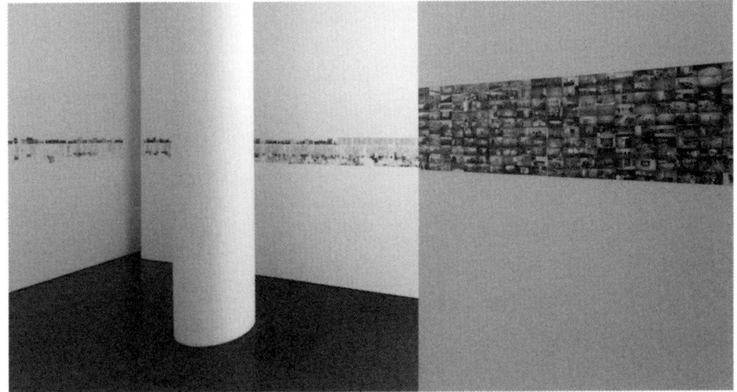

Museum of Parallell
Narratives. In the
Framework of
L'Internationale exhibition,
MACBA, 2011, photo by
Rafael Vargas

IRWIN
Encounters, 2011

In this work, the IRWIN group sets pairs of artworks in dialogue, where one of the paired works is from the East and
the other from the West. The Western works come from the
collections of the Van Abbemuseum and MuHKA, while the
works from Eastern Europe are predominantly from the collection of the Moderna galerija; all three museums are part of the
L'Internationale network.

The works are set in dialogue on the basis of both similarities and differences. In terms of form and subject matter, the
paired works resemble one another, while the differences in
their contexts remain invisible. Similar juxtapositions can be
found today in many museums that include art which until
recently was excluded from Western museums. What we see,
then, are relationships that exist more on a formal level, while
the context is still too little visible and may even seem unim-
portant. In *Encounters*, however, this invisibility becomes what
is most important. Or to put it another way, what seems most
important in this work are the various processes that brought
about the apparent similarities.

A work by Ivan Kožarić from 1963 presents a textual description of casts of the interiors of objects; Rachel Whiteread
(born, coincidentally, in 1963) later made similar casts of interiors in a physical form. In works by the OHO movement and
Guy Mees, three young people display their playful youth—in
the OHO work, they do this in the form of an equilateral

triangle; in Mees's work, this happens in the form of a right triangle. On the visual level alone, such an encounter of similar presences tells us nothing about the fact that the first group did this in order to disrupt the drabness of socialist life, while the second group were playing at a kind of democratic hierarchy. The pairing of works by Gerhard Richter and Bogoslav Kalaš shows us most directly that the couplings are primarily about a difference in causes and methods. While Richter's offset print was created from his famous painting *Kerze* (*Candle*) on the basis of a photograph, Kalaš's picture of a candle was made with a prototype of the painting machine Kalaš himself invented in 1971–1972.

IRWIN's *Encounters* tells us that artworks can encounter each other in very different ways; in museum collections we often overplan such encounters and do not allow for coincidences or collisions that could result from parallel processes. These *Encounters* are, in essence, a kind of Duchampian rendezvous, random meetings where sparks can fly between works that are seemingly incompatible.

Encounter was also the name of a literary magazine that was funded by the CIA in order to promote freedom of thought and to serve the aims of the cultural cold war—a state of affairs that precluded the kind of encounters IRWIN offers to us.

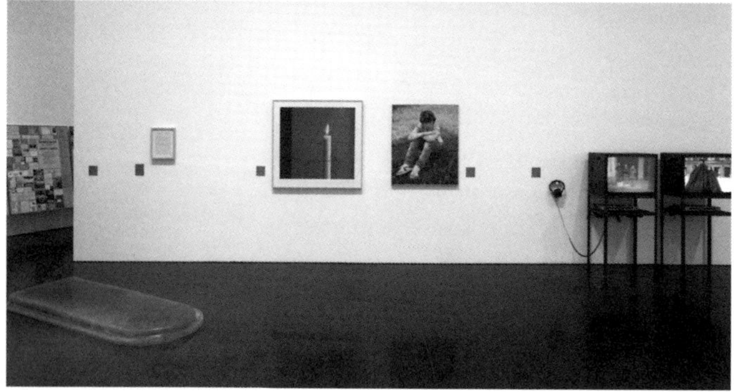

Museum of Parallell Narratives. In the Framework of L'Internationale exhibition, MACBA, 2011, photo by Rafael Vargas

Mladen Stilinović
Hysteria Makes History / After Paul De Vree, 2011

"My concept is perfectly simple. I selected works by Belgian and Dutch artists (with the exception of Robert Filliou) from the 1960s and 1970s. Because the exhibition is large and complicated, I wanted to present works that were simple, legible, and witty. Of course, this is a very personal selection and does not represent any whole. Each work is … what it is."

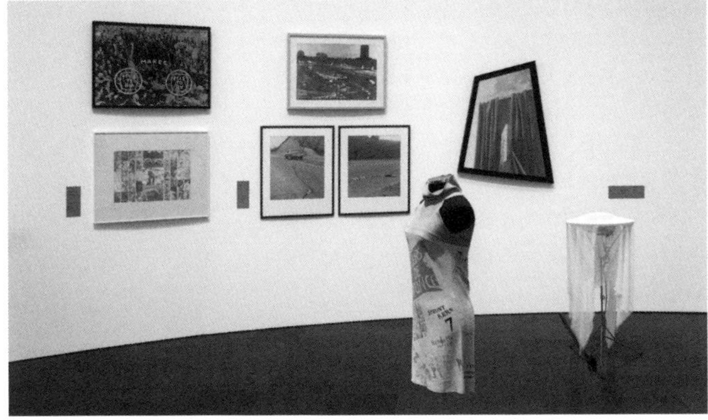

Museum of Parallell Narratives. In the Framework of L'Internationale exhibition, MACBA, 2011, photo by Rafael Vargas

Alexander Dorner
Sol LeWitt—Original and Facsimile, diptych 2011

Sol LeWitt—Original and Facsimile belongs among such works as *Salon de Fleurus* (New York), *Museum of American Art (MoAA)* (Berlin), *Kunsthistorisches Mausoleum* (Belgrade), and a few other projects, which contemplate the history of art as the history of museum collections. Their aim is to assume an external view on art history through the re-enactment of certain famous art collections that contributed to the creation of its canon. What interests these meta-collections is not only the manner in which the dominant history was constructed but also the main postulates of this history, including, for instance, the concept of originality.

Sol LeWitt—Original and Facsimile questions not only identity and tradition, but also the notions of the originality of the artwork and the uniqueness of the author, which are among the basic categories for constructing the historical narrative. It opens up the possibility of establishing a completely different kind of narrative and thus relativises the dominance of the existing "Western Canon".

The original Sol LeWitt work, *Untitled (Wall Structure)* (1972) is borrowed from the Van Abbemuseum in Eindhoven.

The same is true of its copy, which was produced as part of a project by the Danish collective Superflex. At the invitation of the Van Abbemuseum, Superflex selected works from the museum's collection for a special exhibition. The selection was concerned with seriality, repetition, instructions, and process. Among other things, the group set up a metal workshop in the middle of the exhibition, where they produced copies of LeWitt's works. The copies were then distributed to visitors for free. In this way concept and process were underscored as being more important than the end result – the object. The focus became the question of the value of the original work in the collection, as well as the museum's role as a space for critical reflection on production.

The Van Abbemuseum currently exhibits the work *Museum of American Art (MoAA)* as part of its collection. Among other things, *MoAA* also contains the collection *Kabinett der Abstrakten*, which refers to El Lissitzky's room for abstract art. This room was built in 1928 at the invitation of Alexander Dorner, the director of the Landesmuseum in Hanover; it was destroyed in 1936, during the Third Reich. By exhibiting abstract art, Dorner's museum represented an important part of the history prior to the founding of Museum of Modern Art in New York and its formation of the dominant canon of original art.

In the context of the exhibition *Parallel Narratives, Fictive Histories* can be understood as one of the possible external points of view. A similar logic could be transferred to other parallel histories, including that of Eastern European art, which was often characterised as unoriginal and seen as lagging behind the art of the West.

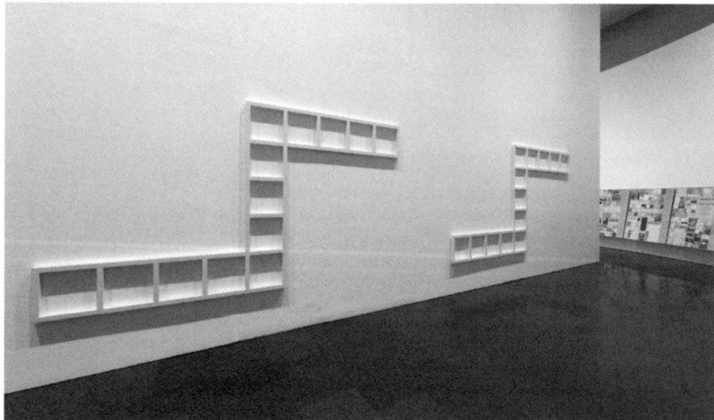

Museum of Parallell Narratives. In the Framework of L'Internationale exhibition, MACBA, 2011, photo by Rafael Vargas

Museum of Affects, Moderna galerija, Ljubljana (2011/12)

The *Museum of Affects* exhibition brings together four important European museums: Moderna galerija, Ljubljana, the Museu d'Art Contemporani de Barcelona (MACBA), Barcelona; the Van Abbemuseum, Eindhoven; and the Museum van Hedendaagse Kunst, Antwerpen (M HKA). The institutions have joined forces to challenge the present canons of art history and replace them with transnational, plural cultural narratives and approaches.

How to go about this? How to address similarities and differences in a new way? The *Museum of Affects* exhibition is one possible approach. It brings together works that emerged out of various events between 1957 and 1986. The circumstances under which these works were produced range from the totalitarian regimes in the former Eastern Bloc and Yugoslavia to the cultural oppression under Franco's regime in Spain and the specific situation in the Lowlands. In addition, pop art, minimalist, and conceptualist works from the then hegemonic North American art system are included in the show.

The main focus of the exhbition is not the formal and cultural positioning of these works, neither is it a comparative analysis between them, but rather the notion of affects, the power of affecting and being affected. We define this power as a resonance with artworks, where artworks become events made of intensities, which leave certain traces in space and time and, above all, on or within our bodies and minds.

Affects involve both feeling and cognition; a sensory experience and an intellectual activity. What is more, affects are also a change, a politics, a rupture, an unknown power. Affects cannot be instrumentalized because they cannot be read or represented. On the other hand, affects can be controversial, especially when linked to certain ideologies and/or totalitarianisms.

What then are the intensities that inform a work? What is the potentiality of an artwork? How do we think of art as event? And how do we work out the antagonisms between affects, representation and the art system in the exhibition itself?

Questions such as these force us to think beyond the defined methodologies of academic art history and its formal analyses, which might incite a different kind of approach towards the exhibited works; or more precisely, the idea of the exhibition is not so much about interpreting the works of art as it is about the specific affective experiences that these works trigger.

For this reason the following groupings were applied: the desire for actual social change through the critique of the system and the media; the desire for symbolic social change and the creation of alternative systems; understanding the world by making invisible structures or energies visible; using the world as material for ironic critique; the desire to articulate the world as semantics and immediacy; and articulating the self in the world as experience.

Bart de Baere, Bartomeu Marí, with Leen De Backer,
Teresa Grandas, Bojana Piškur, curators

1. Desire for Actual Social Change

Translating 'real' politics into art – and especially into art projects that will somehow have a 'real' impact on society – is notoriously problematic. Artists are very serious about their politics, but without letting go of their aesthetic objectives – which are perhaps the only ones that can be attained in art, and anyway the only 'results' that art is well equipped to evaluate and follow up on.

a. Critique of the System
Francesc Abad
Vito Acconci
Luc Deleu
Eulàlia Grau
Grup de Treball
Sanja Iveković

b. Critique of the Mass Media
K. P. Brehmer
Paul De Vree
Ivica Matić

Joan Rabascall
Toon Tersas

2. Desire for Symbolic Social Change – Creation of Alternative Systems

An approach to the art-versus-politics dilemma that may lead to
a 'credible' – although not necessarily pragmatic – stance is the
creation of alternative or parallel systems potentially capable
of improving society. Artists invest much of their credibility
in creating systems that make sense – at least within their own
practice.
Robert Filliou
Jef Geys
Grupo de Artistas de Vanguardia
Andrej Monastirski / Andrei Monastirsky
Muntadas
Skupina OHO / OHO Group, Milenko Matanović
Skupina OHO / OHO Group, Marko Pogačnik
Video–Nou / Servei de Vídeo Comunitari

3. Understanding the World by Making it Visible

There are different methods ('rhetorical' or 'poetic' strategies)
for creating and displaying structure in art, and none of them
is straightforward or unambiguous. There is some overlap between creating your own system and revealing the hidden, but
also important differences – although these are probably differences of degree rather than of kind, just like the difference
between structures and energies upheld here.

a. Making Invisible Structures Visible
Daniël Dewaele
Ferran García Sevilla
Vladimir Kuprijanov/Kupriyanov
Danny Matthys
Bruce Nauman
Gerhard Richter
Mladen Stilinović
Lawrence Weiner

b. Making Invisible Energies Visible
Lili Dujourie
Miklós Erdély
Dan Flavin
Julije Knifer
Guy Mees
Josep Ponsatí
Ilija Šoškić

4. Using the World as Material for Ironical Critique

Creating or maintaining a credible system is not always a
priority for artists. Sometimes the world may be seen as 'material' for whatever they want to achieve, and sometimes the
'nothingness' of the world may provoke actions that are ni-
hilistic in the true sense of the word. It is true that irony was
frequently over-exploited by artists, critics and theoreticians
during the last 30 years. Yet it can still be a sharp and dangerous tool.
Tomislav Gotovac
Hamlet Hovsepian
Miralda
Manolo Quejido
Andy Warhol

5. Enhancing Perception

Enhancing and refining perception as a building-block for art
and a pro-active stance for relating to the world is at the same
time a strategy (an approach particularly well-suited to visual
formats) and a fundamental, almost ontological, attitude to the
possibilities offered by art. The resulting works usually demand perceptual precision also of their viewers, whether they
are focused on the immediacy of an event or on meaning as it
is mediated by various 'languages' available to artists.

a. Articulating the World as Immediacy
John Baldessari
Stanley Brouwn

James Lee Byars
Richard Hamilton
René Heyvaert
Jiři Kovanda
On Kawara
Ed Ruscha
Josip Vaništa

b. Articulating the World as Semantics
René Daniëls
Öyvind Fahlström
Nigel Henderson
Mangelos
Panamarenko
Martha Rosler
Benet Rossell / Cerimonials

6. Enhancing Intensity – Articulating the Self in the World as Experience

Intensity may be both perceptual (on the level of 'input') and expressive (gestural or otherwise, on the level of 'output'), but it is usually just as strategically applied to art-making as are other methods such as reflection or building systems. Yet intensity, also of the physical kind, does not preclude criticality. The artist's Self is articulated in the world, as an image of the world, and can be used as an instrument for understanding and changing it.
Marina Abramović
Eugènia Balcells
Esther Ferrer
Ion Grigorescu
Tibor Hajas
Jacques Lizène
Jan Mlčoch
Carlos Pazos
Petr Štembera
Anne-Mie Van Kerckhoven

Prologue: L'Internationale The Internationale Team
Zdenka Badovinac, Bart De Baere, Charles Esche, Bartomeu Marí,
Georg Schöllhammer, and all our museum colleagues.

In the early years of the 21st century, Europe seems uncertainly
placed between a deep sense of its own historical importance
and anxiety about where it may go in the future. The European
project, which for many of our institutions was a guiding
principle, has run aground on the rocks of neo-liberalism and
an economic priority that forgot about society's political and
cultural dimensions. The national project, on which the foundations of our museums (along with most of Europe's other
cultural institutions) were based, retains little of its 19th century ambitions to progressive, democratic thinking. As a result,
cultural Europe has to chart a new course for collaboration
and for its relations with the rest of the globe. This course has
to take account of Europe's murderous history both inside and
outside its borders, as well as the aggressiveness with which
Eurocentric solutions are still imposed on parts of other continents. At the same time, the construction of democratic ideals, the claims to human equality and many global liberation
struggles have been inspired by popular, academic and cultural
discourses developed in and around Europe, especially when it
was in dialogue with the rest of the world.

It is to try and build on these latter qualities, in the form of
artistic and discursive innovations around artists' works and
collections of European art heritage, that a group of middle-
sized European museums formed themselves into a fledging
transnational cultural institution willing to rethink our shared
European heritage. Internationale—consisting of Moderna
galerija Ljubljana, MACBA Barcelona, Van Abbemuseum
Eindhoven, M HKA Antwerp, and Július Koller Society
Bratislava/Vienna—seeks to work on terms that respect the
relation between artistic voices and localities while searching
for a common understanding of art's potential in the world.
At this point in time, we cannot look to political or economic
leadership to shape our goals, though we will need the active
support of both if we are to build an emancipated vision of
what it is to be a European cultural citizen. Instead, we feel
the need to articulate our own agenda and to do so through

the means at our disposal: common exhibitions, publications, seminars and the sharing of our collections. Through coming together, we can discover more about our individual strengths and weaknesses, we can exchange information and experiences that can enrich our activities in the public domain, and we can cease the pointless competition for cultural capital that reduces art institutions to tools of economic development. We also want to offer an alternative to the "bigger is better" or franchise model of museums based in core northern European capitals, with their apparent desire to deliver a centralized narrative covering European and world art over the last fifty to sixty years. We would claim that the narrative of the last years is still a contested one, and it is our ambition to offer different interpretations from the mainstream as well as to understand how artistic practices are contextual and located. These cannot be simply displaced as objects to construct a single institutional vision of the significance of modern, post-modern and contemporary art today. Neither can they be marginalized as of only local concern when set against the art produced in the urban powerhouses of the continent. If we are to build a genuine vision of a European culture in just dialogue with the world, then constructing the conditions to respect locality while striving for the richest transnational dialogue are an absolute *imperative*.

Our long-term project bears the name of the song "L'Internationale" that proclaims internationalism as a kind of weapon in the struggle for equitable and more democratic societies. In choosing the name and tradition of that particular song we wanted to emphasize a distinction from the modernist understanding of a homogenized, cosmopolitan life or the more recent ideal of a globally networked individual free from a commitment to a particular community or place. Instead, we have decided for the tradition of internationalism represented by the older struggles of workers' unions and intellectuals for international solidarity and fellowship. Their goals were directed at concrete changes beyond the nation-state towards a shared sense of citizenship in which all the dimensions from the personal to the local, regional, international and planetary are taken into consideration.

Parallel Histories/Affective Museums/
Spirits of Internationalism

The first project that the Internationale group has undertaken is
to unite our collections virtually and draw on the total inheritance that we represent to suggest new ways of understanding the period 1957–1986, or the high point of the Cold War
between the US and the USSR. The period is marked on the
one side by the Hungarian uprising at the end of 1956 and the
subsequent invasion by the Red Army that effectively registered the end of any potential for political reform in post-war
East Central Europe. At the other end, 1986 represents the year
of the financial "Big Bang" that reduced the effective power
of political parties within Western Europe to one of economic
management. In between these dates, a vision for a post-Holo-
caust, post-ethnically divided Europe was slowly constructed
on both sides of the ideological divide. This Europe of the
imagination was built not least by artists and academics that
played a significant role in speculating on a new kind of conti-
nental common space that would keep the peace and emphasize
cultural affinities. Even at the height of the East-West divide
there was still some limited cultural exchange, both official
and unofficial, to which a number of works in the exhibitions
bear witness. The artistic efforts to depict and help construct a
peaceful, open Europe out of the shattered imperial ambitions
of the Second World War were shared and understood as the
real responsibility of cultural actors who could offer images
and ideas to counter the dangers of nationalism and ethnic ha-
treds. At the same time, most of these artists were necessarily
active at the most local of levels, in their own cities and towns,
and were working with the means at their disposal. For some
this meant almost underground activities, out of sight of the
cultural authorities, for others it meant particular attention to
their national or regional history, often using their native languages in order to communicate with their immediate environment. These relevant tactics were, unsurprisingly, less noticed
by the international art world both then and still today. With its
English language priority and limited patience for inspirations
or issues not instantly translatable for a non-local public, the art
historical narrative of the years 1957–86 has tended to focus on
New York, especially SoHo, and a limited number of European

centers that were in close contact with the American hub. The ambition of our three major exhibitions, as well as the archival presentations of Július Koller and KwieKulik, has been to recognize parallel histories, as the first title named them. These histories are in no way replacements for the dominant story but are ways of understanding the latter's weaknesses and biases and thus ceasing to put our faith in a single view of recent cultural developments. Each of the three exhibitions in MACBA, Moderna galerija and M KHA/Van Abbemuseum told its own story, one shaped by the host institution's intimate knowledge of its public, environment and own historical needs. MACBA wanted an extended presentation of the collection of Moderna galerija because it felt artists from East and Central Europe needed an introduction for the Catalan public. Moderna galerija chose for another kind of exhibition, that wove the collections of MACBA and M KHA together as a way of introducing different museum models as a way to introduce the permanent displays of their rich contemporary art collection in their new museum building in Metelkova, Ljubljana. Finally, Van Abbemuseum and M KHA wanted to exchange their collections with important supplements from MACBA and Moderna galerija to tell local histories of two neighboring countries with very different cultural and museum policies in the period under discussion.

This publication brings all the diversity of the first Internationale project between two covers, allowing readers the chance to discover the arguments for our selections and the choice of projects, as well as to find out more about particular artistic developments during the period. Alongside extensive visual and textual documentation of the three exhibitions the book develops four main sections, in which methodological concerns, historiographic aspirations, selected case studies, as well as further thoughts on internationalism in the arts are laid out. As this project draws to a close, Internationale is firing itself up for further and deeper collaborations in the future.

Writing History Without a Prior Canon Bartomeu Marí

One of the characteristics that unites cultural contexts as geographically disparate as the Iberian Peninsula, the countries of Eastern Europe and a handful of Latin American nations is the absence of canons as a basis for writing recent art history. Dictatorial regimes have always put more effort into denying than affirming, and culture is one of those areas in which denial, censorship and the lack of freedom have been exercised more thoroughly in these contexts. Ironically, those very absolutist governments and dictatorships are the ones who pretend to be in possession of The Canon.

Artistic creation has confronted situations of censorship and the lack of freedom with similar languages. In present-day China, artists such as Ai Weiwei have ended up borrowing strategies for representation and subject matter that were taken up earlier in the 1960s and 1970s. In spite of all efforts to block, control or censor, there is never a total stagnation of information, and artists have always found alternative circuits through which to gain visibility for their work. The presentation and distribution of art under the conditions of censorship and absence of freedom has spawned uncontrolled networks of information, but it has also produced forms and materials on the fringe of artistic convention. The integration of these forms, materials and attitudes within the present-day narratives of history and heritage is one of the major tasks confronting the museums of our time.

The idea of a canon evokes, in itself, a structuring into a hierarchy of the artistic production of a specific moment, an historical period, an epoch. Who establishes the canons and with what mechanisms? Is it the critics at the present time or the historians later on? Is it possible to conceive of a tool that is instrumental in categorizing or structuring artistic production into a hierarchy that, by way of a canon, can serve as a reliable reference for writing its history? While conventions do not constitute a canon as such, they do, however, exert considerable influence on the way taste is held up as a source of authority. The market and its ability to impose its most highly prized figures on prevailing taste—together with the assiduous complicity of the mass media—has acted as an authoritative source since the end of the 20ᵗʰ century. Moreover, the fact that the majority of the biennials and major collective exhibitions have become art fairs is evidence that the market is capable of absorbing any form, material or product, no matter how much it seems to escape from or avoid the conditions and clutches of commercialization. The very structure of the art auction, one of the most powerful motivators of the market, has inserted contemporary art into its workings. Anything that is contemporary can be auctioned off. Thus, the outcome of the auction and the market prices begin to function as a canon, regardless of whether the critic has taken part in the conversation or the voice of the historian has (not yet) been heard.

Does popular acceptance constitute a canon? Theory tends to answer this question in the negative. But the "new world order" answers it in the affirmative. The corollary of this reasoning and the conclusion that brings us closer seem to question the role of the specialist, whether he/she is the curator of the exhibition—the scientific and technical author of the event—or the journalist-critic. After the Second World War the role of the critic who recognized the genius in the work of an artist became consolidated. As we approached the 21ˢᵗ century, the authority of the critic was diluted and its influence broken up and divided between a series of actors who have almost always been present and are not new, but have passed unnoticed among us until now. The collector will now play a more prominent role, and the freelance or non-affiliated curator, the gallery owner who brings everyone together, the auction house that can overshadow or assume the role of the gallery as the party working to commercialize the work, and the mass media, among other agents, have all taken on a highly relevant or formative role in the formation of the commercial aspect of the canon. These actors frequently converge in the work of a particular artist to the point of suggesting the conclusion that they are all related to each other. This is often the case. But exceptions abound: artists who are considered by critics to be highly significant and of great cultural value do not always command the highest market prices, nor are they commercialized by influential galleries or sought after by a large number of collectors. In contrast, there are those definitively mediocre artists who do not appear on the museum circuit or in important international exhibitions but whose dealers can still maintain their high prices because they end up finding specific collectors for their market. The recent publication of a lecture by Eugene M. Schwartz[1] is a perfect example of the systematization of a passion and a set of intuitions to convert it into a method. What if the history of contemporary art were to be written by collectors and not by historians? Or, to put it another way, what if historians were to "historicize" only that art that has been collected and, as such, outlived its time?

The American historian Robert S. Nelson interpreted the paradox of the canon particularly well in his essay, "Canons of Art in the Space of Our Desires,"[2] when he said that the canon should apply to present-day artistic production. Nelson describes a great contradiction: the canon is a utopia; it has no place among us because it is an ideal construction that never becomes exemplified. At the same time, however, because it seems impossible to write history without canons, the canon, therefore, is necessary. The problem of the canon in contemporary art, in the art milieu of our time, becomes more acute when we observe that the so-called unity of artistic production, the unity of criteria for assuming the value of specific objects, does not exist. Is it possible to conceive of a canon outside the limits established by modernity? What conclusions can be drawn about the make up of what we call "modern"? To whom does modernity belong? The feminist and post-colonial discourses that emerged in Anglo-Saxon intellectual circles in the 1970s have exposed the difficulty of trying to maintain a single and univocal view—white and male—of history and its narratives. If we consider artistic production from the beginning of the 20th century, we can see that its creative centers correspond to those centers of political, economic and military power. In his now canonical work, *How New York Stole the Idea of Modern Art*,[3] Serge Guilbaut analyses the transfer of the "capitality" of art from Paris to the American metropolis of New York in creative, commercial and institutional terms. Even if the canon is a utopia and does not exist per se, the voices of power and authority still have clearly defined geographic locations. In general, the displacement of the the global art capital from the center of Europe to the East Coast of the United States merely perpetuated the role of the Northern hemisphere and the Anglo-Saxon axis as economic and cultural powers capable of

1 Eugene M. Schwartz, *Confessions of a Poor Collector: How to build a worthwhile art collection with the least possible money*, Stuttgart: Edition Taube, 2011 (The New York Cultural Center 1970).

2 See Robert S. Nelson, *Now is the Time: Art and Theory in the 21st Century*, NAi Publishers, Rotterdam 2009.

3 Serge Guilbaut, *How New York Stole the Idea of Modern Art*, University of Chicago Press, Chicago 1983.

organizing and canonizing the art world. In these regions commercial power is accompanied by the power of the academy that provides the criteria and critical arguments. Above all, it is accompanied by the institutional power that, on the one hand, acquires (collects) and, on the other, theorizes; or, in other words, includes a particular type of artistic production within a canon.

We can see the same utopian quality of the canon in the fact that today there is no single canon but rather views of art that exist side by side, that occasionally intersect and are sometimes antagonistic. The variety of narratives that coexist in new critical ecosystems does not produce a stable and lasting canon but rather a network of ideas that interweave a system of interpretation within and amongst themselves. Moreover, we can also see at a given moment how specific canons evolve and mutate. One of the major questions that arises is whether or not the crisis of a particular canon, such as the one we have seen in the transition from the 20th to the 21st century, can produce a new canon. In other words, can it provoke—to paraphrase the title of the MACBA exhibition held in 2011—another type of reference or authority based on a web of multiple or parallel narratives?[4]

Two facts can help us see some discrete but powerful, earth-shaking movements. Until recently The Museum of Modern Art in New York had put painting and sculpture at the forefront of their collections and held exhibitions as their most highly valued artistic genres. Between 2009 and 2011, however, it incorporated a series of relevant works that are very far from the previously defended canon: the Gilbert and Lila Silverman Collection, the collection and archives of Seth Siegelaub and the Daled Collection. These three collections have one important element in common: they are centered on a type of art that was, until very recently, situated on the periphery of the dominant narratives of contemporary art history. Under the heading of "conceptual art" they gathered together a series of experiments whose essential characteristic was a change in the system of values based on the aesthetic of the transcendental and Romantic. This aesthetic holds that the art object contains the qualities of beauty perceived by the subject. But this theory was substituted by another system of values based on both acts and on behavior. This process started at the beginning of the 20th century with some of the most advanced branches of

4 *Museum of Parallel Narratives*, curated by Zdenka Badovinac. Organised and produced by the Museu d'Art Contemporani de Barcelona (MACBA); Moderna Galerija, Ljubljana; the Július Koller Society (SJK), Bratislava; the Van Abbemuseum (VAM), Eindhoven; and the Museum van Hedendaagse Kunst (M HKA), Antwerp.

the historical avant-garde, but it came to greater fruition more extensively in the 1960s and 1970s. The aesthetic of the object gave way to the aesthetic of behavior. The French philosopher Jean-Marie Schaeffer put it this way: "The real objective of the study of aesthetics, before theory, should be behavior, the relationships that connect us to both the world of the works of art and the world per se. These types of behavior are the ones in which ordinary knowledge becomes a source of pleasure, in which subjectivity, acquired talents, memory and sensations all play a part."[5] The aesthetic of behavior begins with the activity of artists whose work disqualifies the previous system. We will probably have to wait some fifty years to witness the incorporation of these works and this new system of values into the canon of art—in other words, into the normal language of the artistic institution.

In speaking of the Seth Siegelaub Collection, Glenn D. Lowry, the director of MoMA remarked: "This collection of works and archives has great historical importance, as many of the works were shown together in critical exhibitions of the late 1960s and early 1970s that radically challenged traditional notions of the art object. [...] This acquisition transforms the collection of The Museum of Modern Art into a pre-eminent center of conceptual art, one of the decisive movements of the 20th century."[6] Conceptual art became a "decisive moment" in the artistic events of the last century and, as such, it is not an anomaly, a marginal gesture or a "systemic error". At the same time, the Getty Foundation in Los Angeles is also carrying out a policy of acquiring artists' archives to facilitate the reading, interpretation and diffusion of art in both the 20th and the 21st centuries.

Two important points can be concluded from these facts. First, museums such as MoMA and cultural institutions like the Getty Foundation have decided to "complete" their permanent collections with those experiments, artists and works that had formerly questioned the centrality and very authority of the institution itself. As the director of MoMA declared: "The Daled Collection is among the most significant acquisitions in the Museum's history and substantially enhances and transforms our holdings of art from the 1960s and 1970s, filling major gaps and also adding considerable depth in other areas of our collection."[7] The art that questioned and caused a crisis in the very

5 Jean-Marie Schaeffer, *Les célibataires de l' art. Pour une esthétique sans mythes*, Gallimard, Paris 1996.

6 See Glenn D. Lowry, "The MoMA Acquires Major Collection of Conceptual Art from Seth Siegelaub," <http://www.artnowmag.com/Magazine/World/2011/Jun/World_Jun1511.html>.

7 Ibid.

nature of the artistic institution is finally swallowed up and digested by the institution itself. Does this mean that one canon has replaced another or that one artistic paradigm can take the place of its antagonist? Of course it doesn't. But it does mean that the official canon has become more flexible in order to be capable of incorporating its opposite.

One of the consequences of this change in the system has been its effect on the internal ordering of the museum, structured in a hierarchical manner and divided into specialized departments: painting, sculpture, drawing, photography, architecture, design, film, and finally performance and new media. American artist Joseph Kosuth relates a story that illustrates the inadequacy of the museum organized into departments to "cope" with the new type of art. When he requested his work *One Art and Three Chairs* (1965) from an important European museum for a temporary exhibition, the registrar department of the museum could not locate the work in its storage section. After frantic searches the work was finally located by way of its different components: the chair was in the design section, the photograph of the actual chair in the photography department and the text in the department of prints. Just as Gertrude Stein foresaw, the modern museum and the contemporary museum would clash head-on.

Another sign that made us think about how the canon is being reoriented was the way the permanent collections of the MNAM-Centre Georges Pompidou in Paris, followed shortly afterward by the presentation of the Tate Modern collections in London, were reorganized. This opening took place in May 2000. The transition to the new century brought with it a new way of displaying the collections that left behind chronological order and the succession of movements and styles. These presentations were based on "thematic environments" within which chronologies have been superimposed until they become random or incidental. Art is no longer explained by a time continuum but rather around formal affinities. History is no longer an unfolding progression in time, but rather a whirlwind that we can grasp by purely ocular sensibility. *Experience or Interpretation. The Dilemma of Museums of Modern Art* is the title of a lecture by Sir Nicholas Sirota in 1995 and published four years later.[8] In it he establishes the foundations for the presentation of the collection of contemporary art in the Tate

8 Nicholas Serota, *Experience or Interpretation. The Dilemma of Museums of Modern Art*, Thames & Hudson, London 2000.

Modern. The back cover of the edition highlights a commentary from the *Architectural Journal*, "[it] Gives a clear idea of what we should expect at Bankside Tate." In other words, the theoretical bases in favor of experience and physical perception beyond traditional understanding had been laid down.

The integration of the Silverman, Siegelaub and Daled Collections on the part of MoMA means that the American institution decided to go a way opposite that of the European institutions. For the Americans, the canon continues to be established within a temporal continuum and is determined by a very specific vocabulary. Even so, it recognizes the viral potential of this type of art for the present organization of the museum: "Cross-disciplinary in nature, the (Gilbert and Lila Silverman) Collection will be utilized by curators from all Departments of the Museum." In other words, the experiences in the art of the 1960s and 1970s correspond to a system of values that will not be allowed to split off into departments or specialties. All the departments, genres and disciplines will come together and intersect with each other.

One of the primary motivations for the creation of L'Internationale consortium has been to establish a vocabulary and a chronology appropriate for the writing of art history produced within the radius of the periphery. This is necessary because, even though these places are close to the centers of power, they are still external to their basic functioning. Vocabulary and chronology are essential tools in establishing a canon: vocabulary identifies objects, ideas and values; chronology locates them in the temporal continuum that situates them in history. The evolution of artistic creation in certain parts of Europe such as the Eastern countries and the Iberian Peninsula has not taken place in conditions similar to those in Central Europe and the Anglo-Saxon world. The Latin American continent has had access to forms and degrees of modernity that were very specific and unique, although different from the canonical forms. Both Africa and Asia have also come into the present by way of varying degrees of access to modernity, in its different political, economic, social and aesthetic aspects and implications. While writers such as Néstor García-Canclini in Latin America have taken up the uniqueness of those "entrances and exits" in modernity,[9] those countries on the periphery of the European continent are now beginning to deal specifically

9 Néstor García-Canclini, *Culturas Híbridas. Estrategias para entrar y salir de la modernidad*, Grijalbo, Mexico 1998.

with their own particular contributions to the History of Art in
capital letters. In Eastern Europe authors such as Boris Groys
and Piotr Piotrowski, among others, have together produced a
substantial bibliography to stand alongside the solid foundations of the contemporary heritage being established on the
part of museums and private initiatives. A country's material
heritage and historical narrative are two symbiotic entities: one
cannot exist without the other. Logically, the acquisition of a
material legacy, a collection of works, objects and documents
precedes the establishment of the narratives that will become
History with the contribution of the pertinent authority.

While it is possible to conceive of a History of Art without a single canon, it is not possible to conceive of a History
without a museum or a heritage. The Getty Foundation and the
Museum of Modern Art in New York have made it clear that
the history of contemporary art cannot be written by starting
only from the study of the works of art per se. It is becoming
clearer that the history of contemporary art has need of the
documents that accompany the making of works and allow us
to translate the varied subjectivities into objectively narrated
arguments. Possession of that heritage enables the institution to
carry out the production of historical narrative. Our museums
in Southern and Eastern Europe are economically fragile and
politically unstable by nature, because we gained access to the
democratic system far later than our Central European colleagues and because we maintain our precarious balance within
the liberal system with less security and tradition. This is why
we have an imperative duty to fulfill and conserve our heritage.
This situation is made even more urgent because our conditions
are understandably inferior when we attempt to develop our
cultural output on a broader scale, given that we are obliged to
compete with the typologies and formats that originate in and
emanate from the metropolis. Our artistic production is peripheral, not because of its geographic condition but because of its
typological material. Above and beyond vocabulary and chronology, it is imperative to invent new narrative typologies.

Translated from the Spanish by Selma Margaretten.

Histories and Their Different Narrators Zdenka Badovinac

The question I find crucial in my work related to historicizing
Eastern European art is who does the historicizing. Who is the
narrator? What is his or her position? These questions immediately place historicizing with its related issues in the context of
politics, which over the last two decades has been, in my view,
the only appropriate way of setting about historicizing Eastern
European art; that is, the art of a territory that is decidedly
geopolitical.

Let me start by explaining what historicizing means to me.
For me, the emphasis in historicizing is on the process that
yields not a single objective history, but a plurality of heterogeneous stories. Unlike history, which presents itself as an objective and impersonal result of study, historicization keeps the
various narrators and their voices in the foreground. It is not
possible to produce a single story from a multitude of different
narratives, no matter how complex the analysis of the various positions; instead, the variety of these positions should be
preserved, as should their narrators. This approach to history
gained prominence as new regions began to open up, regions
whose art could not be understood unless the particularities
of the spaces, the diverse trajectories of art, and its different
interpretive contexts were taken into consideration.

In this text I will outline some examples of historicizing
Eastern European art, i.e., the various processes involved and
the narrators' positions assumed in a range of exhibitions of
Eastern European art staged since the late 1980s.

Over the past twenty years, the agent of history-writing has
often been the focus of interest, in particular of those who demanded a redefinition of the existing art historical canon. Who
is entitled to produce history? This frequently asked question
seeks answers that would break with the former logic of history as a history of winners, and create conditions in which also
the weaker participants could start writing their own stories.

Eastern European art first began to codify in the West. This
is where the first accounts originated, accounts of official art
and dissident art, and of trends and developments in art that

were crucial for the international context at large. A pioneering work on the history of Eastern European avant-garde art was Camille Gray's book *The Great Experiment: Russian Art 1863–1922*, published in 1962. Not only did it reveal to the Western world the Russian historical avant-garde, but it also spread this information in the East itself, sparking the East's interest in its own artistic traditions. It took an outside view for Eastern European art to re-territorialize. The very epithet "Eastern European" speaks of this external position, of a view from the Western side. In the West, the interest in acquiring new knowledge, also about other cultures, had been continuously stimulated both by the tradition of the powerful Western epistemology and by economic and political interests. Such systematic acquiring of diverse knowledge and encouraging a critical view of one's own system produced a sense of freedom, a condition that was often idealized in the East, with the West becoming the object of the artists' desires and fascination. As a result, a general inferiority complex developed in the East, which contributed to local art being underrated and the art of the wider region paid very little attention. This was one of the reasons why a collective narrative of Eastern European art could not develop; indeed, no one in the region was really interested in it until the fall of the communist regimes. It was only this newly aroused interest in Eastern European art that retroactively stimulated the awareness of regional belonging and of the urgent need to define shared characteristics. Thus the East itself increasingly began to use the term Eastern European art, which had not been widely used before. The problematic aspect of this designation, which essentially puts the region in a subordinate position, was seldom observed. A few critics did, nonetheless, point out that the West had in effect usurped universal art, labeling all other art with regional epithets, thus placing non-Western art in pre-modern time, which classified art according to national schools.

"Eastern European art" is a term used by the external narrator. During the time the world was divided into the Eastern and Western blocs, this term referred to some generalized notions of art being produced under ideological pressure in the unfree world. According to the oral accounts of some people such as Harald Szeemann, who were particularly influential on the international art scene during the time of the Cold War, many art professionals thought it somehow best to simply ignore countries under communist dictatorships. Few renowned curators established long-term collaborations with Eastern artists. One such curator was Pierre Restany, whose surviving archive is among the most valuable sources of information on Eastern European art.[1] There was some communication between artists in the East and the West, particularly among Fluxus artists, mail artists, and other representatives of Post-War Avant-Gardes. Not surprisingly it was mail artist Klaus Grohg who edited one of the few books providing a contemporaneous view of the art in the East, entitled *Aktuelle Kunst in Osteuropa* (1972). In terms of exhibitions, Eastern European national selections presented mostly modernist artists at the Venice Biennale and a few other more sporadic occasions, while Eastern Post-War Avant-Gardes were regularly featured at the Paris Biennial, and at a few other events, such as the Edinburgh Festival, thanks to the efforts of Richard Demarco, and at the international event Works and Words in 1979 at the De Appel foundation in Amsterdam.

After the fall of the socialist regimes, however, interest in Eastern European art grew. The first exhibitions of art from the post-socialist countries were staged, understandably, in Austria and Germany. For the most part, they favored artists from the formerly socialist parts of Central Europe. The idea of a shared Central European cultural space did not die, even during the time the eastern parts of it were under socialist order. One of the longest running projects of this type was the Graz biennial Trigon.[2] Covering principally art produced in Italy, Yugoslavia, and Austria, the aim of the biennial was to revive the historical cultural space of "Inner Austria", that is to say, the core of the former Habsburg Monarchy. Immediately after the collapse of Yugoslavia, an extensive show was staged at the Neue Galerie in Graz, entitled Identity : *Difference. Platform Trigon 1940–1990. A Topography of Modernity,* and curated by Christa Steinle and Peter Weibel. Essentially a retrospective of the Trigon series of exhibitions, it aimed to investigate the artistic contributions of these countries to the construction of modernity. Thus, primarily thanks to Peter Weibel, the tradition of Trigon continued in Graz also under the new, changed circumstances. In the early 1990s, Vienna,

[1] The importance of Pierre Restany and his archive was presented by Nataša Petrešin at the Espace 315: "Sources, Archives, Documents and Films" was part of the exhibition *Promises of the Past / A Discontinuous History of Art in Former Eastern Europe*, Centre Pompidou, Paris 2010.

[2] Between 1963 and 1992 the Neue Galerie in Graz staged biennial exhibitions entitled Trigon. The first Trigon show presented works from Austria, Italy and former Yugoslavia. These countries were later joined by "guest countries" like Germany, France, Great Britain, Spain, Czechoslovakia, and Hungary.

too —in particular the Museum of Modern Art (MUMOK) under its Hungarian director Lorand Hegy—stepped its activities up a notch to revive the common Central European cultural space. In 1993, Hegy organized a special exhibition in the framework of the Venice Biennale that brought together artists from the former Yugoslavia, Italy, Austria, the former Czechoslovakia, and Hungary. Significantly entitled *La coesistenza dell'arte,* the exhibition was well in sync with the central theme of the Biennale—transnational multiculturalism and cultural nomadism. What the Austrian Vice Chancellor Erhard Busek wrote for the exhibition catalogue helps explain the dominant narrators' position in Central Europe: "Austria, whose cultural tradition and political psyche are defined in trans-national terms, made this co-existence part of its nascent self-awareness, which is why Austria's identity will always be open and multicultural: Austria was thus predestined to fill the role of mediator in politics and culture, and within the Central European community of states true friendship has arisen from many formerly secret contacts with producers of culture in what used to be the Eastern bloc."[3]

Also Hegy's later show *Aspekte/Positionen, 50 Jahre Kunst aus Mitteleuropa 1949–1999*, staged in Vienna, served the purpose of reclaiming the Central European cultural character lost during socialism. The interest in this common space of Central Europe did not exist only on the part of the former hegemons, but also on the part of the former colonies, both the Austrian and the Soviet. The latter used the new unifying momentum to deal with the traumas of their socialist past. But as Piotr Piotrowski pointed out[4], the revival of "Eastern Central Europe," as he dubbed this part of Central Europe, was in the first place a project of dissident writers, independent and politically committed intellectuals, while far more universalist tendencies prevailed among modernist and neo-avant-garde artists. According to Piotrowski, the last instances of resurrecting the idea of Central Europe can be found shortly after 1989, to be later replaced or overpowered by the processes of identification with Europe and its integration processes. The concept of a shared cultural space of Central Europe, however, survives. One of the things that bears witness to this fact is a collection founded in 2004: tellingly entitled Kontakt, it combines cultural and political interests with the corporate

3 Erhard Busek, "The aesthetic of resistance," *La coesistenza dell'arte, Un modelo espositivo, La Biennale di Venezia,* Vienna: Musuem moderner Kunst Stiftung Ludwig 1993, p. 11.

4 Piotr Piotrowski, *In the Shadow of Yalta: Art and the Avant-garde in Eastern Europe, 1945–1989,* Reaction Books, London 2009. First published in Poznan, Poland by REBIS Publishing House Ltd in 2005.

interests of the Austrian Erste Bank, which has branch offices in most eastern Central European countries.[5]

This interest in eastern Central Europe (that is, primarily the post-socialist world minus Russia) brought together the former hegemons and those who saw the fall of socialism as their liberation from Russian dominance. Exceptions in this development were the former Yugoslavia, which had shaken the shackles of Soviet control in 1948, and Albania and Romania, where the primary source of liberation was having gotten rid of their own dictators. The Balkans has always represented a sphere of interest for Austria. In certain parts, the Austrian cultural influence is intertwined with traces of the long-lost Ottoman period, which is a large part of what makes the Balkans seem so exotic. When the circumstances changed, the wild, underdeveloped Balkans with its different culture became a suitable target for the new European politics of tolerance. In Germany and Austria there were a number of exhibitions dedicated to contemporary art in the Balkan states. Compared to Central European shows, these were made even more in the spirit of respecting difference, the spirit that had helped build the positive image of Europe and the West in general. While the Central European shows seemed to be resurrecting some pre-war cultural space with Vienna, Munich, Prague and Milan as its centers of culture and education, the new exoticism coincided with the contemporary neoliberal spirit. Such exhibitions as *Blood & Honey / The Future Is in the Balkans* (Vienna 2003), *In Search of Balkania* (Graz, 2002), and *In the Gorges of the Balkans* (Kassel, 2003),[6] modernized the paradigm of the art of the Other and put it on the map of the global art market. Those financing the exhibitions fused their narrow regional and broader economic interests. Again it was Erhard Busek who pointed this out in his essay "Austria and the Balkans," where he speaks of the important place the Balkans occupies both in Austria's history and in the processes of European reintegration: "Blut & Honig (Blood & Honey) is a symbol of the seduction and radicalism emanating from the cultural landscape of southeast Europe. Austria of all countries should understand this message."[7]

Regardless of how big a part or which part of Eastern Europe the various regional exhibitions dealt with, that which stimulated the European producers in every case was European

[5] The Kontakt Art Collection of Erste Group, established in 2004 in Vienna, is an association for the promotion of Central, Eastern and Southeast European art with a focus on artistic activities since the late 1950s. Its mission states that it reflects on conceptual forms of art production within Europe's changing political geographies. This involves placing the art of the formerly socialist countries in an international art context and drawing attention to its reciprocal connections and varied practices. Kontakt aims to collect works which play an integral role within European art history while also claiming an exceptional status within a politically heterogeneous terrain.

[6] *Blood & Honey / The Future Is in the Balkans*, curated by Harald Szeemann, Sammlung Essl/Kunst der Gegenwart, Klosterneuburg/Vienna, 2003; *In Search of Balkania*, curated by Roger Conover, Eda Čufer and Peter Weibel, Neue Galerie Graz am Landesmuseum Joanneum, Graz, 2002; *In the Gorges of the Balkans*, curated by René Block, Kunsthalle Fridericianum, Kassel, 2003.

[7] Erhard Busek, "Austria and the Balkans," *Blut & Honig, Zukunft is am*

reintegration politics, which must of course be understood primarily in terms of the reintegration of the markets.

The most extensive exhibition of Eastern European art thus far was staged in Bonn in 1994. Already its title—*Europe, Europe*—pointed to the fact that the fall of socialism reunited something that had been artificially separated.[8] *Europe, Europe* aimed to show that like Europe, art was one and universal. In this sense, the end of socialism meant a reintegration of formerly excluded history into the existing canon. The exhibition and its catalogue aimed to demonstrate that the main task of history was to categorize art within the already existing classification system. Thus the show was organized and represented by various individual groups and movements: symbolism, abstraction, cubism, constructivism, surrealism, socialist realism, systematic tendencies, neo-avant-garde movements etc.

Expressing their regional interest already in their titles, the exhibitions of Eastern European art mentioned so far shared the common ambition of assembling an overview of the art of the region. I would also like to mention two shows that stressed the dimension of time in their titles, indicating a desire to draw a line under a certain period. Staged in Stockholm in 1999, the exhibition *After the Wall* focused on the art in the territories of post-socialist countries in the first decade after the fall of the Berlin Wall. This decade was often referred to as the period of transition, or even normalization. Although opinions differ on when exactly this period of transition is supposed to have ended, many would agree that the watershed mark in the process was the accession of the individual post-socialist countries to the EU. With its range of themes (current socio-political circumstances, history, artists' personal worlds, gender issues) the exhibition highlighted the burning issues with which the region was grappling, demonstrating that the situation in general was far from normal. Or, as the exhibition curator Bojana Pejić wrote in the catalogue: "But if we accept that the 'normalization' of most of the East which started in the late 1980s is now almost over, this cannot mean that life in the region—finally—has become normal. And this should have an impact on the art as well."[9] The time of "normalization" is thus a time when there is still such a thing as post-socialist art, although the issues it deals with are also shared by numerous other spaces.

Balkan / Blood & Honey, The Future's in the Balkans, Sammlung Essl/ Kunst der Gegenwart, Klosterneuburg/Vienna 2003, p. 45.

[8] *Europa Europa – Das Jahrhundert der Avantgarde in Mittel- und Osteuropa*, curated by Ryszard Stanislawski and Chritoph Brockhaus, Kunst- und Ausstellungshalle der Bundesrepublik Deutschland, Bonn, 1994.

[9] Bojana Pejić, "The Dialectic of Normality," *After the Wall, Art and Culture in post-Communist Europe*, Moderna Museet, Stockholm 1999, p. 18.

Over a decade later, the Centre Pompidou in Paris organized an exhibition entitled *Promises of the Past* (2010), which the museum director Alfred Pacquement accompanied with these words: "The wall fell twenty years ago, on the very day that I am writing these lines. The borders have been modified and the limit between two sides of Europe has become obsolete. Artists have circulated in both directions, just as art observers and institutions have developed: the contemporary approach can only be transnational since many countries have joined the European community on a political and economic level. What was still called, ten years ago 'the other half of Europe,' according to the title of a series of exhibitions at the National Gallery of the Jeu de Paume in 2000, now appears to be an outmoded concept."[10] Also the exhibition curators Christine Macel and Joanna Mytkowska problematized interpreting Eastern European art through the East–West duality, advocating instead an understanding of history that can be told in many different ways, as linear history or as several small stories going in different directions. For that show, Polish artist Monika Susnowska made a special architectural structure that took as its point of reference the pavilions at international art fairs and exhibitions. The exhibition catalogue explains that it was exactly these types of events, i.e. art fairs, which gave artists greater scope for experimenting during the socialist period, due to the small dimensions of the works. Unfortunately, this otherwise fascinating architectural concept had the opposite effect in the Centre Pompidou: it became what was merely its historical reference, the art-fair representation of national or regional achievements. The decisive factor in this seems to have been the context of the Centre Pompidou, one of the most influential museums in the West, which made an attempt at a condensed, concise presentation of the art of a region with this show. Although the organizers of the exhibition had explicitly hoped to avoid the East-West dichotomy, this was exactly where the exhibition slipped up, failing to see that—despite the now united Europe—the prevailing power relations had not significantly changed. One of the questions the curators posed was: "What should be done with the art history of the dozen or so countries East of Berlin and West of Kiev that were/are referred to as Eastern Europe?"[11] This question pointed above all to their opinion that the era of trying to define Eastern European identity was over,

10 Alfred Pacquement, *Promises of the Past, A Discontinuous History of Art in Former Eastern Europe*, Centre Pompidou, Paris 2010, p. 13.

11 Christine Macel & Joananna Mytkowska, *Promises of the Past, A Discontinuous History of Art in Former Eastern Europe*, Centre Pompidou, Paris 2010, p. 18.

and that the time of different, plural narratives had come. They grouped the works around narratives related to various topics, such as modernist utopias, modernist positions, micro-politics, feminism, the relationship between public and private etc. After twenty years of Europe's "new democracies," the curators broached a decidedly relevant question: how to proceed in a time when our identities are increasingly merging and the world is no longer (so) divided?

We should stop at this point and ask ourselves whether a change of narrative is in itself indeed a sufficient response to the question how to proceed now that we are done with identity politics. Is the only thing that is different after the past twenty years that we are today becoming more and more similar; or might not this homogenization also represent our greatest problem? And who exactly is best served by homogenization? Do we all contribute an equal share to formulating the new global cultural patterns? The close of the 1980s brought more than just the fall of the Berlin Wall; the processes of globalization and information increased dramatically, as did neoliberalism.

The exhibitions I have talked about so far were all produced in the West and could not have happened without the support of broader political and economic interests that went hand in hand with the reintegration processes in Central Europe and the EU, as well as with the neoliberal favoring of multiculturalism. In most of these projects, curators from the region were involved, contributing not only their knowledge of the art of the region, but also their insight into the current societal processes there. The narratives chosen by the different curators for their exhibitions were not the only possible context for reading the individual shows. Just as the shows brought back memories of a specific geopolitical space, also the space of the presentation contributed its share of the memories. The institutional framework of the presentation greatly impacts the meaning of a show, and this familiar realization should now be incorporated in the medium of the exhibition itself. Nowadays, museums wish to speak in a variety of voices, but usually, the voices are filtered through the existing conceptual and representational models of the institution. When striving for a plurality of narratives, we should keep in mind that already the space and place of the presentation codify the exhibition. What can therefore be done to keep these various voices as undistorted as possible?

This was a question we at the Moderna galerija in Ljubljana
kept foremost in our minds when staging the latest exhibition
of our collection of Eastern European art Arteast 2000+[12],
where we gave room to a number of different narrators. We
underscored the institutional framework with several archives
of exhibitions that represented Moderna galerija's important
contributions to the framing of the Eastern European context,
e.g., the archive of the exhibition *The Body and the East* (1998).
Artists have always played an important role in historicizing
Eastern European art since the inadequate efforts of their local art institutions often forced them to be their own archivists
and even to systemize their (own) local traditions to provide a
context for their work. I have named this approach self-histori-
cizing. One of the most typical examples of such can be found
in the project of the artist group IRWIN entitled *East Art Map*
(2002–2006). This IRWIN project is exhibited in the exhibition of our collection, together with a number of other works by
artists-narrators. A very special place in the exhibition is occupied by oral histories, presented in the form of video interviews
with certain key artists from the territory of Eastern European;
these artists' testimonies are given prominence as one of the
key narratives in our collection. At the same time, oral histories trigger reflection about an exhibition model that would
not be based solely on representation. With the opening of the
new territories and their histories, there has emerged the need
for an exhibition model that would preserve as much as possible the space of unique narratives that cannot be controlled
or transformed. "Oral sources therefore are a necessary (if not
sufficient) condition for a history of the non-hegemonic classes,
while they are less necessary for the history of the ruling class
who have had control over writing and therefore entrusted most
of their collective memory to written records."[13]

How to preserve the collective history of a space that is in a
subordinate position to the dominant spaces with well-developed museum and discursive systems and thus in a position to
control also the history of those weaker than themselves? The
kind of historicizing I advocate should, in addition to providing a variety of narratives, draw attention to various narrating
positions, geopolitical, institutional, and individual. The question of the identity of the art of a region has now been replaced
by the question of the agent of its historicizing. And this is not

12 Arteast 2000+ is the
first collection of Eastern
European art from the
Post-War Avant-Gardes to
the present. It was founded
by the Moderna galerija in
Ljubljana and first publicly
presented in 2000, in the
as yet unrenovated former
military barracks build-
ing in which the Museum
of Contemporary Art
Metelkova—MSUM opened
in 2011.

13 Alessandro Portelli,
"The Peculiarities of Oral
History," *History Workshop
Journal*, No. 12, fall 1981,
p. 104.

an exclusively Eastern European topic. Not only the former
Eastern Europe, also many other regions occupying weak positions in a hierarchically ordered world will increasingly aspire
to participate in informing and shaping the future image of the
world. Not with firmly fixed identities, for this is no longer a
relevant concept; they will contribute their own experiences,
which will not be somebody else's experiences forced on them.
That is why these experiences have to be heard together with
the voices of those recounting them. And this means more than
merely allowing voices to be heard undistorted; it means bringing the various narrators face to face with one another, even
confronting them, in order to understand the various mechanisms involved in history-making.

Translated from the Slovene by Tamara Soban.

Approaching Art through Ensembles Bart De Baere

1. The Ensemble: A Retrospective

An approach based on modes of existence might lead to a situation in which museums acquire not only "works" (sculptures, paintings, drawings, installations) but also ensembles. Relations between constituent parts of ensembles might be specified, as well as the possibilities of exhibiting fragments, separate elements or one single element, the possibilities of including an ensemble in a more extended context or the possibilities of concentrating and dissolving it. We would no longer be thinking of a standard framework with permissible deviations, but instead of a network of relationships that might be realized but does not have to be. Small peripheral elements, which for instance often appear in works by Mark Manders, would be considered desirable rather than problematic. Artists would, in the future, be able to permeate the museum's "permanence" with a desire for change.[1]

It is remarkable how not only the status but also the vitality of words can change. The meaning of the term "ensemble" should be obvious after two decades of fuzzy logic, rhizomatic thinking, processual and performative action, "change management" and the dematerialization of the Self and of our common heritage. In the early 1990s "ensemble" was still a fluffy notion, used as a non-definition to hint at other possible approaches to art, different from the static structures arising from the compelling idea of the artwork as the central unit of art. Just as *This Is the Show and the Show Is Many Things* (S.M.A.K. Ghent, 1994) was in a certain sense a naïve exhibition, it was in a certain sense a naïve act to promote the term "ensemble" as a hypothesis at the end of the preparatory text. The text acknowledged an insight that was up for grabs, and tried to observe it rather than formulate a critique of the system that eclipsed this insight.

This Is the Show... itself arose from the observation during Documenta IX that there was no public space for some of the relevant young artists of the time. Gabriel Orozco, who at that time still worked in the street, Mona Hatoum, whose work seemed to be more about process than slides of her work were

[1] Bart De Baere, "Joining the Present to Now," preparative text to *This is the Show ...*, published in *Kunst & museumjournaal*, 1994–1995, Volume 6, double new year issue, p. 70.

able to show, the fascinating oeuvre of Honoré d'O that had not yet surfaced in the art world but already flourished in his studio and in various alternative locations, the dancing proposals of the Austrian ManfreDu Schu: all these were ultimately left out, although a young Documenta curator would have desired otherwise. The work of one of their peers, Eran Schaerf, which was there, slotted between two Aue-Pavilions, remained practically unseen at this Documenta. The specific complexity in the approach of artists like Jimmie Durham or Cildo Meireles was barely noticed as such within the well-constructed exhibition that Documenta IX nonetheless was. A construction that, moreover, consciously sought to attain diversity in terms of the artworks presented and thereby a more intense composition of the exhibition.

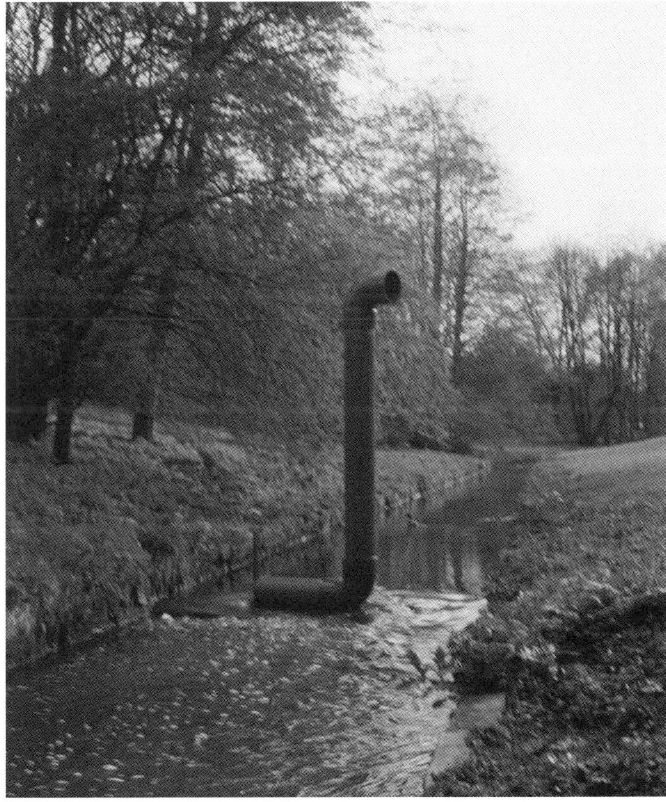

Jimmie Durham, *Die kleine Fulda*, 1992, installation view of Documenta IX, Kassel, 1992

This Is the Show… is now seen as one of the first process-based exhibitions, but was actually derived from the intuitive notion that the space for art could be addressed in a radically different way, i.e. as a modulated "time-space" where a sense of eternity might be juxtaposed with the singular moment and where art would not proceed from the isolation of fragments to the composition of a whole. Instead, it would become manifest as mobile encounters of divergent behaviors, and thereby help define its own space through relations of distance and proximity in a tense and ever-changing continuum. The endeavor was to discover a possible experience that might accommodate an absolutist "stack sculpture" by Donald Judd just as well as gestures and conversations—or, more specifically, Louise Bourgeois's *Liars* and the motocross bike that Jason Rhoades drove round inside the museum. Simultaneously. Articulating each other.

The notion of "ensemble" appeared from around the corner at the end of this line of thinking. Whereas *This Is the Show...* expressed the intuition of a different possibility to show art, the term "ensemble" expressed the need for a different insight into what artists do. Neither the spatial presentation nor the conceptual approach felt revolutionary. They simply felt closer to art. The impression was that the art world had, for a whole century already—the then not quite finished 20th century—ignored the complexity of art and of artists' approaches to it. The early avant-garde was part of this, although the project focused primarily on young artists who appeared to be offering something urgent, with a *raison d'être* that had not yet found its visibility. The project tried to create this visibility, scantily or not at all justified in terms of philosophy and art history and even less supported by the interest in process and the relational aesthetic that were still to come. This visibility was instead negatively determined—by the unacceptable reduction of art to products of a Bonfire-of-the-Vanities-style yuppie-ism, with its new money, its applied technologies and short attention span.

We are now far away from the moment of *This Is the Show...* and the initial use of the "ensemble" notion. We can now see— or hope—that the surge of object-based art, from the *Neue Wilde* to the neo-minimal sculpture that was to oppose them, marked at the same time the beginning of a new phase and the end of an era.

That era of Americanism had extended art history to beyond the bourgeois period in which it was created. It had already appropriated the early avant-garde and stripped it of its intractability. It had reduced Malevich to painting and Rodchenko to sculpture. The early avant-garde was celebrated after the Second World War, but it was as if its body and soul had become separated. The body of the classical early avant-garde, its study of form, had delivered the material for building a bridge from older art to the post-war market system. This bridge made it possible to present the Surrealists without their mad spatiality; it reduced Schwitters to a collagist with an interesting background story, and turned Duchamp into a producer of multiples. The art market, but also the museum system and public presentation *tout court*—they were all based on the work of art.

Since then we have built a somewhat more complex public awareness of what art was proposing in the course of that inspired, passionate 20th century. Russian Constructivism has been liberated from the American reduction it underwent after the Second World War and the surrounding situation has been restored in its polemical complexity. Dadaism has acquired the classic status of a grand public discursive exhibition in Paris. Presentation practice has become a research field in itself. The elusiveness of Situationism has become a cult phenomenon. The big Anglo-Saxon museum machines have endeavored to appropriate non-Western traditions, Post-colonialism has provided an intellectually substantiated diversification of views and the former Eastern Bloc, Yugoslavia and South America have re-valued and marketed their radical Post-War Avant-Gardes with all the intellectual capacity at their disposal.

All this is due in part to the fact that artists, more than ever before, have managed to let the complexity of art infiltrate a market that is becoming less monolithic. On their side there have been sympathetic intellectuals, who are thematizing this complexity, and people in the curatorial niche that has emerged in the meantime, who are reformalizing it. The market, taking guidance from this newly apparent complexity, has established countless new niches and sales opportunities.

2. The Broadening of Art

The bourgeoisie likes counter positions to its vested interests, but (only) in moderation. For a long period of time, art museums have dedicated themselves exclusively to artworks but hardly to any other activities that artists have been engaged in. This has much to do with a tendency to excoriate the uncontrollable passions that avant-garde artists have developed for reigniting the art tradition. The opening up of the area for activity in visual art could be seen as three major movements:

a. The Early Avant-Garde Wanting to Take on the World

After its onset at the end of the 19th century, the early avant-garde presses in the beginning of the 20th century forward to create a new world. Visual art plays a key role: it is a platform for development and a reference for a new grammar and it seamlessly moves on into reflecting and shaping this new world.

Artists at that time often stand with one foot in the traditionally formed patterns of art and the other in a far freer area—one pillar on land and one in the sea, like the Angel of the Apocalypse. Futurist manifestos share a moment with flat paintings, ready-mades with studies of nudes. We might see this as a split, but it is probably more accurate to interpret it as an ambition to hold onto artistic tradition and to imbue it with life, in one broad stroke, to give it a new social meaning. Even the formal French schools stress this ambition to offer a new outlook for society. It is certainly present in Futurism and in Dadaism, which wanted to combine art and life in a Cabaret Voltaire; in early Abstraction; in de Stijl, where fine art, applied art and architecture slot perfectly into place; in Russian Constructivism, which wants to be part of a revolutionary society; in schools like Bauhaus and Vkhutemas that look to connect the new vision with industrial production processes. There, in all sorts of ways, structured or informal, clumsy or flawless, art wants to march out into the world. So the lure of the art museum is doomed in advance: its files become populated by an endless amount of monstrous hybrids that are still—completely, or partially, or perhaps actually—art, but no longer artworks. Instead they are spaces, actions, propaganda designed by artists.

Very much like the Pre-Modern artists of the 15th century, their Modernist counterparts also make work for specific spaces, contexts and small audiences. For other people, to be sure, for new clients: they can no longer count on the support of the nobility and the church but must create the setting themselves, since the days of Courbet with his *Atélier* and the Impressionists with their pastel-colored *Salon des indépendants*. The Modernist artists want to take over the art scene and let art "work". They construct their own spaces and connections, at first often working for small groups of sympathizers. As a collective, artists in fact become their own commissioners, and their task is to reinvent art so that it can become an engine for society; you can only ever be avant-garde if the masses want to follow in your footsteps.

b. The Neo-Avant-Garde Cultivating the Art Space

The neo-avant-garde will have more limited ambitions from the late 1950s onwards. They will try, in different ways, to create an autonomous space for art and thereby articulate a number of alternative possibilities to make art visible for the public. New categories of form are established as genres in their own right with their own distribution channels: performance, video, artists' books, mail art… Socio-political engagement is one possibility—with Joseph Beuys's commitment to the Green Party as the most visible expression—but no longer an inherent, integrated ambition for all art. Jimmie Durham becomes disappointed, despite the rapidly growing appreciation for his work, when he makes art again in New York in the 1980s after his years of political activism. His works do not provoke serious discussion but are only seen as "representation of engagement". Art strives to become a field of values unto itself, which in some segments enters into critical alliances with the market and elsewhere forms alternative networks, such as the Situationist International and Fluxus. In some cases, like that of "visual poetry" in Western Europe, it even remains outside the art world.

Artists request and are granted a place as actors. Again they write manifestos or publish, with the people that surround them, their own magazines and books that in words, images, design and packaging become a radical foundation for what is also happening with their work. "The book, consisting of photographic statements and written testimonies, bases its critical and editorial assumptions upon the knowledge that criticism and iconography only give a limited view of and a partial feeling for how artists work [...]" is the fundamental attitude that Germano Celant formulates in his seminal text *Arte povera* from 1969.

The European powers that negotiate with the market and play its game—from Beuys, Broodthaers or Polke to the Italian *arte povera* artists—play on the duality of object and mental social space, but their thoughts are still mainly disseminated through artworks. To the extent that other expressions of them are collected, this continued to take place (until only recently) in the archival half of the museum. Curiously, such forms were not regarded as art.

For decades after the Second World War the hegemony of the once provincial New York market system is almost total, dominating not only the media but also the art education system. Yet this also allows havens for art to exist in the margins, in places where art detaches itself from the market through internationally networked alternative scenes, the "Innere Emigration" of meditative artists or the political activism of others. Such contexts allow the spirit of the early avant-garde to stay alive.

This has re-emerged in recent years with the renewed public esteem and increasing commercialization of the Neo-Avant-Garde, from French Fluxus to Moscow Collective Actions, from the American outsider James Lee Byars to the Flemish outsider Jef Geys, from Constant Nieuwenhuys's *New Babylon* to Helio Oiticica's *Parangolés*.

c. Freedom as an Element of Commercialization in Recent Decades

When the post-war structure of the world begins to fall apart in the 1980s, the entire range of possibilities for artistic expression pass into common property and artists are no longer compelled to work in niches but can create their own mix of broad exhibition platforms and marketing operations, with or without the initial stakes that lay behind these 20th century traditions. The way of painting of the *transavanguardia* is an expression of this space that was suddenly open, but this is just as true of the new formatting of photography to match the scale and scope of painting, and of the countless hybrid forms that artists are using.

This can be seen as a third stage. It took the art scene a hundred years to absorb the expansion of art into a wider range of activities and formal possibilities. Seen as positively as possible, the present situation can be called an integrated space. The walls and sluice gates of the old system have been torn down. Anything is possible, but therefore perhaps also nothing. The market and event culture are flourishing. What became most difficult is the value judgment that is really at stake here: one that is cultural rather than economic. This cultural dimension is not about convertibility and appropriation in the economic sense, but about non-convertibility and public domain. The limit—the nearly un-thinkable—lies above all in the articulation of the intrinsic value of an artist's proposal, that which can give art sustainable impact. The freedom of the artist has become more obvious today, and therefore also more problematic. This might be a stimulus for institutions to approach the recent past differently.

3. The Inevitability of Particular Topographies, Trajectories and Finalities

These three movements of the 20th century—taking on the world, creating a space for art, playing with a mix of possible expressions—correspond with three major areas in which we may now formulate a notion of art that leads on to ensembles. From this renewed focus of the present, we may approach the historical avant-garde differently and realize that the challenges that have become explicit today were actually (already) on the agenda throughout the 20th century.

a. The Nature of Social Impact

Artists have been recasting the most divergent phenomena in the world as visuality—sex, their own bodies, the mass media, politics, the everyday, the landscape, urban incidents, language, music, architecture, rumors, and it goes on—long enough to create a collective awareness that everything can be art. That nothing can be excluded. Conversely, any action performed by an artist effectively, inevitably and continuously becomes part of his art proposal. The refusal by artists to cultivate their own public persona is as much a part of their practice as doing the very opposite; not appearing at your own opening is as much a part of the media mix as courting collectors.

Artists today are doomed to define their own social impact themselves. While the early avant-garde saw society as its target (with art at heart) and the neo-avant-garde targeted art itself (thinking that this would eventually make society move), no such determined effort can be discerned today. The prevailing criteria for success in the commercial and media markets are not persuasive enough to become valid goals for artists. Focusing purely on them will always lead to a generic product. Such success no longer stands for difference, as before, but for variety marked by a fundamental lack of difference.

What that difference might be is no longer quite clear. To understand this also becomes the task of the artist, who must now not only define his oeuvre and his space but also his production of meaning, his patterns of movement in the most fundamental way: he must determine his own route and the sense it is supposed to make. The *arte povera* hero Michelangelo Pistoletto invests his capital in a foundation at Biella in northern Italy that literally wants art to energize society, while the young Antwerp artist Vaast Colson opts for ephemeral gestures at the edge of visibility to enable art to continuously become one with society.

Slovenian museum director Zdenka Badovinac has advocated the study of the history of regional intellectual contexts alongside local art history—and rightly so, because they form a context that resonates with art proposals, enabling us to better understand how they come together and are brought forward. We can see the intellectual context in the classical sense, as the concrete social and metaphysical insights that feature in an artist's surroundings, how they are justified or challenged and which thinkers create change and when and how.

At the same time there is another context, more difficult to detect: the setting of insights within which artists make their proposals. Art must often—especially in the crucial initial phase—contribute to creating its own environment, the space where it can exist. So artists become symbolic stakeholders, from the very beginning of the situation which brings forward their art, and with which they will remain linked. If we consider this setting for art a constituent part of the intellectual context, Badovinac's approach becomes really interesting. Then we can value the contribution of artists in relation to how social and existential problems are approached at a given moment, and understand that the difference that they make stays relevant beyond that moment, just like important developments in philosophy and theory.

b. A Proper Space for Art

It has become customary for artists to at least intervene in those locations that the neo-avant-garde preferred to cultivate in their efforts to create their own space for art. Publications, invitation cards and other printed matter surrounding a public project, whether an exhibition or something else, are natural components of the framework, just like the picture frame and the color of the wall were for the Impressionists.

Artists are all but obliged to compose their own space for art. They do this by sketching out their own history through actions that accord them special status within the meshwork of traditions that constitute the art scene. The production of artworks as such, and the market that appropriates them, is sometimes just a miniscule part of the total of their activities. They build their own organizations for themselves, and later perhaps their own foundations. They choose their galleries and exhibition spaces not just for their technical qualities but also for the kind of value they embody as setting.

Artists help decide the exhibition title and campaign image, which function as a summary of the project. The title and the basic image are inevitably just as much a part of the art as the works they announce, and not only in a project such as the collaborative work realized at M HKA in 2011 by Lawrence Weiner and Liam Gillick, two artists who explicitly position themselves at the edge of this limit.

Today it is in fact expected of artists that they manage the intellectual circumstances around their work. This too they have already been doing for long, at least to some extent, and now it has become an everyday practice that is often also consciously formalized. Artists govern initial information and reflection on their work, commissioning writers and providing them with input. Such interventions do not amount to the gathering of laudatory speeches to serve as glorified sales pitches. It initiates points of views, modes of approaching the work… When an artist like Luc Tuymans masterminds the content of his catalogues and even makes available detailed access to his visual sources, it is something he considers himself obliged to do as a countermeasure. With this excessive openness he seeks to disarm the anecdotal and content-orientated approach and make it a harmless, liberating measure for conveying anything that concerns him, rather than offering it to viewers as the comfort zone of anecdotes to which they may easily relate. This kind of activity in no way turns artists into manipulative charlatans without belief in the intrinsic value of their own work, like the travelling tailors in The Emperor's New Clothes. Artists undertake this because they are aware of images in a sophisticated way; they know that each small part of an image contributes to determining its reception.

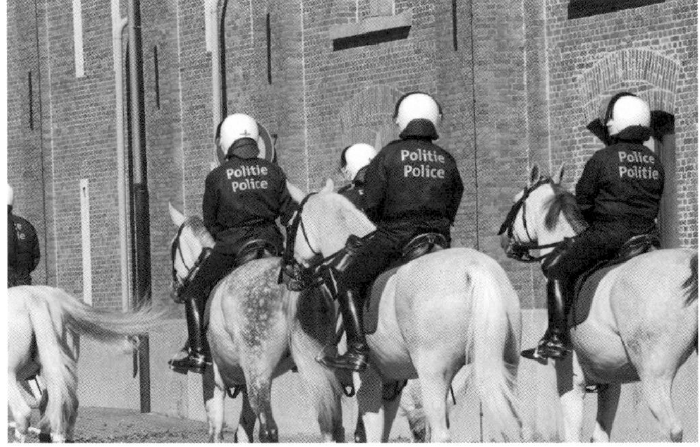

Lawrence Weiner and Liam
Gillick, 2011,
photo by Luc De Jaeger

In an increasingly discursive world artists are also expected to be discursive, and they obviously wish to intervene in the discourse to benefit their art. They take the stage as speakers or become curators to mould the broader view of the art scene according to their perspective. Sometimes, as with Jimmie Durham, who is also an important essayist, discourse is a complement to the work; sometimes, as with Agency, which M HKA presented as part of the *Textiles* project, it is a core component.

c. Composing the Oeuvre

Last but not least, the composition of the oeuvre is just as relevant as what the individual works express; they exist in this setting and are articulated by it. It is therefore important to view artists in the light of their entire production and understand how it has come about. Works are often created and presented in series. Paintings may aspire to their own pictorial finality, but they may also become vehicles for processes that wash over them, or else just a working medium like any other, with which any technically capable painter can work, like a photographer who makes a photograph for another artist or a carpenter who executes a sculpture. In his exhibition at Stella Lohaus Gallery in Antwerp in 2010 Bjarne Melgaard showed self-portraits that M HKA would gladly have acquired had it had the means. He is a gifted painter but he left the painting of the portraits to an assistant and then made adjustments to them; the technicality of representational painting in itself is not what interests him.

Artists communicate mainly with the totality of their actions. They know that individual elements will inevitably be interpreted within the setting of the whole, often literally the moment they appear in a solo exhibition, and in any case implicitly. Members of their initial and (for the artists) crucial audience—whether it be essayists, gallery owners, collectors, critics or other decision-makers—are always aware of artists' broader activities and will assess them accordingly, perceiving and valuing the work against the background of previous knowledge. Much of today's art even relies on this and is only easily accessible with such a context in place. Accidental spectators without prior knowledge must try to grasp an entire process through their experience of the moment, in which the broader picture might not always be very apparent.

Artists compose the diversity of their oeuvre and situate each element of it within a broader framework, of their own history as well as the history of their chosen medium. It is not only painting that has a tradition in which each choice carries weight; the numerous alternative media that have emerged have it too. Prints, artists' books, videos, actions and their documentation, none of these exist in themselves but rather as phenomena in the field of media traditions where recognition continually reverberates. The decision to sign up for one of the many versions of the neo-avant-garde, which developed into genres, is motivated by convention but inevitably also plays with it. Artists may now oscillate back and forth between media that previously seemed irreconcilable, between various manifestations that used to be seen as either avant-garde or reactionary. Sculptures morph into installations that invade

space and are subsequently reformatted to become sculptures
again. Performance artists may also make paintings; painters
may produce videos.

M HKA, just like many Flemish private collectors, possesses
three paintings by Wilhelm Sasnal, in addition to a video work
that he himself considers important and a long series of drawings. Each of these is a work unto itself and could have been
sold as such, but at the Gwangju Biennale Sasnal showed them
as a single coherent work with four interlaced storylines. The
M HKA also has a comic book and a board game by this artist. The passage inside traditions is a role that artists choose for
themselves, a casting of themselves that becomes part of their
proposal. It lends sharpness to a scene in which interdisciplinar-
ity has become the standard. The same material can simultaneously lead to a giveaway publication for Agnès B and to costly
photographs in low quantities for the market. Whereas multiples
were long considered derivative material and the uniqueness
of the work still remained an implicit basic condition, the basic
condition is now the multiple, even in painting, where seriality
has become commonplace. The edition is determined as much
by practical circumstances—what works best in the market,
how much time the maker wants to spend on something—as
by the fact that it has become a decision in itself for artists.
One still remains a valid option, because this number meets the
viewer on an equal footing—that of uniqueness—but five is
also almost one in our overpopulated world.

4. A Respectful Relationship with Contemporary Art

a. It's about insights

When art claimed its independence from the avant-garde by
breaking away from the social consensus it also made itself
homeless, displaced. Art is no longer about something that
is, but about something that might be. The 19th century salon
painters were promptly incorporated into the museums. With
avant-garde art came a disconnection between the production
of art and its societal acceptance, which we might call "mu-
seumization." For a long time the best cases were exceptions,
from artist-driven early modern art museums such as MoMA

in New York and Museum Sztuki in Lódz up to that moment in
the 1960s when the museums' dams were temporarily broken
by now legendary exhibitions.

In the last two decades it has finally become common for
artists not only to receive a place but also to be able to make
their own space in museums. Collecting practice still does not
always know how to deal with this. The tendency is still to
identify a collection with artworks. If collecting practice wants
to retain the context of those artworks, it will normally expand its acquisition from traditionally formatted work towards
whole "installations," thereby petrifying variable ensemble
situations into monolithic, quasi-sculptural arrangements of
diverse elements, setting once and for all a 'correct' and fixed
context. At the same time, however, artists use these same
museums as an integral mobile space. Can collecting practice
accommodate not only the form but also the spirit of artists'
interaction with museum space? Thinking in ensembles might
be a beginning.

Currently, an institution's ready-made knowledge of the
works in its collection is often limited to an A4 summary provided by its mediation service. This is accompanied by a similarly short text on the artist's biography. Various staff members
keep overviews of roughly the same order in their heads. These
are the people who "know the collection." Encyclopedic thinking is a long-lost ambition—in the meantime we have learned
that surveys are not feasible, that they produce at best only a
crude map—but the synthetic *modus operandi* of this mindset
has lingered. The immediately available information of works
in the collection is of the same nature as the information that
fills the Internet or other mass media: good syntheses with accidental areas of depth, but without an organic connection between the surface information and more profound insights.

Yet such insights do pass through the institution. When a
work is purchased more information becomes available and it
is often possible to find proof of this in the archives. Perhaps
a member of the museum's staff is in contact with the artist at
a moment when some problems occur or when a text is being
prepared, and sharper insights may therefore remain in his or
her personal backpack; perhaps an exhibition with the artist in
question is being organized that more thoroughly reveals the
consistency and setting of his or her work.

For such things, however, institutions increasingly rely on external specialists: they let external writers write for publications put together by external publishers. Perhaps this seems more professional and efficient, but in practice it means that afterwards the institution itself may not even possess the final digital version of the text. Indeed, final corrections are made in the PDF that is filed with the publisher, graphic designer and printer. The communication with interested parties is not necessarily connected with institutional intelligence. The mediation system may sometimes be interactive and diversified, but it is also a professionally structured instrument that is self-reliant and, in addition, was often likewise created by external partners.

Since the 1970s museums have kept themselves obsessively busy with completing surveys of their objects, a task they never seem to be able to complete. They have coupled this survey with an ever more perfectionist conservation and management apparatus. Additional information and insights can be appended to the more sophisticated databases of this kind, but this is not the core task of the inventories.

b. Ensemble thinking

The central ambition could also be to gain an understanding of the artists engaged by a museum—a purchase at least gives the impression of engagement—that is in-depth and based on the artists' specific qualities. It would seem natural that an acquisition stimulates further engagement, but this does not always happen. Among its various assets—artists' books, books edited or designed by artists, invitation cards, photographs for which the museum may or may not hold the rights, fragments of stories—the museum could explore and find possibilities for presenting an artist's oeuvre more fully.

The essence of ensemble thinking is that it addresses questions that are otherwise bubbling away at the perimeter of what can be managed and controlled. This is actually what good researchers would do anyway: asking themselves in which setting the object of the research is to be found and to what extent that setting is necessary for the research. Ensemble thinking is a form of mindfulness and self-criticism.

It really should be standard procedure to ask questions about how artists give stature to their oeuvre, how they articulate their own space with the many resources available today, or how they aspire to making a social impact and perhaps also consciously enact this beyond what is traditionally seen as their work. The possibility of developing a collection with the kind of images that give tentative answers to those questions will only tighten the focus on the artwork that might have been the point of departure—unless that work was really not a work but a documentation of something else. Then the focus will consciously shift away from the mutilated piano by Ben Vautier or Wolf Vostell, which then ceases to be a work of art and becomes the documentation of a Fluxus concert.

With this method, artworks are very likely to accrue a broader and more sustainable base of insights. It differs substantially from what is called "contextualization", which was a popular way of differentiation in the recent past through which as yet non-valorized oeuvres were brought to attention, from the standpoint of how they achieved something in a particular situation. This is a relativistic attitude: something derives (its) meaning from its surroundings, not from its behavior (which, of course, is informed through interaction with that environment and may also be more easily read from there).

Ensemble thinking is precisely about finding a platform that is as precise as possible and helps focusing on the particularity of such individual behavior. It asks whether an institution's assets are optimal for the purpose of understanding artists and their work, and if the presentation and framing of these assets reflect their qualities in an optimal way. It seeks significance not only in individual assets but also in their consistent internal interaction as well as in their "outward" consistency. This is the opposite of contextualizing. It is about the potential "outward" effects that are embedded in artistic practice and therefore might influence future appearances of a given work.

The ambition is certainly not to make a shift from the presentation of artworks to a documentary space, as often happens nowadays, or from a *catalogue raisonné* of artworks to an extended version where prints and multiples, invitation cards, public statements, exhibition titles and other such things are added. Yet ensemble thinking does question how and to what extent elements from that long list of possibilities come into play, and how much weight they carry.

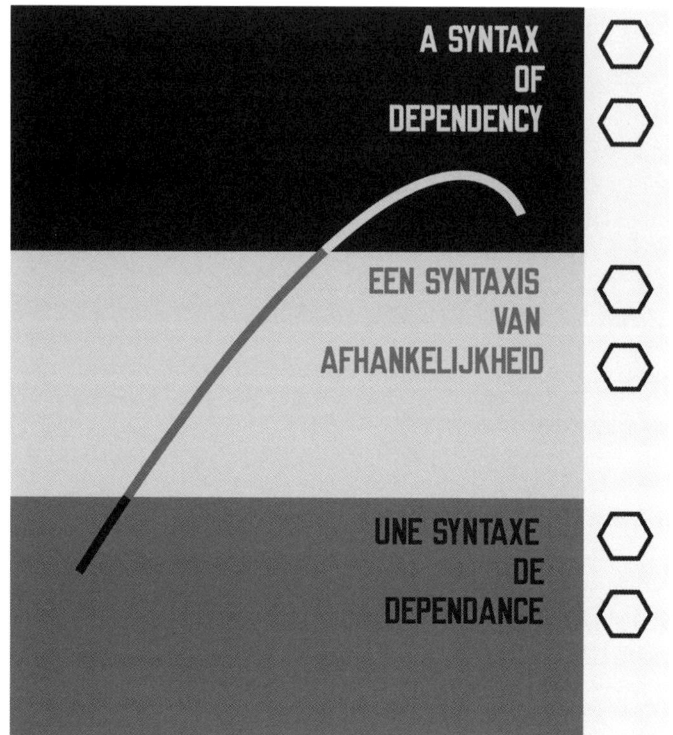

Lawrence Weiner and Liam Gillick: exhibition image *A Syntax of Dependency*, M HKA, 2011; *on the invitation card the use of the three basic colors of the Belgian flag, yellow, red and black, had suggested that this would be a political statement. For the floor piece that made out the exhibition diverging shades of these colors were chosen, however, with an amazing atmospheric effect.* Photo by M HKA

Sometimes the resulting image is panoramic; sometimes it is just the conscious renunciation of important options, a strict refusal, or an understatement that articulates a relaxed way of dealing with things. We can be sure that where an artistic practice itself searched for concentrated forms or syntheses, these will be prioritized anew after all the meandering. Such a reflective glance, which constantly searches for both focus and frame, will turn artists into respected actors. Their actions continue to set the tone, even if questions and discussions about that tone will continue. The task is to always find new connections with artists' activities, a complexity that remains uncertain but that can never be replaced by the most eloquent opinion of the day.

5. Responsible Image-Making: The Art Hypothesis

a. Intersubjectivity

The institutional application of ensemble thinking implies that databases that are rather different from the typical cataloguing software for museums and libraries will become central to the organization. It might seem as if this approach to art, if realized by the institution, will be just another version of extensive archiving. This is not so. In a certain sense it is even an anti-archival approach. Indeed it does not want to look objectively at everything. It wants to focus on making sustainable that what appears to be especially urgent, necessary and meaningful.
It is pro-active and based on choices. It relies on subjectivity and cultivates it not as arbitrariness but on the contrary, as an alternative to the actual arbitrariness and loss of meaning in objectifying methods. It is thus a possible answer to the deficits of encyclopedic collecting practice, which it considers unnecessary (in a time of pervasive visibility), impossible (in a time of over-capitalization) and meaningless (because of having been proven wrong as a project).

Ensemble thinking in the contemporary art museum relies on engagement and effectively deals with the consequences of this. It concretizes engagement into "items" or points of appearance that it finds important. These will often be artworks, but can also be (artists') texts or tools, photographs or moments. It aspires to discover meaningful relationships between the points of appearance of something in which it is itself engaged. It aspires to add "assets" to each of these points of appearance. These contain formatted possibilities for insight. Sometimes they appear to be informative—what an artist says about an item, in which specific circumstances it appeared for the first time—and sometimes essayistic, for instance describing the insights formulated by the institution when and where the item was presented.

Every time an engagement is resumed we search for new insights from the new moment, but at the same time we gather more insights as possible alternative approaches. These are also continuously offered to anyone who wishes to enter into an engagement, becomes interested in an item and wants to think further about it. Ultimately this is not about "content management"—the managing of a "content" that is seen as a fact—but about the continual revival of a quest for insights, and about a methodology and discipline through which bridges can be sustained for this purpose.

This has been about inter-subjectivity from the beginning. Institutional engagements must always be sustained by more than just a single person. It is assumed that this institutional support for ensemble thinking may be extended (to many more people) far beyond the first setting, those who are called the "public", "audience" or "stakeholders", and thereby to society as a whole. A public cultural institution produces proposals that only make sense if people in the community make them theirs, consider them in their own way, and are involved in them for their own purposes; and moreover, if the institution presents itself as accountable to them and is open to changing its proposals. It can achieve this through expressing as specifically as possible how and why it entered into some engagement and how it perceives it at the given moment. This also makes the institution approachable; it is interested in related items and assets that may be added to existing items. It can welcome these and give them a place.

Intersubjectivity is the goal. The institution will therefore ask of researchers working inside or outside it to not only submit conclusions—a text by a writer, an exhibition by a guest curator—but as far as possible also share aspects of understanding that appear earlier in the research. Like the structuring of the materials, and their analysis, so that, to begin with, the museum itself can be involved with the people who work there and are in charge of the project, and then with society at large. This can create an ecology. Now the same basic information often has to be brought together time and again. Members of staff might share more of their internalized knowledge with their peers, and external researchers can leave behind more of the content in their backpack in the institution that engages them. Also quite literally, because as authors they can avail themselves of all that material at a later date without having to archive it themselves in ever-new electronic formats. In any case they will be recognized and respected as authors if their research, through a creative commons license to which the institution aspires, is in the public domain for non-commercial purposes.

To be able to achieve this, the institution must first realize the consequences of its new attitude and not only list what it presents but also motivate this and tell what it has understood in the process. It can only fully live up to this if its actions and thinking merge and if it also tries to formulate the intensity that arises from this double move. Ensembles aspire to be faithful to the art projects they thematize, but at the same time realize they are only a continuous attempt at approaching them. They have no ambition to settle into one definitive story. On the contrary, they provide the cross-link for diverse engagements at diverse moments. It is out of this diversity that an evaluation and validation grows. Ensembles are not aimed at singular art projects alone but will equally find connections between them, because their meaning is also—perhaps especially—in such connections.

b. The art hypothesis

This leads to an art hypothesis. The institution makes proposals, time and again. Its collection is fuelled by these proposals and by the response to them. Its collection is essentially the connections between these proposals, which gives meaning to its elements, situating them within a broad yet concrete image of what art can be; it consists of insights but also of experience.

We may perhaps compare the art hypothesis, as an alternative to encyclopedic thinking, with how a landscape painter paints a landscape. He does not bring all the trees of the forest together, but tries to achieve enough "tree-ness" to infuse the image with sufficient "forest-ness" or "bushiness." To this purpose he focuses on specific trees in a specific landscape, and still it is for him about the landscape as a whole, the world in which we live.

In contrast to museums in the past, which told a master narrative that proffered itself as being definitive and comprehensive, the art hypothesis of the contemporary institution—more or less conscious and articulated—will always be temporary, because it is only sustainable in its variable continuations, and it will always be partial. The art hypothesis consists of choices that open the horizon onto a broader whole, but are anchored in the here-and-now and depart from the focus of past and present engagements. Through these, a consistency is created from and with which we can think ahead.

The big structural change is refocusing from an ownership-orientated view of things (that our items must be catalogued) to a commitment to public domain (to how we can fulfill our public function effectively). The museum is thus no longer a place that has to have, or should have to have, a representative amount of what is "most important" (and thereby will fail ever more tragicomically in this world of ever more multiplying and economizing); it is a space that strives toward a respect for intensities and the complexity associated with them. For its ensembles, this space will search for anchor points in materiality, but it may also envisage memories or references as items. The ensembles may be a phantom body, of which first a pinkie, then an elbow touches the beholder, a fragment that as *pars pro toto* hints at the whole.

In this way, the institution becomes a potential partner for all the other actors, possibly also for those that deal with property rights, and certainly for the authors, who often benefit from the further insights and memories developed around their items. It is possible for the museum to do this without conflicts of interest; it respects holders of rights and simply looks at how and where its engagements can become part of the public domain. It views its own insights, and those of others who continue to contribute, as much as possible from a Creative Commons perspective, whereby non-commercial use is automatically allowed, provided that proper reference is made.

The institution can also stay much truer to what it actually ought to handle in its collection: the presentation of an artistic proposal in its complexity. The possibility of social embedding depends crucially on the insights that can surround items. The institution stands behind UNESCO's thinking regarding Intangible Cultural Heritage. For things, too, it is about the experience and further continuation of the engagement; and this is true for more than heritage phenomena like processions or carillon playing.

The basis of the museum's engagement is then the characteristics of people and societies that cannot be privatized, namely insights and memories. That is what the museum focuses on. While the Internet offers an opportunity for interest to grow *bottom–bottom*, without any further mention of the "up," of a system that should put a value on this interest and put it to work, the museum provides for the sustainability of such "bottom" ratings. It does so through the magnetic attraction of its engagements, but as a listener rather than as a speaker. It seeks engagements that demand to be tested against the insights it receives, and wants to capture these insights and keep them in circulation to fuel further engagements. It wants to preserve insights and let them be included in significant relationships. It can only do this by departing from restrictions, however hypothetical and therefore changeable. These are positive constraints, engagements that it finds it must assume; it bases itself upon the same sort of intensities as those to whom it gives attention.

The museum is by no means the only actor in this. In an art world where more and more takes place in collaborations or is even being outsourced—research, curatorship, production and image-making—it is less of an actor than ever, and the commitment translates into attention for what is happening and into respect for what other parties do and understand. It is editor and subeditor, and knows itself to be a service provider, not a content supplier.

Translated from the Dutch by Jodie Hruby.

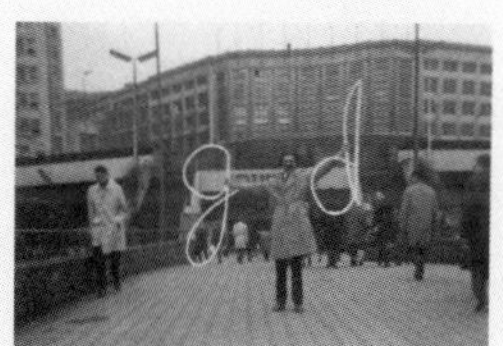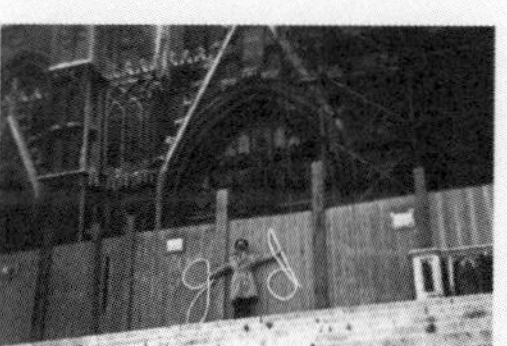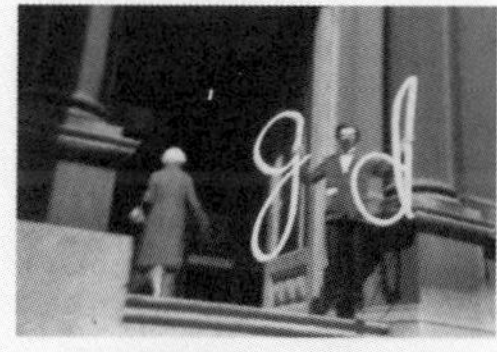

Alain Arias-Misson, *G D Public Poem*, Brussels, 1968, photo by M HKAclinckx, Collection M HKA

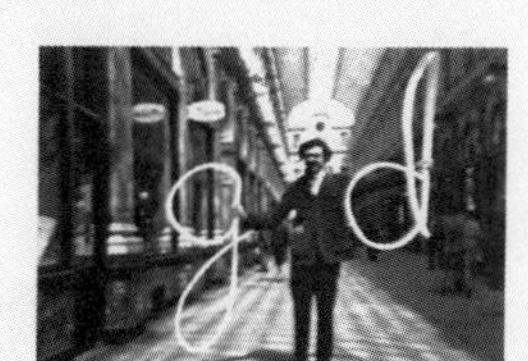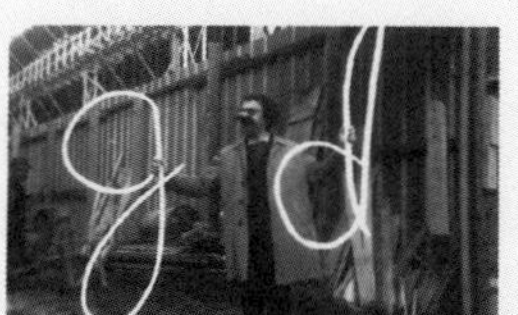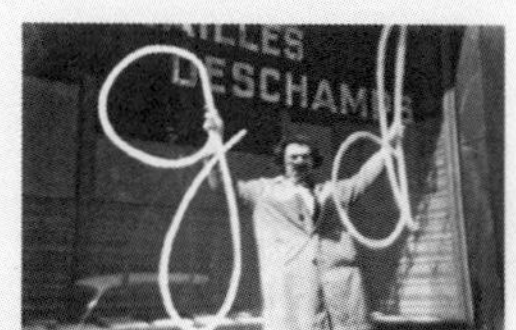

Alain, Arias-Misson, *G D Public Poem*, Brussels, 1968, photo by M HKAclinckx, Collection M HKA

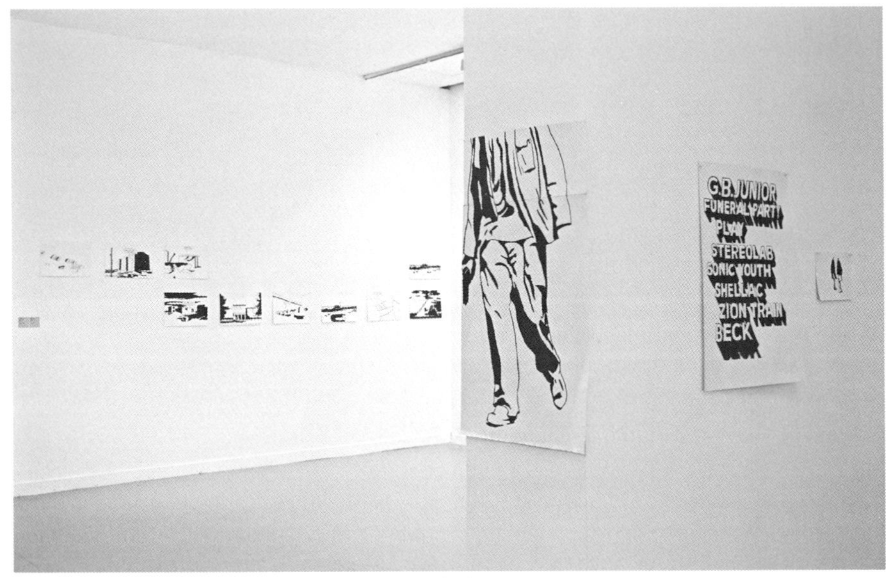

Wilhelm Sasnal, exhibition view, photo by A4A vzw, Collection M HKA

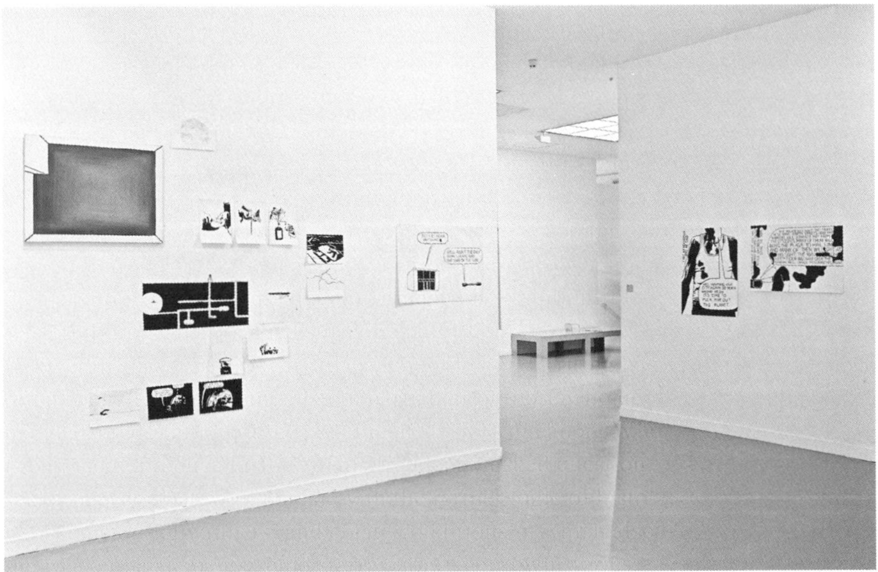

Wilhelm Sasnal, exhibition view 2, photo by A4A vzw, Collection M HKA

An Exercise in Affects Bojana Piškur

The most beautiful thing is to live on the edges, at the limit of her / his own power of being affected, on the condition that this be the joyful limit since there is the limit of joy and the limit of sadness [...][1]

What is power, what is the relationship between power and art? To be more precise the question should be posed differently: "How is it [power] practiced?"[2] This is undoubtedly a difficult if not impossible question. By it we do not mean some kind of representation of power ("power does not pass through forms"[3]) nor the notion of power as a solely aesthetic experience. Neither is power interpreted as a system of certain relations that call its internal operations into being, as for example a museum's legitimation to produce what they name (works of art), making rules establishing what is meaningful, who has the authority to decide, the privilege to speak, and so on. Instead we are interested in something else. Power, as is emphasized in the text herein, is understood as a relation between forces, "a set of actions upon other actions"; in other words, an exercise in affects.

Therefore attention should be turned to Spinoza, for whom the question of power was not a question of moral norms but above all a question of ethics. Let us then begin our investigation on the relationship between power and art with the moment Spinoza asks in his *Ethics*: "What can a body do?"[4] Not only does he break the spell of the power of the soul over the body with this question (for him, the mind and the body are "one and the same thing") but emphasizes that if we are to understand power, we must above all understand what a body is capable of, we must discover its internal structures – or put differently "its degree of power". Ethics is therefore considered an issue of *becoming active*. But there is a crucial moment in understanding this position, and that is when Spinoza turns towards understanding the power to act as a power to be affected: "What a body can do is the nature and the limits of its power to be affected."[5]

1 Les Cours de Gilles Deleuze, Cours Vincennes 24/01/1978, Sur Spinoza (English version), at www.webdeleuze.com (accessed Dec. 15, 2010).

2 Gilles Deleuze, *Foucault*, Continuum, London/New York 1999, p. 60.

3 Ibid, p. 61.

4 See Benedict de Spinoza, *The Ethics*, Part III, at www.gutenberg.org (accessed Dec. 20, 2010).

5 Gilles Deleuze, *Expressionism in Philosophy: Spinoza*, Zone Books, New York 1990, p. 218.
See also Benedict de Spinoza, *The Ethics*, Part III, Proposition II, Note, at www.gutenberg.org (accessed Dec. 20, 2010).

Even though Spinoza's philosophical universe is not in tune with many contemporary philosophical schools (it has often been said that there is always a new Spinoza to be discovered, or that "Spinoza is an anomaly"), his postulates and propositions, especially through the writings of Deleuze, can reveal new insights into an understanding of where and what the points of connection between art and power are. The power of art, in the traditional sense, is understood as the power of emotions. But an emotion is not an affect. When affects (or better, their excesses) are delimited or captured the (relevant) bodies become fixed and so subjectivity and transcendence emerge[6]; subsequently affects are converted into emotions as their residue. Deleuze and Guattari consider this transformation of affect into emotion a political issue, a "politics of affect."

It should be noted that there have been many different interpretations of the relationship between affects and art: Greenberg, for example, understood affects as kitsch, as a "shortcut to the pleasures of art that detours what is necessarily difficult in genuine art"[7] and where affects distinguish an ignorant observer and an uncultivated spectator who, above all, appreciates plastic qualities or a "reflected effect." Jameson, on the other hand, saw the "waning" of affects in the postmodern era where intensities are "free-floating and impersonal"; in other words, in the postmodern world the affects have more or less vanished. But these authors, it seems, recognize affects as a kind of extension, a modification of the "vividly recognizable" representation, or even as a fixed structure of experience (emotion), which is, as Massumi pointed out, "from that point onward defined as personal."[8] But affects are pre-personal; they always precede thought and cannot be owned. It is then impossible to "imagine" affects without first breaking the hegemonic conceptions of art, starting with representation, knowledge and meaning, therefore thinking art beyond representation and of a different "asignifying register."[9] This is not to say that affects are always bringing change towards something *better* (some kind of liberation); on the contrary, affects can bring change for the worse as well (for example, affects as they relate to totalitarianism and that affects can, to some degree, be "orchestrated" etc.).

Art, as we have learned through various narratives and concepts (and here the distinction between Western and

[6] See Jon Beasley-Murray, "Escalón 1989: Deleuze and Affect," *Posthegemony: political theory and Latin America*, University of Minnesota Press, Minneapolis 2010, p. 128.

[7] Clement Greenberg, "Avant-Garde and Kitsch," *Art in Theory 1900–1990* (ed. C. Harrison and P. Wood), Blackwell, Oxford 1992, p. 537.

[8] Brian Massumi, "The Autonomy of Affect," *Parables for the Virtual: Movement, Affect, Sensation*, Duke University Press, Durham 2002, p. 28.

[9] Simon O'Sullivan, The Aesthetics of Affect, in *Angelaki* (Routledge), Vol. 6, No. 3, Dec. 2001, p. 126.

non-Western narratives plays a small role), has to do with
history. More importantly art as we know it through various
forms is already part of the past, and it is, to put it plainly, of
the identifiable and formalized affects that become as such
through numerous encounters with different bodies, objects,
ideas, institutions etc. Both the State and the Institution fear the
unknown affects, because these affects threaten the established
order and, for that matter, anything that is fixed (identity),
confined (aesthetics) and taken for granted (representation).
For Agamben, the Museum is not just a physical place with
collections and exhibitions, but "the separate dimension to
which what once—but is no longer—felt true and decisive has
moved,"[10] in other words, the museum functions as a space that
used to be reserved for a Temple. But something, a force, always escapes this confinement and that is where the encounters
between art and "other bodies" should be investigated. Susan
Buck-Morss has proposed the idea of *somatic knowledge*[11],
which she understands as a way the body senses reality in an
animalistic or biological sense. For her this kind of aesthetics
is a body's form of critical cognition, a knowledge that can be
trusted politically, because it cannot be instrumentalized. And
if we think of art as a "bloc of affects and percepts," then art
= affect is like an electrical shock, which always happens as
"event" and only at "this" very moment. Affects are therefore a
force *in-time*, but this does not mean that all traces of previous
experiences are gone; on the contrary, they can be reactivated
in different relations as an affective memory within the bodies
or as a recovery of the intensities. Similarly Massumi offers:
"[this kind of memory] might not be acted out. […] On the
other hand, it might well catapult you directly into action."[12]

The following registers have molded our exercise in affects:

1. Artists invent new affects. An affect precedes an idea and
is therefore a non-representational mode of thought. "Affects
can be, and are, attached to things, people, ideas, sensations,
relations, activities, ambitions, institutions, and any number of
other things, including other affects."[13] Artists live the affect;
for example[14] Gerhard Richter *becomes-grey* in Grau, Marina
Abramović *becomes-object* in *Rhythm 0*, Mladen Stilinović
becomes-pain in *Pain game*.

10 Giorgio Agamben,
Profanations, Zone Books,
New York 2007, p. 84.

11 Grant H. Kester,
"Aesthetics after the End
of Art: An Interview with
Susan Buck-Morss," *Art
Journal*, Vol. 56, No. 1,
Aesthetics and the Body
Politic, 1997, p. 39.

12 Joel McKim, "Of
Microperception and
Micropolitics: An Interview
with Brian Massumi,
Micropolitics," *Inflexions:
A Journal for Research-
Creation*, No. 3, Oct. 2009,
p. 8, at www.inflexions.org
(accessed Jan. 10, 2012).

13 Eve Kosofsky Sedgwick,
*Touching Feeling: Affect,
Pedagogy, Performativity*,
Duke University press,
Durham 2003, p. 19.

14 All these artists
were part of the exhibi-
tion *Museum of Affects*
in the framework of
L'Internationale, Museum
of Contemporary Art
Metelkova, Nov. 26,
2011–Jan. 29, 2012, see
also http://internacionala.
mg-lj.si/.

2. The first and lowest kind of knowledge (or even "igno-rance") that determines the affects is, according to Spinoza, *affection-ideas* or chance encounters with other bodies. They are also called inadequate ideas, because they are separated from their cause, therefore we know nothing about the bodies or about the relationship between them.

3. Affections are also known as passions and are determined by two affects: joy, which increases the power of acting, and sadness, which decreases this power.

4. The negative affection, or an encounter with a body that mixes badly with our own, is called a "sad passion". Sad passion, according to Deleuze, is "any encounter I have with the body that does not agree with my nature."[15] Subsequently our (my) power to act is diminished.

5. In order to becoming-active and to increase our power to act, something agreeable must be recognized between the bod-ies, a certain affirmation, which is called a "joyful passion." Clarice Lispector put it precisely thus:
Everything in the world began with a yes. One molecule said yes to another molecule and life was born[16].

6. Joyful passions are the next step towards increasing the power of action. But this power (potential) does not come from the external cause as a spontaneous encounter between two bodies as was the case with the first kind of knowledge; instead it comes from the inside, as a "cause of our own affects". It means that we begin to ask what, why and how is that my body agrees with the other affective body; or put another way, what can my body actually do, what is it that is common between my body and another body, what is the "meaning" of the encoun-ter? This is the second kind of knowledge, which is also called *notion-ideas*. Alain Badiou said that with Spinoza (...)

[...] we learn that we have to act, not within the violent disor-der of the chaos, but within
    the cold quietness of the stars, because in the most radical action, we have to persist in the most important positive emo-tion, positive affect [...][17]

15 Gilles Deleuze, *Expressionism in Philosophy: Spinoza*, Zone Books, New York 1990, p. 242.

16 Clarice Lispector, *The Hour of the Star*, A New Directions Book, New York 1992, p. 11.

17 Alain Badiou, "What Is a Proof in Spinoza's Ethics?," *Spinoza Now* (ed. D. Vardoulakis), University of Minnesota Press, Minneapolis 2011, p. 41.

7. There are no unhappy creations in art (Nietzsche: "the tragic hero is happy"). The question is: how is it joy is so often transformed into sadness? This is the point of Mladen Stilinović's work *Dictionary - Pain*, where he adds to all the words in the dictionary the word pain: art - pain, capitalism - pain, communism - pain, comic – pain […] the things, people, ideas, sensations, relations, activities, ambitions, institutions, etc. that affects the artist in a sad way. Sad passions, Spinoza reminds us, are always necessary for the exercise of power, to keep the status quo of the Institution, of the State intact. That is why people who have power (*potestas*) always affect us in a sad way. Pasolini understood this very well when, in his 1963 film *Rage* (*La Rabia*), he repeated the following lines like a mantra:

If you don't cry "Long live liberty!" with laughter, You don't cry "Long live liberty!"
If you don't cry "Long live liberty!" with love, You don't cry "Long live liberty!"

8. The third kind of knowledge, according to Spinoza, is essence-ideas or intuition, which occurs when we "enter into a direct vision."[18]

***

Now to some examples, and to the Museum of Affects[19]. The name of the exhibition is clearly an oxymoron; and, for that matter, a paradox. Generating paradox is, as in Massumi, a good way of breaking the stratified signification and of integrating movement[20] into the everyday and its every detail, to open up the rigid and the stale by setting the systems in motion. Museums cannot "store" affects the way they store objects but their task remains, nevertheless, to preserve all that which makes art art. And art, as we know, is made of affects. On the other hand, a museum itself is an affective body too, which to some extent defines and "orchestrates" other bodies (things, objects, ideas, other affects etc.) But the museum's power lies above all, in understanding its limits of being affected, however paradoxical this might sound. In a strangely familiar way Ismail Kadare in his novel *The Palace of Dreams* writes about the place where all the dreams of all the citizens of an empire are interpreted, classified, and stored, and where dangerous,

[18] Gilles Deleuze, *Expressionism in Philosophy: Spinoza*, Zone Books, New York 1990, p. 301.

[19] An exhibition in the framework of L'Internationale, Museum of Contemporary Art Metelkova (see note 14).

[20] Brian Masumi, *Parables for the Virtual: Movement, Affect, Sensation*, Duke University Press, Durham 2002, p. 15. Spinoza defined body in terms of relations: movement and rest, and this capacity of a body is its power to affect and be affected.

or so-called master-dreams that might affect the stability of the empire, are sought out—similarly, what museums do with affects.

Roland Barthes in *I like, I don't like* makes a long list of things, sensations, books, music, food etc. that he likes and does not like. He likes, for example, cinnamon, realistic novels and the Marx Brothers, and dislikes strawberries, Miró, fidelity and so on. But even though these lists are of no importance to anyone and are apparently without any (particular) meaning, they also mean: "My body is not the same as yours."[21] Barthes writes that it is here where the bodily enigma and the intimidation of the body begin. Similar to Barthes's observations, the most common encounters in art too are chance encounters, affections or passions, where we learn nothing and where our bodies are at rest. Some of these affections are sad and some are joyful. Only joyful affections can shift the potentials of and in the body, and this transition is about a body becoming something else, it is about bodies in movement, since it is only then that we are in "possession" of our power of acting. But it should be emphasized that the affect of joy is not analogous to the emotions of happiness, pleasure, or even beauty. Instead, joy comes from a completely different register, that of the process of having an idea of something that can trigger an emotion; for instance, there is an idea that causes joy, and not a process of feeling.[22]

The questions of how not to be separated from our power of acting and how to produce adequate ideas then become both methodological and political questions, which concern not only individual forces but also collective bodies forming common notions or common relations between bodies (it is a knowledge by causes rather than by sensory effects). For example, if there is a resonance between art and "resistant corporealities", art can eventually become a resource for revolution. At the most powerful, at the point of conversion, these kinds of resonances can become so "overwhelming and bodily that they defy representation."[23] We could then even say that the dream of any art is in finding for itself a receptive "multitude."

However, there is a difference in the way bodies were affected, for example by Tomislav Gotovac, when he cleaned the streets of Zagreb in 1981, and by the residue of that event—a pile of garbage, now at the exhibition; or another event of the

21 Roland Barthes, "J'aime, je n'aime pas [I like, I don't like]," *A Barthes Reader*, Noonday Press, New York 1982, p. 418.

22 See Antonio Damasio, *Iskanje Spinoze: veselje, žalost in čuteči možgani*, Založba Krtina, Ljubljana 2008, p. 15.

23 Gaston Gordillo, *Resonance and Egyptian Revolution*, at http://spaceandpolitics.blogspot.com (accessed Jan. 15, 2012): "Ideology, slogans and speeches are all part of resonance, but at its most powerful moments resonance is sheer affect: bodies joining forces to control space and voicing their passions through openly gestural expressions […]."

same year, where Gotovac walked naked in downtown Zagreb.
This event was an unmediated experience, but only until its
affects were recognized as "signifying gestures", perceived as
a threat to the order of the State (after 7 minutes Gotovac was
arrested by the police). Now, what are the prospects of affects
in the "zone" of a museum? The Museum, as any Institution,
attempts to prevent the appearance of uncontrolled affects.
There are, however, exceptions. Well known is the performance
Rhythm 0 by Marina Abramović from 1974, where she offered
herself to the public in a gallery as a passive object during
which the public could do anything they wanted with/to her.
Abramović purposely exceeded her power of being affected to
such an extreme that after the performance was over the public
could not bear to face the artist any longer. What happened was
that the "threshold of intensity" had been crossed and subsequently a difficult encounter transpired.

Otherwise, however, apart from those extreme cases, it can
not be said that experiences of "performances" affect another
body to a larger extent than a still image or an object in a museum, for this would bring us back into the field of representation
and emotion, but that intensities and reference points of such
events are not the same for everyone. What is sad for one might
be joyful for another. What passes for a chance encounter for
one might be the beginning of an action for another. However,
these experiences also leave traces within the bodies, a sort of
affective memory, which can be activated in other encounters
and actions. All this only goes to prove that a work of art is
itself a little machine, to paraphrase Deleuze and Guattari, and
the questions to be answered are: With what other things / bodies / machines it (the artwork) does or does not transmit intensities? How? Where are the limits of these intensities?

Only to come now to the point where we realize that art's
most important task is to combat sadness. And this is the practical project of Spinoza for today. Sadness as understood in a
political sense—not in a vague sense, as Deleuze reminds us,
but in a rigorous sense. The affects of sadness defeated, so that
(our) life is not dominated or overwhelmed, in the language
of Pasolini, by discontent, anguish and fear. As we already
know, power in art is the transforming of passions and chance
encounters into actions, into potential to act, and towards the
understanding of the relations between bodies and the causes of

these relations, while forming common notions and resonances, only to arrive at the zone where art becomes a "liberation that explodes everything, first and foremost the tragic."[24] So we no longer encounter pain in Mladen Stilinović's Pain but embark on a flight denouncing this sadness instead, "taking as a local point of departure joy, on the condition that we feel it truly concerns us. On that point one forms the common notion, on that point one tries to win locally, to open up this joy."[25] And when we then pass into the domain of adequate ideas, then we pass into the knowledge of causes. We begin to understand sadness, and when this happens we are no longer severed from our power to act, because now we know the limits of our power to be affected. This is the liberation both Spinoza and Deleuze are talking about. And finally, only with profound and versatile knowledge, and an intuitive access to understanding, do we come close to the third and highest kind of knowledge—pure intensity.

[24] Gilles Deleuze, "Mysticism and Masochism," *Desert Islands and Other Texts 1953–1974*, Semiotext(e), New York 2004, p. 134."

[25] Les Cours de Gilles Deleuze, Cours Vincennes 24/01/1978, Sur Spinoza (English version), at www.webdeleuze.com, accessed Dec. 15, 2010.

What if the Universe Started Here and Elsewhere

Steven ten Thije

L'Internationale is a network of museums and artists' archives. These institutes work together not only to realize exhibitions and publications, but also because they sense that the institute of both the museum and the artist's archive needs to be brought up to date with the globalized world of today. In this collaboration the prominent role played by artists' archives is a symptom of today's predicament. Previously, the museum with its discrete collection of artwork was the primary site where art and history were brought together to be ordered, conserved and displayed. Today the practice of historiography and its related activities of collecting and conservation are no longer the exclusive domain of the museum and the artists themselves, as more informal networks of passionate individuals have started to become active in this field as well. This shift appears to mark a restructuring of the way in which art and history are negotiated in society today. The universal narrative of a general art history is no longer entrusted to the institutional machinery of the museum and its academic cousin, art history.

These two modern institutional systems with their bureaucratic, technological schemes of checks and balances are now confronted by smaller, sometimes even individual, players who appear to hijack old institutional models to develop different narratives or champion different histories. Various examples of such come to mind, but the mysterious Museum of American Art with "branches" in New York, Los Angeles, Berlin and Belgrade, is a particularly fine case in point.[1] Another is the recent Latin American network of artist archives Southern Conceptualism that, with the support of Reina Sofia (but not on its initiative), is developing ways in which regional histories can remain a source of reflection and inspiration for a local community and are not "outsourced" to larger museums or collections with global reach. This development raises many issues related to the future role of museums and the discipline of art history, one of which is how this is reflected in the way things are exhibited. How does this development relate to, or even reflect, recent changes within the practices of curating and particularly,

[1] For a discussion of the Museum of American Art see: Inke Arns and Walter Benjamin (ed.), *What is Modern Art? (Group Show)*, exhibition catalogue, Künstlerhaus Bethanien Berlin, Revolver, Frankfurt am Main 2006. For the Latin American network see: http://www.museoreinasofia.es/redes/conceptualismos-del-sur/conceptualismos-museo_en.html (May 30, 2012).

collection curating? Within this text I would therefore like to revisit the discussion surrounding curating, focusing on the theoretical underpinnings of the rise of the exhibition curator in the late 1970s, and close with some reflections on the current situation and some less likely suggestions for future strategies.

For some decades it has become acceptable practice to embed exhibitions in or imbue them with elaborate theories. This development can be seen as a side effect of the more visible role taken up by curators in the later decades of the 20th century. In the 19th and early 20th centuries curators were seen as representing a discipline—art history; or an institution—the Academy, the Museum. In the second half of the 20th century the curator became increasingly independent; curators introduced their own particular perspective, which needed to be specified each time anew.[2] This may now be standard practice, but it is not, by any means, a self-evident standard. Parallel to the rise of densely argued curatorial concepts we also see a corresponding increase in critiques of this model.[3] The presence of a curatorial concept that is based on a variety of different disciplines such as philosophy, anthropology, sociology, political theory and more, continues to infuriate both critics and artists who feel that art is being instrumentalized to illustrate the curator's concept. Even if by now there is quite a stretch of grey area where more balanced and nuanced positions are formulated, the contemporary practice of exhibition making still hovers between two extremes—where on the one side, we find the curatorial concept and on the other, the pure, autonomous artwork. This might seem a horribly old-fashioned division or distinction, but it is, in all its banality, one of the few constants that appear to return again and again in debates on and around curating.

In rather simplified terms one could understand this tension as the result of a rather nasty power-struggle over who has the right to speak or the right to decide. Where once upon a time it was the critic i.e. academic, who had the right to speak and it was the artist who had the right to show. The curator arrived as a horrible hybrid in the middle, both showing and telling, and simultaneously shattering the monopoly of the critic and the artist. Few might admit it aloud, but every time a critic or artist breaks out in a rage against the stifling grip of a curatorial concept, one senses an unarticulated subtext that says: please, let this madness be over, curators have been with us since the

2 For a brief "history" of curating see Beti Zerovc, "The Role of the Contemporary Art Curator: A Historical and Critical Analysis," *MJ – Manifesta Journal*, no. 5, 2005, p. 138–153.

3 A good general example of this in the issue of Manifesta Magazine on the relation between curator and artist. *MJ – Mafesta Journal*, no. 5, 2005.

beginning of modern art, but never at the center, always on the margins; is there no way to push them back, to allow things to return to normal?

Explaining this secret desire to "overcome" curating only in terms of authority lost, however, ignores the more legitimate and epistemological problem that underpins these debates. The unmediated exchange between artist and critic i.e. art historian, that is recalled with nostalgia in the common critique of curating, was formalized throughout the 19th century and was—or still is—the model for a rather delicate epistemological exercise that has political implications for art's functioning in modern society. Even if critics and artists are not required to formulate the nature of this exercise in philosophical terms, they are nevertheless deeply informed by it, and intuitively sense when something or someone is interfering. And curating, unfortunately, always interferes—for in a sense it is the curator's job to interfere. To understand the role of curating in the light of the new institutional and organizational exchanges it is necessary to deploy a philosophical, historical and epistemological approach. To do this, one first needs to describe the exact nature of this epistemological exercise; then, determine its political significance, as performed by the artist, critic and curator; and three, consider what this means for curating and the role of curatorial concepts today.

One: An Epistemology of Experience

The interference of the curator in the domain of art is arguably the late after-effect of a profound shift in the understanding of art as an epistemological entity that is vital to society. The shift occurs roughly at the end of the 18th and in the early 19th century in Western European societies and others close to it. This is more commonly known as the shift from pre-modern to modern society, with the French Revolution as the spectacular kick-start and the philosophy of Kant the intellectual fuel that has succeeded in keeping the engine burning to the present day. In the field of the visual arts it were innovators like Casper David Friedrich, Philipp Otto Runge, John Constable, J. M. W. Turner and others who were pioneers in practicing an understanding of art that revealed traces of this new epistemology.

Central to this new epistemology is an understanding of "experience" as providing an independent contribution to the knowing of the world. Whereas Descartes, for instance, still claimed that "seeing was nothing more than an imprecise form of thinking,"[4] artists like Friedrich believed that experience revealed a part or aspect of the world that was different from, the knowledge acquired through rational thought processes and which was equally important. Friedrich even dealt with this epistemological issue directly in his famous painting *Der Mönch am Meer* (1808–10), which depicts a solitary monk facing the sea. The painting's composition curiously directs the gaze of the viewer not out into the sea, but to the side, and even out of the painting altogether, leaving the viewer frustratingly empty-handed—a disappointment noted by the artist's contemporaries.[5] In response, Friedrich offered that the answer to this frustration lay in the attitude of the monk, who was clearly "thinking", calmly resting his head on his hand in silent contemplation, and not "looking". Friedrich, as he clarified in a comment on his work, denied his monk—and his virtual double, the viewer—because he is not deploying the right "faculty" to break open the mystery of the sea.[6] According to Friedrich's understanding—echoed in different ways by other early modern painters—the subjective experience of the artist in its primordial form, relieved of (rational) intellect and tradition, forms the basis for any legitimate work of art. Only there can one find the precise experiential knowledge that can only be transferred to those less sensitive when it is translated with the utmost care.

This newly-charged concept of experience, found meandering through early-Romantic thinking, is the source for an entirely new form of image that has come to dominate our visual world: the photograph. As Peter Galassi has argued, the beginning of the photographic image is not to be found in technological innovation alone, but also in a new sensitivity towards depicting the fleeting moment in works of art.[7] This sensitivity was even formalized briefly before the "invention" of photography, in the "plein air" oil sketch that was popular in the early 19th century and, for a short time, enjoyed the status of a distinct genre. In the light of this evidence, Galassi argues, photography was not developed simply because it was technologically possible and viable, but also because it was possible to see, from

[4] CraryQuoted in Jonathan Crary, *Techniques of the Observer: On Vision and Modernity in the Nineteenth Century*, MIT Press, Cambridge/London 1990, p. 43.

[5] For a discussion of Friedrich's epistemologically-charged concept of experience see: Werner Busch, *Casper David Friedrich, Ästhetik und Religion*, C. H. Beck, Munich 2003. For an extended discussion of the response by Friedrich's contemporaries (Heinrich von Kleist, Clemens Brentano and Achim von Arnim) see: Christian Begemann, "Brentano und Kleist vor Friedrichs *Mönch am Meer*. Aspekte eines Umbruchs in der Geschichte der Wahrnehmung," *Deutsche Vierteljahresschrift für Literaturwissenschaft und Geistesgeschichte*, vol. 64, no. 1, 1990, p. 54–95.

[6] Busch, op. cit., p. 64.

[7] Peter Galassi (ed.), *Before Photography. Painting and the Invention of Photography*, exhibition catalogue, Museum of Modern Art, New York 1981.

an epistemological perspective, the photograph as a meaningful image medium in its own right. This new sensitivity that began to consider direct observations from nature a suitable approach/subject is in sync with a new epistemological potential located in the world of experience—which Friedrich had actually delineated in his comment on his painting. In this new sensitivity the fleeting moment of experience was considered important precisely because of its ephemeral quality and infinite detail that was now the mysterious reservoir of one part of our selves that had to be treated independently. Knowing the world worked or evolved on the basis of exchange between the rational mind and the senses, and only by developing the specific qualities of both faculties, one could arrive at a full and balanced subject.

Two: The Politics of Experience

This epistemological shift has been the subject of many studies, of which one of the most monumental remains Foucault's *The Order of Things*.[8] More in the realm of art history proper has been developed in various studies by Jonathan Crary.[9] The political dimension of this shift is comprehensively articulated by Jacques Rancière in his discussion of the relation between art and politics. In *Aesthetics as Politics* Rancière sets out to explain the "modern" relationship between art and politics by returning to Aristotle's statement that man is a political animal by virtue of his ability to speak, which is then further specified as "a capacity to place the just and the unjust in the common, whereas all the animal has is a voice to signal pleasure and pain".[10] Politics, according to this understanding, is the negotiation through speech of what is just and unjust. In pre-modern societies, like Aristotle's, it is only the elite who "have time" to gather at the assembly and engage in (this) discussion; in modern times, however, suddenly everybody—the entire *"demos"*—was pressing at the gates of parliament ready to speak. In modern times politics is the struggle to gather and show society at large that observations, feelings and thoughts bear on the common. "Politics occurs when those who have "no time" take the time necessary to front up as inhabitants of a common space and demonstrate that their mouths really do emit speech capable of making pronouncements on the common which cannot be reduced to voices signaling pain."[11]

8 Michel Foucault, *The Order of Things: An Archaeology of the Human Sciences* (first published in French, Gallimard, Paris 1966, translator unknown), Vintage Books, New York 1994.

9 Crary, op. cit., and Jonathan Crary, *Suspensions of Perception: Attention, Spectacle, and Modern Culture*, MIT Press, Cambridge/London 1999.

10 Jacques Rancière, "Aesthetics as Politics," *Aesthetics and its Discontents*, (first published in French 2004, translated by Steven Corcoran), Polity, Cambridge/Malden 2009, p. 24.

11 Ibid.

The consequence of this position is that what is first understood as merely a subjective statement concerning one's wellbeing—in pain or pleasure—is now the seed that brings with it the possibility to evolve into speech that which says something about what is right or wrong. To facilitate this process of discriminating between various declarations, society requires a new practice to identify communications made about the common sphere and the sensations on which they are based. It is within this constellation that the emphasis placed on subjective experience by artists such as Friedrich gains political traction. By making the pure singularity of their experience the basis of (their) art, the viewer is confronted with something radically alien from him or her. To account for this difference the viewer must be open to a new form of sense-experience—one that is felt by someone else—and which is resonant precisely because of these specific demands. As Rancière would have it: "[the] "politics" of art [...] consists in suspending the normal coordinates of sensory experience".[12] Therefore it is important to note that this radical singularity is not understood as being purely private, but as containing a statement about what is general or even universal.[13] Again citing Friedrich as an example, he believed that through these private observations he could communicate something of the divine, of the universal.

Returning to the practice of exhibition making, we can now begin to understand how the place where a work of art is displayed starts to gain new significance in this—to use the Rancièrian term—"regime." The work that is based on the unique experience and sensibility of an artist is extremely vulnerable to transformations in its appearance. How it is shown affects its form, and, as a result, content. To a certain extent this has always been the case, but never so much so as in modern times, where a change in (its) appearance almost resulted in the destruction of the work. In the 19th century this issue was addressed through the installation of both an academic discipline that focused on art (art history) and a public institute that displayed art (the museum). With the help of these two artificial elements it was possible to create a "neutral" platform on which to present art—something that in the 20th century developed into the (in)famous common exhibition model of the white cube in which, by eliminating any art-alien elements, space was created for the artwork and the artwork alone. In the end, the white

12 Ibid., p. 25.

13 In Rancière's text there is further explication of the opposition between "active intelligence" and "passive materiality," which he finds in Schiller's *Letters on the Aesthetic Education of Man*. This division is important for a philosophical understanding, in more precise terms, of the exact position of experience as present in art. Here, however, we have for reasons of space to overstep this refinement. Ibid., p. 27–32.

walls of the museum were the last place the anonymity of the institution had at its disposal to secure a safe environment for the pure subjectivity of the artwork.[14]

Three: The Post-1989 Experience

Later in the 20th century, however, the presumed neutrality of the white walls lost its innocence and was transformed from an invisible background to the normative framework that encapsulated a work of art. The increasing visibility of the curator coincided with an increasing visibility of the frame, and was brought forth in the wake of the general suspicion— on the part of a critical generation of postmodern, postcolonial and poststructuralist thinkers—against anything that was presumed "objective." One might find it paradoxical that the curator as author enters the stage at the exact moment Roland Barthes proclaim the "death of the author," but this is one of its most logical consequences. Where the creative author as a unique, coherent and inspired genius was unveiled as a social construction that was as much "produced" by the reader as by the writer, the neutral and invisible figure of the curator as mere administrator of art history became recognized as historically specific and arbitrary. What took place was a grand inversion in which those who had been "authors" suddenly became constructions, and those bodies long considered neutral systems became charged and in some manner, idiosyncratic authors.

This development gained renewed momentum after 1989, when the collapse of the Soviet-Union inaugurated an implosion of the power-relations that had determined the second half of the 20th century. This implosion was first celebrated as a victory of the West over the East, but has more recently been recognized as inaugurating a far wider redistribution of power specific to today's multi-polar globalized world. For the arts this meant that the presumed universal, authoritative discourse on art, systematized in art history and represented in museum collections, lost its universality and became localized. The early generation of critical thinkers still formulated their theories against the aggressive hegemony of presumed "neutral" discourses such as art history by referring to a near absolute and abstract Other, or an almost metaphysical concept of "difference". In the post-1989 world this Other assumed a face—or

[14] For a philosophical analysis of the role of the museum in modernity see Didier Maleuvre, *Museum Memories: History, Technology, Art*, Stanford Univeristy Press, Stanford 1999. For a discussion of the white cube, O'Doherty's text remains the best source: Brian O'Doherty, *Inside the White Cube: The Ideology of the Gallery Space*, University of California Press, Berkeley/Los Angeles/London 1999.

rather, a thousand faces—located in all of the communities
that now began to produce hybrids comprised of traces of the
Western tradition of art together with their own.[15]

In general the shift that occurred in the wake of postmodern
critique and which intensified after 1989 posed the question:
is the epistemological potential of art still relevant within this
globalized world? Or does globalization challenge the form of
subjectivity that was developed in the modern world along with
its art? Naturally, the scope and framework of this essay cannot
fully address such a question; but what can be extracted from
this discussion is the fact that the subjectivity to which modern
art, with its art history and museums, belonged, was not so
much unique to the West, but to the type of society in which it
organized itself—namely a democratic one. The political function of the epistemology of experience specific to modern art
was connected with the will to make political decisions via a
process of opinion, consensus or enfranchisement, which required constructive forms of and platforms for the exchange of
experiences and ideas. Therefore, even if the universal foundation behind the statements offered in that discourse has become
relative and localized to distinct communities, this doesn't
mean that the political function of art has fundamentally
changed.[16]

This raises a new question concerning the role of the curator
in this constellation. The curator can neither return to the largely faceless entity of the custodian of art history, nor can he/she
aspire to represent a utopian bringer of "difference" or defender
of the Other. Curating in this sense appears to be drawn in and
as an ugly form of impurity, where there exists no solid basis on
which a curator could construct a framework where the work
could appear in (all) its attendant specificity. (As the continued
frustration over the subjective and arbitrary quality of curatorial concepts attests.) One might also wonder, more concretely,
what method might be employed to arrive at a curatorial practice that constructively addresses its compromised, impure
standing in the larger equation.

At this particular juncture it would be improper to formulate, in excessively blunt terms, a solution; it is better, instead,
to state explicitly that one can only speculate. However, this
caveat notwithstanding, what appears to be one of the key developments in the post-1989 world is the shift toward a deep

[15] For a discussion on the effects of globalization on the "white cube" see for instance: Peter Weibel, "Beyond the White Cube," Peter Weibel and Andrea Buddensieg (ed.), *Contemporary Art and the Museum, A Global Perspective,* Hatje Cantz Verlag, Ostfildern 2007.

[16] This does beg the question what happens if this understanding of art is used in societies that use a different political system, as, for instance, contemporary China; but this question cannot be answered here.

"relativism"; perhaps, however, one might better call it a radically shallow relativism, considering the lack of foundation that marks the current moment. Now that the quests for purity and the ultimate Other have concluded, it seems we are left in a complicated world with many traces of things that relate to one another without a privileged viewpoint that can serve as a basis for everything. One tendency within this situation is to subscribe to or practice a sensitivity for the local, the specific, which is now no longer an aberration of some pure form but the irreducible reality in which any thinking and exchange can take place. And while there is some truth to this position locality should not, however, become a new fetish that seeks to simply replace the now vacant place of the Universal or the Other. For, returning to Rancière, the "common" that is addressed by politics becomes xenophobic if it is understood on the basis of an idealized locality. So, even if it may sound paradoxical, within this relative world there is a case to be made for a return to a more traditional discourse of truth that could offer access to the common and which is more inclusive than an unqualified embracing of relativity. Continuously reiterating and rearticulating the idea that there is no solid basis for universal propositions ultimately erodes if not dissolves the relative basis that does exist to make statements. Even someone as deeply suspicious of formalized methods of speaking truth as Michel Foucault was well aware of this when, in an interview late in his life, he commented on the "truth" of his work. Foucault offered that this was the most "complicated" topic for him and that his studies still relied on conventional methods of truth-speaking and would not function when invalidated on that level. He added, however, that the purpose of his studies was never simply to speak the truth, but to offer an "experience" of a certain subject that was of contemporary importance to him and to the community in which he lived.[17]

What this means for curating is this: paradoxically, one imagines a reappraisal of more traditional exhibition platforms, such as the museum. Just as the museum increasingly transformed, in the 1990s, into a model of the "Kunsthalle" and became a site for ever more spectacular exhibitions, it seems at this point that the discursive (and political) possibilities of more traditional forms and practices of collecting and conservation might offer a more promising reservoir from which to draw.

[17] Interview conducted by D. Trombadori and published 1980 in Italian in *Il Contributo*. Translated and published in English in James D. Faubion (ed.), *Michel Foucault – Power: Essential Works of Foucault 1954–1984*, Penguin Books, London/New York 2002, p. 242–244.

A "return" to this model could be a way to (re)establish, with more legitimacy, a common sphere in which a community not only encounters but truly engages with and uses art—as described by Rancière—to its structural political benefit. In this manner we might be able to build a place where one is offered a universal or global understanding of art that allows one not only to account for oneself, but for the other as well, while at the same time recognizing that this universality is based on/in a specific locality. Such a universalism might come forth from a specific site and context, its discourse opening doors to others, yet resisting the colonial reflex to try and draw them in by force.

Major Shifts in Thinking about Art from the 1960s to the 1980s

Trying to recapitulate the period from the mid-1950s to the mid-1980s in broader art-theoretical terms appears a tremendous, complexly challenging and far from easy task. Despite these odds, one can point to several significant shifts that occurred in that period that strongly influenced the way art from that era came to be seen and has been viewed ever since. One of those changes—confining myself to artistic practices stemming from that time—quite generally concerns the role played by theory within those very practices. One might claim that this holds true for art production on both sides of the historical East-West divide, on both sides of the Atlantic, in places remote from the classic "art centers" of that time, in the global North as well as the South.

Roughly from the mid-1960s onwards, what can be witnessed in art scenes all over the globe is not only a proliferation of *theory* in (exterior) relation to art but also an intensified (interior, so to speak) utilization of discursive tools and methods within art production. Evidence of this can be found in a variety of realms, from conceptual art proper, which considered the theoretical framework of art-making as important as its material manifestation, to highly politicized approaches like Situationism, which at a certain point decided to quit art-making altogether in favor of revolutionary agitation and/or theory. One also sees this shift in collective practices like that of the Slovene group OHO, built upon an elaborate philosophical doctrine (*reism*); finally, it also becomes evident when artist/theorist Peter Weibel retrospectively states: "While conceptual artists in New York were discovering the early Wittgenstein (in the mid-1960s), we (in Vienna) were already working with the late Wittgenstein."[1]

Opening up and diversifying artistic procedures—with the crucial help of manifold theoretical tools, even entire sets of theoretical building blocks—was one of the primary, sometimes tacit premises of the wide field that developed in the wake of conceptual, media- as well as action-based art. In accordance with this perspective, theory became an instrument for tentatively extending and exceeding, ultimately penetrating

1 "Sixties, Sweet and Sour: A Conversation with Marko Pogačnik and Peter Weibel on the Beginnings of Their Artistic Careers," *Marko Pogačnik, Art of Life–The Life of Art*, ed. Igor Spanjol, Moderna galerija, Ljubljana 2012.

and undermining existing psychological as well as social and political structures. Artists, it could be argued, at least the more radically and theoretically minded ones, represented the forefront of developing such pre-given structures by means of their *discursively* informed practices. Evidence, again, can be found from the time in such distant places as Warsaw, Zagreb, Bratislava, Antwerp, Kempen, Barcelona, São Paulo, and of course many more.

All this became more overtly apparent in the second and third waves of so-called institution- or context-critical art. But even before that, on the height of the "conceptual revolution" of the mid-1960s, new connective relationships began to emerge across art, theory and other discourse-related realms. Building on these new connective tissues, from the early 1970s onwards, context- and site-related approaches turned their attention to an even wider and more cutting edge field of theory—often in quite selective and fractured manners, with the help of all possible and apparently useful fragments. The higher goal, it might be argued, was to work out a new form of (socially, politically, culturally, economically etc. relevant) critique. What started to emerge around this time was a form of artistic critique conversant with discourse and power analysis, with post-structuralism and deconstruction, post-colonialism and anti-imperialism— informed by, but never fully subsumed within these very fields. This artistic critique drew from fundamental insights of politicized art theory and cultural studies, without descending to the level of mere illustration, or of being a poor copy of these approaches. It ultimately assigned an eminent status to the specifically theoretical configuration within a particular work, or to the critical capacities that an artwork helps mobilize in viewers, without losing sight of the inherently autonomous laws, or the intractability of aesthetic experience. One might claim that what, right up to the present day, characterizes "postconceptual approaches," in spite of their manifold appearances, is the radically altered status they assign to theory: theory not as a discrete domain which is situated above or below, before or after art, but rather as a co-extensive experimental field from which it is possible to borrow or appropriate a wide array of instruments.

The advanced arts of that period were not alone in establishing such a perspective. Around the same time the aforementioned conceptual shift took place, one of the main precursors of a decidedly political understanding of theory asserted: "The role of theory today seems to me to be the following: not to formulate a global system which would assign to everything its place, but instead to analyze the particularities of power mechanisms, to determine their connections and expansions, and to build up, step by step, a strategic knowledge."[2]

Such is Michel Foucault's response, in an interview from 1977, to a question posed by Jacques Rancière with respect to the particular form in which theory may be used to analyze the present. Theory's function as a "toolbox [...], which is available to the new political subjects"[3]—a point of view both Foucault and Gilles Deleuze had treated in great detail in their famous conversation "Intellectuals and Power" (1972)[4]—may easily be applied to the aforementioned artistic practices emerging from the end of the 1960s onward. This becomes even clearer in light of the two postscripts that provide more precise expression to the concept of "theory as toolbox." According to Foucault, it is not a matter of "constructing a system, but rather [...] a *logic* which is appropriate to the power relations and struggles in its environment". Ultimately, such an examination can "only be carried out step by step [...], proceeding from the reflection upon given situations".[5]

This brief formula contains—in condensed form—the orientation that artistic critique took from the mid-60s onwards: firstly, to develop a "logic"—and this means primarily a self-created, both conclusive and incorruptible methodological procedure—which reacts to a given power structure; secondly, not to stop with subjecting "evil" power to mere accusation or moral judgment, but to target its interdependencies and its ultimate imponderability, all the way to its entanglement with the "anti-powers" that act in opposition to it; and thirdly, in order to be able to make such a move, to take as a starting point the local, e.g. institutionally framed situation—even if that means digging up the ground under one's own feet. In these qualifications one might recognize the manner in which theory (in the sense used here) has become productive in art throughout the period in question. Or more precisely, how it could have become productive if its utilization (understood in a positive, non-instrumental sense) had been unswervingly pursued. In this respect, activities carried out by collectives like Grup de

2 Michel Foucault, "Mächte und Strategien. Gespräch mit Jacques Rancière (1977)," *Dits et Ecrits. Schriften, Band III, 1976–1979*, Suhrkamp, Frankfurt am Main 2003, p. 550. (Note: All quotes translated from German into English.)

3 Jacques Rancière in ibid., p. 547.

4 Michel Foucault, "Die Intellektuellen und die Macht. Gespräch mit Gilles Deleuze (1972)," *Dits et Ecrits. Schriften, Band II, 1970–1975*, Suhrkamp, Frankfurt am Main 2002, p. 382–393.

5 Foucault, *Mächte und Strategien*, p. 550.

Treball in Barcelona in the mid-1970s very much testify to a strengthened research- as well as theory-based approach and at the same time—especially via the brief momentum of its short-lived experimentalism—point to the limits of such an approach.

It goes without saying that in order to elucidate this particular usage of theory, a series of further clarifications are necessary, concerning above all the way in which concepts like "power," "critique" and ultimately "politics" are to be understood in such a (art-theoretical) context. Such clarifications, viewed retrospectively, often appear far simpler than the point at which they were offered contemporaneously with the practices they addressed; clarifications which were sometimes just as vehemently advanced in the artistic as well as in the theoretical field; clarifications, finally, which rather than promoting a once-and-for-all mandatory model, might contribute to the avoidance of obvious entrapments that a "unitary model" might imply.

The Academy in Peril

The model, which, from the early 1970s onwards, began to establish itself on the basis of the just-elucidated conception of theory, initially proceeded from a relatively clearly defined opponent, namely *institutional power* in all its flavors and manifestations. In a narrower sense, this could be related to the artistic field, as became obvious in the first wave of so-called institutional critique, whose agenda was primarily to subject the surrounding environment—or the social background of art institutions—to critical, sometimes accusatory examination.[6] Or it could be extended more widely, from particular institutional apparatuses of the state (schools, the military, the academy, bureaucracy, etc.) all the way to social, gender-related or ethnic power structures, all of which entered into art's sharpened field of vision during that period. Common to both variants, regardless of whether the focus lay primarily on the artistic or a social institution, was a simple oppositional pattern: on the one hand, the despotic institution tending towards malignance and concealment of its power; and on the other, the comparatively upright and generally educational gesture of a critique of power which considered itself, in relation to the for-

6 Cf. A. Alberro & B. Stimson (ed.), *Institutional Critique: An Anthology of Artists' Writings*, MIT Press, Cambridge/London 2009, and J. C. Welchman (ed.), *Institutional Critique and After*, JRP | Ringier, Zurich 2006.

mer, as largely independent and external. Regardless of whether it was a matter of the economic intrigues in the innermost reaches of a large museum, or the mechanisms of social exclusion with regard to women or ethnic minorities, this position of a critique of power always considered itself on secure and morally upright terrain, even though it might itself be entangled in institutional relations—entanglements that were not always immediately recognizable. Criticism of the ownership structure behind the Guggenheim Museum could only be effectively presented when, as a recognized artist, one had already entered into proximity to and been short-listed by a museum of this kind.[7] By contrast, artists like Július Koller put forward their brand of artistic critique not by entering into the vicinity of an established institution and trying to critique it from within but instead, by founding their own, much more anarchic and partly fictitious forms—in Koller's case, the *U.F.O. Gallery.*

But a second, long unrecognized, aspect characterized this early form of artistic critique of power. Once the criticism had taken on a certain institution, there could in principle be little inclination to hold back from other institutions situated within, or connected to that very context. If, for example, the primary focus addressed the ownership- and influence-structure behind a particular museum, this inevitably led to a consideration of economic and subsequently political interests, and from there to all sorts of social offshoots—those scattered arenas where the repercussions of real-estate dealings or the armaments/war industry were only too apparent. Naturally, this was clear to the practitioners of early institutional critique to the same extent that it was not always easy to find an appropriate aesthetic form for the highlighting of these entanglements. The "compromise" sometimes consisted in selecting a reduced, serial manner of framing the problematic situation, thus in no way purporting to do justice in a grander style to the actual workings and interminglings of power. It was deemed preferable to reduce an issue to a comprehensible, reconstructable albeit expandable formula, rather than aim at laying claim to the larger political mechanisms that governed society. Nonetheless, the guiding idea of this critical endeavor was long directed at an apparently monolithic power, regardless of whether it consisted of an economic conglomerate, a political lobby, or the state itself. Needless to say the limits of such an approach have sometimes been

[7] This is emphasized for instance by Daniel Buren, when in retrospect he explains, "You're invited by people who like you, people who admire you and probably share your critical position. So you're fighting against a bloc, but ironically inside this bloc you have a lot of friends who have the same attitude." ("In Conversation: Daniel Buren & Olafur Eliasson," *Artforum*, May 2005, p. 212)

met with biting irony: when, for instance, Paul De Vree, in his
piece *Political Poem: (W)AFFE* (1971), plays on the closeness
of the German words for "weapon" and "monkey," both applied
here to a representative of the state; or when Sanja Iveković,
in her photographic documentation *Triangle* (1979), satirizes
the relationship between state politics, publicness, secrecy, and
(public/private) sexuality.

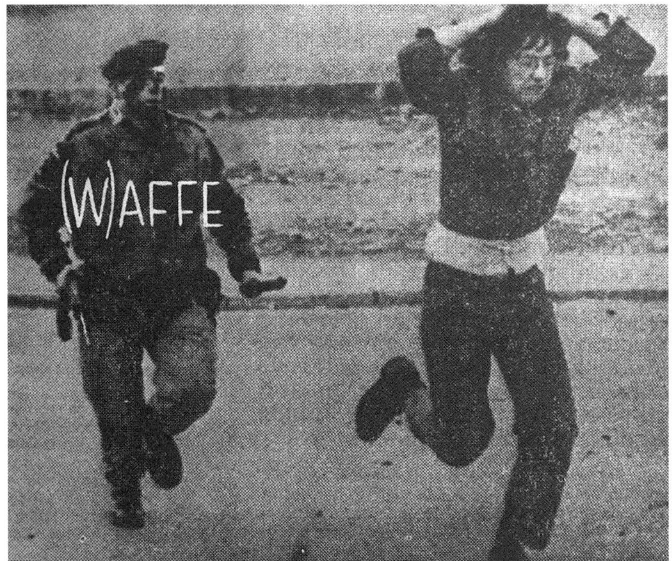

Paul de Vree, *Political
Poem - (W)AFFE*, 1971,
photo M HKA

As is well known, this monolithic conception of power has
almost been completely discarded in the course of poststructuralist discourse catching on.[8] After the period with which
L'Internationale is concerned ended (around the mid- to late-
1980s), relatively little attention has been given to traditional
state institutions such as schools, academies, the military, bureaucracy, or other forms of public administration—which constituted the focus of numerous works during the 1970s. Nor are
the alleged centers of power seen as clearly defined and cohesive in terms of their inherent constitution or a fixable locality.
In short, the traditional model of state power, authoritarian as
it was through the 1970s both in the West and in the East (with
significant differences of course), has come under severe revi-
sion; "states of domination"—as Foucault termed consolidated,
assailable forms of power—can no longer be derived from state
power in any meaningful sense. In short, the idea of dictato-

8 Concerning this and a
succession of related tran-
sitions, see Hito Steyerl,
"The Institution of Critique
(1/2006)," http://eipcp.net/
transversal/0106/steyerl/en
(status August 2012).

rial, one-dimensional, homogenous power structures has not only empirically run up against its limits but no longer holds on any general level either, suggesting a similar shift such as took place with respect to theory in its relation to art.

Towards the end of the 1970s Foucault pointed out the limited extent to which state institutions were capable of serving as the primary focus of an unremitting critique of power. In particular, he countered the critique of an authoritarian and self-contained state totality with an analysis of the plurality of administrative practices—what he summarized in the singular term "governmentality".[9] If the historical prevalence of this type of power manifests itself in the continuous expansion of various policing functions that cannot be derived from a single mode of domination, then the "reflection upon given situations," conceived as a multiplicity of local sites of power, gains new momentum and profile. At first glance, "police"—in the plural, this would constitute the legitimate (though not exhaustive) starting point for a more adequate critique of power— represents that connecting element "which allows the good governance of the state to intrude all the way into the lifestyles of individuals or into the conduct of families".[10] But that is not enough: as soon as the state increasingly retreats into the background—both ideologically and practically—individuals are required, to an ever-increasing degree, to govern themselves. What thus comes into focus and what is thematized or played on in critical art practices throughout the 1970s, are those seemingly inconspicuous everyday procedures that facilitate such self- or mutual-governance: "Parents govern their children, the mistress governs her lover, the teacher governs, and so forth. People govern each other in a conversation through an entire set of tactics."[11] The "major forms of power"—state-run, ideological, etc.—continue to be present in these "relationships of governing and leading which can be established between people".[12] But they hardly constitute their sole focus any longer. Józef Robakowski's film *Market (1970)*, depicting lived experience out on the street, testifies to this change as conclusively as KwieKulik's photographic experiments in life-politics, *Activities with Dobromiercz (1972–1974)*, or Paul De Vree's appropriation of an ecstatic crowd gathering under the title *Hysteria Makes History (1972)*.

9 Michel Foucault, "Die 'Governementalität' (Lecture, February 1, 1978)," U. Bröckling, S. Krasmann, T. Lemke (ed.), *Gouvernementalität der Gegenwart. Studien zur Ökonomisierung des Sozialen*, Suhrkamp, Frankfurt am Main 2000, p. 41–67; reprinted in Michel Foucault, *Dits et Ecrits. Schriften, Band III, 1976– 1979*, p. 796–823. The ominous term "governmentality" includes an entire package of individual measures "which make it possible to exercise this quite specific and yet complex form of power which has as its principal target the population, as its principal form of knowledge political economy, and as its essential technical instrument the security imperative". (*Gouvernementalität der Gegenwart*, p. 64).

10 Ibid., p. 48.

11 Michel Foucault, "Die Intellektuellen und die Mächte. Gespräch mit C. Panier und P. Watté (1981)," *Dits et Ecrits. Schriften, Band IV, 1980–1988*, Suhrkamp, Frankfurt am Main 2005, p. 929 ff.

12 Ibid., p. 930.

The Art of Not Being Governed

At around the same time critical artistic practice found itself engaged in a crucial transition concerning the usage of theory, there occurred a comparable shift with regard to the concept of power, or more exactly, relationships of power. The offshoot ensuing from the new "tool-model of theory" and Foucault's notion of being multiply governed (or self-governed) can thus more clearly be described as follows: What was subsequently required for a sharpened formulation of critique was no longer the idea of a single, grand opposition to state (or ideological) power, but a focus on the numerous practices of (self-)discipline and governing, which are realized far and wide among various social groups and individual persons, even within individuals. Taking this type of decentralization as the starting point of critique this near-impossible, dauntingly immense task has begun to haunt art practices, which have become increasingly confronted with the fact of their own, at times unconscious involvement in all sorts of non-state, extra-institutional practices of governing.

Whereas the orthodox model of power or governance seemed designed to guarantee a kind of closed loop, namely "from the state through the lives of individuals […] back to the state,"[13] the idea of governmentality aimed at exploding this circularity once and for all. And in fact, over the years a series of attributes—national, ethnic, cultural, gender-related, sexual, milieu-related, etc., and all of which constitute relevant points of intersection for power relations—have begun to inscribe themselves not only into the proceeding of artistic critique but more and more into the consciousness of the general public as well. All these attributes are cross sections of various sorts of governmental practices and thereby corrupt the monotonous "song of the cold monstrosity"[14] as Foucault once called the irrational fixation on state power. In an era when the representative civic institutions still demonstrated a predominantly repressive (or at least undeniably authoritarian) character, such a fixation was somewhat comprehensible. But in a period in which the diversity of "life politics"[15] acquires ever more significance, the single vast, "evil" power tends to lose its monstrous status, which in turn opens up a view onto the many scattered arenas of everyday power relationships. It is no longer schools,

13 Foucault, "Vorlesungen zur Analyse der Macht-Mechanism 1978," *Der Staub und die Wolke*, Impuls, Bremen 1982, p. 39.

14 Foucault, "Die 'Gouvernementalität,'" p. 65.

15 Cf. Zygmunt Bauman, *Society Under Siege*, Polity, Cambridge/Oxford 2002, p. 121 ff.

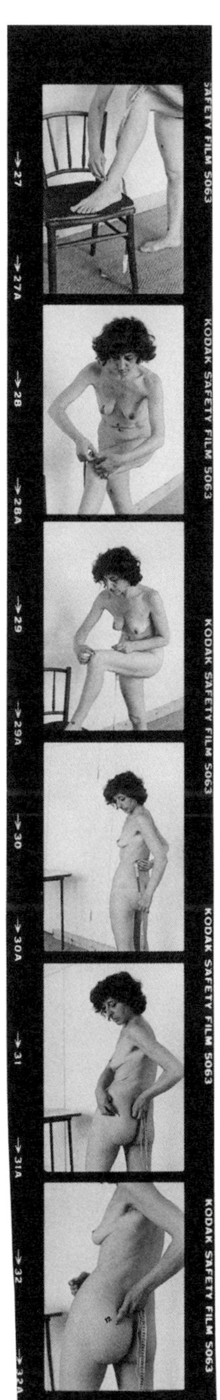

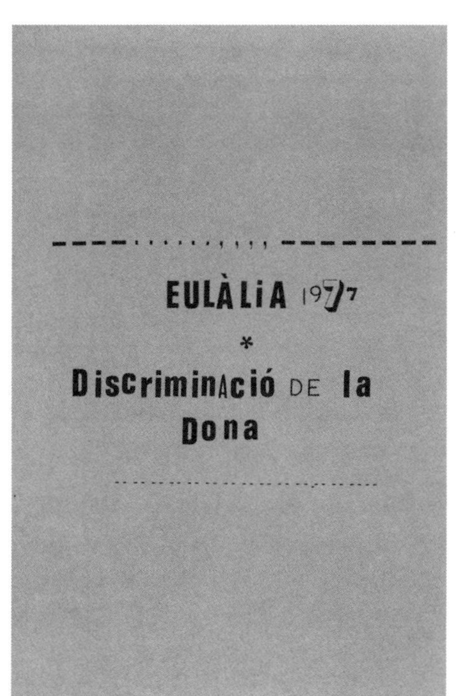

Eulàlia Grau, *Discrimination against Women*, 1977, MACBA Collection. MACBA Foundation. Donation of the artist.
© Eulàlia Grau, VEGAP, Barcelona, 2012, photo by Tony Coll

Esther Ferrer, *Intimate and Personal*, 1977, documentacion of the action at the Studio Lerin in Paris, photo by Ethel Blum MACBA Collection. MACBA Foundation.
© Esther Ferrer, VEGAP, Barcelona, 2012, photo by Rocco Ricci

factories, the academy or the military that constitute their principal stages but instead, familial, group-specific, ethnic or even personal and intimate relationships, wherever they happen to be located. While Francesc Abad's *Tribute to the Man in the Street* (1976–1977) seems still fixated on the excesses of state and/or police power, works like Esther Ferrer's *Intimate and Personal* (1977), Eulàlia Grau's *Discrimination against Women* (1977), or Tibor Hajas's multiple experiments of self-fashioning conducted throughout the 1960s, are clear indicators of a crucial shift.

Mention should be made at this point of another important transition in the field of art between the mid-1970s and mid-1980s. To put it shortly, it was no longer the art institution—the primary target for a first critical wave at the end of the 1960s—that was deemed the carrier of predominantly negative attributes of power, and hence served (negatively) as a projecting surface for fantasies of freedom. Instead, recognition gradually grew that the institution of art, far from being simply located in a material structure like a museum, in fact "imprisoned" all the participants in the art world—or offered them a space of freedom, depending on the perspective. This view of an "internalization"[16] of power- or institution-related aspects made it possible, on the one hand, to set oneself free of the phantasm of a despotic tyrant while, on the other hand, it gave rise to new requirements imposed upon an art practice claiming to be critical. If it was no longer an authoritarian or politically/morally corrupt institution that provided or served as the popular object of attack, then what other modes or sites of control constituted a worthy target? If the "critique of institutions" could not, in the long term, maintain its autonomy in relation to the entities critiqued, then what did this say about its own involvement in power relations? And finally, if artistic critique subsequently felt obliged to turn its attention to the entire field of "the social" (and not simply to the domain of art institutions), then how was it possible to maintain a distinct approach (in marked distinction, for instance, from social theory)?

All of these questions culminated in the problem of what understanding of critique, if any, was appropriate in view of this new, reformulated conception of power. What could serve as the main driver behind critical procedures, inasmuch as their counterpart—formerly conceived as a closed monolith—seems to have all but vanished?

16 Cf. the summary by Andrea Fraser, "From the Critique of Institutions to an Institution of Critique," *Artforum*, September 2005, p. 278–283, as well as the response by Simon Sheikh, "Notes on Institutional Critique (1/2006)," http://eipcp.net/transversal/0106/sheikh/en (status August 2012).

A key to this nexus of questions may lie in finding a "counter-piece to the arts of governance"—something that "is simultaneously their partner and their opponent, as a manner of distrusting them, rejecting them, limiting them and reducing them to their proper measure, transforming them, escaping them or at least seeking to shift them".[17] What this amounts to is the crucial insight that there cannot be a single, accusatory or debunking position in relation to the various forms of governance but instead, that there has to be an entire arsenal of possible forms. This arsenal, historically specific as it may be, can generally be characterized as a "type of mentality" which Foucault, again, delineates in genealogical terms, namely as "the art of not being governed or […] not being governed in this manner and at this price".[18] Critique designates precisely this refusal, which does not exhaust itself in negativity but instead attempts to establish a strategic body of knowledge and its situational application. The historical realization of this attitude, which can easily be discerned as a guiding principle in critical art practices from the 1970s onwards—at least in the context of the transition described above— may be dependent on many different, perhaps innumerable factors. Nonetheless, regardless of how "general, vague and indefinite"[19] it may appear at first sight, it represents a tactical standard through which a variety of power-permeated sites could (and have) become targeted over the past four decades.

If its contemporary implementation inevitably testifies to a sense of waning effectiveness, its historic version, spanning roughly the mid-1960s to the mid-1980s, still reveals or at lease points toward a variety of "just causes": that art could make a difference, that "the international" might be something else, something other than the global market tool it subsequently became, and that change could be sensed around the corner— even though it eventually proved impossible to turn that very corner.

Part of this essay goes back to an argument developed in "How Not To Be Governed–On Defining the Positions of Political and Socially Critical Art", translated from the German by George Frederick Takis, and first published in: Stephan Schmidt-Wulffen (ed.), *The Artist as Public Intellectual*, Schlebrügge, Vienna, 2008.

17 Michel Foucault, *Was ist Kritik?* (lecture, May 27, 1978), Merve, Berlin 1992, p. 12.

18 Ibid.

19 Ibid.

Connect Whom? Connect What? Why Connect?
The World System after 1945 Immanuel Wallerstein

In the project outline of "L'Internationale", the writers state that they wish "to challenge common canons and master narratives of art and to investigate local-to-local comparisons and differences." The reason they wish to do this, they say, is "to build a new, plural narrative and to keep the processes that built it transparent." They say they want to look at "avant-gardes from the decline of modernism to the rise of globalization, 1957–1986." It is not clear to me whether these dates were chosen according to turning-points in the art world or turning-points in the global political arena—perhaps both.

The background text lays emphasis on the large number of authoritarian regimes that existed in various parts of the world at the beginning of that period and presumably fewer towards the end. The text also mentions the rise of globalization, presumably towards the end of that period. The shift that is intended to be discussed is very real, but I would like to offer a slightly different set of temporal cutting-points to illuminate this story: 1945, 1956, 1968, 1979–1980, 1989–1991, 2001–2003, 2008–2010.

1945: This was of course the end of the Second World War. More importantly, it was the end of an intense 30-year-long struggle between the United States and Germany in their efforts, begun in the 1870s, to succeed Great Britain as the hegemonic power of the world-system.

The United States was the triumphant one. It was the only major industrial power to emerge in 1945 with its infrastructure unscathed. It had become the most efficient producer in the world-system and dominated the world market. All of Eurasia—not only the defeated Axis powers but the victors as well—were struggling to reconstruct themselves. The United States was able therefore to assert its hegemonic position and impose a new world order in accordance with and favorable to its interests.

Its only constraint was the remaining military strength of the Soviet Union, whose army was occupying virtually the whole of East-Central Europe. To ratify its hegemonic position, the

United States felt it necessary to enter into an arrangement with the Soviet Union, one we have come to designate metaphorically as Yalta. This arrangement had three components.

First and most important, the world was divided into two spheres of influence: a Soviet zone (the third of the world running from the Oder-Neisse line in Germany to the 38th parallel in Korea) and an American zone (the other two-thirds of the world). Both sides agreed tacitly not to attempt to use force to change these boundaries. There were many tense moments in their relations during the following years, but the outcome of each dramatic uprising or quasi-confrontation was in each case a return to the status quo ante. This agreement remained in fact inviolate until 1989.

Second, each side agreed to remain largely insulated economically. The United States would help to reconstruct Western Europe and Japan—both to ensure their roles as faithful and subordinate allies and to provide markets for the hyper-efficient American industries. Economically, the Soviet zone would stand on its own. This dual protectionism scheme did not hold up near as long, lasting only into the late 1960s.

Third, the two sides were to engage in a very loud rhetorical war known as the "Cold War." The mutual denunciations did not change, were not intended to change, the geopolitical division but rather served to permit each side to control politically its own zone and to ensure that fully loyal governments remained or were installed in power. This was the structural underpinning to the pervasive reality of authoritarian regimes we have seen in Eastern and Southern Europe as well as in Latin America, Turkey, Iran, Taiwan, South Korea, and elsewhere. These regimes would run into trouble eventually, the consequence not of any changed views on the part of American and Soviet authorities, but rather of shifts the two did not control in the wider geopolitical world.

The problem for both the United States and the Soviet Union was that their tacit deal served both of them well, but served as a highly conservative constraint on the changes so much of the rest of the world ardently wanted. With the death of Stalin, the ideological solidity of the Soviet bloc began to erode. The year 1956 marked two major turning points.

First there was the famous (notorious?) XXth Congress of the Communist Party of the Soviet Union (CPSU) and the "secret" speech Nikita Khrushchev delivered there. The speech did not remain secret very long. Khrushchev, speaking essentially on behalf of the Soviet *Nomenklatura*, brought Stalin's endless purges to an end, thereby offering a more stable environment for the lives and the fortunes of this *Nomenklatura*. To do this, he had to expose the Stalinist mythology. Many of the faithful viewed his speech not as "famous" but as "infamous."

The attack on Stalin, as the faithful had feared, undermined, and eventually undid, the worldwide ideological control by the Soviet hierarchy over both the satellite countries and the satellite parties everywhere. One immediate consequence was the two uprisings in Eastern Europe—in Hungary and Poland. While both were repressed, in the Hungarian case with the use of Soviet troops, the unstoppable process of desatellization had begun.

At virtually the same time, Israel, Great Britain, and France invaded Egypt, intending to punish Nasser for the links he was establishing with the Soviet Union. The United States was no more ready to tolerate this unilateral action on their part than the Soviet Union was ready to tolerate the attempts by Poland and Hungary to engage in autonomous political activity. The United States was doubly dismayed, because its allies (and most particularly Great Britain) dared to act autonomously, and because these actions interfered with its own evolving policy of courting governments in the so-called Third World, particularly Nasser's.

So the United States in effect ordered the three powers to withdraw their troops, which they did. All the main actors drew different conclusions from this confrontation. The outcome, however, was once again transformative. The United States would henceforth become an ever more direct actor in the Middle East, seeking to control everything and everyone, and in the long run discovering in this region the limits of the capacities of a hegemonic power.

The 1960s saw the onset of a creeping geopolitical decline for both the United States and its collusive partner, the Soviet Union. Both initially reacted with new kinds of repression. This would, however, not really work in the middle-run. The world-revolution of 1968 was one result to come out of this shift, and it turned out to be devastating for both.

The ideological decline of the Soviet Union was marked by an escalating stretching of the interpretation of Marxism.

In Western Europe, the three most powerful Communist parties—in France, Italy, and Spain—embarked on a path of post-
Stalinist redefinition, which would culminate a decade later in
the concept of Eurocommunism. This new path gave way to a
threefold set of consequences: extricating these parties from
Soviet control and influence; "social-democratizing" their platforms; and despite both of these, or more likely because of both
of these, diminished real electoral strength.

The 1960s also saw the emergence of a cultural loosening
of the Soviet system itself. The most visible aspect of this was
the public emergence of Sakharov, Solzhenitsyn, and ever more
figures the Soviets had deemed "dissidents." In a more obscure
yet important development, an intra-Communist debate was
launched in Hungary and Western Europe around the concept
of the "Asiatic mode of production," which eventually made
possible a return both to actually reading Marx and to a far
wider discussion of Marx's ideas that was less constrained by
official doctrine.

The Chinese Communist Party used this moment to establish its total autonomy from the CPSU—not only politically but
ideologically; and to establish itself as a new global pole in the
larger geopolitical power scheme. The so-called "cultural revolution" (launched roughly 1966) not only created fundamental
social upheaval within China itself but had enormous impact on
all leftist movements around the world.

And, of course, the Czechoslovaks attempted to establish
"socialism with a human face." This led to the invasion by
Soviet and other troops. The invasion was justified by the so-
called Brezhnev doctrine, which did serve to restore Soviet
authority but by the same token turned out to be quite self-
defeating. It both gave way to the political stagnation of the
Brezhnev years in the Soviet Union and it fed, rather than stifled, the thrust toward desatellization.

The political follies of the Soviet leadership from this period
are widely discussed today. We tend to notice less the parallel
imprudence of the U.S. political leadership. In the 1960s, the
integrity of anti-Communist ideology began to be subjected
to increasing scrutiny in the various regions over which the
United States exerted particular influence and/or control.
A left-of-center party was gaining strength in Greece; and
Falangism no longer enjoyed unquestioned status in Franco's

Spain. Salazar's death in Portugal reopened questions about the regime. And throughout various Latin American countries, left or left-of-center movements and parties seemed to be gaining strength as well.

America's version of the Brezhnev doctrine came into play: the Colonel's coup in Greece, Franco's clamping-down on even moderate dissidents in his last days, military coups in Brazil and Chile, the escalating war in Vietnam, and the ouster of Sihanouk in Cambodia. Just as Brezhnev's repression proved effective in the short run but bred its own undoing, so did American repressive thrusts in the late 1960s and early 1970s.

Of course what hurt the United States most was its inability to win the war it was fighting in Vietnam. The Vietnam War not only led to enormous internal turmoil (at home in the U.S.), but it proved particularly draining, both economically and geo-politically. Soon to follow were the moral and political fiasco of Watergate, Nixon's fall from office and let us not forget, the exposure by the U.S. Senate's Church Committee of the nefari-ous exploits of the CIA.

The key turning point was the world revolution of 1968, which pulled all of these pieces together. First of all, it should be underlined that this was a *world* revolution, in the elementa-ry sense that between 1966 and 1970, uprisings of various kinds played out in all three of the dominant geopolitical arenas of the time—in the pan-European sphere, the so-called socialist bloc, and the so-called Third World. Every regional, national and local event or development had, to be sure, its own particular explanation and story. But two underlying themes were com-mon to all of the events in all three zones, and it is these com-monalities that are relevant to our discussion here.

Everywhere protestors denounced the many various expres-sions of U.S. hegemony and the Soviet Union's collusion in these expressions as a result of the unwritten Yalta accords. After 1968, neither the United States nor the Soviet Union would ever again be able to regain the unquestioned loyalty of their presumed allies nor the unchallenged belief in the bright futures each was guaranteeing to everyone.

The second commonality was, if anything, more important: Protestors everywhere called into question not merely the gov-erning doctrines of the Cold War but the honesty, relevance, and real objectives of the traditional antisystemic movements that had inspired and framed popular struggles for at least a century.

All three variations of the Old Left—the Communist parties, the Social-Democratic parties, and the national liberation movements—were branded failures by the protestors. By this time most had come to power in various states and they had not changed the world (for the better) at all, as they had widely promised along their long trajectory from the late 19th century onward. The protestors proclaimed these movements part not of the solution but of the problem. None of these movements would ever be able to recover from the political shock they suffered as a result. These movements ceased in fact to be movements and were diminished to the status of mere parties. They lost the ability to mobilize the faithful, who believed and were ready to sacrifice themselves for the certain glorious future these movements had promised.

These movements had been the movements of modernity. The modern was to have been—and seen—the fulfillment of the struggle, the end of the process, heaven on earth. At the end of these great struggles, all problems would find their (positive) resolution.

It is no accident that, as part of the world revolution of 1968, the world saw the coming to the fore, the flourishing, of all the movements whose (ultimate) causes had been avoided or sidetracked in the name of some larger, more immediate cause; to wait until the conclusion of the process. These were the movements that asserted the rights of the "forgotten people"—the women, the ethno-racial "minorities," the "indigenous" peoples, those whose sexual practices/preferences were other than the hitherto defined and accepted norm. They were also the movements of those who fought for a smarter, more sober world ecology, who struggled for peace, who supported and pressed the necessity for non-violent struggle.

All of these groups were now rejecting the overwhelming primacy of the presumed prime historical actor offered up and installed by the traditional social and nationalist movements, insisting instead on the co-equal primacy of all the oppressed groups. These groups rejected the vertical structures of the antisystemic movements that had long claimed to be the only legitimate movement within their state (present or prospective). They championed instead a more horizontal alliance of multiple groups. And in the process, they began to question the epistemological assumptions of "modernity," which they saw as the hidden (and not so hidden) legitimations of dominance by a small, often unrepresentative segment of humanity—that which had dominated the traditional antisystemic movements.

The end of modernity, the search for the "post-modern," involved the rejection of the assumptions of "inevitable progress" as embodied in Enlightenment thought. This meant not only a different way of thinking about the world, but also a different politics and a different geopolitics; a different approach. And it meant the liberation of the world "left" from the tacitly "centrist" presumptions of the traditional antisystemic movements.

What, however, also emerged out of this (coming essentially from the left) attack on modernity—and what I would call "centrist liberalism"—was a certain liberating of the world right as well, from what had been its equally tacit acceptance of the ameliorative principles of this same "centrist liberalism." Some, in their eagerness to assert the primacy of "culture," failed to realize that as long as we lived in a capitalist world-economy, the economic and political underpinnings of our lives continued to exert enormous influence. The new post-1968 political scene would be one in which not only radicals but also conservatives came to feel freed from the constraints of the formerly dominant centrist liberalism.

This dual-liberation was crucially important because the overall structure of the world-system was entering a cyclical shift. The years 1967–1973 proved a turning point in two crucial ways. It marked not only the end of the unquestioned U.S. hegemony in the world-system, but also the end of the greatest expansion in the global economy the system had ever known. What the French called "les trentes glorieuses"—a typical Kondratieff A-cycle except for the fact that it involved a far larger expansion of the global economy than any previous cycle—soon reached a point of exhaustion. The quasi-monopolies that had sustained the expansion had been sufficiently undermined that the world-system entered a Kondratieff B-cycle of stagnation, one that has remained in place ever since.

What we call today the global financial and economic crisis is simply the culmination point of this long Kondratieff B-phase. The world's Left lived and left the 1970s in search of new organizational forms that would replace those that the Old

Left, the traditional antisystemic movements (now in semi-disgrace), had institutionalized.

The world Right exhibited a far more practical approach. They launched a coherent program to transform the direction of the world-system and to push back against all of the advances in social welfare that had been achieved during the 1945–1967/73 period. They were determined to reduce real wages worldwide, repel all pressures on producers to internalize the costs of combating environmental damage the world over, and to reduce, even eliminate, the benefits of the welfare state. This program was called neo-liberalism.

These forces managed to assume power in the United States with the election of Ronald Reagan in 1980, and in Great Britain—America's key ally—with the Conservative government headed by Margaret Thatcher in 1979. They sought both legislative changes in their own respective countries and changes in the discourse throughout the world. They called for the rejection everywhere of "developmentalism," which had survived as the dominating discourse of the post-1945 period. Developmentalism—promoted equally, albeit in slightly different verbiages, by the United States and its allies, the Soviet Union and its allies, and the leaders of Third World countries—had been based on theories of inevitable progress and the role of states in furthering the values of modernity.

The answer to developmentalism, said the neo-liberals, was globalization: essentially embracing the opening of all frontiers to the free movement of goods and capital—but not labor. The central underlying theme was the freedom of private corporations to seek profit any way and anywhere they could. This was grounded in the explicit ethical undesirability of state interference in any way, shape or form, and on the political incapacity of the states to do so. And there was Margaret Thatcher's famous slogan, TINA— There is No Alternative. If globalization resulted in exaggerated inequalities, this was inevitable, perhaps even desirable. Globalization as discourse was, is, rightwing anti-modernism. And as such it was far more politically successful in the period 1980–2000 than left-wing anti-modernism.

There was, however, a catch to the discourse on globalization. What it did not address was the fact that the 1970s marked the beginning of an ordinary Kondratieff B-phase. Ordinary

B-phases are a consequence of the fact that profits from productive enterprises become very much reduced owing to the decline of quasi-monopolies along with their market-leading products.

Serious attempts at accumulation have, therefore, to seek an alternative route. This alternative route is investing in the financial arena; that is, in speculation. As the years 1945–1970 represented the largest expansion of productive enterprise and profits in the history of the modern world-system, so the years 1970–2010 are those of the largest expansion of speculative profits in the history of the modern world-system.

There are, of course, other features to a standard Kondratieff B-phase, such as significant increase in unemployment worldwide and relocation of productive enterprises to other regions of the world-system in search of cheaper labor. This latter feature fuels the claim by those areas of industrial relocation that they are "developing," and indeed they are the locus of some shift in worldwide capital accumulation.

The crucial feature, however, of financialization as it has come to be known, is that it requires debt, specifically indebtedness. And since debt has to be repaid at some point, the world runs through successive debtors, until it begins to exhaust the possibilities, until it runs out of (new) debtors, which is where we find ourselves today.

One key set of debtors has been the states of the world. In the 1970s, recycled oil rent was lent to governments of the Third World and also to the states in the Eastern socialist Bloc. When they reached the point at which they simply couldn't repay these debts, governments (and the movements linked to these governments) began to fall. The most dramatic of these falls was that of the Soviet Union and the CPSU.

Mikhail Gorbachev does not get particularly good press these days, neither inside nor outside Russia. This is somewhat unfair, and history will see this judgment revised some. I believe his was a heroic, if flawed, attempt to come to terms with the changed world situation and salvage a reformed Soviet Union. The collapse of the Soviet Union and of the CPSU was hailed at the time—and is still seen by many—as a victory for the United States in the long-fought Cold War.

In fact, this collapse signaled the defeat of the United States in the Cold War. The Cold War was not supposed to end but to continue indefinitely. The collapse created two enormous problems for the United States: first, it lost its ostensible enemy and with it the last strong argument why Western Europe (and Japan) should remain tied (and bowing) to U.S. "leadership" and similarly, not stray into the playing of autonomous geopolitical roles.

The second, and perhaps even more important, loss was that it surrendered the Soviet Union's power to constrain its friends and allies from "dangerous" actions that might, in any way, lead to a Soviet-American nuclear war. The most immediate consequence of the collapse of the Soviet Union appeared in Saddam Hussein's invasion of Kuwait in 1990—something the Soviet Union would, in the past, have been able to prevent. The United States responded in 1991 with the first Gulf War, which forced the withdrawal by the Iraqis from Kuwait.

Far from being "the end of history" and a new world order dominated by the United States, the first Gulf War, ostensibly won by the United States, would lead, almost inevitably, to the self-destructive second invasion of Iraq by the United States a decade later.

The growing, repercussive damage to the world's peoples as a result of the policies imposed on the world's states in neoliberal globalization led, in the 1990s, to the beginning of the counter-trend. I trace the counter-movement to the uprising of the Zapatistas (EZLN) on Jan. 1, 1994 in Chiapas, Mexico. The Zapatistas chose the date to make public their struggle because it was symbolic—the date on which the North American Free Trade Agreement (NAFTA) came into force. On the one hand it was the announcement of a struggle that was local—the demand of real autonomy for the indigenous peoples of Chiapas (and elsewhere). But at the same time, the struggle was global—the struggle against U.S. geopolitical dominance and its Mexican (national government) allies.

Chiapas in 1994 was followed (most) notably by the demonstrations in Seattle in 1999 when the efforts of the World Trade Organization (WTO) to enforce neoliberal constraints on governments to resist globalization was stopped essentially dead in its tracks—and has never been able to resume.

The success of the Seattle demonstrations triggered a process that led to the creation of the World Social Forum in Porto Alegre in 2001, which has emerged as the major political force (of an original and unusual kind) fighting for "another world that is possible"—an alter-globalization.

One last word on 2001—that marked the coming to power in the United States of George W. Bush and his administration of "neo-conservatives." It was also, as we are constantly reminded, the year of 9/11, the startlingly successful attack by al-Qaeda on American soil.

What ensued is well known: the neo-conservatives used the attacks of 9/11 to launch their program of so-called "shock and awe"—the invasion of Iraq in 2003. This was a war for which they had been calling, publicly, since 1997. If we are to understand what has happened in the world, we must understand the reasoning of the neo-conservatives who dominated the Bush regime.

The neo-cons formulated the following analysis of the world-system. They believed that the United States had been losing its hegemonic position of power since the 1970s—exactly my own analysis. Their explanation for this decline was, however, quite different. (I have tried to show why hegemonic decline is structurally inevitable.) The neo-cons insisted this was the result of (human) policy error, of the moral and political weakness of past U.S. presidents and administrations from Nixon to Clinton (including, be it noted, Ronald Reagan).

The neo-cons felt the road to reassuming hegemonic dominance was for the United States to engage in unilateral macho militarism that would intimidate everyone (and first all their presumed closest allies in Western Europe) into unequivocal adherence to U.S. policy.

They chose Iraq as the demo-testing field for this exercise. Why Iraq? Because it had humiliated the United States. How so? In the fact that Saddam Hussein had survived the first Gulf War and was still in power. And why was he still in power? Because the then president, George H.W. Bush, declined to march on Baghdad and oust Saddam Hussein. And why did the first President Bush not do this? Because he believed that doing so would lead the United States into a quagmire, out of which it would not be able to extricate itself.

So in 2001, the Bush administration decided to invade Iraq, and it took two years to prepare and obtain (limited) support from some other countries. The neo-cons expected that (1) the invasion would be a simple, easily accomplished militarily exercise, and that the Iraqi public would greet the Americans as liberators; (2) Western Europe would promptly abandon all idea of geopolitical autonomy; (3) would-be nuclear proliferators (notably North Korea and Iran) would immediately cease these efforts; and (4) so-called moderate Arab states would be ready to settle once and for all the issue of Palestine largely along the lines of Israeli terms.

On the contrary, however, the neo-cons turned out to be wrong, catastrophically wrong, on each and every count. Iraqi resistance proved enduring, effective, and is still ongoing. France and Germany teamed up with Russia to give the United States a crushing defeat in the Security Council in March 2003. North Korea and Iran, far from abandoning efforts to become nuclear powers, intensified them. And the Arab states became less willing than ever to accept an Israeli dictation of terms concerning Palestine. The whole fiasco has led, instead, into the precipitate and definitive decline of the United States as a hegemonic power.

In 2008, the next-to-last speculative bubble burst. The world, and most especially the United States, slid, or dove rather, into the so-called Great Recession—which in actual fact is a global depression. And it will be sometime until we emerge even partially from the deflationary consequences.

Now that I have offered my brief and somewhat summary (I hope not too elusive) analysis of the key developments in the world since 1945, and why "modernism" has come under such profound attack, let me turn to what you propose to do about it–establish points of connection. And I have asked, at the outset—Connect whom? Connect what? Why connect?

Let me start with the questions your background text poses:

"How can we define the alternative communal or global interests today? What are new points of connection between these spaces that can serve as points of departure for new subversive global actions?"

The answer as to whom to connect seems to me fairly obvious. It is all those who are searching for alternative communal or global interests. They are of course to be found in the world of art institutions. But those involved in these institutions also comprise, naturally, only a small part of those searching for alternative communal or global interests. They are also to be found in the myriad organizations and movements that already

exist and are constantly springing up everywhere. These
organizations range from those that are markedly local (or
communal) to those organized on wider geographic scales and
levels, even the global.

It seems to me that museums and artist archives can only
do so much autonomously or even jointly. The organizational
question for them is how to create meaningful, working links
with this vast array of movements, small and large, that share
some aspect of your communal objective. Artists, like all
those engaged in intellectual work, are rooted in the social
reality that surrounds them. They reflect this social reality at
the same time, create and modify this reality. It is, to use a
very old phrase, a dialectical relationship, one that has to be
cultivated and nourished, and subjected to constant critical
self-reflection.

So what is it that we want to connect? We want to connect
discussions, debates about reality, short-term and longer-term.
We want to connect concrete actions, of which expositions
are but one mode but surely not the only. We want to connect
moral and political support, since such ongoing connections
will surely come under (negative) criticism from those who do
not share the same views and objectives.

We need always to bear in mind that there are material
underpinnings to the life of museums and institutions as well
as to the life of social movements. They need money to operate. And everyone who needs money, but who wishes at the
same time to engage in "subversive global actions," is caught
in a bind. They do not wish to bend to hostile pressures. But
they often need to bend under such an onslaught. There is no
point in avowing purism. There is every point in trying to
tread carefully on treacherous terrain. The global terrain is
highly variegated, and there are many ways to survive among
the complex range of sources of support—to survive without
surrendering the heart, the essence of what one is trying to ac-
complish. This is vague advice, I know, but the history of the
world shows is rife with movements and institutions that failed
to survive, and therefore failed to contribute to transforming
the world.

And finally, why connect? The answer to that is the simplest
of all. In Mrs. Thatcher's words, there is no alternative. We
are living in an era of fundamental social transformation, one

that I call the structural crisis of the modern world-system. It will not survive. It will be replaced. But will it be replaced by something as bad or even worse; or by something better?

Everyone wants it to be something better—a new world-system that is relatively democratic and relatively egalitarian. But there are many others, powerful others, who want and are working toward another world-system that is at least as hierarchical, exploitative, and polarizing as our present capitalist world-economy.

We can be sure that the present system will not survive. There is no way of knowing what kind of system will replace it. This new system will be the result of an enormous, ongoing political struggle in which everyone, whether they realize or not, will be participating. In effect, this means that there is, at best, a 50/50 chance that the new world-system will better.

But it is also true that, amidst the chaotic and rapid fluctuations of the medium-long period of global transition, every input matters—every input at every moment by every individual and group. That is why we must connect—to have a chance. That is why we must, in your language, "instigate transnational, plural cultural narratives." It is not all we need to do, but it is an indispensable component of a common program. And it is quite wonderful that you are launching such an institutional program.

This essay is based on a keynote address presented at
Points of Connection, The Vienna L'Internationale Conference,
October 27, 2010.

Recycling the R-waste (*R* is for Revolution) Boris Buden

It is odd how simple and transparent the world looks today: one single concept of (post)history, a single economic system, a single political model, a single art-system. Either you are already in or you strive to get in. The picture clearly resembles an ideological delusion. But it is not. Rather it is a cultural one: the belief that the major difference that divides people nowadays is no longer ideological, political or economic but cultural. At least it was Huntington who would have us subscribe to this notion. He also dated this post-ideological turn to the end of the Cold War. Thus, ideology is supposed to have died with communism, but only to make a place for culture that has taken over its function in structuring our reality, both the current and the past one. For it is cultural difference that nowadays governs over both space and time, defining and controlling the boundary between here and there, between now and then.

Where Communism was, there is now East

The best example of such a culturalization of historical reality is the process of transformation known as "post-communist transition" (to democracy, where else?). Curiously, this eminently historical process is usually imagined as a sort of time-space, concretely, as a space of cultural belatedness, mostly in terms of a belated modernism. Its name is "East" and it designates much more than the geographical realm of Eastern Europe. In the post-communist discourse "East" refers primarily to the cultural other of the West. This is how the Cold War divide has survived the collapse of communism—as cultural divide between the West and the East. And this is how the entire historical experience of communism has disappeared from the West—disposed of into the cultural otherness of the East. Now communism not only appears as intrinsically non-western—the West for its part is cleared of all the trauma of the communist past that is still accessible only in the cultural retrospective of the East.

On the ideological level the Western exclusion of the communist past is carried out through the signifier of totalitarianism. It retroactively totalizes a politically, ideologically and culturally heterogeneous experience of historical communism, unifies the space of the East, renders it transparent and finally essentializes its cultural identity.

Now the East, after having been defeated politically and appropriated economically, can be also conquered epistemically and colonized culturally. The first task is assumed by the Western academy, particularly disciplines like the so-called area studies. Not only does the academy produce the knowledge on the East, it also establishes the West as the exclusive subject of this knowledge. In this way the West acquires the ultimate epistemic competence over an historic experience it has allegedly never shared. At the same time, the cultural difference between the West and the East becomes a chasm between theory and praxis in terms of both space and time: theoretical knowledge is here and now (in the West) while the historical praxis is there and then (in the East). Needles to say, the Western theoretical knowledge is always already universal; the Eastern historical praxis, however, is merely particular.

As regards cultural colonization, this unfolds in the form of an accelerated modernization of the East—perceived in the East as the process of catching up with a cultural development it missed. Values, norms and standards of the Western cultural industry are introduced in the East. The same applies for modern and contemporary art. The global (Western) art system with its institutions—large exhibitions, museums, galleries, biennials, curators, art magazines, etc.—penetrates the space of the former communist East. However, there are also some authentic cultural and artistic values to be discovered in the East and introduced in the West. A sort of cultural exchange takes place, but not one between equal partners. The East has much less to offer. It is poor, weak and backward. This is why it suffers a lack of recognition. And this is why the relation in which the East stands to the West can best be described as a struggle for recognition – entirely in accordance with the so-called identity politics that dominates political life today.

The best example of this struggle is the phenomenon of "self-easternization" that marked some artistic projects between the 1980s and the 1990s in former Yugoslavia (Slovenia in particular) and in the former Soviet Union (Russia).[1] At stake artistically was a critical reflection on the so-called

1 See Igor Zabel, "Intimität und Gesellschaft: Die slowenische Kunst und der Osten," B. Groys, A. von der Heiden, P. Weibel (ed.), *Zurück aus der Zukunft: Osteuropäische Kulturen im Zeitalter des Postkommunismus*, Suhrkamp, Frankfurt am Main 2005, p. 472–508. Zabel uses the term "Veröstlichung" (easternization).

historic avant-gardes. But in terms of its ideological meaning the concept of "East Art" actually accepted the rules of the "identitarian" game and claimed an essential otherness in relation to Western art. Let us put aside the question whether the reason for this claim was an attempt to challenge or subvert the Western-dominated art system or rather "simply" a marketing trick—concretely, the opening of a new market niche made possible by the globalization of the art system and the expansion of the capitalist market toward the East during the 1980s and 1990s.[2] The fact that "East Art" is more than a Western ideological projection is important, for it has a real self-proclaimed referent in the East, an art that is not only truly identified with its "eastern-ness" but also with its referentiality to the West.[3]

It is thus no wonder that the Western art system has taken this "Eastern challenge" seriously, especially on the part of its enlightened, inclusivist wing eager to discover hidden aesthetic values out there in the East. If the cultural exchange between the West and the East has, from the perspective of the latter, the form of a struggle for recognition, seen from the West it becomes a sort of simple cultural translation. It sees its task in bridging the cultural difference, embracing the (Eastern) Other and filtering out what is useful and can enrich the (Western) art system—concretely, refurbish the existing canons and so eventually foster their renewal.

But not everything is translatable. What the Western cultural translators address in the East is its cultural heritage, in particular its art history, yet in fact nothing more than a pile of cultural data inscribed into the signs of a foreign culture, respectively the "native informants" charged with delivering this data. By participating in this model of (an always already unequal) inter-cultural translation the "easterners", even if they believe in struggling for recognition, necessarily accept a radical divergence of cultural history and historical praxis with the latter being irrevocably lost in translation. Or, to put it more precisely, it is heterogeneity, contingency and opacity of the historical praxis that is, in this mode of inter-cultural translation, rendered untranslatable. In order to be culturally recognized, the East must leave the truth of its historical praxis to oblivion. This is the price it pays for having a unique cultural identity—identity that necessarily implies the transparency of a common historical experience, a homogeneous cultural space,

[2] The latter option is suggested by Miklavž Komelj in his lecture "The Function of the Signifier, Totalitarianism", in the Constitution of the Field of "East Art'", given at the *Workers'-Punks' University* (Ljubljana) on May 15, 2008. (Manuscript)

[3] Komelj gives the example of an "Eastern" exhibition featured in Ljubljana's Moderna galerija in 2004 under the title "Seven Sins—Ljubljana—Moscow": "The visitor was confronted with a billboard installed in front of the gallery which submitted a definition of 'the Easterners' as clowns who entertain the West (mind the obvious self-irony which is ideally included in this definition). Typically, among the seven constitutive characters of 'the Easterners', beside 'laziness' (we should, of course, read this notion in light of the texts by Kazimir Malevič and Mladen Stilinović) and similar 'sins', one would also read: 'Love of the West'. Thus, an artist is defined as 'Easterner' through his/her love for the West." Ibid.

a shared ideological totality, one is even tempted to say, a common destiny.

If the rules of this game are generally accepted, we get a sort of hermeneutic narrative—a relatively coherent (hi)story of art related out of a transparent historical context, concretely the history of East Art in the context of communist totalitarianism.

Capitalism: An East Side Story

The case of the former Yugoslavia is of particular interest here, for it usually serves as the perfect exception that proves the rule: socialism but with a more or less human face, a closed society but with open borders, a communist rule but not within the Eastern bloc, a one-party system but without a command economy, a Marxist ideology but a respectable cultural production thoroughly comparable to the Western one; and yet, nothing but a communist totalitarian system that collapsed in 1989/90.

Let us try to avoid this hermeneutic trap of providing a specific (Yugoslav) historical context for a general narrative of "Art in the Communist East" and so helping the West to culturally translate the East. The first step in this direction is to shake the entire conceptual horizon that is structured by binary divisions like West/East, capitalism/communism, democracy/totalitarianism, autonomy of art/its ideological subjection and propagandistic misuse, etc.

What follows are a few simple facts of Yugoslav political and cultural history that necessarily get lost in the current Western translations of the Eastern communist past.

In a speech from 1950, Boris Kidrič, a member of the Yugoslav Politburo in charge of the Yugoslav economy, opens the problem of monopolization in a socialist economy, ascribing it to the "Soviet praxis" or more precisely to "the monopoly capitalism that was brought to perfection by Soviet bureaucratic centralism."[4] Elsewhere he writes that "the economic and social role of the Soviet bureaucratic caste totally resembles the role of the capitalist class if it is not, because of its almightiness, even worse." In his *Theses on the Economy of the Transitional Period [CAPS, YES?]*, Kidrič takes the USSR as an example of how "state socialism" cannot be separated "from the strengthening and privileging bureaucracy as social parasite ... from the

4 This and following quotations are taken from Darko Suvin's essay on bureaucracy in the post-revolutionary Yugoslavia 1945–1975. ("Diskurs o birokraciji i državnoj vlasti u po-revolucionarnoj Jugoslaviji 1945–1975," unpublished manuscript). Translations are mine.

suffocating of socialist democracy and general degeneration of
the system" so that it comes to "a peculiar sort of restoration …
a vulgar monopolism of a state-capitalist character."

Isn't this interesting: The crucial part of what is today retroactively perceived as historical communism and identified with
the "East" was labeled—*within* this very historical communism
and by the communists themselves—(monopoly) capitalism
that is even worse than (Western) capitalism itself. Having
said this, I don't insist on a singularity of the Yugoslav position within the communist experience, but rather on an intrinsic heterogeneity of this experience that cannot be subsumed
under one single feature, be it totalitarianism, one-party rule,
Marxism-Leninism, command economy or simply the culture
of the East. To emphasize again: we can think of the "East" as a
place where capitalism was worse than in the West.

However, one might rightly object that the place from which
communism is seen as a form of capitalism that is worse than
capitalism itself is just another self-proclaimed "true" communism. Indeed, this was precisely the case with Yugoslav "as-
sociational socialism"[5], based on the so-called self-management
system, and a peculiar mixture of social welfare state and market economy. But let us take a look at how this "true" communism identified its own political stakes and inner contradictions.

After the split with Stalin of 1948, and contrary to the Soviet
model of state-capitalism, the Yugoslav Communist Party introduced "market socialism": all central plan directives to the
enterprises were abandoned, the labor market was liberalized,
a sort of financial market with a strong role for the banks was
introduced, etc. This resulted in rapid industrialization and
an economic growth rate that averaged 13% annually (1950-
1960s). This, however, also had negative consequences like
massive unemployment[6], a deepening of the divide between the
north and the south, inflation, growing foreign debt and more.

Yet these changes also radically transformed the conditions of cultural production, making possible the emergence
of a powerful cultural industry. To offer but one example, the
famous Yugoslav film industry was capable, already during
the 1960s, of producing some 150 short and 30 feature films a
year. The backbone of this industry consisted in a number of
relatively independent companies, enterprises that were also
the owners of their final products, the films. They provided the

5 This is how, in the
1950s, one very promi-
nent Yugoslav economist
(Branko Horvat) coined—by
the way, in a dissertation
written in Great Britain—
the Yugoslav type of historical communism.

6 This explains one of the
best-known differences between Yugoslavia and the
Eastern Bloc communist
countries—Yugoslavia's
open borders. The borders
were opened not out of respect to so-called freedom
of movement, but rather in
order to cope with the growing masses of unemployed.
They were allowed abroad
to find jobs on the international labour market, mostly
in Western Europe, in
Austria, Germany, France,
Scandinavia etc.

expertise and technology, studios, film-processing laboratories, professional support, etc. On the other side the authors (writers and directors) of the films were not employed by the state. Rather they were organized in free associations of film workers, comprised of screenwriters, directors, actors, composers, cameramen, set designers and more. They were given the status of freelance professionals, freed from direct employment in technical and production companies and were granted the right to negotiate contractual arrangements with the film studios in order to realize various scenarios and film projects. Productions were not financed by the state budget but rather through fundraising from banks, companies, TV and media centers, communal or republic cultural funds, cooperation with foreign film and TV companies and similar.

This doesn't sound like a typically socialist approach to filmmaking, does it? Moreover, this example applies to the broader cultural production in former Yugoslavia, including publishing, theatre, literary and art production.

Altogether, market socialism provided a reasonably friendly environment for the flourishing of all sorts of modernist cultural expression, including contemporary art. It also allowed for a constant and essentially problem-free contact with the international cultural scene and market.

However, there is no market economy—say, capitalism— without crisis. In Yugoslavia such crisis emerged, with all of its political consequences, in the late 1960s.

At the Party Congress of 1971, the elite managed to clearly define the economic core of the crisis: "The surplus value that had been taken from the state hasn't returned to production, to the organizations of self-management labor in the factories, but has flowed over to the banks, insurance and large trading companies, especially those in the export branch." In other words, the Party, as well as society as a whole, loses control over a growing financial sector. One of the leading Party ideologues of the time, Vladimir Bakarić, points to the central problem: "the capital that is accumulated in the banks has become autonomous, is out of any control and restores capitalist relations and conditions wherever it occurs—and it occurs everywhere." He also sees a new subject of power emerging, the so-called techno-managers monopoly. At stake is a new political grouping originating mostly in the banks and other loan-granting and credit institutions "that use or misuse the state in order to push forward the privatization of social income." Bakarić also warns that this new political force is well connected with the positions of power in the Party—he even explicitly complains about himself belonging to a minority within the Party that tries to resist this development—and starts to align himself with the nationalist political opposition in order to take over the state.

Hence, there is one fundamental antagonism that, already in the 1970s, dictates the political life in former Yugoslavia, that between the ideal of a social(ist) welfare state, defended by the "dogmatic" faction in the Party, and the capital concentrated in the financial institutions that strives for overall privatization and in order to seize political power, makes a pact with conservative—in this particular case, nationalist and even fascist—ideology and political movements.

Here one should remember just how completely blind Western politicians and media showed themselves to be during the 1990s, when they personified the main cause of the bloody dissolution of Yugoslavia and the greatest obstacle to achieving peace and democracy in the Balkans in Slobodan Milošević, "that dogmatic communist apparatchik". Certainly he was guilty, on both counts, not as a communist apparatchik but rather as a bank director (having also worked in New York) and economic liberal who seized power precisely by aligning himself with the Serbian nationalist movement.

It is in this context that we must rethink the very meaning of the so-called totalitarian repression against art and culture in communist Yugoslavia, especially the wave of the late 1960s and early 1970s, that targeted, among others, the left-wing student movement of 1968, the films and authors of the so-called Black Wave of Yugoslav cinema, the Marxist and humanist intelligentsia, like philosophers such as the Praxis group and more. However, it is highly significant that this unfolded at the precise moment the warm current of the old revolutionary elite was being replaced by the cold current of the new technocratic apparatchiks, who personified the growing dominance of the market, a return to bourgeois consumerism, and the rise of free-flowing capital together with the banks and other powerful institutions.

Finally there is a well-known image that, in a way, well serves to symbolize the historical failure of communism—a

photograph, essentially black and white, of people desperately
queuing for basic goods. If this photograph had really been
taken in the former Yugoslavia it would have depicted the reality of the 1980s; more precisely, the social consequences of the
so-called austerity measures implemented by the IMF and other
international financial institutions. After having entered the
international market, the Yugoslav economy was also exposed
to both new crises and complex power relations. In the 1970s
these took the form of the energy/oil crises with oil prices
increasing fourfold in 1973–1974, the global recession of 1974–
1975, the crisis of classical Fordism, the implementation of
neoliberal economic policies and their intimate association with
conservative and right-wing politics. By 1980 Yugoslav foreign
debt had mushroomed from $2 billion in 1970 to $20 billion.
From the early 1980s on, communist Yugoslavia was completely dependent on global capitalism and the political will of
its most powerful players. While the Party was enforcing shock
therapy on society at home, as was prescribed by the centers of
global financial and political power, the social(ist) welfare state
was gradually collapsing. The country's standard of living fell
by 40% during the 1980s. Not surprisingly, the full integration
of the former communist Yugoslavia into the global capitalist
scheme, implying of course a fire sale of its entire economy,
was finally accomplished by its violent disintegration in the
wars of the 1990s. The rest is tragedy.

I'm afraid it doesn't make any sense

What does this last act of Yugoslav history bring to mind—a
communist past that has disappeared from our historical horizon with the so-called democratic revolutions of 1989/90? Or
the incalculable social and political consequences of the current
crisis of capitalism; concretely, of Greek society for instance,
that was recently brought to the brink of total collapse by the
debt crisis and the imposed austerity measures? Finally, of what
are we talking here, of communism or of capitalism, of the past
or of the present?

What appears in this story as unresolvable confusion that
resists any clear historical and ideological determination of
the communist past, preventing even a simple differentiation
between this past and our present, or retroactively between two

antagonistic systems that shaped the global politics—of communism and capitalism—of the 20th century, is only the effect of a genuine historical contingency of Yugoslav communism, a contingency that was once induced by a radical revolutionary intervention into the given state of affairs and established power relations. At stake is the Yugoslav socialist revolution 1941–45, the only successful revolution of its kind in Europe after 1917. It liberated an enormous amount of emancipatory energy that subsequently forged entirely unexpected and "impossible" dimensions and developments, like Tito's split with Stalin in 1948, the introduction of market economy and worker self-management, the taking of a leading role in the non-aligned movement, etc. That same energy also fostered cultural production that flourished under the communist rule. It enjoyed freedom, not as a space spared of state intervention but rather as a stake in a struggle. However, the signifier of totalitarianism makes it impossible to entertain an idea of freedom that goes far beyond the meaning of a socio-political or historical condition in which art and culture were produced—a freedom that was seized by art and culture in order to create this very socio-political and historical condition; in short, a freedom that did not serve to provide a context for art and cultural production, but rather was its very text. What made this freedom possible? What made this possible was clearly the revolution. In his seminal work on partisan art, Miklavž Komelj[7] argues that the partisan "contemporary art" was able to co-create its time, and not, on the contrary, simply adapt to it. What this art at that time actually did was rather to challenge its own impossibility and in that way, symbolically articulate the turn of impossibility into possibility. This is precisely what we call revolution.

To end with a question: does it make any sense for a contemporary knowledge on art to rummage through the dustbin of history in search of some recyclable artistic R-waste ("R" is for revolution)? From a position that historically legitimizes itself precisely in its having thrown its own revolutionary experience into this same dustbin; and is now able to enthusiastically embrace the idea of revolution only if it is being actualized somewhere else—in another remote and belated culture—or one forensically recovered from the scrap heap it calls the cultural heritage of the East?

7 *Kako misliti partizansko umetnost (How To Think Partisan Art)*, Založba cf./*, Ljubljana 2010.

PART I. The King's Conscience

1. What is [the] "mousetrap"?

The play-within-a-play (a play inserted within the action of another play) has long been known as an effective narrative technique. In William Shakespeare's *Hamlet*, one of western culture's greatest literary masterpieces, this technique was used to show how the haunted hero utilized the medium of theatre to expose the guilty conscience of the King and the corruption of his court. Hamlet cunningly referred to his early modern "interventionist" device as a *mousetrap*, and described his creation as a "thing" in which he planned to "catch the conscience of the King". As an early modern rendition of the "Trojan Horse," the *mousetrap* became a metaphor of tactical surprise in art, relationships and war. Always crafted with the purpose of destabilizing the sensing being's perception of the surrounding reality, the *mousetrap* fulfills its function by producing an uncanny effect of discomfort and uncertainty in those who get jammed in its machinery.

2. The father's command

The *mousetrap* is the invention of a modern hero *par excellence*. Due to his theatrical behavior, his ambiguous speech, his puns and his tricks (his "antic disposition") Hamlet became a prototype of the modern artist. His urgency to catch and display the King's conscience (instead of just carrying out an act of revenge) is driven by the urge to know whether the conscience of the one who governs is worthy or guilty, and if the power to which he is asked to submit is legitimate or usurped.

Freud recognized Hamlet as a successor to Oedipus Rex. In The Interpretation of Dreams, Freud noted that despite the shared traits linking Oedipus and Hamlet (the "Oedipus complex") there are also enormous differences in the psychic lives of these two characters, grounded in the distance between the epochs in which their authors lived. Jacques Lacan further developed this observation by analyzing the difference in the contexts surrounding patricide. The murder of the father in Hamlet, unlike in Oedipus, was committed secretly; after being heinously planned, it was only indirectly (unconsciously) connected to the hero through a web of complex family relations.[1] In other words, Shakespeare's hero was involuntary mobilized into a wicked drama of power, sex and murder for which he was not directly responsible; he learned about it from his father's spectral authority, which summoned him for revenge. Revenge would, however, require committing another murder, not motivated by his own free will or passion, but by the necessity to follow the imperious father's command.

3. Lights! Lights!

The *mousetrap* was constructed as an artistic (compensatory) solution produced out of the necessity to resist conflicting commands: a father's spectral authority on the one hand and the authority of the living legitimate King on the other. The "double bind" which blocks Hamlet's action is, as Bill Readings observed in *"Hamlet's Thing,"* further thematized by the medium of theatre itself, that is to say, by utilizing the quintessential gap between the lure of visual representation and the grip of the voiced (father's) command.[2] The *mousetrap* achieves its goal precisely by staging the previously voiced narrative of the dead king's absent authority as a "dumb show" and, as a consequence, triggering an involuntary expression of the living King whose conscience is nagged by guilt. When he is confronted with the public display of his hidden deed, the King interrupts the show, demanding "Lights!" Although he never overtly confesses, his behavior clearly displays and confirms his crime to those who already doubt his integrity and suspect what his conscience (most probably) hides.

4. The net for the birds

During the modern era, *Hamlet* became a formative artwork in shaping the dialectical consciousness necessary for the building of national state cultures and for the impending revolutionary culture. Shakespeare sensed the phenomenon before it was named (concepts such as individualism and revolution were not common currency when the play was written), pre-articulating

[1] According to psychoanalytical interpretations (most notably Ernest Jones's in his seminal book *Hamlet and Oedipus*, 1976), Claudius realized Hamlet's unconscious desire to kill his father, usurping his mother and the throne.

[2] Bill Readings, "Hamlet's Thing," Mark Thornton Burnett, John Manning (ed.), *New Essays on Hamlet*, AMS Press, London/New York 1994.

the perceptive apparatus which would be further characterized
and conceptualized in the discourse of later epochs. As Lacan
emphasized in his study of Hamlet, what was recorded on the
page by Shakespeare some centuries ago is nothing other than
structured language, words on a white page, words organized as a net encoding the social constellations, players and
symptoms from which the political and psychological *modus
operandi* of the modern world would later emerge. Lacan called
Hamlet a "net for the birds." He characterized it as a tragedy of
desire, which is structured as an empty frame for the emplacement of anyone's desire to go with it. And exactly, he said,
because "this frame, this apparatus, this net, net for birds is so
well structured, everybody can recognize him or herself in it".[3]
The success of Shakespeare's *Hamlet* is inseparable from the
success of its hero's construction of the *mousetrap*, where theory (words & thoughts) is demonstrated in practice (images &
actions). By using the meta-theatrical technique of "induction",
Shakespeare showed that his own plays are not just "words"
but also "things"-miniature counter-apparatuses reflecting the
larger social and political apparatuses. In the case of Hamlet,
the King's guilty conscience proliferated into modern state
apparatuses-reaching and inhabiting every individual social
subject regardless of his or her relation and involvement in the
incriminating governmental affairs.

3 Jacques Lacan, *Hamlet*.
Transl. Marjan Šimenc,
Jelica-Šumic Riha, Stojan
Pelko, Slavoj Žizek, Mladen
Dolar, Miran Božovic,
Analecta, Ljubljana 1988
(my translation from
Slovenian).

5. Breaking the art/life divide

Bill Readings noted that, structured as a "dumb show," the
mousetrap anticipates contemporary performance, which uti-
lizes the specificity of the medium of theatre and its irreduc-
ibility to a purely aesthetic form.[4] Performance is an art that is
simultaneously "artificial" but also "authentic" and "real"; it is
at once "art" and "life". This double character of the performative phenomenon has the power to create, but also to undo the
experiences of the "real" by affecting the experiencing subject's
ways of seeing, perceiving and deciding what is real and true
for them. Thus the desire to understand the mechanisms of
vision and perception of the human agent became as characteristic for art as for science, politics and war. Long before any
such art/science/war division existed, the Trojan Horse was
created as an ingenious enterprise of science, technology, arts

4 Bill Readings, "Hamlet's
Thing."

and crafts inspired by the necessities of war. The early modern obsession with meta-positioning as a way of simulating and taking over a (dethroned) "God's" view was as characteristic for Jeremy Bentham's *panopticon* as it was for Shakespeare's *mousetrap*, and attained its full realization through successive generations of modern technologies. From *camera obscura*, photography, film, video, and television to computer modeling and satellite imaging technologies, the entire world has gradually become enmeshed in an endless *mise en abyme*; in a condition of mirror within mirror, image within and image, story within story and play within play. Interactive optical traps discovered and utilized through the unfolding of modernity not only play upon our desire to see ourselves seeing but also "expose us to observe from a point of view within as well as from without with which we can never really merge".[5]

[5] Barbara Freedman, *Staging the Gaze: Postmodernism, Psychoanalysis, and Shakespearean Comedy*, Cornell University Press, Ithaca 1991.

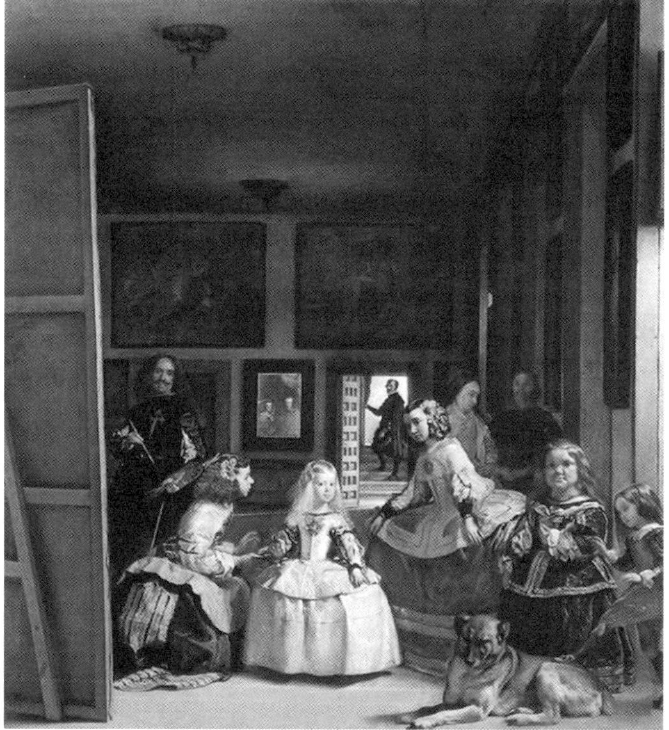

Famous example of mise en abyme from the history of painting: Diego Velázquez, *Las Meninas*, 1656

During the modern era, the potential of vision expanded far beyond the naked retina's imaging capacities, but in doing so the inherent incapacity of vision to provide any view beyond itself was exposed. According to Bill Readings, *Hamlet* is about a certain "failure of representation, an inability to show the enigmatic "thing" that compels action or grounds representation". (The other name of this "thing" is "Ghost", but it may also be called *language or unconscious*.) [6]

PART II. Hamlet-Machine

1. I was Hamlet (family album)

Heiner Müller's lifelong obsession with Shakespeare's *Hamlet* began when he first read the play at the age of thirteen. Indeed, as Lacan argued, this play functions as a "net for the birds," a trap that reveals more about the reader and his or her time than about the play's protagonist, who is considered un-interpretable.[7] Over the course of modernity, many "geniuses" that desired to be "free like a bird" and to live in a perfectly organized world recognized their own predicaments in Hamlet's. As much as it was a story about a character in a play written by Shakespeare, it was a story about them.[8] By mapping the enigmatic "thing" without ever being able to fully grasp it in a form of enunciation, *Hamlet* become a repository of modern subjectivity—a subjectivity that had been shaped through the struggle to reconcile the conflict between authority, desire and the share of guilt for deeds belonging to the darkest sides of modernity.[9]

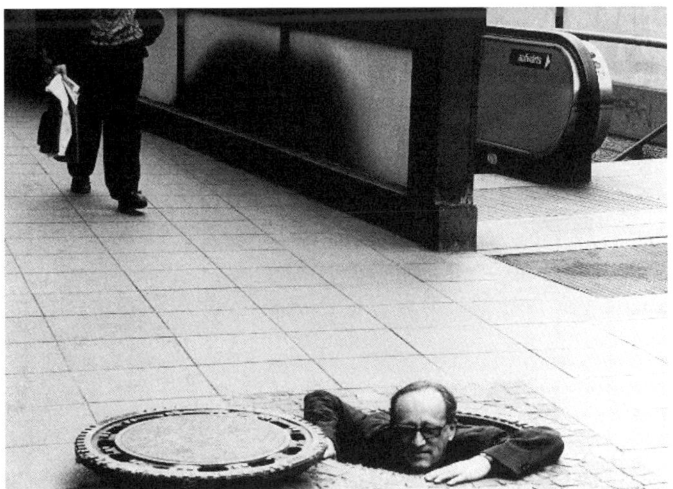

Heiner Müller, 1982, photo by Joseph Gallus Rittenberg

[6] Bill Readings, "Hamlet's Thing."

[7] Müller's most frequently quoted statement about Hamlet is that he is "much more a German character than English [...] the intellectual in conflict with history". Heiner Müller, *Hamlet-Machine*. Transl. & ed. by Carl Weber, John Hopkins University Press & PAJ Books, Baltimore & New York 1984.

[8] To name just a few: Henry Mackenzie (1780), J. W. von Goethe (1795), S. T. Coleridge (1808),

[9] In his lecture "Shakespeare a Difference" Müller articulated an idea similar to Lacan's metaphor of the "net for birds," asserting that the invasion of the times into the play constitutes a myth which is an "aggregate, a machine to which always new and different machines can be connected". Heiner Müller, Carl Weber, *A Heiner Müller Reader*, John Hopkins University Press & PAJ Books, Baltimore & London 2001.

Müller wrote the first words of what would became *Hamletmachine* in 1956—a critical year in European history. (In February 1956 Khrushchev revealed the full scope of Stalin's reign of terror. Berthold Brecht, who most elaborately employed the *mousetrap stratagem* in his dramaturgy, died on August 14th, 1956. Three days later, the Communist Party of Germany was banned in the Federal Republic of Germany. In October, efforts to reform the Communist system in Hungary escalated into a revolution that was crushed by Soviet forces after a weeklong civil war.) He spent more than twenty years working on this text of just a few pages, which, along with his other "plays," represents the ending point of drama and theatre, as we knew it (but also the beginning of something else).[10] In his writings, Müller frequently evoked tropes of "the end". In the poem *Theaterdeath* (1994), he portrayed theatre as a "dying man who now resembles none but himself."[11] Elsewhere, Müller announced that he was looking for a new approach to writing because "the historical substance has been used up for me from the vantage point I tried to employ while writing about it […] The author can't ignore himself anymore. […] If I don't talk about myself I reach no one anymore".[12]

The first scene of *Hamletmachine,* called "Family Album," begins with the actor (acting Hamlet) saying: "I was Hamlet. I stood at the shore and talked with the surf BLABLA, the ruins of Europe in back of me."[13] As the play unfolds, two photographs are torn apart. In the second scene ("Europe of Women") Ophelia announces: "With my bleeding hands I tear the photo of the men I loved and who used me on the bed on the table on the chair on the ground." In the final scene ("Pest in Buda/Battle for Greenland") the script calls for The Actor Playing Hamlet to deliver the final monologue while "Tearing the author's photograph". After that the actor ends the ritual by saying:

"I force open my sealed flesh. I want to dwell in my veins, in the marrow of my bones, in the maze of my skull. I retreat into my entrails. Take my seat in my shit, in my blood. Somewhere bodies are torn apart so I can dwell in my shit. Somewhere bodies are opened so I can be alone with my blood. My thoughts are lesions in my brain. My brain is a scar. I want to be a machine. Arms for grabbing legs to walk on, no pain no thoughts."

10 Müller's and Beckett's "end-plays" represent two different sides of the Janus face: one facing the frontiers of modernism, the other dissolving in an open-ended post-modernist virtuality. The most significant difference between Beckett's and Müller's "ends" of drama and theatre is their different treatment of the relation between literature and theatre. Beckett insisted on staging his text strictly according to his instructions (didaskalia). He authorized his agents to prosecute directors and theatres that disobeyed his rules. Müller's plays, on the other hand, are not structured as dialogical anymore, but as endless monologues (repositories of quotes) scripting the idea; an algorithm to stimulate the performance to happen (differently with each new translation of words into actions and images).

11 *A Heiner Müller Reader.*

12 Ibid.

13 Heiner Müller. *Hamletmachine and other texts for stage.* Ed. Carl Weber, PAJ Books, New York 1984.

2. My father (In memoriam)

We are all born into a continuing play called history, and it falls
upon each of us to learn what happened in the previous scenes
so that we can take up the roles and to be able to act in the coming ones.

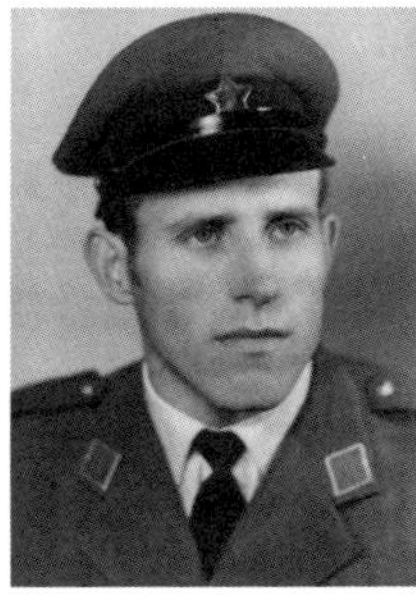

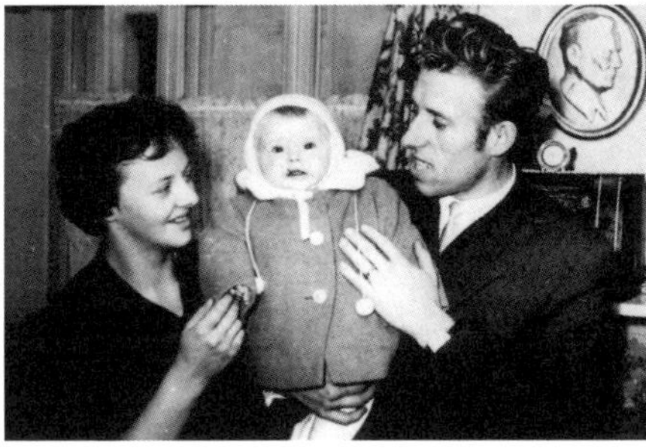

Silvester Čufer as a
police officer, 1960
(from family album)

Čufer family in 1961
(from family album)

My father, Silvester Čufer, was born in a small Belgian
industrial mining town, to which his Slovenian parents had
migrated for work. In 1940, after Hitler attacked Belgium, the
family was repatriated to the land that is today Slovenia—a
territory that was then under Italian occupation. During the
war, the family first lived in an abandoned hotel, but in 1943,
when the German army destroyed the hotel, my grandparents
and their three children became refugees, moving from place
to place, from one barn to the next. After the war ended, my
father finished primary school and got a job in an iron factory
in the heavy industry town of Jesenice. A decade or so later,
in 1958, he was given the opportunity to enroll in secondary
school. Immediately following graduation, he was invited to
join the police force of the Republic of Slovenia, part of the
new post-WWII state of the Socialist Federalist Republic of
Yugoslavia. The choice to become a policeman turned out to be
a very good one for my father. He believed strongly in socialism and the superiority of the new socialist state as opposed to
the former organizational traditions and structures dominated
by the church and wealthier classes. The new socialist state of
Yugoslavia *de facto* blossomed into a successful project during the 1960s and 1970s, offering its citizens opportunities and
prosperity that were unimaginable before.

By 1965 my father had a wife, a daughter, a car, and a TV.
One of my first concrete memories as a child is the sensation

of excitement when the first TV screen lit up our household.
I remember my father carrying the box into our house after
work one day, explaining to my mother and me that he bought it
after seeing the first televised images of the Moon through the
window of the small local appliance store. So this was March
24, 1965, when *Ranger 9* impacted the Moon at the *Alphonsus
Crater* and transmitted the first pictures of the Moon shown on
live TV in the minutes just before its (planned) crash landing.

The socialist reality passionately fought for and won by our
fathers was very good to them; it later felt like a cage to my (the
second but also the last) socialist generation.

3. I caught myself captured (Laibach-Machine)

Laibach concert, Križanke, 1982: Laibach's frontman, im-
personating a creature resembling the fascist leader Benito
Mussolini, is reading our (Slovene) constitution. He speaks
about our—the people's—rights, but he does so as if those
rights were our sins, our unforgivable guilt, and not the rights
that would support and empower us.

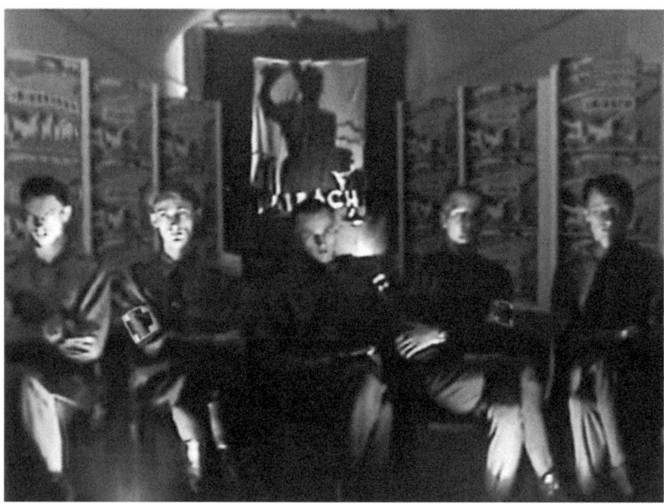

Laibach-Pengov interview
in Tednik, TVS, 1983 (photo
of the screen)

As I stood in the crowd, watching the concert, I experienced
a sense of acute anxiety. The conflict between the message (the
freedoms granted in the words of the constitution) and its enactment (in that authoritative voice and militaristic demeanor)
opened a gap, a split, between what I was hearing and seeing

and what I was understanding. The text that granted me rights was suddenly materialized in a voice that commanded my social behavior.

The concert in Križanke in the fall of 1982 was, however, only a prelude to another more memorable event. Less than a year later I watched the evening news and saw a stunning image on the screen. Uniformed Laibach members were sitting in a stage-designed environment, ready to give an interview to the then popular TV host Jurij Pengov. Watching that scene unfold, I had a sudden insight into the mechanisms captured in Shakespeare's *mousetrap* (which had been the subject of the theatre academy classes I was attending at the time). What shocked me most was the extent to which the event I was watching had been staged—its bold theatricality. Only later did I learn that Laibach had accepted the invitation to give an interview for Slovenian National TV subject to certain conditions: that the interview be filmed in the exhibition space (within Laibach's own installation in ŠKUC gallery, Ljubljana); and that Laibach members would receive the questions from the journalist in advance. In setting these conditions, Laibach refused any kind of spontaneity or interactivity that would have been "normal" for TV interviews. What we eventually saw on TV that evening in 1983 was Laibach's lead-voice sitting among his pals, reading the pre-written answers to the questions like a programmed robot, while the other members of *Laibach* posed in silence as if frozen in an old looped photograph.

In its postmodern rendition, Laibach inserted its little "disturbing scene"—not within the action of another play but within the protocol that would define the postmodern tele-communicative era. When the journalist asked them: "Can you tell us anything about yourselves? For instance, who are you, what are your professional occupations, how old you are? Are you all here or are there more of you?" the reply was offered in verse:

We are the children of the spirit and the brothers of strength,
Whose promises are unfulfilled.
We are the black phantoms of this world,
We sing the mad image of woe.
We are the first TV generation.

Laibach's urge to challenge the power of the TV medium underlined the entire interview. When the host provocatively asked:
"So far you have been spreading your ideology, your ideological provocation in writing. Was your decision to acquaint some
600,000 to 700,000 members of the public with your ideology
by appearing on TV in any way difficult?," Laibach answered
as if declaiming from a Marxist manual:

"Apart from the educational system, television has the leading role in the formation of uniform opinions. The medium
is centralized, with one "transmitter" and a number of "re-
ceivers," while communication between these is impossible.
Being aware of the manipulative capacities the media possess,
Laibach is exploiting the repressive power of media information. In the present case, it is the TV screen."

The operation was conducted with great precision, leading
to the "mousetrappian" tactical reversal of the places of viewing. Just as the King in *Hamlet*, after seeing his own doings
suddenly commands everyone's attention by screaming for
the lights, so did we—the home TV viewers of the Laibach
interview—by being mousetrapped in between the internal
image of our present behavior (sitting still and watching TV)
and the reflection of that behavior disturbingly repeated on
the screen—produce a scream that reverberated for years after
the event (which took the form of theatre-without-theatre and
Hamlet-without-*Hamlet*[14]).

4. I want to be a machine. (Theatre-Without-Theatre)

Writing on the decline of literature in the 1960s and 1970s,
Heiner Müller argued that writers could no longer come to grips
with the macro-structures (of society); therefore from now on
"the problem is the micro-structure". His comments found an
epochal equivalent in the theory and practice of the Situationists
and their most reverberated charge—that contemporary society
was becoming a "society of the spectacle" where "life is presented as an immense accumulation of *spectacles* ..." and "everything that was directly lived has receded into a representation".[15]
Or in Andy Warhol's *Factory*, which inspired the final words
of *Hamletmachine*: "I want to be a machine".[16] Müller understood that within spectacularized post-industrial society, theatre
(separated in its own social, spatial and temporal frames) lost its

[14] Referring to titles of
two separate productions:
"Theatre Without Theatre,"
MACBA (exhibition),
Barcelona, 2007; *Hamlet
Without Hamlet*, book by
Magareta de Grazia, 2007).

[15] http://www.bopsecrets.
org/SI/debord/1.htm

[16] "I want to be a machine"
is a statement by Andy
Warhol ("The reason
I'm painting this way is
because I want to be a
machine. Whatever I do,
and do machine-like, is
because it is what I want
to do.") According to
Müller's own reading, the
title of the play refers to
Warhol's mechanized art
factory and to Duchamp's
"Bachelor-Machine," giving
HamletMachine the initials
H.M. = Heiner Müller.

power to produce meaning (and consequently access to hearts and minds of audiences). Yet most of Müller's plays were and still are staged in the standard theatre boxes proudly maintained by numerous theatre institutions across Europe.

In their TV interview, Laibach on the other hand inserted their theatre into the vortex of the larger social spectacle, within the protocols of one of the most powerful modern and contemporary codifiers of reality—the TV network. In doing so, Laibach's performance enacted the final words of Muller's *Hamletmachine*: "I want to be a machine," but it delivered the message as an image, distributed from within the ongoing, real-time play enacted by TV transmission. As such, Laibach's intervention not only reflected an image of an automated bureaucratic, depersonalized, emptied society, but also gave us— the viewers—a little lesson about how this kind of society is created, and by whom.

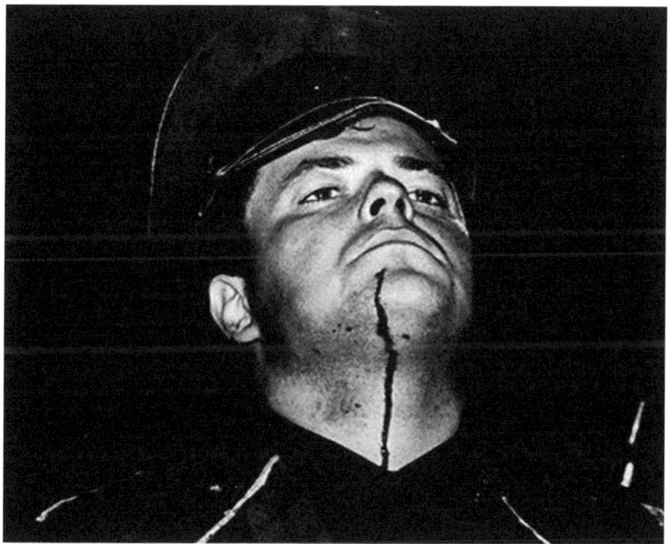

Jane Štravs, *Tomaž Hostnik*, 1984, Courtesy of Moderna galerija, Ljubljana

Television, which brought the simulacrum of theatre into people's living rooms, became a "game changer" during the Cold War. The Space Race between the USA and USSR that brought the first TV set into my family's living room had already become quite irrelevant by the 1970s, by which time it was already evident that not the rockets but television would be the victorious vehicle of the future imperialist wars. A little over a decade later, Laibach's TV appearance succeeded

in becoming a performance that produced a scandal the goal
of every good "mouse-trapper". Many people were screaming "Lights!, Lights!" that evening—and they screamed for
very different reasons. There were many fellow Slovenians
and Yugoslavians watching Laibach that evening that, like my
father, grew up during WWII, and sincerely liked the world
they had created out of resistance to Mussolini, Hitler and other
dreadful imaginaries that *Laibach* bluntly brought back onto
the central stage.

5. Over-identification (Žižek saw it in a word)

Slavoj Žižek was a genuine spectator of early Laibach. A
skilled "trapper" himself, he managed to catch in a concept
exactly those levels of the Laibach phenomenon that were commonly experienced at Laibach events, although few people
knew how to articulate, let alone theorize, the uncanny and
discomforting collision of feelings that put most Laibach spectators in a virtual state of trance during their performances.

Laibach unraveled, according to Žižek, the fact that ideology, any ideology, does not engage its subjects through the
power of argument so much as through unconscious automa-
tisms. An open revolt used by political dissidents of the early
Cold War period—or the era when it was still meaningful to
"deconstruct the subject" on the stage—became, as Müller
also announced, utterly ineffective by the late 20th century.
Therefore Laibach's dramaturgy (which was part of the *punk*
strategy of audience-address, explained Žižek) did not target
the consciousness of the spectator directly but rather played on
the automated realms operating beneath the layers of daily consciousness. In "Ideology, Cynicism, Punk", published shortly
after the TV event, Žižek introduced his first reflections on the
public reception and functioning of early Laibach.[17] He was
intrigued by the fact that Laibach performances represented a
peculiar challenge to the so-called enlightened, critical parts
of its audience, as opposed to the audience who either flatly
rejected or immediately identified with its manifest contents
composed of an "inconsistent mixture" of visual and verbal
residues of the darkest sides of European history (fascism,
Nazism, Stalinism, historic avant-garde art, social realism, Blut
& Boden, Nazikunst etc.). In analyzing the public reception to

17 Slavoj Žižek,
"Ideologija, cinizem, punk,"
*Filozofija skozi psihoana-
lizo*, Analecta, Ljubljana
1984.

the Laibach TV interview, Žižek referred to Peter Sloterdijk's *Critique of Cynical Reason*, where Sloterdijk equates cynical reasoning with post-modern critical consciousness. The contemporary cynical subject is fully aware of the falsehood of the ideological script according to which he or she performs but nevertheless keeps acting in it. The place of naïve ignorance of what Marx called "false consciousness" is taken over by a directly schizophrenic, pathological split, according to Žižek: "a perversely complex structure of contemporary reflecting consciousness" which is in many ways much more miserable and pitiful than the naïve, passionate "false consciousness" of those who truly "don't know" and naively identify with it.

Between 1988 and 1994 (the years of Yugoslavia's disintegration and war), Žižek summarized his reflections on early Laibach in two subsequent texts, "The Enlightenment in Laibach" and "Why are Laibach and NSK not Fascist?" Here he first explicitly discusses Laibach's effect on late-socialist audiences as a form of *over-identification*.[18] "The ultimate expedient of Laibach," he said, "is their deft manipulation of transference: their public (especially intellectuals) is obsessed with the "desire of the Other"—what is Laibach's actual position, are they truly totalitarians or not? – i.e., they address Laibach with a question and expect from them an answer, failing to notice that Laibach itself does not function as an answer but a question." [19]

Yes, Laibach functions as a question and as a command that demands us to "name it"! And in responding to it, one has a choice to name "what it is" (the desire of the Other), or "how it works" (the mechanic of the socio-machine).

Leftist critics, Žižek noticed, tend to read Laibach as the ironic imitation of totalitarian rituals; however, their support of Laibach was always accompanied by an uneasy feeling: "What if they really mean it? What if they truly identify with the totalitarian ritual?" Or: "What if Laibach overestimates their public? What if the public takes seriously what Laibach mockingly imitates, so that Laibach actually strengthens what it purports to undermine?"[20]

These questions, he argued, are backed up by the assumption that ironic distance is automatically a subversive attitude. But what if the contemporary "post-ideological" universe feeds exactly upon cynical distance toward any public values at all? Müller already noticed that the macro-structures of society

[18] "Die Aufklärung in Laibach". First published in the Croatian magazine *Quorum* 4, No.1, 1988 and translated into English and published as "The Enlightenment in Laibach" in 1994 in the British magazine *Art and Design* 9, No. 3-4; "Why are Laibach and NSK not Fascist?," *M'ARS* 3-4, Moderna Galerija, Ljubljana 1993.

[19] From "Why are Laibach and NSK not Fascist?".

[20] Ibid.

had become dead channels through which artists can no longer address audiences. So what if this internal distance practiced by enlightened audiences, Žižek asks, "far from posing any threat to the system, designates the supreme form of conformism, since the normal function of the system requires cynical distance?"[21]

Within Žižek's equation, the Laibach-Machine reaches the hearts and hopefully the minds of its beholders (the society's micro-structures) by knowing precisely what behavior will be most frustrating to them. Laibach exposed the fact that ideology, any ideology, does not engage its subjects through the power of argument so much as through the enactment of social "automatism". One way or another, each of us is a mere link in the chain of social reproduction. Contrary to common belief, the performative dimension of ideology is not just a set of rules implemented by a certain society or community, rules that we can ignore and go on living as if we were free individuals. The power of ideology is that it incorporates itself into every one of us and speaks through each of us in everything that we do, every day. The most basic material practices of everyday life are exactly the kind of practices, as Žižek would say, that make one Slovenian, American, Christian, Communist, Muslim, professor, student, artist, pilot and so on—the things that give us this or that kind of prescribed social role but that also cut us off from other parts of our potential selves that might otherwise be open to different ways of acting. Excessive identification (*over-identification*) with these externally inscribed social identities can as well produce the possibility of its opposite—"de-identification" (from automated identities)—giving one the chance to experience the volumes and voids of alienation and openness to the potential selves.[22]

6. Epilog (1989, 2001)

Significant structures and borders established within the unfolding of modernity (from the 16th century on), irreversibly collapsed by the end of the twentieth century. "Art and totalitarianism are not (any longer?) mutually exclusive," said *Laibach* in its 1980 manifesto. Likewise, the King's guilt and the hero's desire, politics and art, are now as inseparable and interchangeable as the auditorium and the stage. In the last thirty years, so

21 Ibid.

22 The mechanics of over-identification as explained by Žižek resemble explanations of de-alienating effects that art could perform on the audiences in modern industrial and post-industrial society, such as estrangement, de-familiarization (*ostranenie*), alienation effect (*Verfremdung*), schizo-analysis, etc.

much has been said about the inevitable deaths (of author, god, subject, literature, painting, theatre, history, society, politic, etc.) that the issue has almost become a cliché. Müller's or my father's generation (who experienced fascism, Nazism, and the sweet promise of socialism and communism followed by their collapse) contemplated "death" through different moral scales than my, "the first TV generation", to whom real and fictionalized death were, from the outset, presented through one and the same mode of (virtualized) experience.

The dematerialization of the object of art, which was institutionalized sometime during the Cold War era, coincided with the mass-media take-over of industrialized cultures at large, turning societies themselves into living objects that generate themselves according to one kind of social algorithm or another, until reaching their limit and miserably collapsing.

Müller is partially right when he qualifies Shakespeare's *Hamlet* as "an attempt to describe an experience that has no reality in the time of its description. An end game at the dawn of an unknown day." In contradiction to his deconstructive and dystopic thinking, he seems to also have believed in the existence of a world which Shakespeare's mirror would not be able to reflect anymore: "We haven't arrived at ourselves as long as Shakespeare is writing our plays."[23] Developments in art and politics after 1989 have revealed, however, that the world can perhaps survive without Hamlet (hero and author) and even without theatre (art). But there will always be the "mousetrap," as it is a meta-generative mechanism (effective in art as well as in politic/life), which can create and destroy peoples' realities *ad infinitum*.

The Cold War (and the crucial role of the mass media in supporting this new form of inverted psychic/moral warfare) turned social realities into a permanent swindle and deception in the service of "higher" (state, market, corporate etc.) interests. In 1967 Marcel Broodthaers opened his "Museum of Modern Art, The Department of Eagles" in his private home and introduced it with a truly Shakespearian theory of "deceptive art": "A museum that is a deception has something to hide. There is," he said "a Freudian aspect to the personal lie. But what the personal museum seeks to hide is only the real museum." [24]

This kind of *reductio ad absurdum* mode of argumentation (proof by contradiction) became a familiar feature of post-1989

[23] In "Shakespeare a Difference," *A Heiner Müller Reader.*

[24] Marcel Broodthaers, "Musée d'Art Moderne, Dépatement des Aigless," A. Alberro & B. Stimson (ed.), *Institutional Critique*, MIT Press, Cambridge/London 2009 (The text is taken form an interview with Broodthaers conducted by Johannes Cladders in 1972).

and post-2001 military and artistic strategies wherein completely new intensities of mimicry and deception were introduced—
not to mention new levels of blending the borders between the
territories and their inhabitants, between the imaginary and
real, between the authentic and fake, and between the capacity
for truth and the necessity of the lie.

The German composer Karlheinz Stockhausen was widely
criticized for his un-self-censored comments on the 9/11 terrorist attack on WTC in the context of an interview about the new
section of his opera *Licht* (*Light*, work in progress 1977–2003).
Asked if the figures in his opera represented real historic figures or just material appearances of abstract ideas, he answered
that there is no difference, as abstract ideas always inhabit real
historic people. To support his point he offered the example of
Lucifer (a cosmic spirit of rebellion, anarchy and destruction
who is incapable of love) who had just completed the "biggest
work of art there has ever been," that everybody could see in
the footage of the terrorist attacks on the WTC in New York
(which had happened a week prior to the interview). Apart from
the monstrosity of his statement it would be hypocritical to
deny that Stockhausen failed to censor himself in uttering what
was actually the very first thought that many people familiar
with the idioms of avant-garde art had when looking at TV
footage of the 9/11 attack for the first time.

9/11 was of course not the biggest artwork ever, but it was an
artful tactical military operation that employed aesthetic means
to create a unique 21st century mousetrap-like reversal of power
that exposed the King's guilty conscience and morally handi-
capped its reign. Its success was grounded first in the artistry of
locating the 21st century global court, and second, in presenting
the cause in the image of the enemy's own theatre of permanent
war, which generated a generation of subjects lethally susceptible to "experience its own destruction as an aesthetic pleasure
of the first order".[25]

Based on notes from a lecture delivered in 2010 at "The Cold War Avant-garde
Seminar" at Moderna galerija, Ljubljana, this text will appear as a chapter in
the author's forthcoming book, *Art as Mousetrap*, written with the support of a
grant from the Creative Capital/Andy Warhol Foundation.

[25] Walter Benjamin, "Art in the Age of Mechanical Reproduction," *Illuminations*. Ed. Hannah Arendt, Fontana Press, London 1973. In this semi-nal text, Walter Benjamin eighty years ago anticipat-ed the upcoming structural reversal of the roles of art and politics permitted by new technologies of repro-duction and moving images which would eventually lead to the formation of audiences conditioned to enjoy virtual experiences of destruction and demise.

Should Ilya Kabakov Be Awakened? Viktor Misiano

The present text was brought to life by a real event. More precisely, it was born from a desire to clear up the questions that the event spawned, and to overcome a misunderstanding that it left behind. We are here talking about a massive retrospective of Ilya Kabakov, which took place in Moscow in 2007, crowning his triumphant return to Russia after an absence of virtually twenty years. The exhibition venue was the newly created Garage Centre for Contemporary Culture, established by the Russian oligarch Roman Abramovich. It was in "Garage," in the giant space of the former Bahmetiev bus park— built in 1926 by the extraordinary constructivist architect Konstantin Melnikov and the no-less-extraordinary engineer Vladimir Shukhov—that the main retrospective project, the exhibition-installation of the "Alternative History of Art" unfolded. One autonomous component of this event was a reconstruction of the installation "Red Wagon" ["*Krasniy Vagon*"], created by Kabakov for an exhibit in the Kunsthalle Düsseldorf in 1991. Another its reconstruction, the installation "Toilet," ["*Tualet*"] created in 1992 for *documenta IX*, was sited on the territory of the so-called "WINZAVOD" gallery cluster. His installation, "From the Life of Flies" ["*Iz zhizni Mukh*"] was also exhibited there, various forms of which the artist has been developing since the 1980s. Finally, in the Pushkin State Museum of Fine Art, the most respected academic museum in Moscow, a new exhibition called "*Gates*" ["*Vorota*"], featured a series of objects and painted canvases created especially for the Moscow retrospective.

Kabakov's chosen genre of a monographic retrospective, i.e. of showing works created over an extended period of time (and in this case, in the twenty-year period of the artist's time outside Russia), was duplicated and thematically enhanced by the central work of this entire undertaking—an exhibition-installation, the "Alternative History of Art." In substance, this work was made similar in style to a chronological retrospective of the art of three, obviously fictional, artists of different generations, whose work was meticulously reconstructed and displayed in the "Garage" in twenty-three separate rooms he constructed inside the hangar. The first hero of the "alternative museum" is a certain Charles Rosenthal, an artist of the Russian avant-garde[1], whereas Kabakov's second character, Ilya Kabakov, was born in 1933, the same year that his namesake was born, and the same year Charles Rosenthal died. The creative period of the fictional Kabakov—an ardent follower of Rosenthal and his spiritual pupil, falls in the period spanning the 1970s–1980s, i.e. the time the real Kabakov was working in Russia. At the same time, the third hero of the "alternative history," a young man by the name of Igor Spivak, was active during the 1990s, i.e. when the real Kabakov was actively working in the West. What binds these three personae and what justifies their inclusion in a communal "alternative" artistic tradition is a combination of both avant-gardism and traditionalism in their work. Or, more precisely, in the calling card of modernist innovation— the combining of geometrically abstracted elements in the artists' painted pieces, and contrastingly, elements of figurative realism that have hitherto resisted extinction.

Moreover, one of the components of the event was not only Kabakov's display of artwork at the exhibit, but also his public performative behaviour, which provoked a profusion of questions and misunderstandings. Exaggerating the oligarchic expanse of his retrospective, and bringing the dramatization of the "return of a grand master" to its dramatic conclusion, Kabakov (on his own initiative), was received at the Kremlin by the acting president of the Russian Federation, Dmitry Medvedev. (The artist had left Russia after the opening of the exhibition, but returned to Moscow from Tokyo for one day, especially for this meeting). At the same time, Kabakov did not express any sympathy for the new Russia: he refused to communicate with the local press and the cultural bureaucracy, and in the single interview he granted in the lead-up to the exhibition opening, he labeled the Russian artistic milieu—i.e. those who would be expected to attend the exhibition the very next day, and in large numbers—"pink puss." Finally, Kabakov's most effective performative gesture in Moscow played out during the press conference for the exhibition: present at the podium, he refused to take the floor, and sat with his eyes closed for the entire two hours. For the openings (of which there were three, for each exhibition space, held on different days),

[1] In substance, this part of the "Alternative History of Art" is another one of Kabakov's already completed works included in the retrospective exhibit. In 2000–2001, under the name *"Zhizn' I tvorchestvo Charlia Rozentalia"* [The Life and Art of Charles Rosenthal (1898-1933)], this fictive exhibit was already shown as an independent work at the Staedelmuseum in Frankfurt/Main.

everyone who addressed Kabakov was greeted with an annoyed reply: "What do you want from me? Can't you see that a person is sleeping?!"

How is it possible to bring together these seemingly contradictory actions? On the one hand, the dramatization of a triumphant return to the city and to the country that he had consistently avoided for twenty years, and on the other, a demonstratively *a priori* disgust with what he supposedly encountered there? Is there consistency in Kabakov's chosen line of behavior if, on one hand, being present in Moscow, he dramatized his absence ("a dream"), and on the other, invited himself to a reception with the head of state? What did Kabakov want to say by selecting precisely these (art)works from his extensive legacy? And why did the "alternative history" at the center of the exhibit bring together two seemingly incompatible poles of 20th century art? And if the Moscow retrospective was a summation of his many years of creative work, as well as the experience of his entire generation—and, it seems, that it was precisely this that the artist invested into his grandiose retrospective—how can one understand and formulate the meaning of his message? And generally, what worlds did the "sleeping" Ilya Kabakov inhabit? And should he not, all the same, be awakened?

Kabakov belongs to a generation born out of the culmination of Stalin's modernization, which matured during its test of strength and final triumph—the period of war and victory. However, when the eruption into modernity was effected through public violence and disciplinary excess, it is common to call the result an archaic or conservative model of modernization.[2] Sociality born of this type of social development has the form of a depersonalized, convulsively aggressive collectivity, which Kabakov, along with his companions in Moscow conceptualism, called "the communal body."[3] The metaphor for this communal heterotopia is Kabakov's famous piece, the "Toilet," which he included in the Moscow retrospective. Because from Kabakov's point of view, alongside the (regime's) permanent and spontaneous aggression, the second psychological regime of a communal society was a state of permanent euphoria. That was precisely how the communal body reacted to the constant victories of modernization—the launch of new

2 About conservative modernization in the USSR see A. G. Vishnevsky, *Serp I rubl'. Konservativnaya modernizatsiya v SSSR* ["Sickle and Ruble. Conservative Modernization in the USSR"], Odintsovkiy State Institute, Moscow 1998.

3 In the *Slovar' Moskovskogo Konseptualizma* ["Dictionary of Moscow Conceptualism"] <http://www.conceptualism-moscow.org/files/Esanu_Dictionary_Web.pdf>, *Kommunalniye tela* [Communal Bodies] "refers to collective bodies in their early stage of urbanization, when their aggression is intensified under the influence of unfavorable environmental conditions".

factories or electric power plants, a good harvest, or triumphs in the spheres of science and technology.[4] The images of exalted celebration are Kabakov's dominant motif in many works of art, including the paintings and canvases in the museum of the "Alternative History of Art."

This counterpoint and the interpenetration of archaism and modernization was relevant to Soviet society later as well, at the outset of the creative careers of Kabakov's generation. Nikita Khrushchev, the new Soviet leader, proclaimed the goal of "catching up to and overtaking America," thus admitting that the USSR lagged in social and technological developments and excusing the (his) use of the term "catch-up modernization" in his modernizing program of the 1950s and 1960s.

The constant counterpoint between the traditionalism and modernity of Russian-Soviet reality did not just become one of the themes in Kabakov's art, but a structural principle of his artistic language. As mentioned above, the construction of images of his works in the "alternative museum" presenting the history of 20th century Russian art is composed precisely of elements of figurative imagery canonized by Soviet socialist realism, as well as motifs of modernist geometrical abstraction. Kabakov's "Alternative History of Art" is alternative precisely because its conservative vestiges were constantly reproduced, resulting in hybrid forms coupled with regenerative impulses; its progression void of linear self-development based on innovation—as the case may be with the normative history of Western modernism.

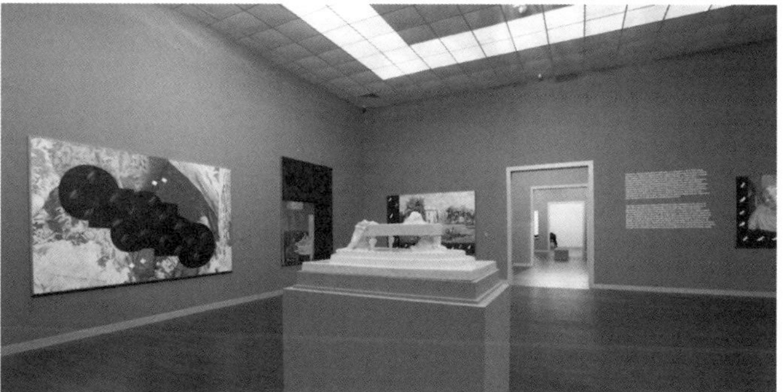

Ilya & Emilia Kabakov, The Alternative History Of Art, Ilya Kabakov, Moscow 2008, photo by Igoris Markovas

For Kabakov, the depersonalized, aggressive nature of the so-called communal body—the primary social product of a conservative or catch-up modernization—was undoubtedly a

[4] Mikhail Riklin, a philosopher with close ties to Moscow conceptualism, dedicated an entire investigation to Kabakov's descriptions of the spaces of euphoria in his works (or, as Riklin called them, "spaces of elation"): M. Riklin, *Prostranstva likovaniya* ["Spaces of Elation"], "Logos", Moscow 2002.

source of panic-stricken horror. His first experience of Soviet collectivity was a fine arts boarding school, and then a residency at the Surikov Institute. His only refuge during these years was to be found in the cultural infrastructure—museums, libraries, the music conservatory, etc. "During childhood," remembers Kabakov, "when I lived at the fine arts boarding school, the museum was the only place where I could save myself from life. It was an island on which one could save oneself from reality…"[5]. This is why upon returning to Russia—amidst relentless horror—Kabakov creates a museum in the Bahmetiev bus park, the penultimate monument to Soviet modernization, a museum capable of sheltering he and his art "from reality."

It is interesting, however, that although Kabakov shields himself from the excesses of modernization in an oasis of cultural infrastructure, it is easy to apprehend a dialectic of traditionalism and modernity fundamental to Soviet society within it. This giant, multifaceted infrastructure was nothing more than the creation of an enlighteningly motivated Soviet modernization; however, the ideology behind this infrastructure was extremely traditional, having a metaphysical, almost sacral understanding of culture and its institutions. Moreover, Kabakov and his understanding that the museum is found "outside of reality," share the same transcendental understanding of culture. For him, the museum is a place where the linear constitution of time ceases to exist, where the future is transformed into a metaphysical timelessness. Thus, "not everyone is admitted" as Kabakov insists, "into the future."[6]

A telling metaphor for this temporal transition from time into timelessness is Kabakov's theme of the gates, that the artist presents as the foundation for a series of works he created for the Moscow retrospective, and which he programmatically exhibited at the Pushkin Museum. The installation featured giant, wooden gates with open shutters installed at the center of the exhibition hall. These same gates were represented on the painted canvases that hung on the walls of the hall. The central motif of the gates was faintly recognizable against a generally murky background in these sluggish, monotonic images, which must have created the impression that they had created by an artist who has crossed the threshold of reality and immersed himself in nirvana-like transcendence. This time, what is especially important, is the fact that we are not dealing with a fictive

[5] See the interview with Irina Kulik in the periodical *Kommersant*, 27.08.2008.

[6] See the chapter *V budushee voz'mut ne vseh* ["Not everyone will be admitted into the future"] in a recently published book of Kabakov's conversations with the philosopher Mikhail Epshtein, *Katalog* [Catalogue], Gherman Titov's Library of Moscow Conceptualism, Moscow 2010, p. 442–444. See also Kabakov's text *V budushee voz'mut ne vseh* ["Not everyone will be admitted into the future"] in Ilya Kabakov, *Texti* ["Texts"], Gherman Titov's Library of Moscow Conceptualism, Moscow 2010, p. 550–568.

"alternative," but with a real academic museum where the spectator has to proceed through the entire space of the exposition, passing through halls rich with Rodin, the impressionists, the postimpressionists, Matisse, Picasso, Derain, and so on, in order to reach Kabakov's "*Gates*." What is at stake is a museum that enjoys the reputation of the most respectable museum institution in Moscow—and for Kabakov, exhibiting there has long been an *idée fixe* (he even created several compositions based on this idea). It seems that accomplishing this goal was rivaled only by the idea of being received by President Medvedev.[7]

Thus, the exhibition of the "*Gates*" in the Pushkin Museum could be understood as part of a performative dramatization of Kabakov's triumphant return to his native homeland—one which had previously exiled him and now accepts him as a "grand master," on the same level as a head of state. From here stems the performative element of "sleep" enacted at the opening of the retrospective: it is impossible to anticipate in reality, the presence of the one who returns from the "gates" of eternity, from the timeless future that "does not accept everyone."

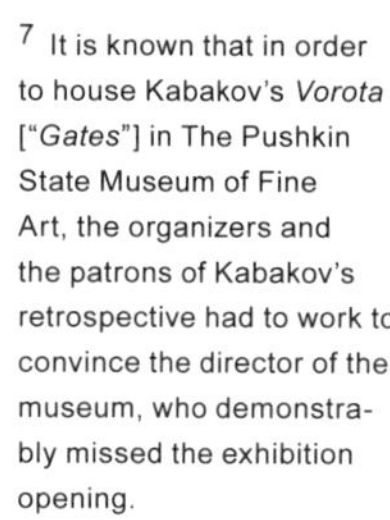

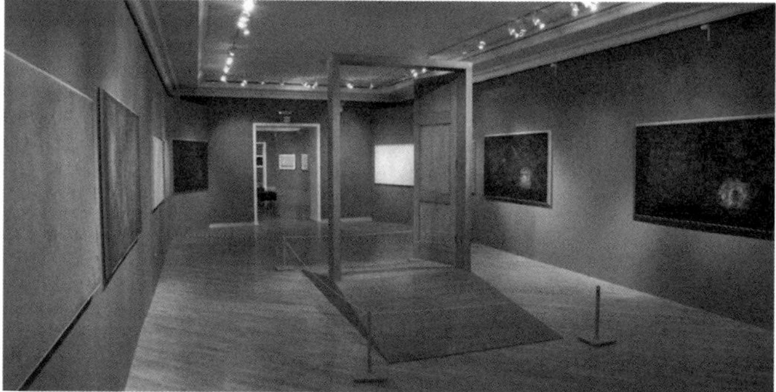

Ilya & Emilia Kabakov, The Gates, Moscow 2008, photo by Igoris Markovas

However, Kabakov's transcendental, and in substance, traditional understanding of culture is characteristic of many artists of his generation—and on the whole, for the majority of critically-oriented Soviet intellectuals, who in their criticism of conservative modernization resisted not only the conservative, but a modernizing beginning; and moreover, resisted it from a conservative position. Thus, for Kabakov, the sacral and the transcendental remained the generative creative substance, at least as a Russian artist: "I think that Russia is like cabbage: its outer layers are splitting, secularizing, but the dark, national, sacral nucleus remains."[8] Describing Kabakov's disposition,

7 It is known that in order to house Kabakov's *Vorota* ["*Gates*"] in The Pushkin State Museum of Fine Art, the organizers and the patrons of Kabakov's retrospective had to work to convince the director of the museum, who demonstrably missed the exhibition opening.

8 See Ilya Kabakov, Boris Groys, *Dialogi (1990–1994)* ["Dialogues 1990–1994"], Ad Marginem, Moscow 1999, p. 85–86.

like the disposition of others of his generation—Joseph
Brodsky or Andrei Tarkovsky—a contemporary historian of
literature and culture, Mark Lipovetsky offers: "the Soviet experience was perceived by many in the 1970s (and is perceived
that way still) as a distortion of some 'normal' path of Russian
culture, represented, for some, in the classics of the 19th century, and for others, as modernism of the 1910s and 20s, and
as a replacement of true 'transcendental signifieds' by their
simulacras. Based on this kind of perception, there is a tempta-
tion to return to 'non-distorted' trajectories, which became the
source of many illusions for non-official, as well as late Soviet
art. This is why the new, non-official and nonconformist art
born out of the 1970s had frequently combined the deconstruction of the Soviet myth with a particular kind of interest in the
transcendental."[9]

However, if the "normal path of Russian culture" is under discussion here, then Kabakov's idea of what exactly this was is
somewhat more complex. Obviously, he did not identify himself with the official Soviet aesthetic doctrine. For him, Soviet
artistic officialdom was the product of a "collective body," the
foundation of which—the dual permanent states of violence
and exultation—was a source of a similarly permanent terror.
Thus, his own artistic search as well as the search of those in
his creative circle gravitated towards a different aesthetic order
of things. As witnessed by Kabakov himself: "the dominant
thought of an artist from the 1960s was an assumption that
there is also a different history... The main conviction of 1960s
artists is that our life must be comparable, correlated to this
big history."[10] This other history is, in substance, the normative
history of Western modernism, inaccessible to a non-official
Russian artist in all its vast complexity. As a result, Kabakov
admitted to experiencing an acute sense of his shortcomings
and marginality, finally admitting to an inferiority complex
running through his entire life.[11] Kabakov's uncritical and
exalted, forgiving perception of the Western art system stems
from this as well, of which he gave a detailed account in a
speech at the Congress of the International Association of Art
Critics in Stockholm in 1994.[12] Moreover, despite the fact that
he had already lived in the West and was enthusiastically accepted there, he continued to suffer from this same inferiority

[9] See Mark Lipovetsky, *Paralogii. Transformatsii (post)modernistskogo diskursa v russkoy kulture 1920-2000h godov* ["Paralogs. Transformations of (Post)Modernist Discourse in Russian Culture 1920s–2000s"], *Novoe Literaturnoe Obozrenie* ["New Literary Review"], Moscow 2008, p. 289.

[10] See Ilya Kabakov, *60–70e... Zapiski o ne-ofitsalnoy zhizni v Moskve* ["1960s–1970s... Notes on Non-official Life in Moscow"] NLO, Moscow 2008, p. 28.

[11] About the inferiority complex, see Kabakov, Epshtein *Katalog* ["Catalogue"], p. 11–23.

[12] See *Povest' o 'Kulturno-peremeshennom litso'* ["A Story of a 'culturally-displaced individual'"] (talk given at a critics' convention), Kabakov, *Texti* ["Texts"], p. 550–568.

complex. It remained impossible for him to completely identify himself with that (Western) system, and despite enjoying a comfortable position, felt himself a stranger—or as he described himself, a "culturally displaced individual."

This paradoxical nature of Kabakov's views is exacerbated by what was fully apparent to him—genetically, such polar opposites as Western and Russian-Soviet art history have, nevertheless, common roots. Thus, Malevich, whom Kabakov ironically calls "the big boss," but whom he had also called a "commissar", accusing him of (active, implicit) involvement in Soviet modernization, is for the artist one of the undeniable founders of modernism. And that is because the totalitarian nature of official Soviet art stems from the totality of the Russian avant-garde. Boris Groys's concept of *"Gesamtkunswerk Stalin"*[13] was based precisely on this thesis. Groys, a like-minded friend of Kabakov's, formulated the idea that the development of art from the Russian avant-garde to Socialist Realism represented not a "distorted," but a causal trajectory. Moreover, what fascinates both Groys and Kabakov in the Soviet project is its unequivocally larger radicalism than that which evolved in Western modernism. And thus, the "horror" that Soviet reality provoked in Kabakov, provoked an increasingly larger trauma, that simultaneously proved, however, to be the main theme and stimulus to his art.

Thus, it is revealing that Kabakov's consciousness is built on several layers of contradictions. While well aware that he is the subject/product of Soviet modernization, he also sees this as a secondary influence compared to the primary influence of Western modernization; yet the Soviet variant too is simultaneously primary, since its inherent modernizing potential is actually enhanced, greater due to its archaic nature. Framed as such, the experience of a conservative modernization is fundamentally significant, but it must be represented in the West, since its context is referential. This referentiality of the West, not at all (immediately) apparent to critical Western consciousness, appears more evident to a "culturally displaced individual," perceiving the West from a distance—as the bearer of an external consciousness. Accepting the superiority of the object of perception, and subsequently, his own inferiority complex and imperfections in his "Promised Land," the "culturally displaced individual" has its/his own advantages. This is because a

13 See "Gesamtkunstwerk Stalin," Boris Groys, *Isskustvo Utopii* ["Art of Utopia"], Fond Pragmatika Kulturi ["The Pragmatic Culture Fund"], Moscow 2003. Boris Groys, *Gesamtkunstwerk Stalin*, Hanser Verlag, Munich/Vienna 1988.

distanced gaze sees the perceivable reality as a whole, whereas someone living through practical experience apprehends it only in parts. Two alternative models of modernization meet in the "Alternative History of Art," a model example of such a holistic gaze; and in their meeting are subject to elimination. Thus, the inferiority complex transforms into a mania of superiority— "metaphysics" as the reverse side of "horror."

One of the characteristic traits of Russian (although, similarly most any) catch-up modernization is the intermittent character of social development. The jolts of modernization are interspersed with long periods of stagnation (or, as it became common to say in Russia—stasis [from *zastoi*]), which are again replaced by periods of brief but accelerated development. In these short periods, long-lasting closure is replaced by openness as well as an omnivorous interest in anything that had long remained inaccessible. One such period in Russian-Soviet history emerged in the mid-1950s and was nicknamed Khrushchev's "Thaw."

In 1957, when Kabakov finished his studies at the Surikov Moscow State Academic Art Institute, the legendary International Festival of Youth and Students took place in Moscow, instantaneously revealing a broad view of the contemporary outside world to a closed Soviet society. The presentations of contemporary Western art shown in the context of the festival were supported by an entire succession of other events, shattering long immutable canons upheld for decades. Thus, contemporary art from the USA and France, a large monographic retrospective of Fernand Léger and Giorgio Morandi, as well as of the artist-primitivist Niko Pirosmanashvili (Niko Pirosmani), much liked by Russian avant-gardists, was shown at many different exhibition venues. During those years, canvases by the French impressionists and post-impressionists, as well as the early work of Matisse and Picasso began to return to the permanent exhibition of the Pushkin museum, also simultaneously at the Tretiakov gallery, and although both highly selective and condensed, the work of the Russian avant-garde, too, began to be shown again.

Thus, in the span of but a short period, a young Kabakov who had just finished his academic training, became acquainted with a previously unknown history of art—from impressionism and naïve art, to Pollock's "drippings" and Georges Mathieu's calligraphy. Almost a century of art (history) appeared within a very constrained time frame. As a result, Seurat's pointillism struck the young Kabakov as poignantly as did Rauschenberg's early pop art. This experience of living through the history of art not as diachronism, but as synchronism left a profound impression on the consciousness of Kabakov's generation. Everyone who lived through the period of the "Thaw" held the capacity to experience the past as present with great acuteness, and to see the roots of history in the present. This is how Kabakov's contemporary and colleague, artist and poet Dmitry Prigov wrote about it: "nothing that appeared in the social-cultural perspective withdrew into historical perspective, but persisted in its continued relevance. Thus, one could be shedding the same tears for example, for a recently deceased mother, or the premature death of poet A.S. Pushkin, who has died a century-and-a-half earlier. Precisely this constant displacement, flashing, flickering between these many, eternally relevant cultural-historical layers, gave rise to the specificity of Russian consciousness."[14] Thus, the first elements of postmodern consciousness[15] were formed in Kabakov's circle, almost simultaneously with their acquaintance with the modernist—or more precisely—Western modernist tradition. In other words, (their) enthusiasm for modernism coincided with the beginnings of its deconstruction.

Both of these historic models—the diachronic and the synchronic—are simultaneously present and parallel in Kabakov's Moscow retrospective. Thus, his "Toilet" represents an ahistorical temporality of a "collective body," whereas the "Red Wagon" represents the history of Soviet modernization in all its gradual historical development. This work, which took up a large part of the exhibit, is presented immediately at the entrance to the "Garage." However, Kabakov re-routed the entrance to the exhibit through the emergency exit. As a result, the spectator first arrived to the "Alternative History of Art" and then, walking through the halls and becoming acquainted with this new work, they would encounter the old work of the "Red Wagon." Moreover, the museum itself combined both synchronic and diachronic approaches: the showcase of three artists unfolded diachronically, whereas the history of innovation and tradition in their works saw consistent correspondence in synchronism. Thus, the alternativeness of Kabakov's

14 From the text *Tretie Perepisivanie Mira* ["The Third Rewriting of the World"], mashinopis' ["typescript"] (D. A. Prigov archive).

15 The term *proto-post-modernistkiy* ["proto-post-modernist"] was first used by Boris Groys in *Russkiy avangard po obe storoni 'Chernogo Kvadrata'* ["Russian Avant-Garde on Both Sides of the 'Black Square'"], Voprosi Filosofii ["Philosophical Questions"], Moscow 1990, p. 11. But it was likely coined during the home seminars of Moscow artists/nonconformists at the end of the 1970s, in which Prigov, Kabakov and Groys participated.

"Alternative History of Art" converged on the fact that it deconstructed both "historiosophies" (philosophies of history)—the modernist and the socialist realist—equally.

However, it is important to add that the experience Kabakov's generation lived through in the second half of the 1950s and early 1960s held not only great emancipatory potential, but was accompanied by trauma as well. "What will I do now, with my professional mastery?" said Kabakov's friend, artist Erik Bulatov, describing the trauma experienced by he and all of his generation upon realizing that mastering the language of figurative painting, to which they had dedicated many years, exposed its own insolvency. But most significantly, many of the artists of Kabakov's generation, having lost a sense of identity with the Soviet artistic language given them, did not exchange it for an identification with the newly discovered language of Western modernism. What Prigov termed "proto-postmodernism" assumed that the shock experienced by the artists also brought them to recognize the conventional nature of artistic language in general. The direct result of this discovery became the formation of the so-called Moscow conceptualism, which established the study of language as the foundation of its practices.

However, Moscow conceptualist understanding of that language could only go as far as the events that had allowed it to come into being. Because the Moscow conceptualist circle was unplugged from channels of public communication as a product of non-official culture, it was immersed in the experience of personal inner communication. Similar cultural conditions were branded by the conceptualists "speech (pan-linguistic) culture."[16] Thus, the subject of their interests did not emerge as language as such—the codes, systems of signs and rules of usage, i.e. what was at the center of attention of Anglo-Saxon conceptualism, but instead the language in action, i.e. the work and exchange of people in using a code or system of code or language. In other words, what interested Moscow conceptualists is what semiology refers to as "*la parole*," and Kabakov himself calls "speech acts."[17] Also characteristic of conceptualism was a shared interest in the investigation of "speech culture" with the Russian Tartu-Moscow semiotics school, which programmatically investigated what it termed the pragmatic level of language, i.e. usage as lived in social practice. Finally, Merab Mamardashvili, a key figure in Russian philosophical thought

16 See the section *Yazikovie deystviya: govorit' I slushat'* ["Speech Actions: To Speak and to Listen"] in Kabakov, Epshtein, *Katalog* ["Catalogue"], p. 136–144.

17 About this, see the article in the *Slovar' Moskovskogo Konseptualizma* ["Dictionary of Moscow Conceptualism"]: Speech (Pan-Speech Culture (Speech Sight), p. 113, <http:www.conceptualism-moscow.org/files/Esanu_Dictionary_Web.pdf>.

at the time, had similarly categorically refused to elaborate his ideas in written form, and insisted on the "Socratic," i.e. on the exclusively oral level of their existence.

Kabakov and his colleagues' involvement with "speech culture" had several key effects. Firstly, understanding their place in the outpouring of oral speech, Moscow conceptualists recognized their participation in the communal body, immersed in affective, convulsive communication. Out of this was born the term "Moscow Communal Conceptualism"[18], and from this, conceptualism came to be defined as a reflexive component of communal speech. Secondly, the result of these reflexive efforts became led to the discovery of a typological diversity of the communal body. Appropriating sociological methodology, Kabakov proposes different versions of a similar typology in some of his work (for example, in the installation, "The Fly" ["*Mukha*"]), fixating on various social types present in late-Soviet society. In his memoirs on the artistic world of the 1960s and 70s, he describes the artistic environment as having splintered into different closed circles and environments.[19]

The next step was to discover a particular mode of describing social types, called "character creation," assuming that the artistic object is created by an artist from the perspective of an imagined character.[20] Three characters-authors of the "Alternative History of Art" stand as an example of a similar concept of authorship, although this time the typology carried a historic-artistic, and not a merely social, character. Finally, Kabakov and the Moscow conceptualists made another important discovery in the intersection of creativity rooted in the "speech act" and character development: art becomes inseparable from the performative behaviour of the artist. The artist, having become aware of the affinity of any expression of individual and group forms of life, begins to connect their own expressions with a particular behavioural strategy. Dmitry Prigov had realized this conceptualist discovery in the most coherent and radical way in both theory and practice, having presented himself for the majority of his artistic life as Dmitry Aleksandrovich Prigov—the extent of correlation between this identity and the author himself remaining unclear until the end. Kabakov termed this conceptualist, as well as personal, trait expressing his poetics, as "being the character of oneself."[21]

18 See also "Moscow Communal Conceptualism," p. 67–68, as well as Viktor Tupytsin, *Kommunalniy (post)modernism* ["Communal (Post) Modernism"], Ad Marginem, Moscow 1998.

19 See Kabakov, *60–70e… Zapiski o neofitsalnoy zhizni v Moskve* ["1960s–70s… Notes on Non-official Life in Moscow"].

20 For Kabakov's understanding of character types see "Hudozhnik-personazh" ["Artist-Character"] and "O 'hudozhnike-personazhe" ["Of the 'Artist-Character'"], Kabakov, *Texti* ["Texts"], p. 501–510 and 611–619; Kabakov, Epstein, *Katalog* ["Catalogue"], p. 296–303.

21 See "Kak I gde ya stal personazhem samogo sebia" ["How and Where I became a Character of Myself"], Kabakov, *Texti* ["Texts"], p. 68–73 and 230 ff.

During the Moscow retrospective, Kabakov had, at on at least two occasions, presented himself as a "character of oneself," having invented Ilya Kabakov, and under whose name he had created some of the expositions at the "Alternative History of Art" and similarly, dramatizing the "dream" at the press-conference and the opening of the exhibition. However, in complete accord with the poetics of Moscow conceptualism, the extent to which the identity of this character/characters related to the author remained, once again, unclear. Thus, if Kabakov's "dream" at the opening of the retrospective was (very likely) a dramatization, then it did not become obvious which of the real Kabakovs—real or virtual—visited the Russian President at the Kremlin. And if it is obvious that the real Kabakov created the author of the "Alternative History of Art," then it is not apparent which Kabakov is the author of the other works in the retrospective; for example, the canvases in the installation *"Gates,"* obviously drawn by the same hand as Kabakov's paintings in the "alternative museum."

In other words, we are once again confronted with a series of insoluble contradictions, converging on Kabakov's insolubly contradictory understanding of authorship. As a "proto-postmodernist," he preserves his connection with the romantic modernist understanding of authorship from both his Soviet and his Western understanding-experience. The metaphysical horizon appears here, which can be gleaned from the figure of an artist he presented in Moscow—the "big master," a wakeful dreaming genius. However, having gone beyond the boundaries of the modernist paradigm, he deconstructs that figure himself, turning it into a thematic object, into an intertextual game and dramatization. And this is how Kabakov's "The Dream of the Author" is different from Roland Barthes's "The Death of the Author." The author does not die under the Russian proto-postmodernist, but instead finds himself in a space of dreaming, or in the hollow center, from which he continues to invisibly control the artistic structure.[22] The artist, representing himself sleeping at the greatest triumph of his life offers himself as a reference—at the center of a web of unresolved and unsolvable contradictions dispersing in all directions.

Translated from the Russian by Gregory Gan.

22 Mark Lipovetsky discovers these ecstatics of the transcendental alongside its analytical deconstruction in many texts on Russian culture of the 20th century, and calls it an effect of *'vzrivnih aporiy* ["explosive aporias"]; *Paralogii. Trasnformatsii (post) modernistskogo diskursa v russkoy kulture 1920–2000h godov* ["Paralogs. Transformations of the (Post)Modern Discourse in Russian Culture from 1920s–2000s"].

Forgotten in the Folds of History Wim Van Mulders

Daniel Dewaele, Paul De Vree, Jacques Lizène and Marinus Boezem: regarding art in the Benelux

So much information, and why do we know so little?
Noam Chomsky, from a lecture in Brussels, March 17, 2011.

1. Adorno has drawn attention to the history that so far has been written from the standpoint of the victor yet had better have been written by the vanquished party. Yet it is necessary to simultaneously turn to what is not recognized in this dynamic, what remains laying by the wayside—in a certain sense, the waste and blind spots that escape dialectical history; that which is not well suited to the historical laws of motion.

What remains laying by the wayside is the most interesting because it is not immediately identifiable, recoverable and consumable. The blind spots threaten to disappear in the authoritarian discourse of art criticism and art history dictated by the illusion of power over the canon. By holding onto fixed diagrams it is at first difficult to grasp what, for example, happened in the Benelux region in the 1970s and 1980s.

2. It is natural to assume that New York in the 1960s and 1970s is the most efficient art production machine. The art metropolis possesses a clearly structured distribution of tasks between gallery and museum, artist and collector, art and business, public and private, production and promotion, myth and mystification. The role New York appropriates for itself is the making of a history by means of a custom-tailored authoritative voice backed (and furthered) by commercial success. And spoken in such a loud voice, talking about the construction of an artistic highway of "masterpieces" with the metropolis as final destination. Thus the tendency arises to glorify a specific cultural history and to accept the corresponding dominant social order as benchmark. In 1975, in *"On Practice,"* Mel Ramsden lashes out at the idea of the hegemony and dominance of New York. He asserts that "the administrators, dealers, critics, pundits" are now "masters," and New York artists have become "imperialist puppets".[1] He forgot, however, to mention the fact that he was the one who

[1] Mel Ramsden, "On Practice" (1975), Alexander Alberro and Blake Stimson (ed.), *Institutional Critique. An Anthology of Artists' Writings*, MIT Press, Cambridge MA 2009, p. 170–199.

had taken advantage of that dominance to then, as a revanchist and anarchist (he quotes Bakunin), turn against authority himself. One could not afford such a critique in the Low Countries because of the distance, although Marcel Broodthaers and Jef Geys suspected that a small region increased the potential to identify a discordant point operating beyond the agencies of authority and destabilize the juggernaut from below. Where there is power, there is counter-power.

3. As Serge Guilbaut illustrated, in the Benelux we often experienced the miracle of America as no more than the authority, the pressure and the manufacture of a range of models that were considered the incarnation of power and freedom.[2] Wanting to be an artist in Belgium in the 1960s and 1970s required becoming aware of the (surrounding), indifferent, even hostile cultural environment. The lack of a solid infrastructure is consistent with the lack of an intelligentsia who saw no good in a professional relationship with contemporary art. There was painfully little prospect of a successful career as an artist. Moreover, artists were not given grants or subsidies with which they could hope to compete in international markets.

Obviously there is an enormous difference between the art worlds of Belgium and the Netherlands during this period. The exhibition "*Op Losse Schroeven, situaties en cryptostructuren*" (On Loose Screws, situations and crypto-structures) at the Stedelijk Museum in Amsterdam in 1969 received major international attention. It guaranteed a paradigm shift in art. Amsterdam and Eindhoven, Cologne and Dusseldorf, Antwerp and Brussels play a decisive role in the discovery of the new art because many constructive contacts are made and maintained. Jan Dibbets, Ger Van Elk, Marinus Boezem, Bas Jan Ader and Stanley Brouwn enjoy international recognition, immediately or in due course. In his search for the identity of the Belgian province, Broodthaers placed question marks on art under a national flag. What did a flag and artwork have to do with each other? In an action in the MuHKA (Museum van Hedendaagse Kunst Antwerpen) of 2009, Jacques Lizène responded to Broodthaers by equipping banner wavers with flags depicting a symbiosis of half a "Flemish Lion" and half a "Walloon Cock." He uses *communautaire* ("of the (EU) community") contrasts and plays with "identity as fiction" that originally serves to

[2] Serge Guilbaut, *How New York Stole the Idea of Modern Art. Abstract Expressionism, Freedom, and the Cold War*, The University of Chicago Press, Chicago 1983.

define his own group. But of the four artists who constitute the
subject of this essay, none will probably ever be as deeply embedded in the official hierarchy as Marcel Broodthaers.

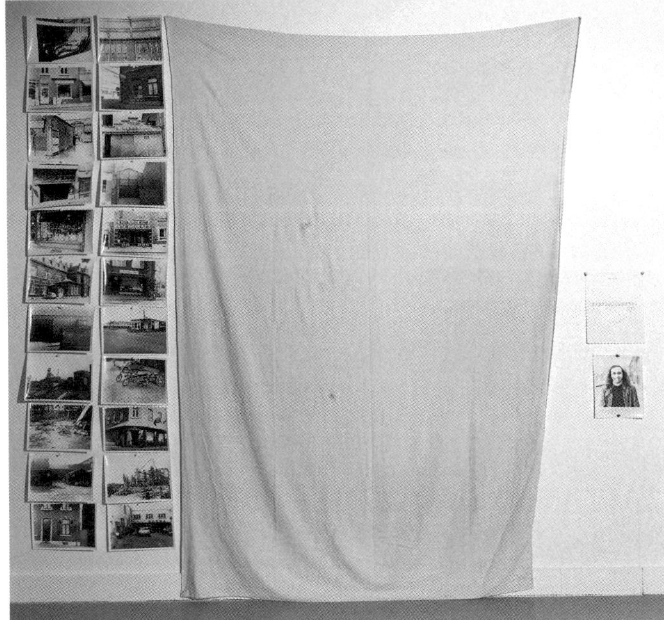

Jacques Lizène, *Rapport d'un voyage*, 1973, Collection M HKA

4. In the 1970s, Daniel Dewaele, Paul De Vree and Jacques
Lizène are present in the meager Belgian exhibition circuit. The
contrast with today could not be greater. They tread the path
of the in-between, the not quite, the stimulating deviation. I
saw their work at a time when it was scarcely acknowledged as
valuable art—this for those who have forgotten how negatively
and paranoid the then official art milieu behaved.

At that moment Marinus Boezem is a familiar name, as
he's present at the two pioneering international exhibitions
"*Op losse schroeven*" and "*When Attitudes Become Form*".
Boezem's work is the result of encounters between different
forms of experience, where thinking and doing function com-
plementarily. Until the realization of his Gothic works he glides
along smoothly in the Dutch and international circuits.

5. By closely following the four artists in their respective trajectories it became clear to me that they had developed a practice
that would not be unproblematic for the viewer. There was no

social support for art. This was an art that was only relevant
on the condition that the spectator developed an almost professional interest in information and research. With his work, the
active artist made an appeal to an activated observer.

There are references to Modernism that, as a project, are
not so much repeated as further considered and developed. The
Avant-garde is distinguished in its search for a place for alternative, utopian worldviews. In this area, in the 1970s, one notes
a certain utopian stagnation in a culture and consciousness
industry that contemplates the status quo. Artists realize what it
is to make visible those things excluded from the existing order
through the unknown and unnamed. They turn the media they
use inside out in order to convey social conflict in an artistic
dimension of analysis and construction.

The subculture that is visible in the work of Dewaele, De
Vree, Lizène and Boezem once again surrenders the "I" for the
"we". They consider the modern masses not as a threat but as
the victim of a consciousness industry expanding into a culture
of spectacle. The spectacle does not need to be understood as
purely negative. The spectacle reveals what producers can do.
Finally, the culture industry, with the spectacle at heart, is one
industry among others. Opposite standardized cultural products
they place an art that necessarily situates adversarial processes
at the center. They believe, in moderation, in progress and
accomplishment. With much reservation, they consider the
predicted decay and decline of a culture. The *"poesia visiva"*
by Paul De Vree is regarded as a prefiguration of art's social
relevance. Social engagement guaranteed liberation and eman-
cipation. The engagement of that time is now an underlying
dictate that weighs on the expectations of global art.

They sought an artistic and social perspective in the folds of
history.

Over their world hung the threat of the Cold War, with a
furious ideological battle the result. The difficult to digest post-
colonial past with all attendant associated guilt, the protest
movements of May '68, an oil crisis with serious economic
consequences, and a nuclear holocaust, were all real threats.
Another grim insight suggested that the West could only continue to flourish economically at the expense of prolonged
Third World poverty[3].

3 Immanuel Wallerstein,
*Historical Capitalism with
Capitalist Civilization,*
Verso, London/New York
1983, 2011.

6. We know that the endless chain of the "fracture in art"
teaches us nothing more about the dynamics of art, because
in the end we perceive great continuity in the fracture. The
idea of a fabric as the structure of art (Victor Burgin) is, for
example, much more useful than linear evolution schemes. In
a carpet there is occasionally a flaw that gives space to more
unorthodox shifts and displacements. The place of the artist
skips, like the insect that sits in wait in a web or slips through
the mesh. In "Canons and Contemporaneity," Terry Smith
discusses the impossibility of arriving at a naturally ordered
visibility. "Contemporaneity consists precisely in disjunctures
of perception, mismatching ways of seeing the same world, in
the coexistence of asynchronous temporalities, in the jostling
contingency of various cultural multiplications, all thrown together, that highlight the inequalities within and between them.
This is the world as it is now. It is no longer "our time", because
"our" cannot stretch to encompass its contrariness. Nor is it
"time", because if the modern was inclined above all to define
itself as a period against past periods, any kind of periodization
of contemporaneity is impossible."[4]

7. In its first ten years of existence, the International Cultural
Centre in Antwerp (1970–1998) is the place where international
figures including Dan Graham, Joseph Kosuth, Daniel Buren,
Vito Acconci, Laurie Anderson, Bill Viola and others exhibit.
The icing on the cake is the non-preserved "Office Baroque"
(1977) of the prematurely deceased Gordon Matta-Clark. He
raised the status of the I.C.C. to that of an international phenomenon. With the exception of Boezem, the aforementioned artists
are present at the I.C.C. and later at the MuHKA (from 1986
onwards). Paul De Vree will be shown four times in the course
of *"poesia visiva"* and *"lotta poetica"* events. In 1976, 1979 and
1980, Dewaele comes on board (in 1980, with the publication
of the book *"No Trespassing"*) and as of 1972, Lizène appears
regularly on stage together with the collective CAP (Cercle
d'Art Prospectif, with Ransonnet, Lennep, Nyst, Courtois and
Lizène), with presentations, videos and performances.[5]

8. Aware that spatial dimensions and other such issues are
poorly treated Daniel Dewaele realizes a work at the Actuel
Art Gallery in Knokke in 1977. The floor is black and the

4 Terry Smith,
"Coda: Canons and
Contemporaneity," Anna
Brzyski (ed.), *Partisan
Canons*, Duke University
Press, Durham/London
2007, p. 309–326.

5 Johan Pas,
*Beeldenstorm in een
spiegelzaal. Het ICC en de
actuele kunst 1970–1990*,
Lannoocampus, 2005.

number 223,921 cm^2 is painted on it in white.[6] The work allows Dewaele to represent the *psychophysical problem of space.* The number expresses a physical identification with the space. In leaving the studio, Dewaele critically reviews the distinction between art versus non-art, art versus society, artist versus the dear, unattainable spectator, and art versus institute. Dewaele is one of the first artists, in line with Jef Geys, who seeks out a wider audience by acting in the public arena (the street).

"I would like to exhibit those surveyed museum spaces as open sculptures, i.e., sculptures around which the visitor is free to move [...] the work is very concrete (so many square metres) and at the same time, due to its immateriality as an artwork and as an exhibition, completely virtual." Unlike Yves Klein in *"Le Vide"* in 1958, where mystical, occult and cosmic sensibilities assume form, Dewaele links the empty space, independently of any metaphysical interpretation.

Dewaele claims the accessible space and interprets it as a virtual playground.

In the letters from the project "24,800 m^2 Sculptuur" (1977–1980), Michael Compton of the Tate Gallery responds: "The size of the space devoted to temporary exhibitions in this museum varies from about 600 to 1000m^2."

Dewaele draws no theoretical conclusions from the results of the correspondence. This contrasts with Hans Haacke's *"poll"* of 1972 in the John Weber Gallery in New York. By means of a tally, Haacke establishes that 75% of gallery visitors are professionally involved.

A similar paradox guides the work *"Art and Society. Are there solutions?"* from 1982–1985. Is there a rift between contemporary art and society? The sixty-nine artists' responses appear in facsimile in a book. Wolf Vostell chooses not to answer the question, but sends a number of catalogues of his work and asks Dewaele outright to distil an answer. Dewaele refuses and aloofly states: "It was in no way my intention to pass judgment on the answers. So I do not. This is not a scientific work. This is not a study."

The stubborn refusal to interpret and make himself invisible as an artist indicates distance and detachment. The artist sets processes in motion but ignores the logical conclusion. Is this one of the reasons Dewaele's work has had so much difficulty reaching and penetrating a larger public?

6　Wim Van Mulders, "Daniel Dewaele", *+-0, Revue d'Art Contemporain,* n° 28, November 1979, Anno VII (Genval), p. 33–35. The artist was given the opportunity to realize an artist's page. This work also exists as business cards that Dewaele handed out during openings.

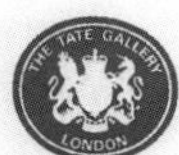

THE TATE GALLERY

126/MC/VAE.   18th January, 1979.

Daniel Dewaele, Esq.,
Baron Ruzettelaan 146,
8320 Brugge,
Belgium.

Dear Mr. Dewaele,

Thank you for your letter of 7 January. The size
of the space devoted to temporary exhibitions in
this museum varies from about 600 to 1,000 m2.

Yours sincerely,

Michael Compton,
Keeper of Exhibitions and Education.

THE TATE GALLERY MILLBANK LONDON SW1P 4RG
TELEPHONE: 01-828 1212 TELEGRAMS: TATEGAL LONDON

Daniel Dewaele, *24800 m2 sculpture*, 1979, detail, Collection
M HKA

STADT AACHEN
NEUE GALERIE - SAMMLUNG LUDWIG

Herrn
Daniel Dewaele,
Baron Ruzettelaan 146
8320 Brügge

51 AACHEN
TELEFON 47/2581
INFORMATION 47/25 71

Aachen, den 18.1.1979

Betrifft : Ausstellungsangebot

Lieber Daniel,

Herzlichen Dank für Deine Mitteilung Nr 44 vom 7.1.1979. Der
Partizipation habe ich als Museumsleiter immer den Vorzug
gegeben. Zugleich interessiert es mich, den Museumsbesucher
ästhetische Realität klar erfahren zu lassen, weil die zu-
ungeordnet ist, zeige ich ihm die Wirklichkeit.

Deine Partizipation, in Kürze, Deine Ausstellung, würde darin
bestehen, dass Du mir angibst, wieviel m2 du benötigst. Dadurch
bekäme ich einen Begriff von der Energie Deines Freiheitsbedürf-
nisses.

Ich hoffe auf Deine Teilnahme und danke Dir im voraus für Deine
Mühe.

Herzliche Grüsse
Dr. Becker

GEÖFFNET: DONNERSTAG BIS SAMSTAG 10 BIS 13 UND 14 BIS 17 UHR, SONNTAG BIS DIENSTAG 10 BIS 13 UND 15 BIS 19 UHR, MITTWOCH GESCHLOSSEN

Daniel Dewaele, *24800 m2 sculpture*, 1979, detail, Collection
M HKA

MODERNA MUSEET

Stockholm February 2, 1979

Daniel Dewaele
Baron Ruzettelaan 146
B - 8320 Brugge

Dear Daniel Dewaele,

In a way,the museum is in all its functions,its rooms,its open-hours,
for one artist's work.Even though the collections of Moderna Museet
count a number of some 3.700 oeuvres (together:the living memory),
each oeuvre is here on its own,is to be regarded regardless of all the
others (a collection is also a collective).
Take a sculpture by Brancusi,Le Nouveau-né,in all its height:16,5 cm;
the walls continue to stand around it also as you pass the door
bringing the piece with you,in your mind.Then,if you are lucky,Klein's
Monochrome demands your eyes and occupies your mind,and very quickly
the museum turns out to be full of "on its owns",side by side; they
are participation.Whoever spoke of anything else?
I should say that your participation,on your own,has nothing to do
with the space of the museum.You should take,the least to the whole
if "neccessary".
Or take Air de Paris,1919,by Marcel Duchamp,a certain amount of air.
I suggest your freedom of movement (liberty of action?) will that
of your subject,and later the second viewer's and-so-on.Your distinction
between any kind of space and the definite will have to be objectified,
or at least defined,before a dialogue can take a start. (We all know what
infinity means,or?)
If it is a matter of space,please don't hesitate,if it isn't,we'll see.

Best regards,

Nina Öhman
curator

Statens Konstmuseer Moderna Museet Skeppsholmen Box 16382 S-103 27 Stockholm Sweden Telefon 08/24 42 00

Daniel Dewaele, *24800 m2 sculpture*, 1979, detail, Collection
M HKA

In *"Wat zegt u het I.C.C.? Komt u er soms? Waarom? Waarom niet?"* (What does the I.C.C. call to mind? Do you sometimes go there? Why? Why not?) Dewaele relies on the participation of the casual passer-by in the street. The answers acquired the status of a global statement on art and its absence from social debate. Dewaele appears as the gadfly. Still, the work has since found its way into the MuHKA collection.

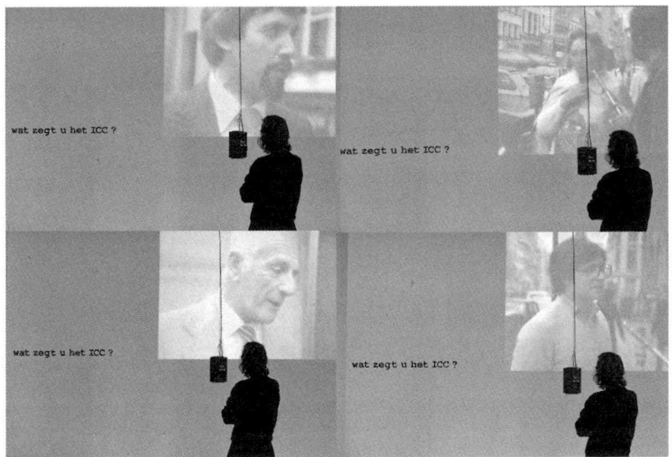

Daniel Dewaele, *Wat zegt U het ICC* (What does the ICC Tell You), 1980, Collection M HKA

No singe occurrence remains without consequences, and every occurrence is the cause of yet other occurrences. Nevertheless, it is significant that Dewaele, although scarcely visible in the local history texts, still appears today in numerous art centers and group exhibitions with uncompromised sharpness.

9. In an inimitable mixture of attitudes, Jacques Lizène criticizes "great men, great works, great moments, great styles, great books and great art."[7] In response to a reading by Pierre Restany about Daniel Spoerri, in which the guru of *"Nouveau Réalisme"* asserts that Spoerri is no *"petit maître"*, Lizène claims the qualification of *"Le petit maître Liégeois de la seconde moîtié du XXe siècle"* and *"Artiste de la médiocrité et de la sans importance"*. There is a pseudo-identity with the negatively connoted terms *"sans talent, médiocrité, sans intérêt, petit maître, mysogynie,* une oeuvre emmerdante". In reversing the dream of fame and fortune, Lizène punctured, in a provocative manner, irrational, mythical illusions.

[7] See the publication accompanying the exhibition *"Jacques Lizène"* at the MuHKA, *Jacques Lizène. Tome III*, Editions Yellow Now, L'Usine à Stars, Crisnée/Liège 2009. The thick book (488 pages) includes a special contribution inspired by the encyclopedia *Larrousse Illustre* entitled "Le Petit Lizène Illustré. Une tentative inachevée d'abécédaire autour de l'oeuvre du Petit Maître."

There is a real biological center to be found in the work of Lizène. In 1965 he approaches the cycle of life with a radical materialism. He decides not to reproduce and undergoes a vasectomy, which becomes the core of his artistic universe. He refuses to give shape to future generations because the vasectomy represents a closure whereby the tap is definitively turned off. This is to be taken literally and serves as a dominant metaphor throughout his oeuvre. He interprets the demoralizing world situation with its then terrifying population explosion. Through biological injury and mutilation Lizène dissociates himself from the instinct for (re)production and procreation. The highly common "HA! HA! HA!" is the Lizènian laugh, which rises from the body and varies in range from the loud laugh, the heavy laugh, the evil laugh, and the dark laugh, to the sneer. Sometimes one gets the feeling that the broad smile, cramped and artificial, is linked to an infusion of seasoned humor. He finds himself in the paradoxical situation of the jester, who confirms the power that he bombards with his humor. As such, humor does not destroy the institutional structures, but keeps them properly intact, enabling them to be played with.

Through playing, he develops a passionate attitude towards the existential seriousness in which art is imprisoned. In this way, "le petit maître" is the lucid figure that practices "non-theorizing". Working with personal fecal matter also indicates closeness, intimacy and energy. He trembles, anxiously, for the detached objectification and reification of art. His preoccupation with the biological leaves the "I" soaking in a warm gulf stream of libidinous force with his intuition, feelings and eroticism.

The preoccupation with art exists as parody, as theatre, as self-denial, as futility. It's as if Lizène embraces the collapse of great art and puts small, inconspicuous bagatelles in its place. It is as if he, together with Nietzsche, looks to the "last man" who no longer has great ambitions and has submitted to mediocrity but without accepting domestication.

10. Paul De Vree defines his visual poetry as poetry that just wants to be itself, a poetry that faithfully records, coolly describes, and where the emotions of the poet are irrelevant. The contents of the poem correspond to the visual features in which it is manifested. Thus, this poetry slides into visual art but also into social reality. De Vree revised the crisis of Western consciousness. The oil crisis of the early 1970s and the associated severe economic and financial crisis are directly expressed in one of his last works. One sees a pitching drilling platform with the text: "what does not capsize?". This statement from 1981 again embodies acute topical value.

In the 1981 catalogue *"Paul De Vree – XX Centuries"* I quoted from Althusser who offered conflicting interpretations of the crisis. "In the first sense we are dealing with a negative definition of crisis. The crisis is a critical condition that precedes destruction or death. But there is a second sense that is positive. The positive is hidden behind the negative. With Descartes the positive could mean: *"larvatus prodeo"* (go forth masked). Thus, one speaks of a growth crisis, a puberty crisis; one speaks of a crisis in order to understand that in the old man something new is in the process of being born."[8]

In one of his better-known works, De Vree lets the term "revolution"—an interpretation of the anti-authoritarian impulses of May '68—rotate round a circle while the circumference of the circle horizontally cuts through the word. The shifting of the two halves creates a pattern that expresses the disruptive character of a (r)evolution. Visually, the revolution is in continuous motion. Due to their ethical commitment, the traditional political podiums and forums of union, party, elections, government and parliament, lose their credibility.

De Vree was convinced that conceptual art was a commercially organized movement. Although this is a simplification of a historic, disparate phenomenon, De Vree's conviction held a certain truth. "Conceptual art" seemed highly saleable and had failed in its aim to circumvent the marketing mechanisms. Moreover, this art never dematerialized as Camiel van Winkel has well demonstrated.[9]

Visual poetry unwittingly maneuvered its way into a deadlock situation, choosing the literary magazine as the forum in which to show new work, and in so doing involuntarily limited their visibility radius to those who bought the magazine. Still, during his life, Paul De Vree was highly "visible" in both literary and visual art circles. He was a poet, author, publisher, artist, art critic and organizer of important exhibitions of contemporary art, such as the international *"Forum"* exhibition in Ghent in 1962 and 1963, in which Rauschenberg, Johns and Pop art first appeared.

8 Wim Van Mulders, "Een tekstbeeld van de (r) evolutie," *Paul De Vree – XX Eeuwen*, Provinciaal Museum Hasselt, 1981, unnumbered pages.

9 Camiel van Winkel, *Moderne leegte. Over kunst en openbaarheid*, SUN, Nijmegen 1999, Part II: Openness as a condition. Also see: Camiel van Winkel, "Het dwangbeeld van een puur idée," *Conceptuele kunst in Nederland en België 1965–1975*, Stedelijk Museum Amsterdam, NAI Publishers Rotterdam, Amsterdam 2002, p. 28–47.

According to De Vree it is the fault of the bourgeoisie that
he, the artist, regards man as an isolated individual who is blind
to collective realities. The poet/artist leans strongly towards existentialism in the way he integrates linguistic ambiguities. He
accepts the imperfection of human existence—a world without
anchors—from which he developed humanistic ethics and morals. Man possesses the freedom to make choices, with the result
that he bears responsibility for the values he chooses and the
deeds he performs. In this sense of responsibility, De Vree saw
a way to firmly embrace his own time.

11. In 1960, Marinus Boezem, a contemporary of Jan Dibbets,
Ger Van Elk, Stanley Brouwn, Bas Jan Ader and Wim T.
Schippers (creator of absurdist television shows) sets out with
a sculptural attitude that rapidly evolves. In 1964, he walks
around with a briefcase containing projects that can be realized
on demand—projects about growing impoverishment and a
flattening of human communication. Boezem's most typical or
telling work revolves around the direct application of natural
forces. His "bedding", with white sheets and pillows, in the
windows of the Stedelijk Museum, literally and figuratively
intended to blow a fresh, harsh wind through the rigid institution. An interpretation of the forces of nature leads him to
visualize wind and its effects on fragile installations. "Wind
is so immaterial that it was interesting for me to try to make it
into a sculpture."[10] He signs a fan, as an instrument that creates
wind, and lays tables with thin white tablecloths that flutter in
the flow of air from the fan. Wind and temperature play a role
in his "weather forecasts". For an entire month he sends, on a
daily basis, a number of art friends and museums the weather
map from September 26, 1968, depicting the high-pressure
areas, depressions, wind speeds, etc. In so doing, Boezem explains the conditions and dynamics of the airspace for an immense ever-changing work of art. In the iconic work *"Signing
the Sky above the Port of Amsterdam by an Aeroplane"* (sic)
from 1969, the name Boezem dissolves in the air. It is one of his
most spectacular and ironic works, his signature taking possession of the airspace, but at the same time he distances himself
from it through its definitive disintegration. Just like Richard
Long, Boezem sees nature as a material that is unapproachable
and manipulable. He is not a romantic. A place in the Dutch

10 See catalogue raison-
née *Boezem*, Thot, Bussum
1999, p. 107.

polder (low-lying reclaimed land) takes on a reflective dimension by way of a simulation of the Reims Cathedral. A total of 174 poplar trees are planted following the ground floor plan and dimensions of the cathedral. The thin, sharply rising trees stand so far apart that any romantic-religious associations and experiences connected with the mystery of nature are minimized. The dating of his largest project *"1978/1987–Present"* marks the beginning of the metastasis and dissemination of the cathedral within his oeuvre. The endless embroidering on this project gives the impression that 1987 signifies a relative yet abrupt endpoint. The sublime moments in his personal history clarify once more the fact that such waves are of short duration. Is Robert Motherwell's distinction between "mode of invention" and "mode of variation" relevant here?

It's strange, but with this realization and the voluminous 1999 catalogue of his oeuvre, the figure of Boezem fades inexplicably away in a busy, crowded art scene. In the tragicomic descriptions of art history one discovers a parabolic curve with a wave whose every rise is followed by, leaves behind, a trough.

12. Belgium now has professional museums and art venues while the Netherlands is still dominated by a far greater number of institutions, despite the imminent reduction that is discounted in the draconian cuts within the cultural sector.[11] The struggle with insufficient budgets once again induces a spirit of frustration in curators and artists. Today's abundance demands a rigorous selection based on "exclusion," the choices of which lie at the junction of our diverse experience of the world and divergent points of view.

This interpretation requires us to employ nuance, and to understand that calling a porous period difficult can appear superfluous. Today the artist occupies a more central position than ever before. And the reading of a work leads, to some measure, to an in-depth dialogue with the artist. A lot of ink flows on strategies and machinations through which the viewing of an individual artwork (the "close viewing" of T. J. Clark) appears to come second.[12]

The place of an artist constantly shifts and has a preliminary character. There is no end to the speculative tendency to position artists. Each conclusion is an artificial fortiori.

[11] Merijn Rengers, "De botte bijl. Over de onverwachte effecten van de bezuinigingen op de culturele sector," *De Witte Raaf*, n° 154, November – December 2011, p. 13–14.

[12] T. J. Clark, *The Sight of Death. An Experiment in Art Writing*, Yale University Press, New Haven/London 2006. Also see Bart Verschaffel "Omzien naar 'choses plus apparentes que les paroles': T. J. Clark over Nicolas Poussin," *De Witte Raaf*, n° 125, January – February 2007, p. 9–11.

Over a period of thirty years (which historians call a change-of-generation), one can see how quickly the museum, that many-headed body, reorients itself to new, young art *and* to rediscovering forgotten art. Myriad cultural, sociological and political actors positively assess the blazing speed of art production. Yet, through overproduction, many artists gain a distorted image of their own chances of success and estimate the(ir) chance(s) of breaking through unrealistically high.

Therefore it is instructive to recognize that a historical phenomenon like the ready-made remained dormant for more than half a century: not until the 1950s did artists assume in their work the problems the ready-made posited. At the same time, its endless exegesis begins through education in the arts.

Today's successful generation is freed from the local and the regional, and arrives on the international stage. Still, their supporters do not limit themselves to artistic criteria. They praise solipsism, self-positioning, assertiveness, professional management, corporate culture and global-market-thinking. Some get lost in the slightly absurd belief that art is the most reliable investment in uncertain economic times. That the heroes of today can become the false lights and fire fighters of tomorrow does not occur to the entourage. It is also a mistaken assumption that the value of each work of art always increases with time.

Thus, a silent generation stands opposite an internationally successful generation. But success and depth are not directly synonymous nor even correlative.

13. The recovery of forgotten artists in the Benelux is motivated by a genuine reappraisal. Rehabilitation and the urge to rewrite the canon are the domain and duty of the museum of contemporary art. Yet it is a vain intention, if only—in the style of the lonely and adventurous explorer—to guide a forgotten artist in the canon. The corrections are made in dribs and drabs because the artistic truth is a matter of consensus and (still) depends on the authority of experts. In the art world democratic principles do not—if were they present—apply. Inequality in the arts is far greater than in other labor markets.

In the discussion on "Celebrity Culture," the supporters or pro-contingent offer that we live in the best of all possible worlds (Leibniz) and that we will again discover the masterpieces in a democratic way.[13] By seamlessly linking celebrity

[13] Isabelle Graw, *High Price. Art Between the Market and Celebrity Culture*, Sternberg Press, Berlin/New York 2009.

to culture, one narrows the discussion down to the offending history of the tenors. While many, starting with Warhol, enthusiastically enumerate the benefits of "Celebrity Culture," star architect Rem Koolhaas asserts: "People can no longer imagine that a normal person can fulfill the role of architect (artist). They want you to be a celebrity. Subsequently, every attempt at real communication is doomed to fail."[14]

The image has the opportunity to achieve that point at which the personal grows together with the worldview. The image with imagination, the image that is a representation, exists largely as a residual of the artist's global energy. Each image has its margins and its silences. Even though the lost generation is disposed to maladjustment and distress, the creative impetus, which expresses a certain vitality, nonetheless attains great authenticity. Sometimes the distribution of their art (the four artist-subjects discussed herein) went very smoothly (Boezem until 1987), sometimes uncertainly, sputtering and difficult for the other three.

The museum as a concept is nothing more but also nothing less than a culmination of the public domain. It possesses an openness in which self-examination and self-justification of art and artist play out and receive a permanent position.

Although there is now a broad professional infrastructure, for the artist who does not fit into the gallery-controlled art world it still remains tremendously difficult. In the bustle of the international art market, there is little room for unknowns. He/she who does not make news is sidelined. Many sought-after artists are significantly more expensive. Artists who receive little attention risk—for so many obscure reasons—being just as ignored as their counterparts from the 1960s and 1970s. Here is what prevails: the reality of art is that which is communicated about it.

This text is an attempt to think, to interpret and to correct the canon and its [perceived?] evolution as a single generation. Time only proceeds thanks to our participation, so we support the events: today is yesterday and tomorrow is today.

Translated from the Dutch by Jodie Hruby.

14 Interview by Jannetje Koelewijn with Rem Koolhaas, *De Standaard* (newspaper), December 3, 2011.

Art and Francoism

The second half of the 20th century in Spain was marked by the dictatorship of General Franco from 1939—after three years of Civil War that did away with the Second Republic—until his death in 1975, which signaled the beginning of the democratic reconstruction of the country.

In 1969 one of the biggest business scandals in Spain at the time broke. It was significant not only for its widespread economic consequences but also for its political implications. The company in question, Matesa, had swindled the Spanish government out of thousands of millions of pesetas through the fraudulent use of credits for the export of textile machinery. The Catalan businessman, Juan Vilá Reyes,[1] a member of the ultraconservative Catholic Opus Dei and with close ties to several of Franco's ministers, was accused of unlawful appropriation of government funds and sent to prison.

[1] "Suddenly Matesa ceased to be the project that, according to Vilá Reyes, 'summed up the human virtues of sacrifice, effort, risk and ambition... an example that we wished to convey,' to turn into a scandal." Bernat Muniesa, *Dictadura y monarquía en España. De 1939 hasta la actualidad*, Editorial Ariel, Barcelona 1996, p. 124.

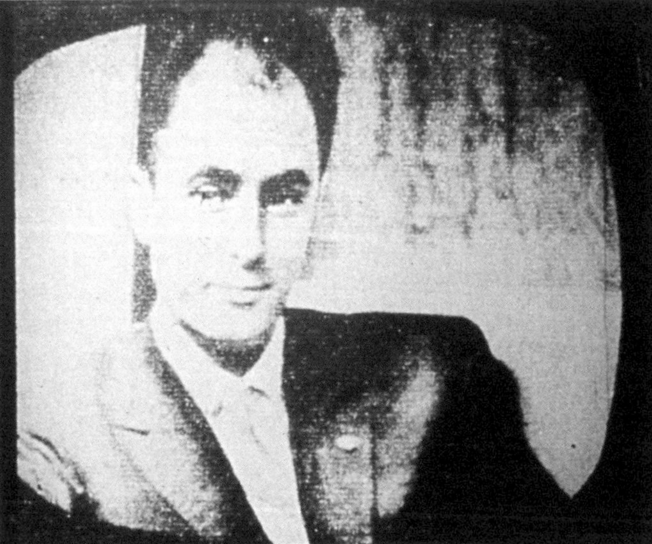

Eulàlia Grau, *...We, too, can invent...*, 1976, silver halide photographic print on wood with printer ink on silver paper. Detail of one photograph of a total of 21, artist's collection, © Eulàlia Grau, VEGAP, Barcelona, 2012

Later, in 1976, the artist Eulàlia Grau created a work entitled *...Inventemos también nosotros...* ("We, too, can invent"). This parallel narrative tells the story of the businessman Vilá

Reyes and Diego Navarro, a construction worker who was wounded during a demonstration and detained by the Civil Guard. The story reveals that it was never revealed who shot him, nor which doctor saw him and refused to remove the bullet, and that he was put in prison in Tarragona where he was found hanging in his cell. The lack of information and absence of images in this narrative stand in direct contrast to the abundance of iconographic material documenting the industrial and social activity of the businessman. Vilá Reyes was pardoned in 1975 in spite of the severity of the charges, the prison sentence and the fine imposed on him. Eulàlia Grau's work makes use of the two diametrically opposed stories to highlight the unequal treatment and application of justice in the context of and relation to the social standing of the persons involved. The result was a polarized portrait of triumphant power and the losers.[2]

Several decades earlier, in 1937, in the midst of the Spanish Civil War, the anarchist syndicate CNT produced a film directed by Fernando Mignoni called *Nuestro Culpable* ("Our Guilty One"), a comedy satirizing bourgeois society and its relationship with justice. A thief is surprised in the act of robbing the house of a banker by the banker's mistress, who herself absconds with the loot. The alleged thief is unjustly apprehended and put in jail where he receives special treatment thanks to the protection of the banker. The apparent insignificance of the narrative does not exclude a criticism of the complex social framework of Spanish society at the time, and the mechanisms of economic and judicial power by which it was governed. Its underlying message is that the only way the bourgeois order can get around the law is via the genre/process of the picaresque. In this sense it is close to what Valle-Inclán termed an *esperpento*, the idea that one can take advantage of the decadence of Spanish society to ridicule, satirize and deform reality in a decidedly grotesque manner.[3]

Almost forty years separated Mignoni's film and Eulàlia Grau's work, almost the same number of years that this country spent living through one of the darkest periods in its history. On 18 July 1936 there occurred what the historian Pierre Vilar claimed was the "Military uprising" led by General Franco against the legal and democratically constituted Republican government. Three years later the Civil War was over, the rebel army had emerged victorious and a dictatorship was installed. The 1936 rebellion was consecrated as a "National Uprising"

2 In this regard, Eulàlia Grau produced another interesting work: *Cancionero de los hombres verticales y de los hombres horizontales* (1975) ("Songs of the Vertical and Horizontal Men"), depicting the winners (vertical) and the victims and losers (horizontal).

3 "The tragic sense of Spanish life can only manifest itself with a systematically deformed aesthetic..., because Spain is a grotesque deformation of European civilisation." Valle-Inclán, *Luces de Bohemia* (1924).

and in 1939 the dictatorial regime of General Franco was implanted in Spain that was to last until his death in 1975. Once the war—henceforth to be known as a heroic and evangelizing "crusade"—was over, the new regime devoted itself to persecuting and in effect annihilating the Republic and its followers as its raison d'état. Franco self-styled himself as "Caudillo de España por la Gracia de Dios" ("Caudillo of Spain by the Grace of God"), which gives us a clue as to the two great pillars of the new construction of the Francoist project: Catholicism and the military. This brings to mind Unamuno's definition, in 1936, of the history of Spain as "the marriage between the sacristy and the barracks." The Church dictated the moral order and controlled education from primary school through university. Spain, defined from then on as *"una, grande y libre"* ("one, great and free"), was transformed into an authoritarian and repressive state that censured any possible deviation from the conservative values that imposed themselves on a single, unified thought. Until 1950, Spain lived through a period of economic and political autarky. The United Nations's condemnation of the new regime was accompanied by diplomatic isolation and the withdrawal of ambassadors. The declaration of the General Assembly of December 12, 1946 condemned the imposition by force of Francoism and its connivance with Nazism and Fascism. This news was covered in the NO-DO, the sole official newsreel created in 1942 to maintain "the proper guidelines for national cinematographic information". From 1943 on it was shown in all the cinemas in the country before every film, and featured mass demonstrations of the Spanish people mobilized in support of Franco. Nevertheless, beginning in 1950, Spain's strategic position in Europe and its potential for economic growth enabled the establishment of bilateral relations with the United States government, initiating a policy of loans to the regime. In this regard, we should mention the 1953 film *Bienvenido Mr. Marshall* ("Welcome, Mr. Marshall"), directed by Luis García Berlanga and written by Juan Antonio Bardem, two outstanding filmmakers of the period.

Because most of the prominent Spanish intellectuals had gone into exile, this left a notable absence of prominent (intellectual) figures in the Francoist ranks. The world of culture was reduced to a small nucleus, given that censorship filtered every aspect of publishing, radio, and public events, and its (explicit) presence

was felt only in demonstrations of a patriotic nature with a tendency toward Francoist exaltation and opportunism. During the 1940s culture took on a rather reactionary and backward-looking character, tending to shy away from any trace of innovation.
In 1948, however, the first symptoms of the revitalization of an avant-garde began to appear in the Escuela Altamira, in Dau al Set (more attentive to the pre-war avant-garde) and in the first October Salons. On the other hand, by establishing a framework of economic cooperation with the United States, the regime itself was interested in presenting a more open image to counteract an unusual political situation. The Hispano-American art biennales, the first of which took place in Madrid in 1951, were diplomatic operations that facilitated the exhibition of abstract art in contrast to the earlier academicism. In this regard, most avant-garde art was used as propaganda to promote the regime abroad.[4] The lectures on abstract art delivered during the summer course at Santander in 1953, in conjunction with the Exposición Internacional de Arte Abstracto, represented an attempt to normalize the artistic debate.[5] Finally, the exhibition of American art organized by MoMA in Barcelona in 1955 confirmed Spain's inclusion in the circuits promoting American art, together with the signing of agreements with the United States and the admission of a diplomatic delegation to the United Nations.

President Eisenhower's visit to Spain in 1959 contributed to enhanced recognition for the regime at a time when it had decreed Abstract Expressionism (Informalism) to be the dominant tendency, and selectively promoted artists such as Tàpies, Saura, Millares, Oteiza or Chillida. It is interesting to note that while the most conservative informalist tendencies were being reinforced, the opposite was actually developing in architecture and design. Artists were already experimenting in these disciplines with the most advanced and transgressive innovations, in many cases under the auspices of civil society in the absence of public institutions. An example in architecture is Grup R (with Bohigas, Coderch, Sostres, Gili, Moragas, Valls and Pratsmajó), which created the pavilion at the 1951 Milan Triennial, combining architecture and design with ceramics, popular art and works by Miró. In this same line and in the following decade, the role of the design schools in Barcelona was fundamental. Eina, founded in 1967, taught art and design from a multidisciplinary perspective involving various types of

4 See Jorge Luis Marzo, *Art modern i franquisme. L'origen conservador de l'avantguarda i de la política artística a l'Estat español*, Fundació Espais d'Art Contemporani, Girona 2007.

5 These lectures by Sebastià Gasch, Alexandre Cirici, Gaya Nuño, Jorge Oteiza, J. M. Moreno Galván and Camón Aznar, among others, were published under the title *El arte abstracto y sus problemas* (1956).

experiences.[6] Many critics, philosophers and artists participated in Eina, where an important constituent of the artistic avant-garde later to emerge in the 1970s was trained.

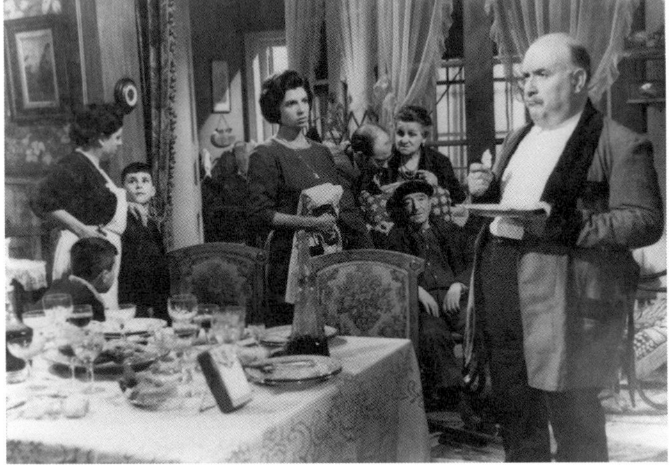

Photogram of the film *Plácido*, 1961, directed by Luis García Berlanga, courtesy of Jet Films

In 1961, Luis García Berlanga made the film *Plácido*, a satirical portrait of Spanish reality. The film depicted an ironic presentation of Christian charity understood as a way of salving the bourgeois conscience toward the underprivileged classes. Beneath the slogan "Ponga un pobre en su mesa" ("Seat a poor person at your table"), there is an unforgettable scene of a raffle for the poor for the chance to have Christmas dinner in the home of a wealthy family. It was biting commentary on a society that lacked everything, was extremely unequal and was governed by bureaucracy. A year later, Fraga Iribarne was appointed Minister of Information and Tourism. Censorship was reinforced in all types of media and communication, and in 1966 the new Press Law went into effect.[7] Fraga was also responsible for launching the campaign to attract foreign tourists with the slogan "Spain is Different". Thus, a pleasant, friendly, dynamic and carefree image of the country under the sun was projected. The Catalan artist Joan Rabascall satirized this image in a series of the same name between 1975 and 1977. The outline of the Iberian Peninsula on the one hand, and the shape of a television screen on the other both incorporated images of seaside tourist sites at the precise moment urban-driven speculation was beginning to invade and transform the country's coastal beaches. These images were interspersed with

7 This law affected newspapers, magazines and the only television channel in the country, in addition to films, theater and literature. It remained in effect until after the death of Franco and, among other things, enabled the government to confiscate anything that attacked the Falangist movement and its principles.

imaginary everyday populist life based on football, attending church and the sale of arms. This self-complacent iconography took place against a background of social malaise and the role of university resistance, strikes and the *Caputxinada*, a notorious incident that took place in Barcelona in 1966.[8]

The beginning of the 1960s saw the opening up of the art market with the recognition of Spanish Abstract Expressionism (Informalism) abroad—a fact that was further enhanced by Spain's invitation to participate in the Venice and São Paulo Biennales. Parallel to this turn towards the culture of consumption was a highly politicised reflection, in art, on reality, as seen in the graphic work of Estampa Popular and other groups such as Equipo Crónica and Equipo Realidad. At the decade's close and into the early 1970s, a series of developments unfolded in the artistic milieu that revolved around experimentation and the problematic considerations of the work of art itself, its means and circuits. At the same time—and in some cases—art was openly critical, both socially and politically. In addition to the developments at the design schools, other artists began collaborating with experimental spaces such as the Centro de Cálculo at the Universidad Complutense in Madrid, that from 1968 on organized seminars and exhibitions on the generation of plastic forms by means of computers.

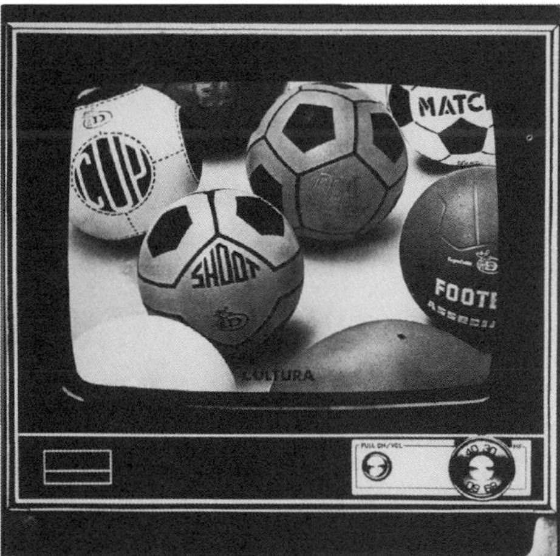

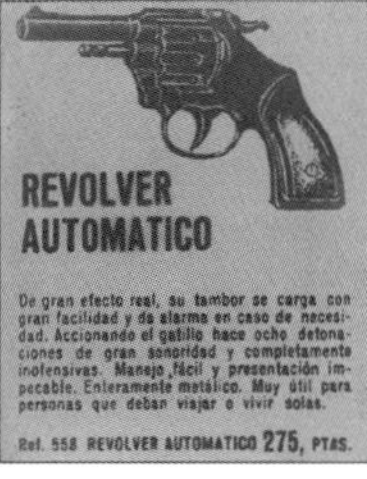

Joan Rabascall, *Automatic Revolver* (from the series *Spain is Different*), 1975 MACBA Collection, MACBA Foundation.
© Joan Rabascall, VEGAP, Barcelona, 2012, photo by Rocco Ricci

Joan Rabascall, Culture (from the series *Spain is Different*),1975, MACBA Collection, MACBA Foundation.
© Joan Rabascall, VEGAP, Barcelona, 2012, photo by Rocco Ricci

The culture of consumerism, coupled with economic prosperity, had its repercussions in the domestic environment and life's domestic necessities. The home was the ideological framework by which the majority of the middle class consolidated its social position by means of the dwelling and its furnishings. As Alexandre Cirici remarked, the bourgeoisie, "satisfied with its feeling of security, experienced a particular craving for luxury, which showed itself in its preference for antiquated styles of homes and furniture. Imbued with the new ideas of history and hierarchy, it tried to emulate the aristocracy by bringing about a gigantic falsification of furniture, objects, tapestries and lamps in imitation of the ancient nobility."[9] Here we should mention the articles by *Jack el Decorador*[10] (the alter ego of the writer Manuel Vázquez Montalbán) for the interior design magazine *Hogares Modernos*, published between 1969 and 1971. These articles were a kind of satirical chronicle on bourgeois taste, with war cries like "¡Guerra a la metalistería psicodélica!" ("Down with all this psychodelic metalwork") and encouraging everyone to eat sardines with "!Viva el rigodón y el porrón de vino tinto!" ("Long live the rigodoon [dance] and the glass wine decanter").[11] He ranted about the consumerist proliferation of monstrosities and the lack of good taste. This outcry against the excesses of the so-called society of wellbeing in contrast to the harshness of the very real social inequality, violence and injustice that prevailed was also reflected in some of the components of Eulàlia Grau's *Etnografías* (1973–1974).[12] The home was also understood as the conceptual framework of the family that was ruled by paternal masculine authority. The husband not only constituted moral authority, but he was also the holder of legal power over his wife and/or daughter (who needed his permission to apply for a bank loan or a passport). This is an example of the tremendous inequality in the social consideration of women, who were assigned a subordinate role within the family. During the 1970s several artists portrayed and denounced this situation.[13] The publication of photo romance novels aimed at a female audience contributed to the reinforcing of certain stereotypes about the woman who complements and helps the male figure and ends up surrendering to him for love, as in Eugènia Balcells' work *Fin* (End) of 1977. These photo romance novels that sought to create expectations within a specific moral and social order contrasted greatly with the comics that proliferated in Spain during the 1970s within a circuit of marginal and counter-cultural publications. These comics were highly critical of bourgeois customs and were rife with explicit references to sex

9 Alexandre Cirici, *La estética del franquismo*, Gustavo Gili, Barcelona 1977, p. 149.

10 Jack the Decorator' (in Spanish a play on words alluding to "Jack the Ripper", the English serial killer).

11 Quoted in "Las andanzas de Jack el Decorador. Ni se compra ni se vende el cariño verdadero. El Drugstor de Bilbao o la resurrección metálica de Gallardo," *Hogares Modernos. La revista de la decoración, el mueble y la arquitectura*, no. 40, October 1969.

12 She continued to develop this theme in a later work, *Vivendes…Vivendes* (1976), on how the home reflects the conditions of the life of its inhabitants and reveals its social inequalities.

13 Noteworthy examples of this are: *Standart* (1976) by Fina Miralles, *Discriminació de la dona* (1977) by Eulàlia Grau, the works of Esther Ferrer, Olga Pijuan, and the films and videos of Eugènia Balcells.

and drugs, in addition to linking up with other practices, alternative art and design spaces, bars and music venues. Nevertheless, their position was closer to anarchism than to actual political criticism. They were frequently subject to censorship owing to their offensive morals, sanctions, kidnappings, fines and trials, but they were highly prolific, and some even managed to exist for years. Barcelona served as an important center, together with Madrid, with smaller groups active in other cities like Valencia.

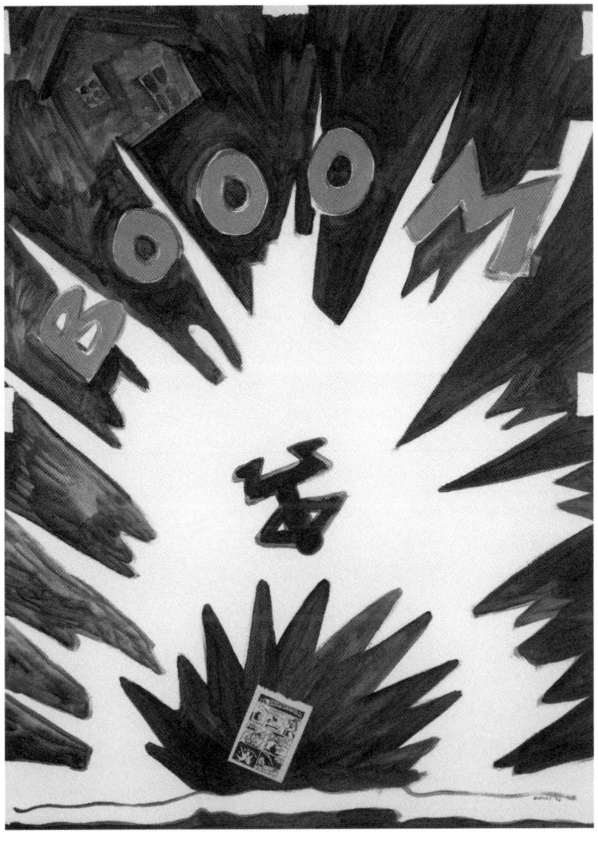

Manolo Quejido, *Boom*, 1976, MACBA Collection, MACBA Foundation. Gift of the Fundación Catalana Occidente, Manolo Quejido, VEGAP, Barcelona, 2012, photo by Tony Coll

The Matesa affair—which opens this essay—is interesting because of the political implications surrounding it. In 1965 the Opus Dei had brought about a change in government in order to control the mechanisms of the political future. Several ministers and important government officials were clearly implicated in Matesa because of their close association with the firm, and because they were directly responsible for the concession of the fraudulent credits. Nevertheless, no one was brought to trial or prosecuted except the businessman. A campaign to dethrone the Opus by exposing the scandal was orchestrated by their opponents in the press, but this only succeeded in having some of its members removed and replaced with others from the same organization. The affair, however, was responsible for exposing the confrontation between the two powerful political factions; and Franco's difficulty in controlling them in the last years of his dictatorship. In June 1973 Admiral Carrero Blanco, an expert in dealing with the various political families and a symbol of continuity of the regime, was appointed Head of Government. But on December 20 of the same year a commando of the Basque terrorist organization, ETA, attempt on his life en route from the church he attended daily in Madrid.[14] In 1977 the artist Ferran Garcia Sevilla presented, at the X Biennale de Paris, the work *Lectura per semblança i contacte de lletres, pedres i colors* (1974), a triptych comprised of the front and first two inside pages of *La Vanguardia*, one of the most prestigious Catalan newspapers, with images of the Admiral's car completely demolished—the explosion was so powerful that the car landed on top of a six-story building. In addition to the images and captions, Garcia Sevilla's analysis centered on the process of how the images were chosen, laid out and displayed, as well as the intent and arbitrariness of the media and censorship. The tragic feeling of the image forms a counterpoint for and complements the irony underlying the work, and takes us back to the *esperpentic* vision of Spanish society. This image has its pictorial correlate in the cartoons of 1974–1976 by the Seville-based artist Manolo Quejido. The uncomfortable climate created by Spain's political situation and its changes is clearly revealed in these works in which Quejido uses a traditional pictorial medium but overlays it with both a biting critical component, and a background personifying the social reality of the day. On September 27, 1975, barely two months before the death of the dictator on November 20, and in the last, dying moments of the regime, the execution of two ETA militants and three members of the FRAP (Frente Revolucionario Antifascista y Patriota) was ordered—the last of those to be condemned to death in the Franco era.

Translated from the Spanish by Selma Margaretten.

14 The assassination of Carrero Blanco hastened the executions by *garrote vil* of the Catalan anarchist Salvador Puig Antich and Georg Michael Welzel. Prior to this, in 1970, the death penalty had been overruled in the Burgos Trial against the ETA militants. Those who had been condemned to death had their sentences commuted in a gesture of "clemency" in the face of international pressure.

When Zofia Kulik and Przemysław Kwiek began their complex experiment to collaborate as KwieKulik in the beginning of the 1970s—analyzing and reflecting on their everyday life, their private and public existence as a couple, and their creative work with socialist concepts—their work was accompanied by political considerations and artistic demands for a new role of the artist in society. The forms of representation of these considerations and the questions they raised related to the status of contemporary art in general, and provided a thematic framework for a particular project that developed over a period of nearly two decades. It is a project that finds few analogies in European art of this period: a couple that reflected its artistic and private existence as a model for an ongoing aesthetic/political action, as a reformist-motivated, praxeological workshop for the education of an emancipatory society within the framework of state socialism.

It was a specific moment in Polish (art) history when Zofia Kulik and Przemysław Kwiek began their artistic partnership and their semiological and analytical reflection on the relationship between societal form and practice, that aimed at the rejuvenation of everyday life under socialism, riddled as it was with bureaucratic routine. The Moscow *nomenklatura* had just put a stop to the cultural warm-up exercises of the modernist "Sweet Sixties" in the post-Stalinist Soviet Empire. The new conservative rigidity of cultural politics after 1970 was, among other things, intended to prevent the reformist ideas embodied in and personified by the Prague Spring from taking a stronger hold. While everywhere else in the Soviet Bloc the neo-avant-gardes that formed were pushed out of the public perception into internal or real emigration, the seemingly liberal political climate and the rhetoric of social reform of the early Gierek years allowed the second generation of the Polish neo-avant-garde, young, pop-spiced late- or post-conceptualists an audience and even a space for public representation within the institutional frameworks of the official art system. Envy of these Polish liberties spread beyond the Warsaw Pact states.

Though these ultimately remained gestures whose symbolic integrationist power was not enough to secure a lasting legitimacy of the system, they had opened up prospects of reformist possibilities and a clearer insight into the insoluble contradiction between the imaginary space of socialist power and the real space of everyday socialist life. These new prospects for KwieKulik, when reconsidering the social role of the artist, seemed to be, at the very least, opening possibilities of actuating educational processes aimed at open and emancipatory structures in both artistic practice and its institutional frameworks.[1] Contrary to most of their co-combatants of the second generation of Polish conceptualists who neglected this perspective and addressed themselves to a rigid formalism, private mythologies, media self-reflection or a hippie, pop-cultural and alternative cynicism,[2] the couple took the call for reform literally, but with a specific task in mind: namely framing the analysis of regimes of form and discourse on the aesthetic as a social and political project. For KwieKulik, the cultural forms of the 1970s were seen and treated as the most distinct symptoms of that which works in the absent something—the social.

KwieKulik's attempts to decipher the 'modi' of the production of form regimes within the structure and dynamics of cultural procedures started in their late years as students at the Academy of Fine Arts in Warsaw; more specifically in the classrooms of Jerzy Jarnuszkiewicz and Oskar Hansen, and against the background of the corrosion of the universalist modernist paradigm of sculpture, architecture, and urban planning with which these teachers had worked. Hansen in particular had criticized modernism's visions of spatial appropriation and purity as incompatible with the reality of a world burdened by increasingly apparent social contradictions.[3] This too had transpired in the so-called West: Conceptual Art and Minimalism were the first high water marks in the deconstruction of Modernist paradigms, which in Poland found its analogy in the first generation of conceptualism in the visual arts that was triggered by linguistic methods of concrete poetics or by a theatrical abstraction in the "Foksal generation." But the method that was rebuked via these strategies was imaginary, staged, and, in the course of its transmission, often fell precisely on the arguments that had led to the critique of modernism in the first place. Hansen's concepts indirectly attacked

[1] This direct address and confrontation with the authorities started with *10 deka papierow Kwieka* (1971). The fact that later, after criticizing the State Visual Art Workshops (PSP) on the occasion of an exhibition in Malmö in 1975, KwieKulik were slapped with a travel ban and the use of their passports restricted for years is not a direct consequence of these critical interventions.

[2] As portrayed in Łukasz Ronduda's recent book, *Polish Art of the 70s.* Warsaw 2009.

[3] For a detailed and in depth contextualization of KwieKulik's practice see Łukasz Ronduda's essay "From Alternations of Red to Alternations of Grey. Art and Politics in the Work of KwieKulik between 1971 and 1987," *KwieKulik. Forma jest faktem spo³ecznym. Form is a fact of society. Guidebook,* BWA Awangarda Gallery, Wroclaw 2009, p. 9–19.

these positions from the viewpoint of a theory of Open Form[4], and the exercises in Jarnuszkiewicz's class triggered the grammar of a modernist-formalist logic through the integrating of everyday and vernacular objects into the artistic practice of sculpture and performative processes.

In the late years at the Academy and early on in their collaboration, Zofia Kulik and Przemysław Kwiek took these challenges—then in friendly communication and cooperation with a larger circle of artists and students, among them J. Wojciechowski, A. Wiśniewski, Pawel Kwiek and K. Zarêbski—and elaborated the critical concepts of their professors into performative extensions. The scores of Activities they had started—juxtaposing and confronting traditional representations of art with objects, situations and relations, including the object and the method of situative collage—was more than a reinterpretation of the formal canons of modernist art. It aimed at demonstrating exactly how the beautiful clarifying of a thing and a change of methodology could transform the aesthetic value and social constellation of a situation.

Unlike in Western conceptual art of the same period (which continues to dominate the international canon and heavily influenced the young Polish generation), and in contrast to the first generation of Polish Conceptualism, KwieKulik's work was, from the outset, less focused on the question of the absence of material and the primacy of the immaterial concept. Instead it focused more on a movement towards new materials and media (which included performative strategies, gesture, fragments, found objects from nature, games, methods from other disciplines, and more) appropriated by the artists within a specific range of formal means of expression. In these years, a grammar and typology of actions developed a certain register that was constitutive for the later development of KwieKulik's visual narrative. Their work traced the paths of transportation and the changes in the requisites of form apparatuses. It described these in terms of a social model and in relation to a specific situation or reality, and tried to make comprehensible their ossification in conventions, or the modulations of their meaning, when it shifted from one mode of usage to another.

Open Form and Beyond

Already with their first collaborative works, like the Hansen-
influenced film *Open Form*, or *Excursion*, a *dérive* through
Warsaw where the artists were equipped with devices for the
mechanical recording of images, KwieKulik charted their actions in real time and interpreted them through a game theory
lens, transcribing them into a symbolic space, abstractly interpreting the subject/object relationship of the constellations. In
Excursion they were interested in the clash of different spatial-
urban situations, the provocation of interpersonal interaction,
and the possibility of linking particular photographic shots
through similar formal elements. Later, in a group of works
they entitled *Visual Games*, scored events were unified by a
generative scheme in which participants were invited to revaluate a specific situation or reality in relation to a social model.
One of the most striking examples of these formalist manoeu-
vres of the designation of everyday life in abstract relations
between objects is *Activities with Dobromierz*. From 1973
onwards, immediately after the birth of their son, KwieKulik
began incorporating their child into their constellational and
semiological arrangements in their apartment and other places.
Their approach was role-less and completely transcended any
conceptual or neo-avant-garde perspective. So dramatically
juxtaposed with the conventions of the new subjectivism, with
the hippie and pop-culture attitudes of their generation, inevitably gave rise to mutual misunderstandings and estrangement
with their milieu.

Considering a more general critique—an insistence that art,
like life itself, is fuelled by formal oppositions and that it is the
power of interpretation that comprises the "control and reality
principle of a society"—KwieKulik experimented with form as
a social agent with which to grasp the essence of the common
in a way that might be called a 'now' of perceptibility of the
ossification of society in the simple, banal facades and spatial
figures in everyday life's occupations and movements in conventions. The artistic interventions they conceived sought to
provoke modulations of meaning, shifting perception and the
creation of terrain for social agency.

A new paradigm of production was implied in this move
towards an artistic understanding of the self, which could be

called (to historicize and mutate a term by Antonio Negri) "social factory" aesthetics.[5] These new ideas had, superficially considered, similarities to Western conceptual thought and practices which looked to expand their contexts to the analysis of social spaces. The fact that KwieKulik established their practice in models of a missing public sphere was both an element and an expression of this "logic of informatization" on which KwieKulik's work in the mid- to late-1970s was based—a linking of physical localities, practice and forms of documentation.

5 See Michael Hardt and Antonio Negri: "Biopolitical Production," *Empire*, MIT Press, Cambridge MA 2000, p. 37–55.

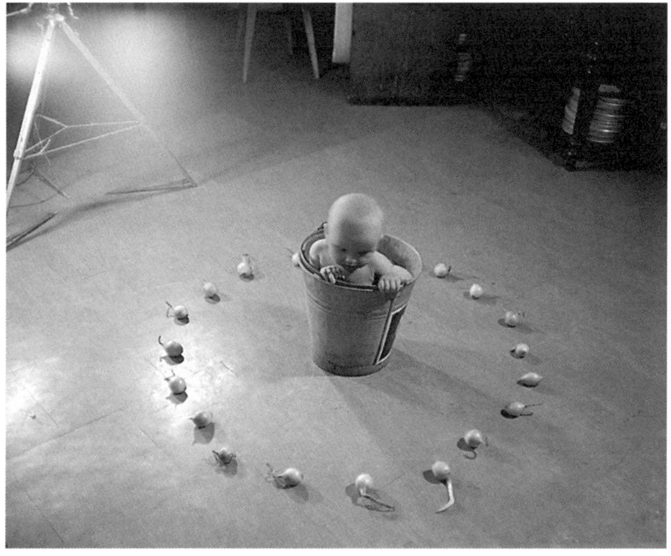

KwieKulik, *Activities with Dobromierz (I)*, from a series of black-and-white and colour photographs, Warsaw 1972–1974. Courtesy of Zofia Kulik for KwieKulik (Przemysław Kwiek and Zofia Kulik)

In late 1975, after they had opened the PDDiU (Studio for Activities, Documentation and Popularisation) in their shared Warsaw apartment, KwieKulik's ongoing negotiations with the institutional system of a state socialist art world was represented in this para-institution that simulated the functions of an official gallery and art documentation centre—which was in fact a living room, atelier, and workshop for the couple and their artistic production. Planning and production of pieces and activities, exhibits, communication and documentation, services for other artists, and finally, product design for the socialist state (which they had to accept in order to earn their living) turned towards explicit themes and had embedded in it an ethos of "honest work". "We were labourers," Kulik later offered in an interview[6]: proletarians who loathed the aristocratic attitude demonstrated by the hero-artists who were celebrated by society and the media and that survived in the habits of some of their neo-avant-garde friends and enemies. In contrast to the positioning of oneself outside the system, Kwiek and Kulik considered themselves artists who interpreted their own private and semi-public domain as the almost metaphysical substance of the political, working with it as a form with which to confront the reality of an institutionalized art system with the singularity of a particular politics. KwieKulik's Activities with the so-called Pot-Boiling works, most of them commissioned by the State Visual Art Workshops (PSP), was perhaps the most provocative variation of this acting out of the contradictions of their practice in relation to (the state-level) modernism's prevailing forms and pseudo-universalistic language of design that represented more than the logic of official art production (in the political, cultural, and administrative sense). According to KwieKulik's definition, Pot-Boiling work was a "job for money, one that was supposed to be creative but in which we felt limited by the strict instructions of the commissioning body". Working on their consecutive commissions, KwieKulik did not cache from their other work but dealt, offensively, with the double situation. In a sort of hybridization of the plates, inscriptions, decorations, and monuments they produced for official commissions, they interacted on and with them using tools, objects, and configurations of their own "independent" aesthetical repertoire. Thus, again in an act of playful signification and transposition, the vocabulary of modernist design liberated itself from its political functionality.

The photographic (and sometimes filmic) notations of these semiotically structured settings and activities initially followed a praxeological score relative to the cybernetic theories they had studied in the Academy of Fine Arts in Warsaw. A systematic act of inscriptions and comments—a seemingly endless discursive reconfiguration and reconsideration of attitudes of the work—deconstructed the hidden strand in the logic of representation, leading from the point where the visual experience of seeing was not knowledge but spectacle, to where the artists were fighting for a social agency of visual art. Furthermore, this approach also entailed seeing artistic work as in no way a random, formative process within society, but as a process in

6 Tomasz Załuski, "Anatomia KwieKulik," *Art & Business*, 11/2008.

which the individual's wishes and desires are confronted with a social agenda embodied by the state institutions.[7] It visualized the opposition between the official status of the artwork and the procedural techniques of the new and emancipatory artistic practice KwieKulik had in mind.

To think politics entails giving consistency to an event; to "faithfully" think through a complex artistic activity "in its own other medium, by its own other art", is, in a sense, suited to understanding whatever there is to understand with whatever elements the observer brings to the task. Understanding this event in its truth is an act of inner ethical labor or *ascesis*, oriented towards a certain kind of self-transformation.

7 See Jean-Luc Nancy, *La comparution. Politique à venir*, Bourgois, Paris 1991, p. 47ff.

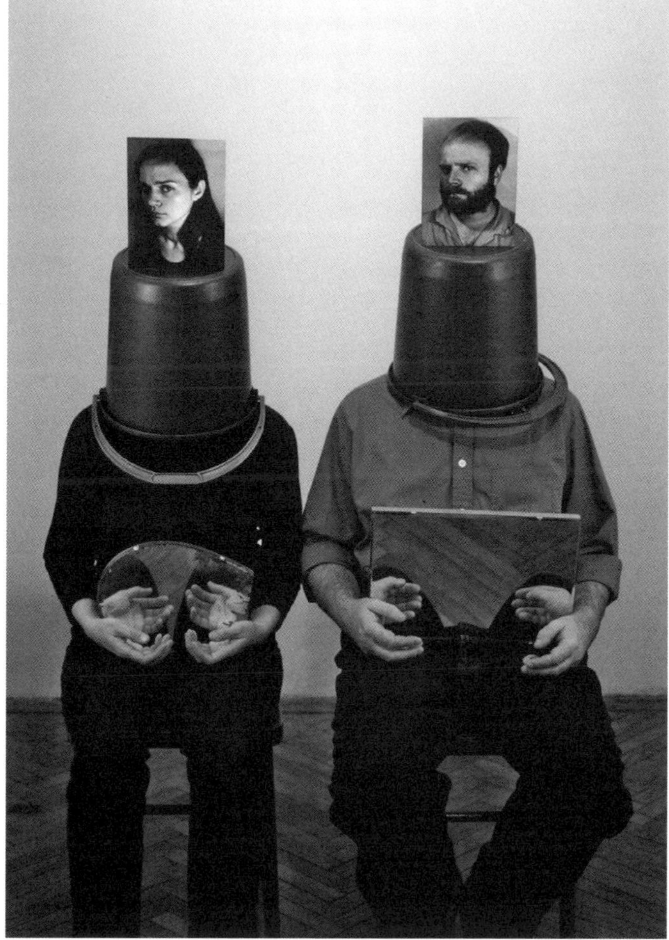

KwieKulik, *Banana and Pome-Grenade; Mercury*, Pracownia Dziekanka, Warsaw, November 24, 1986.
Courtesy of Zofia Kulik for KwieKulik (Przemysław Kwiek and Zofia Kulik)

Expanded Media

KwieKulik's undertakings spanned a vast array of projects, actions and media: producing their own critical media in the form of photographically reproduced postal mailings, the Mail-Outs sent to officials and representatives of the art world critically commenting on its structures; stamps in the tradition of the international mail art movement like *Art on the Run*; conceptual (group) painting (*October Revolution 77* or *Acronyms*); and installation-based sculptural arrangements (*Mediolan* or *Logical Window*). By the same token, collecting and montaging visual evidence of the social as an aesthetic act found another medium in performative and installation-based multi-channel projections. With these expanded cinema-like Activities comprised largely of slide projections, KwieKulik developed a unique and specific format that processed all the fixation work the camera did in documenting the Activities, their surroundings, and the Activities of other artists. In the moment of projection, the juxtaposition of imagery itself became the theme of the installation, which simultaneously brought the perception-dependent status of the image within the realm of physical and cognitive experience. The camera, its actions, and the artists who manipulated the projection devices were also on view as part of the presentation, which occasionally took the form of a political spectacle (like in *Proagit I* and *Proagit II*), or a didactic play, so it was as if the act lifted itself up out of its own perspective and destroyed the illusion of the narrative that it was capable of creating.[8] With these projections, which made use of photography as a model for structural analysis of the creative process and societal formation, KwieKulik raised fundamental issues related to structure, event, and agency, just as their *Visual Games* had privileged discussions on performative, societal, and political identity. In KwieKulik's concepts every perception became an act of creation in which the perception opened as many circuits as there were memory images attracted by this new perception, making of every perception a qualitative multiplicity of space figures, forms and constellations of form. And all of this captured in the theatrical act of presentation focusing on the semiological and structural analysis of the 'social fact' of exchange.

Theatricality and the use of images in the performative presentation and multimedia displays of the 1970s had already

8 See Maurizio Lazzarato, *Videophilosophie*, b_books, Berlin 2002, p. 91ff.

included acts and actions by the authors and various forms
of viewer participation. In the 1980s, mainly in the series
KwieKulik performed in Warsaw at the Dziekanka Gallery,
the staging and setup shifted in methodology, transforming the conceptual and imagological analysis of society and
the politics of the image into an enigmatic political theatre
of form and object. Some of these performances referred to
painful personal experiences, others related to more abstract
concepts, all creating an endless chain of poetic associations.
What distinguishes this imagological mapping from a 'classical' metaphorical or symbolical transformation is its exclusive
orientation toward experimentation in contact with "the real."
KwieKulik's performative theatre did not reproduce an unconscious closed in upon itself; it constructed the unconscious.
It was open and connectable in all of its dimensions; it had
multiple entryways, as opposed to a tracing that always comes
back "to the same."

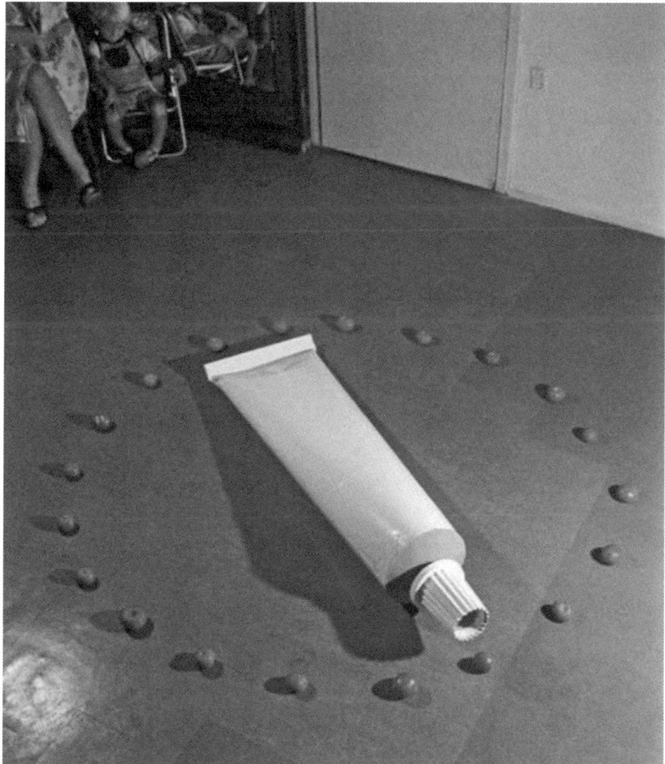

KwieKulik, *Activities with
a Tube*, from a series of
black-and-white and colour
photographs, PDDiU
(Studio of Activities,
Documentation and
Propagation), Warsaw,
August 1975.
Courtesy of Zofia Kulik for
KwieKulik (Przemysław
Kwiek and Zofia Kulik)

This object/subject theatre was characterized by the surfacing of a certain intellectual conduct —in short, the abstention from empiricist or positivist ideologies through insight into their sleeping symbolic structures. One can suggest that this moment represented an unexpected and remarkable dissemination, a second-order operation performed on the field of existing theories and sciences, not in the sense of meta-language to object language but in the sense of an act of inner self-problematization and self-transformation of society performed on art that was conceived to be constituted as merely factual or 'natural' for the purposes of the exercise. As Fredric Jameson once said, 'form is a fact of society'.[9]

This essay was first published in *KwieKulik. Forma jest faktem spo³ecznym. Form is a fact of society. Guidebook*, BWA Awangarda Gallery, Wroclaw 2009, p. 20–29.

[9] Fredric Jameson, *A Singular Modernity: Essay on the Ontology of the Present*, Verso, London/New York 2002, p. 31.

Július Koller / Dialectics of Self-Identification Daniel Grúň

A. I proclaim my absence in the act of exhuming the corpse of art; B. By my absence I proclaim my distrust of modernistic and exhibitionist attempts on exhuming art; C. By my involvement in anti-art I proclaim my detachment from the modernistic exhumations of art; D. I proclaim my involvement by artistic absence at the burial feast of art; E. I announce my absence in the experiments of resurrecting a dead art.[1]

Július Koller (1970)

Art practices established in the arena of institutional critique in the former East of the bipolar division of the world have not been comprehensively explored and still raise many questions and doubts. If the 1960s were characterized by the criticism of institutions that represented social forms standing for restriction and oppression, anti-authoritative statements were not exceptional, neither in the countries of the Socialist camp.[2] De-Stalinization and the criticism directed at the cult of personality after 1956 in these countries wheeled at a different pace, and the revolt against the doctrine of socialist realism was gaining momentum by tying severed bonds with the interwar avant-garde. In the second half of the 1960s, one would find in some countries such as Yugoslavia, Poland, and Czechoslovakia a critique of the modernist tendencies in art, which did not revolve around the Zhdanov Doctrine but rather the mannerisms of modernist styles and image concepts, mostly *Art informel*.[3] I would like to explore some of the ambivalent practices of individual subversion against the centrally controlled state apparatus of the Socialist art institution and to reflect on the political situation after 1968. Parallels drawn between official and unofficial art and their distribution apparata accounted for only one instance of the conceivable interaction between art and politics in real socialism. The particular art scene was not, as such, "definitely divided into two adjacent zones" as Piotr Piotrowski claims.[4] Between "official" and "unofficial" lay zones of interaction, infiltration and significance, not to mention direct participation of artists engaged in the unofficial scene involved

[1] Július Koller mailed this notice on November 19, 1970 to the artists who took part in the unofficial exhibition held in Rudolf Sikora's house that was titled 1st Open Studio on Tehelna street in Bratislava. He also enclosed a telegram containing the following statement *UME? NIE!* (splitting the Slovak word denoting "art" into two parts – ART? NO!). The excerpt from the manifesto in which he distanced himself from the "modernist exhibitions" of his colleagues, introduces his anti-art, which he channeled by using various paintings, text, and performative means of expression and which he started in 1965 with his *Anti-happening* manifesto. The documentation on the exhibition is available in the publication as follows: Marián Murdoch, Dezider Tóth (ed.), *1. Otvorený ateliér*, Sorosovo centrum súčasného umenia – Slovensko, Bratislava 2000, p. 70–75.

[2] Blake Stimson, "What was Institutional Critique?," Alexander Alberro, Blake Stimson (ed.), *Institutional Critique. An Anthology of Artist's Writings*, MIT Press, Cambridge, MA 2009, p. 22.

[3] "In the first half of the 1960s there was a simultaneous development of *Art informel* painting and of work growing out of the critique of painting: object- and action-based art." In: Piotr Piotrowski, *In the Shadow of Yalta. Art and*

in the production of official art. Július Koller gives the impression of a typical proletariat artist yet his plain appearance is more reminiscent of a clerk in the marketing department than an avant-garde artist. Even though he does not fit any of the social schemes of the art scene, his practices challenge the universalist demands applied both to the ideology of the Socialist art institution, as well as to the ethical ideal embraced by the dissident resistance against this ideology.

the Avant-garde in Eastern Europe, 1945-1989, Reaction Books, London 2009, p. 213.

4 Ibid., p. 248–249.

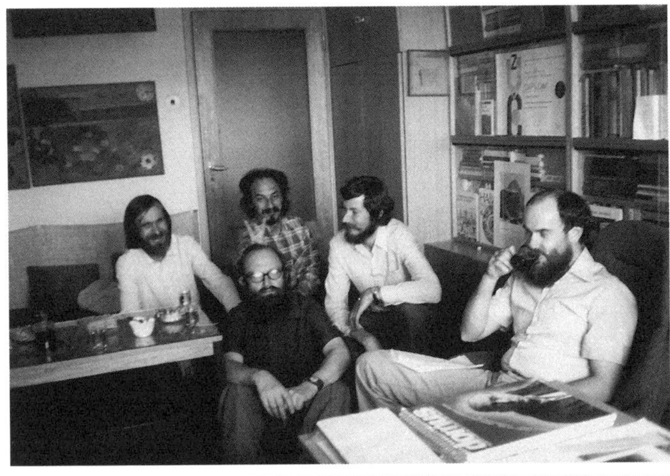

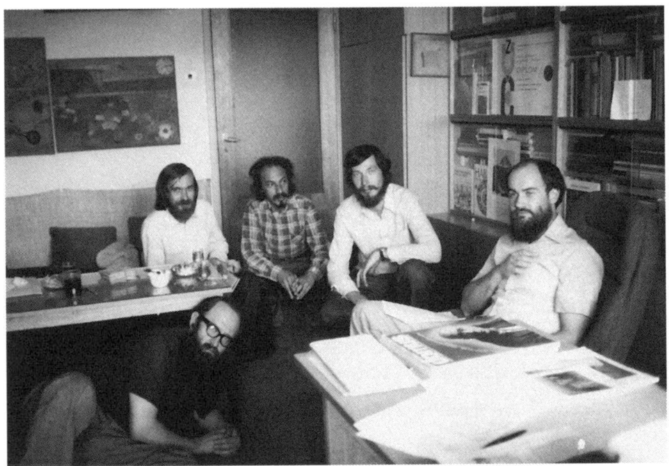

Július Koller, U.F.O. Gallery Ganek, *Organisational Committee*, 1982, photo by Květoslava Fulierová. Property of the Július Koller Society.

One might wonder who Július Koller, the professional academic painter and conceptual artist of the 1970s, really was. With regard to his problematic social identity, the answer is just as inconclusive as the coiled loop of a *Möbius strip* and its "double reference" that represents one of the key discursive features of his works. Besides his concept that "defies *a priori* any institutionalization of art", as pointed out by Georg Schöllhammer, the artist's performative self-identification with the institutional apparatus of Real Socialism transforming into a fictitious society named *Univerzálna Futurologická Organizácia (U.F.O.)* cannot go unnoticed.[5] Numerous documents—voluminous hand-written notes and correspondence from his archive, stratified over the course of many years spent in a prefab flat with the documentation of his projects and the amassed collections of magazine cut-outs—comprise the most convincing reference material of his permanent activity. Privatization of the political discourse and collective mental territory by daily archival work with a whole spectrum of periodicals, be it the daily newspapers or popular magazines, takes place as routine practice rather than after the collapse of collective property, as Boris Groys would suggest.[6]

In his book titled *Obnovenie poriadku / The Restoration of Order*, on the Real Socialism typology in post-1968 Czechoslovakia, the philosopher Milan Šimečka asserts that information control was the fundamental requisite of order: "Information is a neuralgic spot of Real Socialism—the whole organism of the Socialist society reacts alarmingly to each undirected piece of information, immediately enfolds it in conjectures and treats it as a faulty signal in the system of total control. This sensitivity has developed over years of following the newspapers, radio, and television. It often took as little as an unusual photograph, article edit or absence of a familiar phrase in the usual place to stir up speculation."[7] This is where Július Koller's incursion with his "poetic" lingo takes place. Thus, taking into account his continuous commentary, debunking and demystifying linguistic conventions rooted in the institutionalized art discourse, his work challenges the system of total control. Long-term situational actions such as *Univerzálne-kultúrne Futurologické Operácie / Universal-Cultural Futurological Operations (U.F.O.)* were performed by Július Koller as contact with non-identifiable objects and phenomena. His "culture of life" proceeds without detachment from day-to-day reality, and represents a return of the fantasmatic dimension, repressed and ousted beyond the symbolic field of Real Socialism.[8]

5 Georg Schöllhammer, "Július Koller: Cosmologist, Skeptic—and Player," Petra Hanáková, Aurel Hrabušický (ed.), *Július Koller. Science-Fiction Retrospective*, Slovenská národná galéria, Bratislava 2010, p. 61.

6 Boris Groys, "Privatisations, or Artificial Paradises of Post-Communism," *Art Power*, MIT Press, Cambridge, MA 2008, p. 167.

7 Milan Šimečka, *Obnovenie poriadku*, Archa, Bratislava 1990 (orig. publ. Index, Köln 1979), p. 52.

8 Slavoj Žižek, "The Fetish of the Party," *The Universal Exception: Selected Writings*, Continuum, London 2006, p. 91.

Koller's institutional critique is evasive, as it pertains to both the "unofficial" art scene and official art with its bureaucratic production mechanism that he confronts with his own existential non-identification. Artists' archives are a testimony to his permanent process of demystifying the Socialist institution of art, in which he publicly participated in his own way and which he could not escape. Koller produced dialectical language games that he distributed as notices—text cards with stamped letters, manifestoes and conceptual statements proliferated via mail. His frequently mailed "post-communication" replaces the gallery space and effectively reaches a wide spectrum of addressees. The use of anagrams and word games makes room for the linguistic expression of repressed phantasms. The games of verbal mechanisms of denial and identification use a tautological shift of positional demarcation and self-identification. Dialectical linguistic operations confront the field of subjective activities with the field of objective and real facts. Koller created them in the spirit of dialectical materialism to debunk the false consciousness and to demystify the social hypocrisy in Socialist Czechoslovakia.

Now we return to the exhibition *1. Otvorený ateliér / 1st Open Studio* to clarify the context for Koller's declarative method. What was a collective exhibition of avant-garde proponents held to express a stance against restrictions imposed on exhibition making, was also a reaction against the pressures which were altering the cultural and social landscape in the country after the occupation of 1968. Several prominent Czech and Slovak avant-garde artists of the 1960s were invited to the venue—Alex Mlynarčík, who had already presented his works in the Paris Biennial and was renowned for his contact with Pierre Restany and Nouveau Réalisme; or Jindřich Chalupecký, a respected authority in art criticism. Koller's contribution to the exhibition mirrored the spirit of his dialectic nature: he nailed two painted notice boards resembling real ones on a building with flaking plaster. One read POZOR, PADÁ OMIETKA / BEWARE, PLASTER FALLING OFF, the other PAMIATKOVÝ OBJEKT / HISTORICAL MONUMENT. Both pseudo-notices that simulated regular notice boards placed on dilapidated buildings signify the "cultural situation" of an exhibition site with a clear connotation: avant-garde is merely a relic with the plaster falling off.

Koller's position is a unique one, because of his conscious relativism opposing the quasi-dissident character of a modern artist. Jindřich Chalupecký's thesis on the ethical dilemma of a modern artist in Socialism absolutizes the necessity to autonomize art. Artist must choose between the roles of a pro-regime promoter and resign to art, or follow through with his/her artistic mission vows and act ethically on them.[9] Koller did not dedicate himself exclusively to the unofficial scene; he also sent his works to various official regime exhibitions. As he proclaimed in his own words, he did not perceive his work as art but rather as a life culture: "My current work is a professional expression of skepticism towards painting (painting practices), the resignation of the visual (traditionally modern) style and the personal painting endorsement. It refers to the illusion in its illusiveness and the illusion of style that represents only an illusionary subjective world that ignores objective facts. My work (…) is a culture that harnesses the painting craft to discuss and meditate on life and culture. It is a philosophy that does not use words to express itself, but visual art. My "painting" inquires about the significance of painting in the present day."[10]

In the official exhibitions of the 1970s and 1980s, he presented his simple latex paintings that depicted an urban landscape in line with the widely distributed postcards and popular magazine reproductions. Realist landscape paintings styled after comic strips, monumental sights such as the Prague or Bratislava castles, the Red Army monument in Banska Bystrica, environmental and development issues, or various features in the Slovak landscape—all of these aspects projected Koller's official profile. He put his paintings up for review to the selection committees for the state-run company "Dielo" (Artwork), which was administered by the Slovak Fund of Visual Artists where Koller was registered as a free-lance artist from 1972, after his candidacy in the "elite" organization of Socialist art, the Association of Visual Artists, was revoked. No matter how trivial selling paintings via a state-dedicated enterprise might seem, even with respect to securing a sufficient, if not only supplemental income, it entails an elaborated intervention in(to) the economic mechanism of the state institution. On one level, this intervention presents a consistent reflection of the bureaucratic apparatus, tracking administrative correspondence and detailed recordkeeping of sold and unsold paintings.

9 Jindřich Chapupecký, "Osud jedné generace (1972)," *Cestou – necestou*, Nakladatelství H&H, Jinočany 1999, p. 154. The essay was originally published in Notiazario di Arte Contemporanea 1972, č. 10, Octobre, p. 10–14.

10 Hand-written text on paper card, signed J. Koller, 1977. Archive of the Slovak National Gallery.

He relays the monstrous bureaucratic apparatus into his own
pseudo-official documentation and often targets it directly in
his conceptual projects. Koller's critique of the centralized state
institution and total control of artistic operations by means of
his total life work occupies the other side of the spectrum. It is
the self-historicization that is perceived to be a model of institutional critique in the former Eastern European countries.[11]
Koller's archive is more than a collection of oddities and obscu-
rities published in the mass media: it is also a particularly constructed arrangement of self-historicization; a labyrinth pieced
together from innumerable attempts to define and proclaim the
principles of his own work.

[11] Zdenka Badovinac,
*Prekinjene Zgodovine
/ Interrupted Histories*,
Moderna galerija, Ljubljana
2006, pages unnumbered.

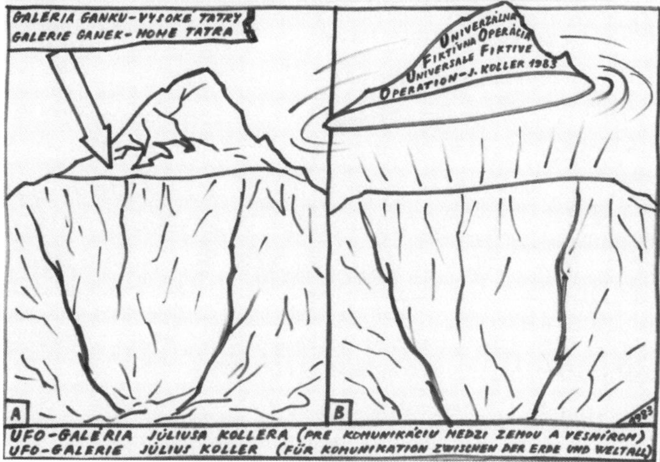

Július Koller, U.F.O. Gallery
Ganek, 1983, marker
drawing on paper, 21x29,8.
Property of Květoslava
Fulierová.

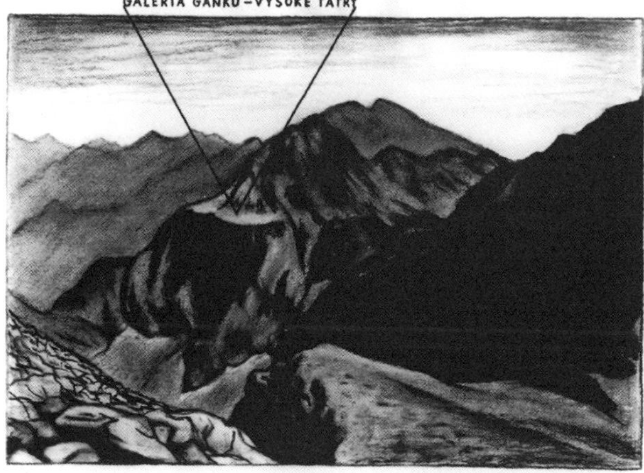

Július Koller, U.F.O. Gallery
Ganek, 1982, drawing on
paper photographed and
sticked on paper, 21x30.,
Property of the Július Koller
Society.

The fictitious gallery project titled *U.F.O. Galéria – Galéria Ganku, Vysoké Tatry / U.F.O Gallery Ganek, High Tatras* best conveys the evasive parallelism of Koller's institutional critique. The project's concept originated in 1971. Initially it took the form of a preserved natural history magazine, *Vysoké Tatry / High Tatras,* named after well-known Slovak mountains, to visualize the situation in which a natural setting transforms into a 'U.F.O. Gallery'. Later, between 1980 and 1983, Koller laid out statutory principles and convened an organizational board to propose an exhibition plan for the fictitious gallery.[12] The founding articles of the gallery consistently imitate the jargon used by the administrative and bureaucratic machinery of a state art institution and create the impression of a real-life project. The discursive wording in the gallery's statutes follows the premise that the institution's own account makes for the most reliable source of understanding its own totalitarian character. The Czech literary critic Petr Fidelius proposed an analysis of language used by the Communist regime and showed that this language reflected a specific ideology constructed as a cohesive system rather than the real world. He asserts that in Real Socialism a mechanical relationship between words and reality to which they refer is established—notions are reduced in content; they become void; they intermingle and fuse until they turn into interchangeable codes for one and the same thing.[13] For this reason, the linguistic aspect conveyed in the inauguration of the fictitious gallery stands in deliberate contrast to its aim, which was to facilitate the contact of alternative subjective participations dedicated to the communication with unidentified phenomena. The *Gallery Ganek* project might seem escapist to some, but its double reference to reality and fiction forms a parallel dimension for free thinking.

Translated from the Slovak by Jana Krajnakova.

12 Organisational and advisory board of the U.F.O. Gallery – Gallery Ganek was founded in 1981; its members were Milan Adamčiak, Pavol Breier, Igor Gazdík, Peter Meluzin and Július Koller. Documentation from the archive of the Július Koller Society.

13 Petr Fidelius, *Řeč komunistické moci*, Triáda, Praha 1998 (orig. publ. as samizdat 1978, 1989), p. 196.

Gorgona / Beyond Aesthetic Reality Branka Stipančić

Gorgona was a group of colleagues and friends that was active in Zagreb from 1959 to 1966. Painter Josip Vaništa headed Gorgona, whose members extended to painters Julije Knifer, Marijan Jevšovar and Djuro Seder; art historians Radoslav Putar, Matko Meštrović and Dimitrije Bašičević Mangelos; and sculptor Ivan Kozarić and architect Miljenko Horvat. The group took its name from Mangelos's poem "Gorgona," published in 1959 in the portfolio *Eulalia*. Alongside their individual work in painting, sculpture and criticism, the members of the group collaborated on a wide array of joint-actions: they managed the exhibition venue Studio (G for Gorgona) in Zagreb, they proposed a number of projects, evolved various forms of artistic communication, and published the anti-magazine *Gorgona*.

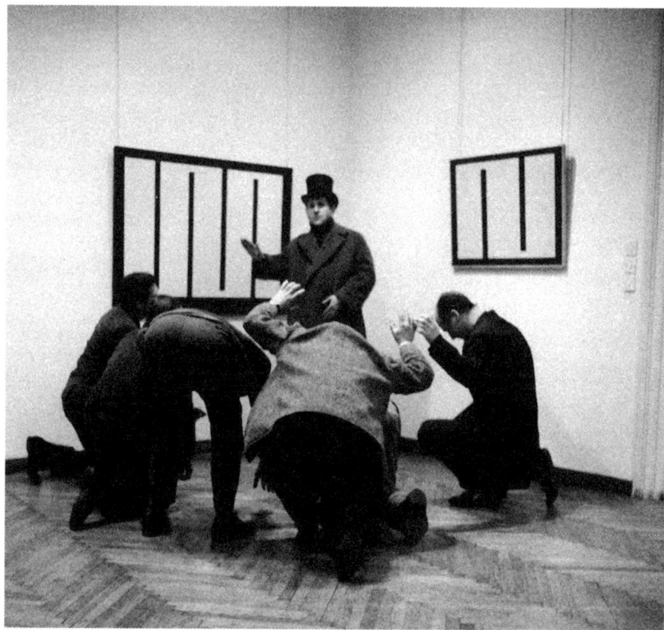

Members of Gorgona at Julije Knifer´s exhibition in the Gallery of Contemporary Art, Zagreb, 1966, photo by Branko Balić. Courtesy of the Institute of Art History, Zagreb

"Gorgona was not a painters' group," claims Josip Vaništa in his *Notes*. "Its goals were set beyond aesthetic reality. Reticence, passivity, indifference were above the ironic denial of the world we lived in. No importance was attached to actual works, activities were extremely simple: group walks in the city surroundings, a committee inspection of spring, as Putar used to say jokingly, ordinary conversations outdoors."[1] What drew them together? "It was the risk, the absurd, the striving for what is hidden. An interest in something beyond painting."[2] Today their work would be described as conceptual rather than aesthetic. In the spirit of the late 1950s and early 1960s, Gorgona turned to neo-Dadaist trends as well as to the reductionism and philosophy of Zen Buddhism. Many members emphasized that their works were anti-paintings. Julije Knifer believed that a form of anti-painting could be achieved by a reduction of the visual content through the use of minimal means and extreme rhythm-generated contrasts: he always painted the same sign, using meandering black and white vertical and horizontal lines. His (approach to) painting is based on categories of continuous flow, rhythm, endless patience, asceticism and, as he himself once put it, "non-development." Repeating a single motif since the time of Gorgona until today, he has become a modern Sisyphus, closer to existentialism than the neo-constructivism of the "New Tendencies" exhibition series[3] with which he began exhibiting. Marijan Jevšovar demonstrated his anti-aesthetics with his *Gray Surfaces* (1961-1962), where he degraded the canvas with repeated coats of paint to achieve a lifeless, dirty gray surface. Gorgona witnessed the first attempt to "dematerialize" a work of art that Josip Vaništa pioneered. After a series of monochrome surfaces crossed only by a single line he realized, in 1964, a work in text only:

"Landscape format canvas/ width 180 cm / height 140 cm / the entire surface white/ through the center runs a silver line (width 180 cm, height 3 cm)."

Mangelos also negated painting using various techniques, one of which was the *anti-peinture* series. With the statements "Negation de la peinture" written over scratched-out or blacked-out painted reproductions, Mangelos continued a long line of negation characteristic of 20th century art, from Marcel Duchamp through Renée Magritte to Marcel Broodthaers, rejecting painting as simply not stimulating enough. Characteristically, Mangelos never negated painting using painting as the medium; he intervened in reproductions and his negation appears conceptual, negating the very idea

[1] Josip Vaništa, *Notes* (Knjiga zapisa), Moderna galerija and Kratis, Zagreb 2001, p. 294.

[2] Ibid, p. 296.

[3] Cf. Ješa Denegri, "Erkundung des Objektiven," *spring-erin* 1/2011, and Armin Medosch, "Overcoming Alienation," in this volume.

of painting. The reproductions employed spanned various
styles and periods, from Thomas Gainsborough to the Croatian
painter Josip Račić. The last of them Mangelos entitled *anti-
hommage à Račić*, as an ironic aside about Croatian art whose
most revered protagonists of the early 20th century lagged considerably behind the practitioners and developments seen in the
larger international art-scape.

This tendency to negate the aesthetic properties of art
(work), striving for a monochromatic experience, this need for
a "ground zero," brought the members of Gorgona together
and close to artists from around the world: the Zero Group,
Azimuth, Fluxus, John Cage and others with whom Gorgona
enjoyed direct or indirect contact.

Like Fluxus, Gorgona opened the question of what could be
art. It promoted an open atmosphere, a veritable cult of freedom, something its members discussed with great enthusiasm
even years later. Gorgona was playful, funny; and it strove to
redefine the term art, seeking art that would not result in objects but rather in concepts and experiences.

In 1963, Ivan Kožarić proposed a "collective work," the project *Cutting Sljeme*, a semicircular incision into the mountain
near Zagreb, as well as a set of instructions for a project that
involved making plaster casts of the interior of the heads of all
Gorgona members, the interiors of several cars, studio apartments, trees, even an entire park—in general, of all of the city's
important hollows.

Gorgona approached the concept of exhibition as a separate
and distinct phenomenon, something that was fully to evolve
in conceptual art. In addition to other projects, Vaništa mailed
invitations to everyone on the gallery's mailing list with (just)
the text "You are kindly invited to attend" (1962), in a dada-like
provocation without details as to where, when and what.

The anti-magazine *Gorgona*, founded by Josip Vaništa in
1961, was a particularly important group activity. It was called
an anti-magazine in accordance with the members' affinity for
anti-art, anti-drama and anti-film, but also because the review
did not contain any art-related information. Gorgona held a
special place among magazines published at the time. While
artists' magazines such as Dieter Roth's *Spirale* (1953–1964)
published lavish reproductions of woodcuts and linotypes
of famous artists, or the more modest Spoerri's *Material*

(1957–1959) published visual poetry, and Manzoni's and Castellani's *Azimuth* showed work by various artists, each issue of *Gorgona* was the conceptually unified work of a single artist, an individual artwork in its own right, conceived in close relation to the medium. In the early 1960s Gorgona proved to be a forerunner in what was later described as magazine as artwork," after Germano Celant's term "book as artwork." *Gorgona* contained and communicated primary rather than secondary art content, with conceptual works presented in a cool, sophisticated layout scheme. Between 1961 and 1966 eleven issues were published. In the first issue (1961) Vaništa reproduced identical photographs of a plain shop-window, laying emphasis on the emptiness and monotony of the motif by repeating it across all nine pages, similar to the photographs in Ed Ruscha's book *Twenty-six Gasoline Stations* (1962). But while Ruscha's photographs function as a "collection of facts," Vaništa's *Gorgona* highlights the immobility, drabness, even irony of and in relation to the expected reception-experience. Two of Vaništa's *Gorgona* issues deal with emptiness: in one issue he inserted a card with basic information on the magazine between its blank pages, another consisted solely of a photograph of the front page between the covers. Like Manzoni in *Life and Works* (1963), the artist was entering the sphere of entropy and the concept of physical non-entity. Other issues of *Gorgona*, produced by Knifer, Kožarić, Jevšovar and others, were equally radical both in their approach to content and awareness of the medium.

Gorgona's members were highly educated and maintained extremely high standards in intellectual discourse. The ties the group established with the international avant-garde circles—particularly in connection with the anti-review *Gorgona*—further served to confirm both their vision and their ability to recognize kindred spirits. Dieter Roth, Victor Vasarely and playwright Harold Pinter realized works in *Gorgona* magazine, while the projects of Piero Manzoni and Enzo Mari, among others, were never executed. The body of Gorgona correspondence contains letters from Manzoni, Lucio Fontana, Robert Rauschenberg, Otto Piene and others that express their admiration and support. Through New York publisher and bookseller George Wittenborn, *Gorgona* was included in the Museum of Modern Art in New York library as early as 1968.

Although little was known in Croatia about the Gorgona group during their prolific and most active years, they lay the foundations of virtually all important components of the art structure: they formed a group of spiritually kindred artists, set up their own exhibition space, founded their own anti-magazine and established contacts with artists abroad. Communist regimes were notorious for not tolerating private galleries or publications, and most private initiatives in politics, business or culture were suppressed. Nevertheless, there were loopholes and exceptions that could, with cunning and determination, be employed and exploited. The Gorgona group used a picture framer's shop to mount exhibitions. They organized the printing of the *Gorgona* anti-magazine themselves, bypassing the censors that appeared less strict there, than in other communist countries where illegal publications led to prison sentences. As a group and a force, they constituted an oasis that realized and enabled unhindered work; at the same time Gorgona was an isolated ghetto whose members had no impact on other artists until their exhibition in 1977 at the Gallery of Contemporary Art in Zagreb (today the Museum of Contemporary Art), after which many artists came to embrace them as role models.

OHO / An Experimental Microcosm on the Edge of East and West
Ksenya Gurshtein

An Experimental Microcosm on the Edge of East and West

The history of OHO—a Slovene collective that fluctuated between being a broader cultural movement and a tight-knit group in the years 1965–1971—encapsulates perfectly, if on a miniature scale, most of the possible responses to the historical conditions to which this book gives greater exposure and theoretical grounding.[1] Emerging in a place considered peripheral to the hotbeds of neo-avant-garde activity, OHO produced a body of work whose diversity and inventiveness—encompassing drawing, object-making, poetry, book and journal publication, manifesto writing, newspaper design, comic strips, urban performances, Land Art, photography, film, installations, and communal life—make it anything but marginal.

In large part, this work responded to the realities of contemporary Yugoslavia, whose leaders sought a socialist society different from the Soviet model, yet demanded, if somewhat less stringently, a similar kind of total ideological buy-in from it's citizens. At the same time, the work also responded to both local avant-garde histories and to the political and cultural shifts of the 1960s whose impact transcended national borders. Indeed, OHO's history allows us to speak of the international connections that experimental artists from outside the traditional centers of the art world forged before the days of globalization, even as we also note the communal and inward-looking nature of art collectives, particularly common in Eastern Europe, which emerged under repressive regimes and in the absence of art markets.

OHO's ties to its local avant-garde roots can be established through its interest in the 1920s publications *Zenit* (published in Belgrade and Zagreb) and especially *Tank* (published in Ljubljana and banned after two issues). Looking at these historical precedents allows us a richer understanding of the centrality of print media to OHO's early projects. Just as they did in the 1920s, the home-grown publications of the 1960s gave their creators a way to participate in an otherwise distant international conversation. Even more importantly, these publications emphasized the critical discourses that framed the group's

[1] While the conceptual framing of OHO's intellectual history offered in this text is my own, my work owes a great debt to the research (including precise chronologies) and analysis offered in the histories of the group written by Slovene art historians Tomaž Brejc and Igor Zabel. For their most extensive texts, see Tomaž Brejc, *Oho: 1966–1971*, Študentski Kulturni Center, Ljubljana 1978; Igor Zabel and Moderna Galerija Ljubljana, *Oho: Retrospektiva = Eine Retrospektive = a Retrospective*, Revolver, Frankfurt am Main 2007, second edition. I am also deeply grateful to the former members of OHO—Marko Pogačnik, Iztok Geister, Naško Križnar's, Tomaž Šalamun, Andraž Šalamun, Milenko Matanović, David Nez, Matjaž Hanžek, and Tomaž Brejc—who allowed me to interview them in 2009-2010. My conversations with them were essential to my research.

activities in all its iterations.[2] Art and its theorization were intertwined for the group, as were works that explored ideas across multiple media. The group's neologism of a name comes from putting together the Slovene words for "eye" (*oko*) and "ear" (*uho*), and such "mediality," as the group called it, forms yet another link to the ethos of both the historic avant-gardes and OHO's international artistic contemporaries.

In its first iteration, even before the name for the group existed, the future OHO was ushered in by the 1965 collaborative publication of poetry and drawings two high-school students from the town of Kranj, Marko Pogačnik and Iztok Geister. Their journal was juvenilia, but its creation radicalized its makers when local school and Communist party authorities reacted to it in a heavy-handed and repressive way. Afterwards, Pogačnik and Geister, along with like-minded students whom they encountered in Ljubljana in 1966 (and only a couple of whom were studying art), became sensitive to the often dormant but ever-present political potentiality of work that defied accepted aesthetic norms or, more importantly, tried to redefine the function or boundaries of the aesthetic.

OHO's work tried to do just that. Influenced by an internally contradictory but potent combination of existentialism, semiotics, philosophy of language, and anti-consumerism, OHO's early work set itself the goals of imagining—in a way that was intellectually provocative, if not long sustainable—new relationships between humans and everyday objects, as well as readers and text. The philosophical term that came to denote this desire to liberate objects from having to be useful and text from having to have meaning is *reism.*

2 For information on *Zenit* and *Tank*, see Dubravka Djurić and Miško Šuvaković (ed.), *Impossible Histories: Historical Avant-Gardes, Neo-Avant-Gardes, and Post-Avant-Gardes in Yugoslavia, 1918–1991*, MIT Press, Cambridge/ London 2003, p. 298–302 and 308.

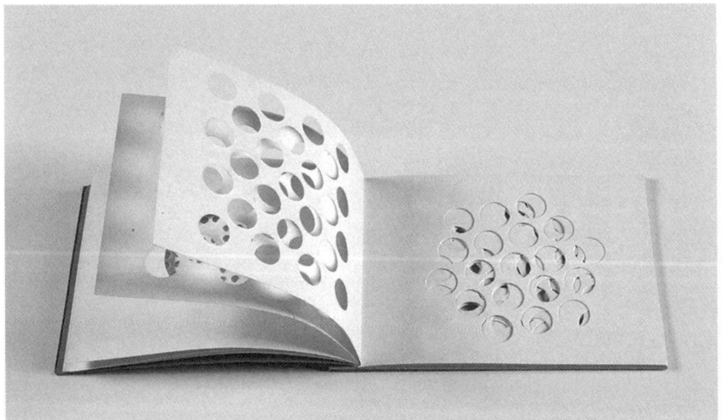

OHO Group, Marko Pogačnik, *Item Book*, 1966, Courtesy of Moderna galerija, Ljubljana

Perhaps the single object that best captures the spirit of *re-ism* is Marko Pogačnik's *Item Book of 1966,* the first in the OHO Editions series. Its status as "article" (the word is used here in its "item of goods" sense) positions it as a new kind of thing, between a totally utilitarian object and a reified work of art. It thus tries to shake off the constraints of existing discourse on the ontology of things, but remains, at the same time, obsessed with the functions of language, making the holes in its pages into the basic units of a "text" that visualizes both the yearning for the complete (literal) transparency of language and the possibility that it is nothing but an opaque string of (again literally) empty signifiers.

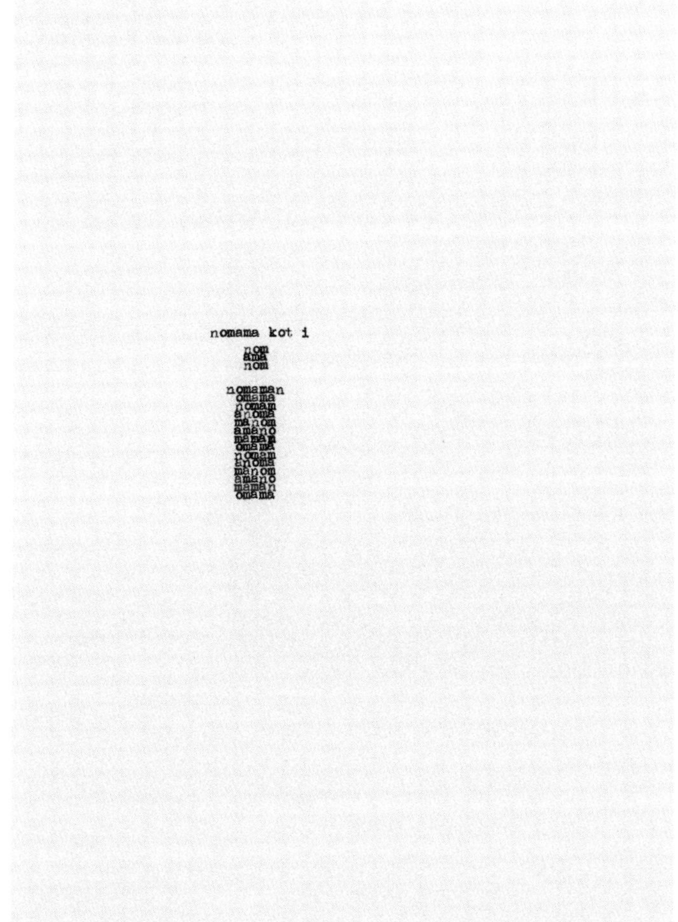

OHO Movement, Matjaž Hanžek, *Nomama as letter i*, 1967, Courtesy of Moderna galerija, Ljubljana

Print media were central to OHO's earliest period, largely
for practical reasons. The publications *Tribuna* and *Problemi*
provided the fora where the young radicals could put their
ideas into circulation, as well as publish foreign thinkers.[3] At
the same time, the self-published OHO Editions books, cards,
and boxes—objects that still strike one today with their power
of estrangement from the ordinary—were a way to bypass any
need for official support of experimental literary and visual
forms. Over time, the language OHO first developed in print—
its references, special vocabulary, and neologisms—began to
demarcate a separate, private sphere that spanned multiple media, as in the case of Matjaž Hanžek's *Nomama* poems, which
became an eponymous 1967 film by Naško Križnar, the group's
prolific filmmaker.

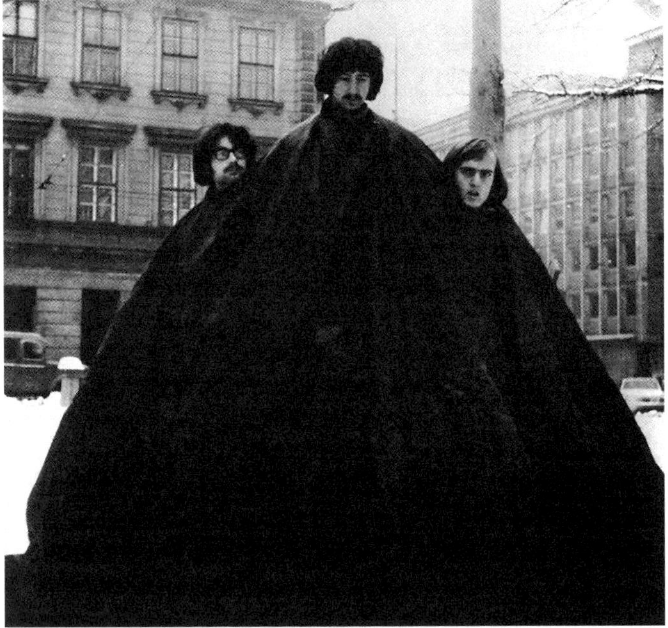

OHO Movement, Milenko
Matanović, *Mt Triglav*,
1968, Courtesy of Moderna
galerija, Ljubljana

Dissemination of its ideas in the culture at large had been
from the start OHO's stated goal for the creation of its objects,
and films, even if they often met with indifference or negative responses. In 1968, the special world OHO had created
spilled out briefly into public space with actions that took place
in Ljubljana's Zvezda park. These culminated in December
of 1968 with *Triglav*, a witty performance staged by Milenko

---

3 Particularly important
to OHO's creativity was
Tribuna, the student newspaper of the University of
Ljubljana for which several
OHO members were edi-
tors and contributors. One
can appreciate the intel-
lectual breadth that reading
the newspaper offered
when one considers that in
1967 alone, the newspaper
published translations of
texts by Bertrand Russell,
Francis Picabia, Bob Dylan,
Witold Gombrowicz Roland
Barthes, Pyotr Kropotkin,
and Julia Kristeva, as well
as reviews of contemporary
Austrian literature and
French films, articles on the
psychedelic revolution and
anti-Vietnam War protests,
and analytical texts on literary and social theory.

Matanović and David Nez (an American studying art in
Ljubljana) together with Drago Dellabernardina. Mt. Triglav
is Slovenia's tallest mountain and a symbol of national identity whose name means "three-headed" (because it has three
peaks). Taking this as their cue, the young men used ladders
and cloth to arrange themselves so that their bodies became
the mountain, their heads forming the three "peaks." Still
channeling the spirit of *reism*, the performance "liberated" the
mountain by using a pun to make visible the linguistic sleights
of hand that can turn the literal into the abstract and vice versa.
The action, moreover, had an obliquely political overtone in the
idea of self-identification with a symbol of national identity in
an absurd visual form and brought such ambiguous commentary into public space.

This, however, was the greatest extent of OHO's ambivalent
engagement with politics.[4] In an environment that constantly
threatened to politicize any gesture (despite the fact that
Yugoslavia was, relatively speaking, far less repressive than
the Warsaw Pact countries of Eastern Europe "proper"), OHO
appears to have deemed it most worthwhile to use art to make
politics visible only negatively, by acting *as if* it were not a
shaping force. In taking its art to the streets in 1968, OHO was
engaging with the discourses of the global New Left, but this
engagement also extended to the period when OHO moved
into the privacy of rural nature. The ambivalence of the New
Left's understanding of the relationship between social change
and art was articulated in the writings of Herbert Marcuse,
and OHO seems to have become a living embodiment of such
ambivalence.

In the 1968 *An Essay on Liberation,* Herbert Marcuse de-
ployed the term "new sensibility"—a term the critic Tomaž
Brejc would be using in 1969 to describe OHO's first prominent
exhibition, *Pradedje,* which took place in Zagreb and presented
the collective as one now focused exclusively on visual art.
The works in the exhibition exposed the tension between the
conflicting positivist and metaphysical tendencies that defined
much of OHO's existence after its earliest period. While some
works were still rooted in *reism,* several works seemed already
to share the interest in raw materiality found in *arte povera*,
to which OHO members had a personal connection through
Tomaž Šalamun, the older brother of Andraž Šalamun and the

4 OHO's founding member,
Marko Pogačnik, performed
more overtly political
gestures by staging one-
man protests against the
Vietnam War, but because
these were not aimed at the
Yugoslav political regime,
they did not carry the same
risks as gestures that
could be construed by the
authorities as disturbing the
peace at home.
For an alternative view on
OHO's political engage-
ment, see Miško Šuvaković,
*Skrite Zgodovine Skupine
OHO [Hidden Histories of
the OHO Group], Zavod
P.A.R.A.S.I.T.E., Ljubljana
2009.* Šuvaković argues
that OHO participated
in creating "countercul-
tural urban gestures of
resistance",born of the
"urban and non-directional
politicality of youth on the
Ljubljana scene". While
this was true in 1968,
Šuvaković's argument does
not address OHO's ambiva-
lent relationship towards
politics that became
increasingly apparent from
1969 on.

curator of the exhibition, who had lived in Paris and Rome a
few years earlier.

Pradedje marked a key shift from a broader movement in
which individuals worked together on specific projects to a
group in which four members—Milenko Matanović, David
Nez, Andraž Šalamun, and Marko Pogačnik (who had returned
from a year of military service)—worked as a unit that focused
on exhibition-making, occasionally publishing documentation
of interventions in nature that became a big part of the group's
output. These latter works shared philosophical and formal
affinities with certain other Land Art practices, such as that
of Richard Long, whose work the Slovenes knew. At the same
time, OHO's group dynamic in which every new work became
a new experiment helped it retain its singular character.

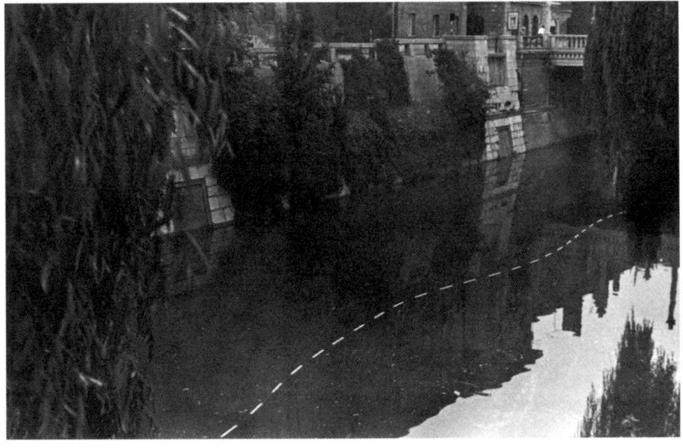

OHO Group, Milenko
Matanović, *Snake*, 1969,
Courtesy of Moderna
galerija, Ljubljana

What emerged more strongly than ever in OHO's work in
1969, when the group started to invent what Tomaž Brejc would
call "transcendental Conceptualism," was a tension between
arbitrariness or chaos and systematicity. In some pieces—like
Milenko Matanović's *Snake* (1969)—this produced work that,
in the true spirit of Conceptualism, elegantly made invisible forces, in this case the current of a river, visible. What's
more, such work could potentially "make it" in the Western art
world, as evidenced by OHO's participation in the exhibition
Information at MoMA and a show at Aktionsraum 1 in Munich,
both in 1970.

For reasons both personal and philosophical, however, OHO
members decided that existing in the separate, commercial

sphere of the Western art market was not for them. In late 1970, at Marko Pogačnik's urging, the group tried to organize its very existence into a complex systematic attempt of fully merging art and life (fig. 5 shows the kinds of elaborate experiments and mental constructs OHO devised), but the effort quickly proved untenable.

The subsequent careers of OHO members, however, do bear out their commitments to exploring the ultimate avant-garde question of the ways in which creative interventions can bring meaningful change into the world. Of the four core members of OHO's last incarnation, Marko Pogačnik led a commune in the village of Šempas for decades and is now engaged with healing the Earth through lithopuncture; David Nez works as an art therapist while also continuing to paint and create collages; Milenko Matanović founded The Pomegranate Center outside of Seattle (U.S.A.), which helps communities design and build common public spaces; and only Andraž Šalamun remained true to a traditional career in art as a painter—his works can be found in major museum collections in Slovenia. OHO, moreover, has been an influence first on young artists in Serbia, including the group of actionists from which Marina Abramović emerged in the early 1970s, then on the artists of the IRWIN group in the 1980s, and on a whole generation of young Slovene artists since the 1990s, having gained in the mid-1990s the status of the germinal artistic development in post-war Slovene history.

What remains now is to add OHO to an expanded map of global neo-avant-garde and conceptual tendencies and recognize the richness and unusual significance of its history. Despite its brief existence, the group, living at the seam of Cold War East and West, managed to make visible in a hybrid manner inner tensions that characterized both systems. Like so many artists in Eastern Europe, OHO opted for a collective practice to pursue a low-tech, "intermedia" aesthetic that privileged the creation of a common mental space and alternative modes of behavior over the development of a personal style, the lack of an art market and "art world" serving in this regard as both a constraint and a source of freedom.

At the same time, the focus on local realities was inflected by a deep curiosity about the West, as well as earlier avant-gardes, and a desire to be in dialogue with both. What's remarkable about this dialogue—its peripheral location being, again, a mixed blessing—was the intensity and earnestness with which the group engaged ideas ranging from Wittgenstein to the New Left, applying them to the fraught issues of the social role of art and the possibility of utopian artistic action. For several years, OHO's philosophical searching manifested itself in its discourses and its formal explorations of the extremes of both entropy and systematicity. Ultimately, life superseded art, but with that, the group's disbanding became in a certain sense the most fitting utopian gesture to end its experiment.

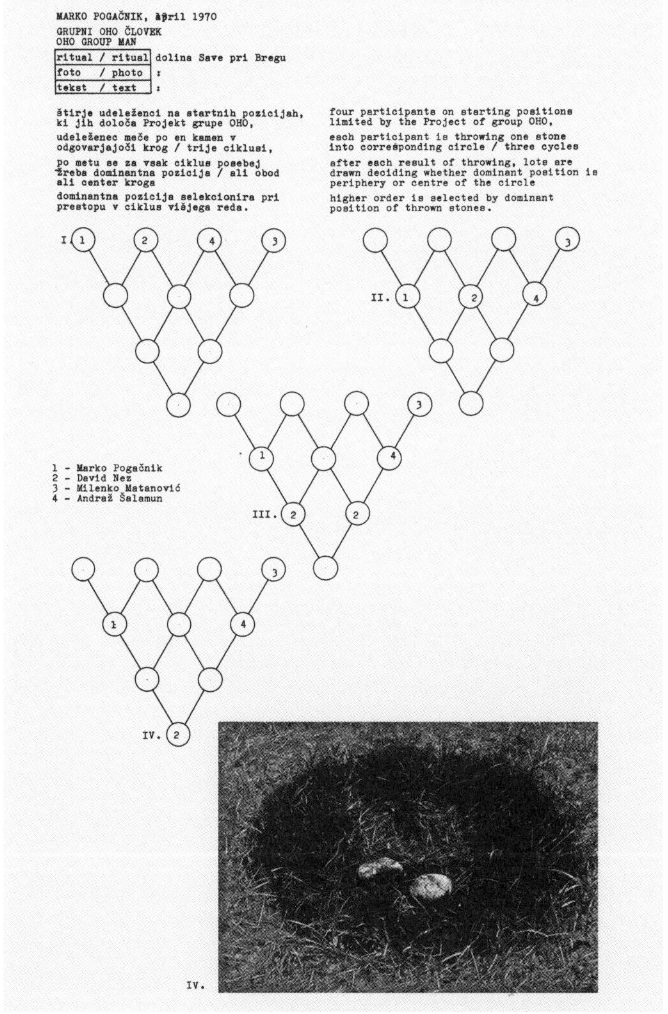

OHO Group, Marko Pogačnik, *The OHO group-man*, april 1970, Courtesy of Moderna galerija, Ljubljana

Jef Geys and Marinus Boezem / Taking Care of the Frame

Steven ten Thije

At first glance, the work of the Belgian artist Jef Geys and the Dutch artist Marinus Boezem is similar neither in subject matter nor in method.[1] Jef Geys's work is deeply influenced by a research-driven attitude. He makes lists, inventories, and maps; he collects "evidence" and experiments. Marinus Boezem, on the other hand, can be better described as a transcendental poet. He makes the invisible visible through small or simple gestures that can assume monumental scale. Geys is uncomfortable around particularly big words; Boezem recognizes them everywhere. However, even if their methods are radically different, both artists developed their working methodology in direct response to specific social conditions and struggled with similar questions on how to position art in society. Reviewing their work together therefore has the merit of allowing us to see how similar questions regarding the place for art can produce two very different answers. To understand how these different practices share some specific similarities, it is helpful to first discuss the work independently and then go on to describe the common ground. As a starting point, I have chosen the works presented in the last exhibition of L'Internationale's collaborative project: *ABC École de Paris* (1959–1961) by Jef Geys and the *Soft-Table* (1968) by Marinus Boezem.

Jef Geys's work *ABC École de Paris* exists in various different versions. One is a collection of A4-size drawings, the second version consists of 15 large A1 size cheap brown paper sheets that each contain one "lesson" from the "ABC École de Paris" drawing course. Geys signed up for this "expensive" drawing course to learn the illusionist tricks used by the "great masters". The drawings are often reiterations of similar subjects in different forms on the same page, and are testimonies to one or even several "lessons". A sheet might be filled with shoes, or with studies of muscles or skeletons, or with animals, or an exercise on linear perspective. All in all, the drawings are imbued with an air of study, and are sometimes even graded. The cheap paper emphasizes the sketch-like nature of the images—they are only one stage in the development towards something else.

1   I would like to thank both Jef Geys and Marinus Boezem for their generosity in discussing their work. The final text is deeply informed by these discussions.

The only thing that questions this unfinished status of the work is the monumental size (in the second version), some comments written next to or over the drawings, and the certainty of the "line." The drawings are not only studies, they are close to flawless studies, as though Geys decided to save only those drawings that register a successful execution of the assignment.

This fateful execution produces pages that appear banal at first sight, but through their banality develop a subversive and critical argument. If we look, for instance, at one page in more detail—a page framed in a slightly bigger frame in the second version, making it stand out some from the rest—we see a variety of attempts to draw a head or skull. At the top of the page are two heads and a skull of relatively small proportions drawn in red ink. Immediately below those three heads, to the left, is the profile of a woman, executed in a deep black profile line. Next to it, on the right side of the page, is a type of cartoon box that contains a "buste" portrait of a man wearing a hat and suit with tie. Almost on top of it—or more underneath it, for the lines are thinner—are three faces, of which only the profile line is drawn. The profiles each contain a "dotted" support line—a straight line that is placed either straight or in a curve against the "nose"—allowing the jaw to come more to the fore and the forehead to retreat into the rear. Below these three profiles are studies of skulls that use similar support lines. There are four skulls, aligned left to right by a horizontal support line at the height of the nose; and next to these is a vertical support line for each skull, straight on the left side and taking on a sharper curve toward the right. As a result, the skulls remind us of illustrations of the process of evolution, in which the higher oval shape of the human skull gradually transforms into the lower, flatter oval shape of the ape skull. In the left corner is written," reinforcing the sense that one is looking at an illustration from a (pseudo-)scientific text. Below this is written, in French and Dutch, "fig 6, Greek classics, white race, negro, monkey." At the bottom of the page are three standing rectangular boxes, subdivided into smaller rectangles, each containing a human head, en face, en profile, and three quarter, the rectangles helping to define the "correct" proportions. This segment is also captioned, with the French at the top and the Dutch at the bottom, reading: "the ideal proportions of the head". Overall, the drawings are executed with a straight ink line, and in a style that is slightly reminiscent of illustrations in children's books or educational literature—a schematic style that doesn't ridicule but rather simplifies.

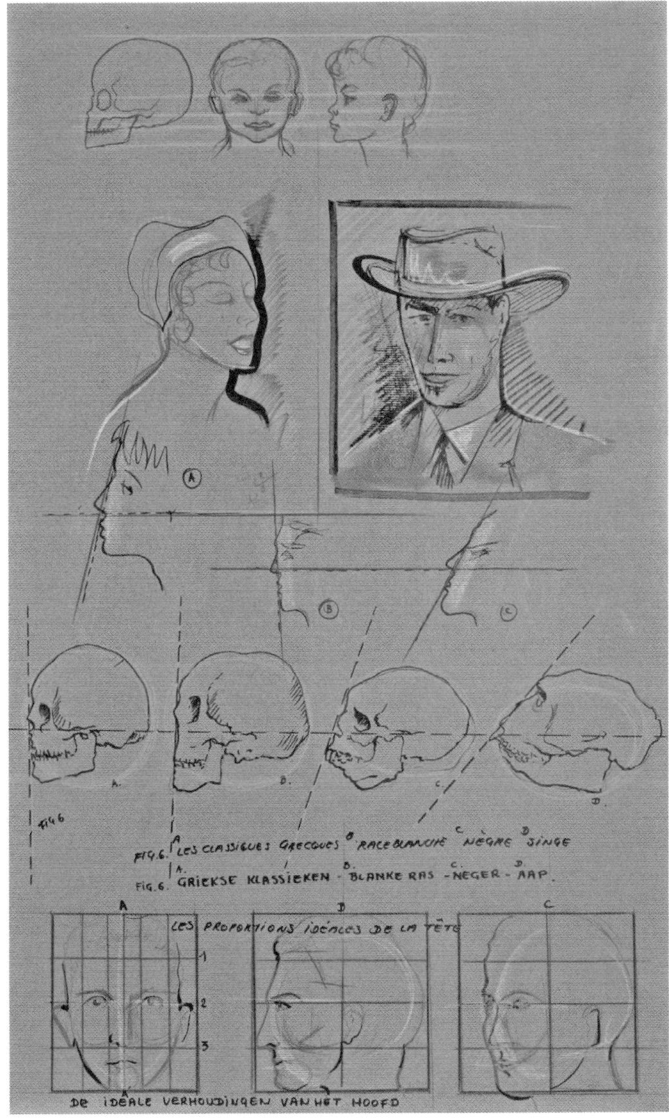

Jef Geys, *ABC*, Ecole de Paris, 1959-1961, photo by Syb'l. S.

Not every page has a similar complexity or structure: some pages contain less variation, consisting, for instance, only of women's shoed feet, or hands and arms. The page described

above, however, has the quality of containing a variety of elements that together expose something of the basic logic of the
ABC École de Paris series. The first impression the page im-
parts is a relatively random group of drawings that deal with
the same subject: the depiction of the human head. There is no
clear storyline, but more an order that places one thing next to
or below the other. The drawing even appears to be sandwiched
by two series of three heads, with the more scientifically (ac-
curately) proportioned drawings at the bottom, together with the
skull and two heads in red, that blends somewhat into the brown
background at the top. It is clear that the page, as a whole,
reflects a moment in the process of studying. One sees the attempt to understand the relationship between the skull and the
face, and from the face to a hat and clothing. In some sense the
drawing evokes a kind of matter-of-fact-quality that suggests
that what is learned are "merely" correct proportions. But when
reading the captions it becomes clear that what appears neutral
or objective is profoundly defined and infected by norms and
even judgments. The four skulls are neatly divided into a "classic Greek"-side that is close to the "white man." and the animal,
monkey-side that is close to the "negro." Something that is
underlined by the fact that the proportions of the head below—
which is clearly a "white" head, for the profile line of the nose
mirrors the one of the "white man's" skull—are "ideal." This
then further defines the entire page, affecting the man with the
head, which is now no longer a skull, but with added flesh and
clothes becomes a gendered figure, who occupies some middle
ground between a type of cowboy and a bourgeois male.

The subversive "content" of the page might appear today
somewhat disappointing. The awareness that seemingly neutral
drawings are ideologically defined and charged is not surprising anymore. There is a certain nostalgia attached to this kind
of "critical" art that is reminiscent of the great unmasking
practiced in the 1960s by thinkers like Roland Barthes and his
Mythologies or Foucault's genealogical studies, that demonstrated how what was presumed self-evident or "natural" was
nothing more than an arbitrary construction resulting out of
encounters between various hegemonic interests groups. This
association is not incorrect, as Geys's work was influenced by
the critical spirit of structuralism or post-structuralism, but it
obscures the artistic method used to articulate this critique.

What is important about the *ABC École de Paris* is not just that it exposes the normative pattern that is, as it were, hidden in the surface of educational material, but the conscious and complex appropriation of this normative pattern through practice. The drawings are not just copies of educational material, but are themselves specimens of the process of apprehending or learning how to "use" the material. They are—and here Geys's practice breaks with many of his contemporaries—deeply connected to the "subject" Jef Geys. Where the minimalists or the conceptual artists were negating the presence of the biographical subject, or Pop artists, inspired by Dada and Marcel Duchamp, played with the subject as a readymade, like Warhol's "machine" ambition, Geys allowed himself to "appear" in the work, to become not just the one who conducts the experiment, but also the guinea pig. If there is something troubling about Geys's artistic strategy, it is the lack of divide between himself and his work, without the work ever dealing with issues of "expression."

This requires some further enumeration. To state that Geys's work is "subjective" does not mean that it either reflects the "subject" or even that it has some unique quality—some genius —because it is based on the subject "Jef Geys." Instead it suggests that Geys has been faithful to this subject—himself—in a manner that has been defining for his work. This subject was, thereby, never an isolated or Romantic entity, but was—and still is—a social *and* organic construct. This duality is perhaps best expressed in two simple facts: one, he never left his birth region of "Kempenland"; two, he worked for close to thirty years as an art teacher in the local school system. So on the one side, as though he were a plant that couldn't survive "relocation," he has stayed "true" or at least close to his roots—even though he did travel for work or other reasons when necessary. On the other side his educational work always inspired him to look at people not just as finished products, but as developing entities that could—to some degree—be molded and that in any case, inevitably transformed. These two things—his home region and his educational work—are two recurring elements in his work, and they are, in some idiosyncratic sense, documented in his own publication series, the "Kempens Informatieblad" (the Kempen Information Leaflet) that he produces parallel to his artistic projects. Often the social web of students and his own family help him respond to the requests made of him by his own (partial) habitat—the art world. Either by taking them as subject or employing their help, these relations help him produce his work—not always, but often.

This inconsistency is, thereby, perhaps the complicated "center"—which is actually a type of "anti-center"—of his working methodology and the place where the organic and the social exchange and where *change* takes place. By always allowing the duality of roots and change to be present there is never an immobile core to the work. Much more than a core, there is a space between two things that is produced by time and that produces a change. In the case of the *ABC École de Paris*, this in-between space is constantly produced on the page and between the pages, showing the laborious and time consuming route of the appropriation of models. But more generally there is an in-between between the educational material and the pupil—in this case Geys. If the work directs attention to some ideological confusion or misconception, this problematic point is not positioned in a definite, ideal "space"—the work, even if related to the process of education, is never didactic. The works asks of those who engage with it to allow themselves to observe the process of change or transformation from within. Change formulated as such can only be measured in reference to a fixed point. Or perhaps better expressed, change occurs through the encounter of two moving bodies that travel at different speeds. Culture, tradition, family, friendship and science all have their different paces, merits and flaws. They come together in the haphazard entity of a historically specific subject, bouncing against and off each other or forming temporary alliances. This encounter is the organic process of growing that in the end grounds the relative values of these historical forms and enables them to become real in the physical life of the subject. Geys is aware of both the danger and the potential of this process, and appears to despise those who take it lightly. Those who take the time to engage with the work—and time is a factor—will have to study its careful inconsistency, which is perhaps the only "logic" therein.

The work of the Dutch artist Marinus Boezem differs in many ways from this "logic."[2] A first glance at *Soft-Table* from 1968 makes this clear from the outset. The work consists of a standing table 120 cm high with a round, 50 cm-diameter

2 For a comprehensive article on the entire oeuvre see: Edna van Duyn & Fransjozef Witteveen (ed.), *Boezem,* Thoth, Bussum 1999, p. 11–55.

tabletop that rests on a thin leg taken from a music stand. Over the table lies a white nylon tablecloth, while mounted underneath the centre of the tabletop is a fan that blows into the tablecloth through a circular hole, producing a small cushion of air that collapses when the fan is turned off. The work produces a delicate, poetic sensation with the use of simple, everyday elements. There is something magical about the little air cushion that lives as long as the fan is switched on. It is clear that the heart of the work lies in the ephemeral quality of the air blowing against the nylon, but there is more to the work than just air.

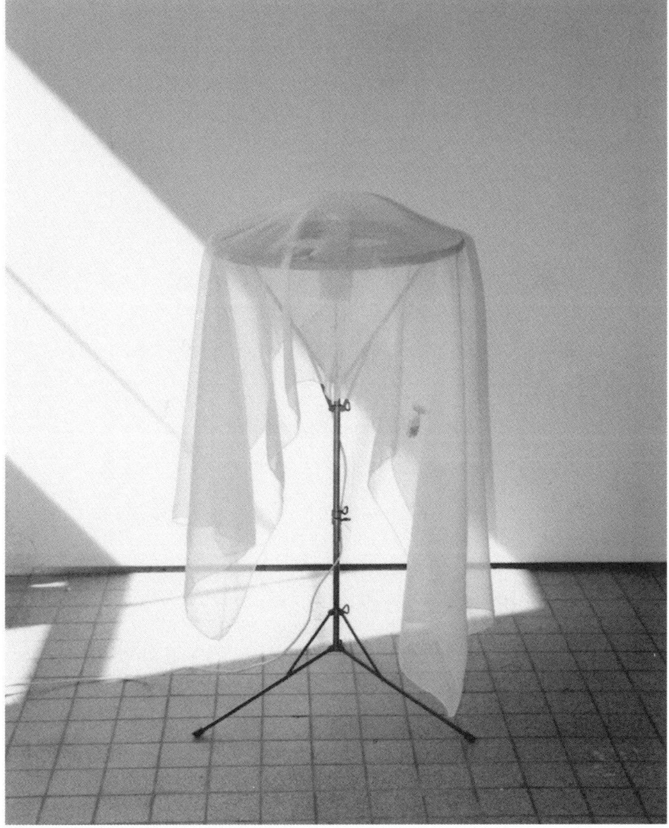

Marinus Boezem, *Soft Table*, 1967, Collection Van Abbemuseum, Eindhoven

The table, present in the form of the work itself and repeated in the title, adds a particular dimension to the work. The table belongs to everyday life, even though the connection between this particular table and the everyday is more metaphorical than a direct reference, since the table is too delicate with its thin

leg to function as a normal table. The table stands there not just
as table, but as an image of a table, a sensation of a table. The
work serves to change something that at first seems apparent.
The table with its reference to the everyday appears to invoke
the character or identity of the "readymade"; the work is merely
using something already there by transforming its banal materiality into something else—into art. However, on second inspection, when the table is revealed as a fraud and not a real table,
as only a reference to a table, the work transforms. Both the air
and the table are there as image. They are placed there to produce a sensation that is not grounded primarily in the intuitive,
physical understanding of a human being relating to a table.
The table cannot activate that embodied memory of how it is to
lean on it, for it is clear it would collapse. What the table acti-
vates is a mental domain in which the idea of the table is stored.
The magical or dreamlike quality of the work comes forth out
of the "mental materiality" that it addresses. The work builds
not from the physical body that through reflex memorizes,
but—even if the difference is subtle—through mental reflexes
that exist in the mind and that appear to control us when in a
state of dreaming.

Throughout Boezem's oeuvre, air remains the one recurring
element: from a dramatic proclamation in 1967 that in the year
2000 "air" would be the most important creative element, to
exhibiting newspaper weather maps tracing air currents; from
his many installations using fabrics that dance in the wind
(produced by fans), to "the artist" vanishing in the thin air
(represented by two empty shoes standing on the railing of a
bridge), through his monumental work of a complete cathedral
made of trees, which record the wind in their leaves and mark,
through the air between them, the walls of this holy building.
Air is a central motif in all of these works, but is also always
approached as an immaterial concept that materializes as a sen-
sible image. The image-quality of the work defines the mode in
which one is affected by the work. The work releases an energy
that is present in the world, which sparks a dialogue between
everyday sensations and profound mental concepts—a mental
domain that, as it were, precedes our everyday understanding of
the world. The air is not just the element that surrounds us, but
it is (much) more the spiritual element that unites and connects
us. Seemingly without effort the mind is able to associate with

the world in a holistic manner, drawing lines between past, present and future that exceeds the singular, physical living organism. The air that Boezem "uses" is not just the air necessary to keep the biological machine working but is also the fuel for the spiritual machine as well.

What is relevant here is that this spiritual "machine" is not dealt with in an abstract manner, nor is it approached in isolation. The last component of Boezem's work that is important to describe here is its social and historical dimension. This aspect is easily overlooked, for the spiritual nature of the work appears to direct one's attention away from the specific, historical moment of creation towards a "higher", "eternal" dimension. But the image produced in the work of Boezem is never a pure or abstract image. The work never seeks to isolate this spiritual faculty of man in some form that is entirely universal or a-temporal. The work recalls either a specific moment or a distinct social condition in which the mental reflex of the spiritual is inserted. The tables, for instance, are also images of a social sphere. They trigger a sense of conviviality, of gathering at a table. Also the use of technology is significant here. The fans, or the airplane Boezem once used to "sign" the sky, belong to a specific historical moment, in which each time the transcending sensation of the spiritual is relocated anew and needs to be circumscribed again. Art has to be anchored in this social, historical domain and should actively contribute to the social community by revealing these places of transcendence that transform this collection of individuals into a social "body."

This social dimension is exactly the point where the works of Geys and Boezem meet. What connects the two is the awareness that there is no division between this social dimension and art. Even if the artist has the possibility to operate in a singular and idiosyncratic manner, giving space to the ego in a way that in other fields is impossible, the stake of this game is informed not by the identity of the artist alone, but by the social system in which this figure has a function. Geys makes visible the complicated procedures of subjectification and does so not from an abstract outside—only in a reflective manner—but (truly) through practice. By doing certain things with both himself and with others he is not just offering a theory of how things are, but he is mapping the way they affect the living subject who is both body and mind —rooted and free. Boezem has a more

mystical sensitivity—even if presented with a fair dose of irony—but his artistic practice can also be understood as offering
a "service" to the community in which he lives. Making visible
the invisible spirit that surrounds and combines a community,
he translates a social function that used to belong to institutions
like the church into a secular and profane practice that is still
effective.

This distinct understanding of art as having a social function has produced one of the few points of similitude or correspondence in their working attitude and approach, which is
deeply suspicious of the art market—where they thought this
social function dried out and withered. Even if both artists have
sought to establish a position within the art world and have sold
work, made exhibitions and contributed to spectacular art festivals, they have done so with care and ambivalence. Both coming of age in the 1960s they were part of a specific generation
that sensed that a new "order" was possible. The experimental
art made over that decade also enabled imagining this art
would function differently from the more discrete paintings and
sculptures that so well suited the logic of the market. However,
in the end this art was not impervious to the gravitational pull
of the market. Even if fashioned from the most profane of materials, this art could still serve or be seen as a form of class distinction. Where some other artists may have believed that in the
end the work could survive this almost inevitable corruption,
Geys and Boezem both sought to build counter-structures to
determine whether the potential of art could not be better realized elsewhere. Geys has done so with the consistent production of his information leaflet, which allowed him to frame and
position his own work in a manner he felt appropriate. Boezem
did so by retreating from the art world somewhat and working
in various teaching positions between 1971 and 1986.

A certain similarity between the two emerges not only out
of some specific professional choices—the way they developed
practices combining art making and teaching—and out of,
perhaps, an expanded notion of "materiality" that is invoked
by the work. Whereas artists like Donald Judd would make a
case in the 1960s for "specific objects" as artworks constituting
clear constructions that avoided anecdotal relations to existing
"traditions," Geys and Boezem have allowed tradition and relationships to remain primary elements in their work. In Geys's

practice these relationships are more human and semiotic in
character; with Boezem these relationships are more spiritual
or transcendental, connected in a careful and sensitive way
to a more religious tradition. In both practices, however, this
has produced a resistance to the tendency to separate the work
from its context, to isolate it as if its potential significance were
contained in the object alone. The practice of making works
always remains connected to a care for the context and an active engagement with the social network of relationships that, in
the end, surround and frame the artwork, be it through teaching, curating, or writing. Producing an affect at that precarious
point where subject and object meet could, in their view, only
function if the artist took responsibility not just for the work,
but for the frame as well.

Paul De Vree and Toon Tersas / Hysteria Makes History

Lars Bang Larsen

The works of Toon Tersas and Paul De Vree represent two extremes in Belgian post-war art. Yet in spite of the differences between them, their respective projects don't stand in direct contrast to each other either. Instead it seems fitting to address their work together, for one thing since the two artists represent positions that the national art system couldn't comprehend. In the case of Tersas, this was because he worked in relative isolation and rather hermetically; in the case of De Vree, because his work was dispersed across disciplines—between poetry, sound and visual art—as well as geographically, in European networks of artists' magazines. If Tersas's work was infra-national, hardly part of a local art scene, De Vree's was trans-national and dialogical, as he produced and distributed work with other velocities and within other communities than those to which the art institution at the time was attuned.

Paul De Vree (1909–1982) was not only internationally oriented: he was in himself, as Henri Chopin put it, an international.[1]

One can approach De Vree's work through concrete poetry. Even if, according to him, this art form was only one phase in his work, concretism offers a genealogical perspective—or represents at least a bone of contention to De Vree himself—in a family tree of works and strategies that sits "between poetry and painting."[2] He also talked about his work in terms of visual poetry and phenomena of artistic *Vermischungen* (amalgamations or fusions) between literature, visual art and what we today call sound art.[3]

As over-used as the term is today, it seems apposite to call concretism a social art—if only because in the 1950s and 1960s, "everybody did it," according to the German artist Thomas Bayrle.[4] It was an art that promised new and transparent relations of production between signs and materials. It could be created anywhere, typically with a piece of every(wo)man's technology—a typewriter—and traditional, academic parameters of skill and training were eradicated in favor of the sheer material presence of paper, ink, and linguistic sign. Much like

[1] Henri Chopin, "The International Paul De Vree," *Lotta Poetica*, series 2, year 2, nr. 5 (January 1984), p. 18–26.

[2] Op .cit.

[3] Paul De Vree, "Visual Poetry," *Konkrete poezie, klankteksten, visuele teksten*, Stedelijk Museum, Amsterdam 1970, p. 1.

[4] In conversation, November 2011.

certain kinds of minimalism and land art, concretism was an (anti-)style that cultivated the weak signals of egolessness and anonymity, of systemic process, and the poverty and commonness of the materials used. As a non-spectacular art form it was present in social space by dint of its *haecceity*—the objective 'here it is' of its materials, procedures and technologies. Yet at the same time it was 'cool,' because it phased out aesthetic fundamentalisms of expressivity and engagement. In concretism there is not much space for abstraction, nor for individual mythology or indignation. What you see is what you get.

There are many strands and inflections of concretism in the mid-20th century, and many geographical locations of its articulation. A shared feature between the different versions—whether derived from Bauhaus concretism or Surrealist poetry—was the undoing of conventional structures of meaning in order to unleash new signification that may remain uncharted by religious and psychological myth. What is at stake is the irremediable presence of that which has been removed or taken apart: the concretists played in the ruins of language, tonality and motif, as they debunked ideas of the artwork's whole and closed form. Concretism was one of the big destroyers of traditional aesthetic tropes and media boundaries, at the same time as it re-constituted the relation between sign, image, word and material trace, and made this relationship susceptible to the slightest ripple of new meaning. De Vree's classically concretist concern with language as the work's *prima materia* that undergo a series of permutations can for instance be seen in *Explositieven* (1966), *Tsjechoslovakije* (1969) and *Eerootic* (1971). In De Vree's poetry, language matters as a factual presence between images, sounds, symbols, and signs. As language descends from the heaven of meaning it becomes a bodily concern: in *People* (1974), five dancers drape their limbs around elementary structures that spell the work's title.

One can argue that the representational logic of the concretist work is a kind of pointilism, as it wavers between its minute constitutive elements and forming an image, a *Gestalt*. The work is often internally constituted through many punctual, irreducible events, and relates on its outside to its historical milieu as a small part in a larger reconstruction; the work and its maker are in themselves little dots in a larger crowd or movement that will eventually reform society. It is not so strange, perhaps, that this intention of poetically massaging the social realm was seen to fail. At least De Vree lost his patience. In his essay "Notes on Poesia Visiva" (1972), he scoffs that "even though [concrete poetry] blew a little oxygen into the veins of poetry, it remained too strictly defined by its protagonists and it never dared to descend into the arena, much less into the street. It continued to think that its task was to harmonize the world by means of 'aesthetic signals,' and it remained hypocritical and harmful beneath its pretensions to being democratic."[5] Instead he at this point rather favors an "anti-conformist revolt," based on the "constructive destructions" undertaken earlier in the century by Dada, and one that is aware of its "clear and precise ideological responsibility."[6] On this Leninist note, and by way of a certain brutalism, De Vree intended to fuse artistic and social critique by substituting the space of the page for that of the street. He would burn motifs or words into the paper, for example by laconic reference to conflict zones such as Santiago, Beirut, Belfast, Soweto, Cape Town, Notting Hill. These works are *brandwonden*, fire wounds. As Jan De Vree puts it, his grandfather's work "hovers around the contrast between rest (being adapted, wellbeing, acceptance, interiorization) and unrest (non-conformism, rage, refusal, accusation/complaint). As he grew older the latter became more dominant."[7]

Even if concretism according to De Vree failed its ideological responsibility, it was not uncommon for artists to employ the idiom to address historical conflict (think of Franz Mon's brilliant mushroom clouds composed of machine-typed letters). On his side, De Vree proposed a poetic critique of repression and violence, and—even if he declared that in the 1970s he moved "from sociology into politics"—of the (party) political human being.[8] Thus in *De mens* (1973), four silhouettes of a person represent different types of human being: "uomo utopico," "uomo normale," "uomo economico," and "uomo politico." They are ordered according to their degree of humanity, represented with diminishing sizes of hearts: 'utopian man' has the biggest heart while 'political man' has none at all. To De Vree, a socio-poetic utopia was the only way of conceiving of freedom. Paraphrasing Herbert Marcuse, he wrote that "utopias have to be thought of not as impossibilities but rather as postulates of things to look forward to."[9]

5 De Vree, "Visual Poetry," p. 2.

6 Op. cit.

7 Jan De Vree, "Some Tendencies in Paul De Vree's Poetry," unpublished essay, 2004, transl. Nicole Hunter, p. 2.

8 Paul De Vree Interview by Sarenco, *FUTURGAPPISMO. Comunicato numero I*, April 1978, p. 2.

9 Paul De Vree, "Notes on Poesia Visiva," *Lotta Poetica* 13–14, 1972, p. 3.

The work and persona of Toon Tersas (1924–1996) is a far
cry from the cosmopolitanism of De Vree. Self-taught and
employed for most of his life in a post office, he infrequently
exhibited his work—and with a few exceptions only did so in
Belgium. A family photo that shows the artist with his wife
and eight children in front of their home is probably a truthful
picture of his working conditions: not the studio or the café, but
the suburban bungalow.

Paul De Vree and Toon Tersas share an aesthetic of textual
pleasure. Thus for Tersas, too, art seems to have had a psychophysical source that is turned toward social space through language. Where De Vree remained faithful to the internationalism of the historical avant-gardes through a poetics that would
join forces with insurrections in the streets, Tersas re-employed
a vanguard predilection for language experiments via his hermetic passions. "After you, dear language," wrote André Breton
in the first *Surrealist Manifesto*, as if he were holding the door
for a prominent visitor; an invitation that Tersas could also have
pronounced—if only to lock himself up with language like a
mad monk in his cell.

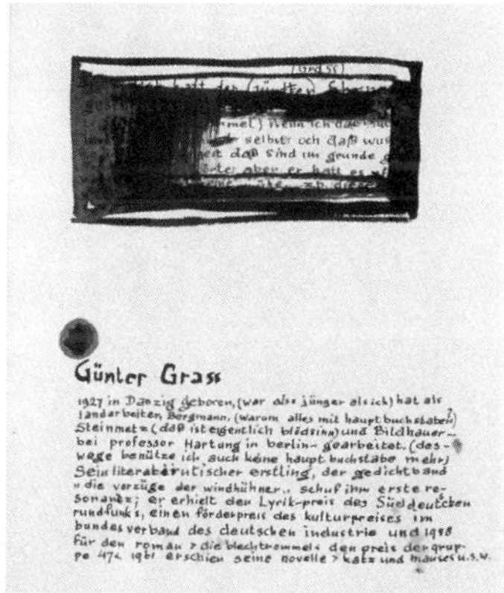
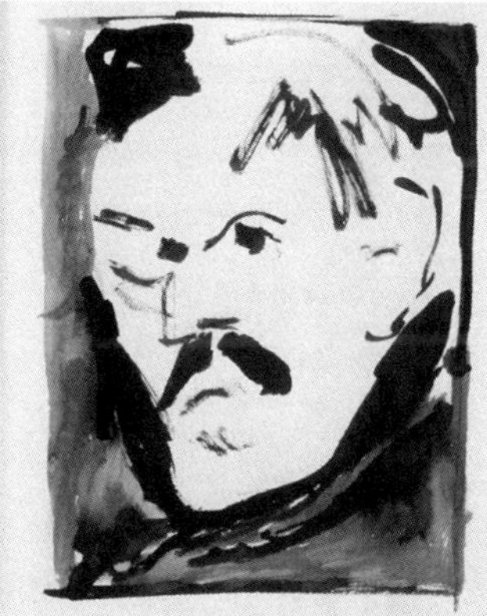

Toon Tersas, *Tolles Gehirn*,
1971, Collection M HKA

The concern with the appearance and depiction of text,
typography and already reproduced images is prominent in
Tersas's work. Confronting the technologically reproduced
image with the pre-Gutenbergian technology of ink, paper
and pen, he proceeded with the copyist's fidelity to his source,
copying film stills, logos, postmarks, bills, entire pages from
books and newspapers: sometimes with apparent care to make
an exact reproduction, sometimes quick and impressionistic,

sometimes mirrored. Products of his own imagination are rendered in pseudo-encyclopedic form, such as the extravagantly titled *Tolles Gehirn (Fragmenten)* (1971), an ink drawing emulating a German-Flemish dictionary through more or less alphabetized entries, mainly—but not exclusively—with the letter "e." A newspaper article on the death of the Shah has seemingly been transposed into a pastiche of a medieval manuscript; other "copies" are produced by montage-ing various sources. Tersas's objects include a homemade book with a white, furry cover titled *Erotiek in de grafiek* (1973), which he exhibited in a padlocked box with a glass top and a pink interior.

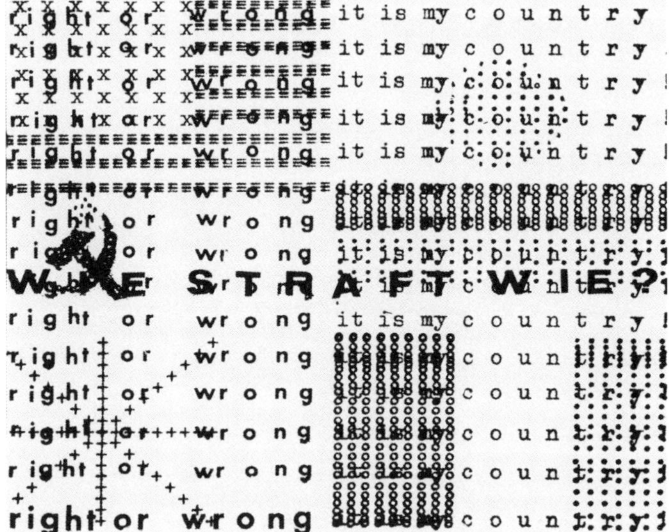

Paul De Vree,
Wie straft wie, 1971,
photo by
M HKAclinckx,
Collection M HKA

There are artists who are considered strange birds because their work is seemingly ruled by their idiosyncrasies: Jim Shaw, with his drawn recordings of his dreams; Cecilia Edefalk, with her paintings of copied copies of images; or—as an art historical example with which Tersas's early paintings resonate—Picabia's refusal of a signature style. But rather than the conventional notion of artistic idiosyncrasy, one could argue that these artists, like Tersas, operate with singular aesthetic laws of their own making. Their obsessions are not qualities of an artistic talent, but systemic rhythms and abstract machines that are set free from individuality. The work of another Belgian graphic artist, Henri Michaux, also comes to

mind here: more explicitly than Tersas, Michaux worked on the
site of affect, but similarly favored a kind of automatism that
allowed him to proceed robotically, like a plotter, in his calligraphic improvisations.

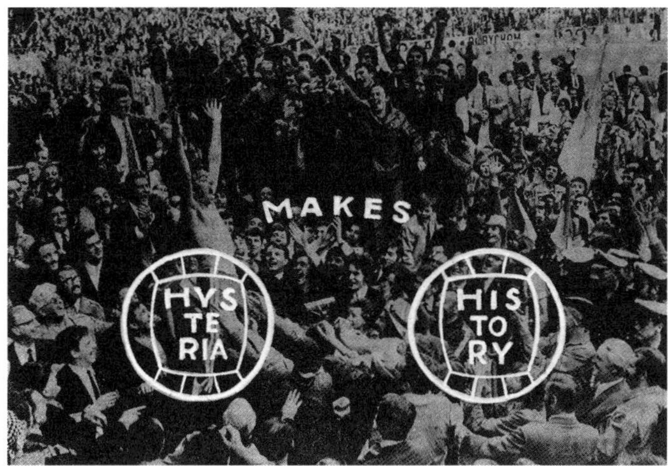

Paul De Vree, *Hysteria makes History*, 1973, Collection M HKA

Also Luc Tuymans's signature style of painterly precision
and chromatic discretion echoes in Tersas's black and white
ink drawings. However, the reality that Tersas re-produces in
his work is one that cannot be contained in a single image, resulting in a work that is fragmented and insufficient. Perhaps
Tersas can more productively be seen as a quirky forerunner
of appropriation art in the vein of Jef Geys and Guillaume
Bijl (circumstantial evidence of this would be the correspondence between Geys and Tersas, and quirky works such as *Jef
Geys. Eet meer Groente* ["Eat more vegetables"], 1968). The
Belgian tradition of appropriation differs from the ready-made
tradition by turning away from the object. Moreover it is not
unequivocally the author who selects the object, but rather an
environment (Bijl) or, more abstractly, a logic of image production (Geys) that ironically "selects" the author. Such strategies
cannot be reduced to the approach of Duchamp, who acted as
a high priest of art initiating profane everyday objects into the
realm of high art; nor is it aligned with Yves Klein's even more
emphatic and gestural employments of authorship, as when
he signed the world. Toon Tersas is no such (self-)empowered
author. Instead he reproduces the already represented world,
disowning authorial intention in the process. Still, one can

attempt to trace Tersas's motivation for his selection or "curating" of the sources he depicted: articles from German newspapers about the Rote Armee Fraktion and its members, articles
from Flemish newspapers about art, Nazism, and lesbianism;
and a copy of an advertisement for industrial components under
the poetically meaningful headline "Système aux variantes
infinies" (*Lithos recto/verso*, 1972).

Maybe Tersas's approach was a way of honoring the truth
that Paul De Vree articulated pithily in a work from the early
1970s: *Hysteria Makes History*.

Grup de Treball and Vídeo-Nou / Two Collective Projects in 1970s Spain Teresa Grandas

This text will discuss two diachronic collective projects in the Spanish state that took place immediately before and after a significant event—the death of Franco in 1975. A study of the Grup de Treball (1973–1975) and Video Nou/Servei de Video Comunitari (1977–1983) will enable us to trace the complex relationship between artistic experimentation and the socio-political situation of the time. These groups cannot be understood as isolated cases. Instead, they acted as transmitters for permeable action and interacted as critical settings and stimuli for innovative attitudes, in which artistic activity goes beyond the mere formal fact and is insolubly linked to socio-political practices. In this regard, it is important to take into account that Grup de Treball evolved in the last years of the dictatorship, against a background of political repression and, in Catalonia, a reaffirmation of its identity. In the case of Vídeo-Nou, the project was born already immersed in the pre-institutional democratic models of construction.

"DUE TO THE TEMPORARY absence of the country, direct information is wanted about the reality of same Visits 5–7 or write Muntadas Comercio 64, Barcelona 3. T. 3190930."[1]

Grup de Treball gathered together a heterogeneous aggregation that included artists, filmmakers, art critics and the occasional politician. Among its participants were artists such as Francesc Abad, Jordi Benito, Alicia Finguerhut, Xavier Franquesa, Muntadas, Àngels Ribé, Manuel Rovira, Dorothée Selz and Francesc Torres; the filmmaker Pere Portabella, the musician Carlos Santos, the poet and artist Santi Pau, the writers Carles Hac Mor and Antoni Munné, the historian Imma Julián, and others such as María Costa, Jaume Carbó, Josep Parera and Enric Sales. The coordinator of the group was Antoni Mercader.[2] Their involvement in the project was diverse, uneven and sporadic. There were also occasional contributions from the designer and artist Alberto Corazón and the artists Olga Pijuan and Luis Utrilla.[3] Although they all continued to work

1 *Anunciamos* was a series of 17 texts inserted in the classified ads section of the newspaper *La Vanguardia Española* between June and July 1973 by the Grup de Treball. The text combined the printed word with the characteristic red circle marking the parts that were deleted by the censor.

2 The list of members was furnished by him.

3 They signed the reply to Antoni Tàpies as part of a public polemic (see note 4). This was not the only controversy that arose with other artists, although it received the most publicity.

individually between 1973 and 1975, they combined their activities with a collective project under the name "Grup Treball," which revolved around a critical perspective of conventional artistic practices while stressing the social function of art.

The group was marked by its strong political commitment and emphasis on ideology. It was no accident that it took shape during the final stages of Francoism, precisely when the agonizing regime was in its most repressive phase, having ignored the ever-increasing need and demands for democratization both from inside and outside the country. In February 1973, in conjunction with the show *Informació d'Art Concepte* ("Information about Conceptual Art") within the space of the Llotja de Tint at Banyoles, the guidelines and aims of the group were drawn up in a work about the circulation of information. This document appealed to the public to think about and discuss the situation. From his tribune as a collaborator in the newspaper *La Vanguardia*, the painter Antoni Tàpies branded them as "a naïve version that wants to be aggressive and politicized."[4] The reply, supported by a wide spectrum of people, was published in November of the same year in the review *Nueva Lente*, no. 21.

The group was formally presented in summer 1973 at the fifth Summer University in Prada de Conflent. During those years meetings were frequently organized in smaller towns throughout Catalonia, in which papers were read and artistic and political questions were debated. At the same time, experiences—in many cases short-lived—were presented that questioned the usual art circuits and reflected on the work of art per se, including the very notion of authorship, as an alternative and awareness of artistic anachronism and commercialization. These encounters acted as settings for creative and intellectual stimulation, not only strictly in the realm of art but also in music, architecture, film, design and politics.[5] These were by no means isolated happenings, for they were also included places and events like gallery spaces or venues devoted to other activities as well as artistic presentations.[6] At this point it is important to emphasize two negative factors in regard to these circumstances: on the one hand, the lack of freedom prevented a display of discordant or even critical attitudes; and on the other, there was a noticeable lack of infrastructures and an absence of supportive institutions. Nevertheless, these adverse circumstances actually facilitated a wider diffusion of ideas and a

[4] Antoni Tàpies, *La Vanguardia Española*, 14 March 1973, p. 13. He goes on "…but without anything to support it and so ill-adapted to the needs of our country that it ends up as a mere anti-establishment declamation, with all the typical childishness that is often counterproductive. Moreover, we should recall that while here they exalt the subversive side that runs contrary to the system that they claim for conceptual art, it is sold almost everywhere in galleries, collected in museums and admitted to the official competitions of that very system."

[5] A good example of this is the congress of the ICSID held in Ibiza in October 1971. During its sessions there were artistic events such as a ceremony of colors on the occasion of the inauguration of the conference organized by Miralda, Dorothée Selz and Jaume Xifra, with the musical collaboration of Carlos Santos and the construction of a large inflatable structure by Muntadas and Ponsatí. The *Instant City*, an ephemeral inflatable city was also build to house the students, and Jordi Cerdà presented his films within the framework of the congress. Muntadas, Selz and Santos became members of Grup de Treball later on.

[6] A few examples of this are the Galerías G, Mec-Mec and Ciento in Barcelona, artistic spaces such as B5-125 at the Universidad Autónoma, the Sala de Personal in the Caja de Pensiones and the Espai 10 in the Fundació Miró in Barcelona and the Sala Tres in Sabadell. Venues devoted to other activities such as the Sala Vinçon in Barcelona also

series of events that linked together different types of creative activity and developed a methodology for work and visibility.[7]

Grup de Treball called into question the different artistic languages as a way of disseminating the dominant ideology. It also questioned the concept of style, the work of art itself, the autonomy of artistic activity and the art circuits; in other words, the art market. The "work" or artistic product was conceived as a form of political and social mobilization. Through their participation in various events they would analyze the organizational structures, the control mechanisms and their determining factors that influenced the participants and the opportunity and opportunism that they entailed. A good example of this was the work presented at the aforementioned session of the Universitat d'Estiu at Prada de Conflent, denouncing the system. In this work, they established a relationship between the name of the artists who had participated in the Kassel Documentas 4 and 5, and the value or price of their works. The interrelation between art and economic power was also the basis for their *Encuesta a 24 galerías de arte de Madrid* (Survey of 24 art galleries in Madrid) in 1974. On the occasion of the the IX Biennale de Paris in October 1975, they presented *Champ d'attraction. Document. Travail d'information sur la presse illégale des Pays Catalans*, an important work on the illegal clandestine press in the Spanish state. The passing of the antiterrorist law in 1975 and the introduction of the state of emergency forced them to present the work anonymously, and it was excluded from the catalogue because of fear of reprisal (the last executions under the death penalty were still very recent).

included artistic contributions in their programs. The German Institute in Madrid and Barcelona and the College of Architects also played an important role.

[7] The magazine *Ajoblanco*, no. 4 (April 1975) published the text that Grup de Treball had presented at the *Mostra d'Art Múltiple* and was shown at the FAD (Foment de les Arts Decoratives, one of the forerunners of stimulating interest in design in Catalonia) at the end of 1974. It consisted of a criticism and protest against the opportunism of the competition and the acts associated with it. *Ajoblanco* was founded in 1974 "with a spirit of inquiry and out of necessity", with a plurality of interests (counter-cultures, underground and alternative movements, ecology, art, film, philosophy, etc.), "because we want to intervene, provoke, facilitate and make use of a creative culture". (Editorial no. 1). During these years other publications appeared such as *Star* and *Ozono*, which were interested in criticizing culture and daily life. Parallel to these magazines others appeared, such as *El Viejo Topo*, which were more theoretical-political oriented, even though they shared common concerns.

Grup de Treball, poster of the Group "Solidarity with the Workers' Movement", 1973, printed ink on paper, 50 x 80 cm MACBA Collection. Government of Catalonia Art Fund, © Grup de Treball, 2012, photo by Rocco Ricci

Internal disagreements within the group, the sporadic commitments of various members and the new political situation that was opening up after the death of Franco all played a part in their dissolution, which happened in 1975.[8] It is important to place the Grup de Treball in context in relation to other coetaneous artistic projects. Traditional histories have tended to group them all under the same heading of Conceptual Art in Catalonia. This, however, does not allow for individual differences and limits creative activity to the merely artistic, rather than taking into account the affiliations and networks of connections with other circles and in relation to clandestine projects and opposition to the regime.

Like Grup de Treball, Vídeo-Nou (1977–1978), which later became Servei de Vídeo Comunitari (1979–1983), grew out of the context of the struggle for democracy. But this time it appeared in the post-Franco era, precisely in the same year the first democratic elections since the Second Republic were held in Spain. This was "the first independent video collective in the Spanish state that worked in the field of social intervention to promote the contextual use of electronic communication".[9]

This arose at a time when expectations of freedom and the need for transformation in the country were at their highest point. This collective saw its project as inseparable from the historical context and social mobilizations, as part of a process of the decentralization of power and social autonomy.

In this regard, the appearance of portable video equipment provided the technology that enabled the activation of projects involving communication in alternative spaces that were decentralized and on the periphery. We should recall the precursor work of Muntadas, who in July 1974 organized a "Workshop of works with videotapes in groups," on the use, possibilities and projects with portable systems in the Sala Vinçon in Barcelona together with William Creston. That same month Muntadas did his *Cadaqués Canal Local* (Cadaqués Local Channel), which many believe was the first example of local television. Even if it was not exactly a television channel per se, it did, however, anticipate the community video projects of Vídeo-Nou. In 1976 he had already developed another similar project called *Barcelona Distrito Uno* (Barcelona District One), where he gave the neighborhood association in that district a voice with which to speak out, and utilized the space of the Galería Ciento

[8] Antoni Mercader believes that the last public appearance of the group took place in 1977 when they presented their work on the illegal press at the Fundació Miró in Barcelona as a part of the exhibition *Vanguardia artística y realidad social en el Estado español, 1936–1976*. This work was shown a year before at the Venice Biennale. See Antoni Mercader, "Sobre el Grup de Treball", in *Grup de Treball*, Museu d'Art Contemporani de Barcelona 1999, p. 8.

[9] As defined by one of its members, Carles Ametller. Quoted in Carles Ametller, "Vídeo-Nou. Servei de Vídeo Comunitari," *Banda Aparte. Revista de cine. Formas de ver*, no. 16, October 1999, p. 46.

as an information centre. The journalist and cultural activist, Josep M. Martí i Font, underlined Muntadas's contribution with an opportune reflection in relation to Vídeo-Nou:

"With his artistic activity Muntadas was filling a gap that should have corresponded to the neighbours themselves, that is, the unmasking of information by proposing to the individual the inevitable comparison with official television. When would there be a community television? Would it ever be possible for television to revert to the hands of society and free itself from official power? Because an artist's work can only indicate a road to follow at a certain point; it only sets down the guidelines for action, but it does not actually carry them out."[10]

In fact, Vídeo-Nou was born out of the will to foster an alternative type of communication in a country with only two public channels, both controlled by the state. It would be similar to the local television models in the Francophone regions of Canada, France and Belgium, rather than a guerrilla-type television. VN/SNC arose out of the VII Encuentros Internacionales de Vídeo organised by the Centro de Arte y Comunicación-CAYC of Buenos Aires that took place in the Fundació Miró in Barcelona in February 1977. Margarita d'Amico and Manuel Manzano, two Venezuelan experts in social communication and new technologies who participated in the symposiums on art, architecture and communication, offered to organize a workshop with Muntadas's portable equipment, and Vídeo-Nou was born.[11]

This project of collective communication was made up of people of diverse backgrounds and training, a fact that made for great versatility and intersecting interests. Many of its participants were former students of film from the CIPLA of the Institut del Teatre in Barcelona. Carlos Ametller had a degree in Fine Arts and Graphic Arts; Esteban Escobar was trained in anti-psychiatry; Albert Estibal studied medicine and journalism; Xefo Guasch was an architect and photographer; Marga Latorre, a sociologist; Pau Maragall (Pau Malvido), an economist; Maite Martínez, an urban planner; Luisa Ortínez, a lawyer; Lluïsa Roca, a school teacher; and Joan Úbeda an engineering student.[12] What they all had in common was their will to participate in social and political transformations of the time and an interest in appropriating the means of production of audiovisual information. While the mass media was being

[10] Josep M. Martí i Font, "Alternativa a la TV", *El Viejo Topo*, November 1976, p. 66. *El Viejo Topo* (1976–1982) was a journal that dealt with cultural topics from very marked sociological, philosophical and political points of view.

[11] They used Muntadas's portable system in their first interventions until they were able to buy their own equipment in Germany.

[12] Carles Ametller, see above, note. 8. Other participants mentioned in "Vídeo-Nou. Dossier 1977–1978" are Genís Cano (psychology graduate and research worker in educational sciences), Juan Cardona (electronics student) and Sylvie Poissenot (a television producer who had collaborated on projects with Muntadas). The academic and professional references of the members of the group refer to their occupations at that time, even though they may have worked in other fields later on.

manipulated and controlled according to the interests of those in power, this group was interested in the possibilities for transformation offered by the new technical resources.

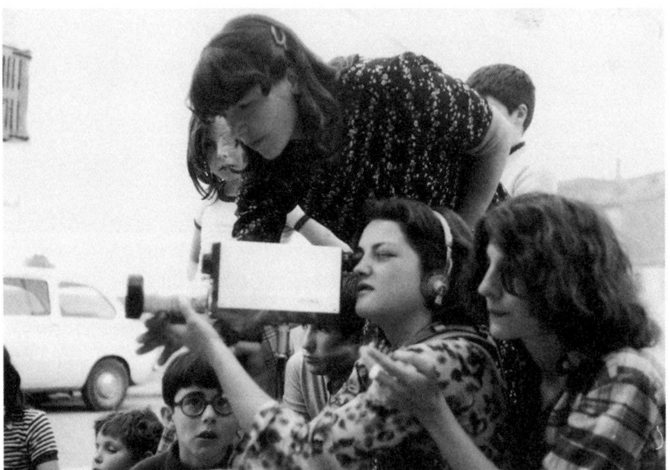

Vídeo-Nou, Photograph of the campaign of the Catalan League for the towns of Girona. Vídeo-Nou, 1977, left to right: Lluïsa Roca, Lluïsa Ortínez and Marga Latorre. MACBA Collection. Study Center. Vídeo-Nou Fund

Vídeo-Nou began working in social intervention and mediation with close ties to the industrial belt of Barcelona and immigration. Its aim was to create a network within local popular communities who, in turn, would become active participants in helping to transform their daily lives. They were also closely linked to popular culture and underground circuits in the city.[13] They spread out their activities in different fields of video application. One sector concentrated on social animation, that is, the study of forms of life and popular culture in the different sections of Barcelona. Films were made in which the participants became very involved in the subject matter, and they were then shown in cultural centers, bars, civic meetings and neighborhood associations.[14] A second field of action was the diffusion of information about politics, given that it coincided with the years when political parties and labor unions were being legalized and the first democratic elections were held.[15] A third activity was the making of documentaries on various subjects.[16] A fourth section worked in the artistic sphere, in particular, activities relating to the counter-culture and underground scenes.[17] The fifth activity involved the actual integration of audiovisual media in the field of teaching and in conjunction with

[13] Pau Maragall, one of the members of Vídeo-Nou/Servei de Vídeo Comunitari, signed his articles with the pseudonym "Pau Malvido". These chronicles, which were published under the heading "Nosotros los malditos" ("We the Damned or Cursed Ones") in *Star* magazine, contained a brief rundown of the counter-culture of the country. Vídeo-Nou/Servei de Vídeo Comunitari also recorded many of the activities of people and venues, galleries and spaces within this counter-cultural context.

[14] Examples of this type of video intervention are the films of the petrol station strike (1977) and intervention in the Can Serra district in L'Hospitalet de Llobregat (1978) in which neighbourhood associations were closely involved.

[15] Campaña por la Lliga de Catalunya (Campaign for the Catalonian League), April-May 1977; Las Jornadas Libertarias Internacionales de Barcelona (Barcelona Libertarian Days), June 1977, with a political and festive component; and the meeting of the U.G.T. Socialist labour union at Monjuic, Barcelona, December 1977.

[16] The first political elections held after the death of Franco in 1977; the first legal celebration of the Diada Nacional de Catalunya (the National Day of Catalonia) 11 September 1977; the demonstration for gay rights demanding the repeal of the Law of Social Danger for homosexuals (1977); and the bicycle demonstration by ecologists (1977).

schools.[18] Finally, the group worked in the professional sphere in advertising and film production.[19]

In 1978 they had already realized that it was impossible to attend to all the requests they received and that the material they had produced lacked a steady outlet for distribution. Thus, the Servei de Vídeo Comunitari (Community Video Service) was created.[20] Its purpose was to put at the disposal of cultural entities and community associations the training, loan of equipment, technical assistance and orientation of distribution at accessible prices. Following the line begun by Vídeo-Nou, its purpose was to present audiovisual language as a dynamic factor in the cultural life of the community. Its point of departure was the potential created by the city councils arising from the new democracy. At the same time, these proposals formed part of a criticism of the institutional processes within the politics of social planning. They conducted workshops to train people in the use of video as a means of communication in Barcelona and in other cities around the country. As Pepe Ribas, one of the founders of the magazine *Ajoblanco* pointed out,[21] Pau Maragall's contacts with the Socialists enabled them to establish relations with the new political leaders. An agreement was signed with the Barcelona city council between 1980 and 1982 to finance their activities in the different districts of the city in relation to everyday problems and topics of popular culture. Nevertheless, the agreement was not renewed in 1983, because the Socialist municipal government curtailed the autonomy of social initiatives in order to centralize them. This marked a critical moment within the associative movement and signaled the end of SVC. At the same time, several members turned professional and some became incorporated into the new autonomous television network of Catalonia. The end of the activities of this collective coincided, to a certain extent, with the institutionalization of the experimental cultural projects initiated under the democratic governments which, in turn, put an end to the expectation of possibilities for change.

Translated from the Spanish by Selma Margaretten.

17 The taping of a parody of the official television program with a news broadcast by Montesol and Onliyú (June 1977); participation in the Canet Rock music festival (July 1977); Ocaña's exhibition in Galería Mec-Mec in Barcelona (1977); Mariscal's exhibition *Gran Hotel* at the Galería Mec-Mec (1977); Lindsay Kemp's rehearsal at the Teatre Lliure (1977); the recitals of Sisa in the Saló Diana and Casavella in Zeleste (both in 1978), and Pau Riba's performance in Zeleste (1978).

18 Didactic programs for a kindergarten (1977) and a pilot school (1978), and the introduction of video media in a highschool (1978).

19 Publicity casting, translation and dubbing of a tape, television movies for a film, taping of a fashion show, collaboration on a film by Bigas Luna and the Muntañola report on urban games for the Colegio de Arquitectos.

20 Núria Font, Josep M. Roca and Francesc Albiol joined the group at this time.

21 See Pepe Ribas, *Los '70 a destajo. Ajoblanco y libertad*, Ediciones Destino, Barcelona 2007.

Retroavantgarde is not so much a contradiction in itself than a complex—and contested—object with various meanings. First of all, it is the title of an installation by the Slovenian artists' collective IRWIN created in the late 1990s. Secondly, the notion, which was coined and used respectively by Laibach Kunst, Peter Weibel, Marina Gržinić and IRWIN, is meant to identify an art movement on the territory of ex-Yugoslavia that developed during the 1980s. First used by Laibach Kunst in 1983[1], Peter Weibel in 1992 "re-invented" the notion without, however, referring to its origins.[2] In 1997, Marina Gržinić wrote that "in the 1990s, Peter Weibel re-launched a discursive matrix […] in which he coded the ex-Yugoslav territory from 'outside,' subsuming the productions of Stilinović, (the 1980s) Malevich and IRWIN under a common moniker: the 'Retro-avant-garde'. The trio repeated this matrix themselves in an exhibition entitled 'Retroavantgarda' (or 'Retro-avant-garde') in Ljubljana in 1994."[3] Finally, in 2003, the notion found its way into the seminal publication *Primary Documents: A Sourcebook for Eastern and Central European Art since the 1950s.*[4] Used as a chapter title ("Onward, Toward the Retroavantgarde") the notion is used to describe artistic movements in Eastern Europe in the 1980s and 1990s in general.

However, it has to be underlined that *retroavantgarde* neither existed as a clearly defined movement nor does it stand for a general trend in Eastern European art. Rather, it designates, if we follow Peter Weibel, a specific relation to, and a re-evaluation of, the historical avant-garde.[5] Retro-avantgarde is a "third avantgarde between early avantgarde and neo-avantgarde".[6] While Western neo-avantgarde was largely naïve in the sense that it took over and developed further only the formal innovations of the historical avant-garde, Retro-avantgarde "remembered not only the great and central contributions of the East to Western modernity, from Malevich to Ionescu, but also thematized remembrance, and therefore remained aware of the historical social experiences of this modernity."[7] Retro-avantgarde is about the destruction of historical naiveté.

1 Laibach Kunst: Monumentalna retroavantgarda – AUSSTELLUNG LAIBACH KUNST. Galerija ŠKUC, Ljubljana, 21 April 1983. *Neue Slowenische Kunst*, AMOK Books, Zagreb/Los Angeles 1991, p. 26.

2 Peter Weibel, "Probleme der Neo-Moderne," Peter Weibel and Christa Steinle (ed.), *Identität: Differenz. Tribüne Trigon 1940–1990. Eine Topographie der Moderne*, Böhlau, Vienna/Cologne/Weimar 1992, p. 3–21.

3 Marina Gržinić, *Fiction Reconstructed. Eastern Europe, Post-Socialism & the Retro-Avantgarde*, Edition Selene, Vienna 2000, p. 41 (originally published as *Rekonstruirana Fikcija. Novi Mediji, (Video) Umetnost, Postsocializem in Retroavantgarda: teorija, politika, estetika 1997-1985*, Ljubljana 1997).

4 *Primary Documents: A Sourcebook for Eastern and Central European Art since the 1950s*, MIT Press, Cambridge MA 2003.

5 Inke Arns, *Objects in the mirror may be closer than they appear! Die Avantgarde im Rückspiegel. Zum Paradigmenwechsel der künstlerischen Avantgarderezeption in (Ex-) Jugoslawien und Russland von den 1980er Jahren bis in die Gegenwart*, PhD dissertation, Humboldt-Universität zu Berlin, Philosophische Fakultät II, published

IRWIN's installation *Retroavantgarde* (1999) construes a fictive art movement for the geographic space of Yugoslavia, the "retro-avant-garde", whose roots can be traced back to various images and the artists allegedly belonging to this movement back to the 1910s and 1920s: the art movement Zenitism of the 1910s and 1920s (Belgrade), the artists Mangelos (Zagreb), Malevich (Belgrade, 1986), Goran Đordjević (Belgrade, 1980), Mladen Stilinović (Zagreb), Braco Dimitrijević (Sarajevo/ Paris), Necrorealism (St. Petersburg), Laibach Kunst (Trbovlje, 1981) and IRWIN/NSK (Ljubljana). According to Eda Čufer and Roger Conover, *Retroavantgarde* is a "complex artistic statement reflecting on the absence of a stable historic narrative on modern and contemporary art in Slovenia, Yugoslavia, and in Eastern Europe in general. The artistic achievement of these places never managed to become a part of the Western canon, or even develop its own consistent meta-narrative."[8]

November 22, 2004, http://edoc.hu-berlin. de/docviews/abstract. php?id=20894.

6 Peter Weibel, "Arteast: Retroavantgarde," Zdenka Badovinac and Peter Weibel (ed.), *2000+ ArtEast Collection*, Folio, Vienna/ Bozen 2001, p. 8.

7 Ibid.

8 Roger Conover/Eda Cufer, "IRWIN," Roger Conover/Eda Čufer/Peter Weibel (ed.), *In Search of Balkania. A Manual*, Neue Galerie Graz 2002, p. 67.

IRWIN, *Retroavantgarde*, 2000, View of the exhibition IRWIN Live, Moderna galerija, Ljubljana, 2000, photo by Lado Mlekuž, Matija Pavlovec, photo Courtesy of Moderna galerija, Ljubljana

As a reaction to this two-fold lack, the IRWIN group refers, with a gesture typical for them, back to an entity that was central to the definition and derivation of modernism: Alfred H. Barr's *Diagram of Stylistic Evolution from 1890 until 1935*.[9] This diagram, developed in 1936 by the founding director of New York's Museum of Modern Art (MoMA), lists the European avant-garde movements as precursors—almost in the sense of an aesthetic evolution theory—of the abstract art of modernism, both geometric and non-geometric. With a similarly arrogant attitude, IRWIN transfers this scheme onto Yugoslavia, here in the form of a reversed genealogy of the "retro-avant-garde," which extends from the neo-avant-garde

9 See Astrit Schmidt-Burkhardt, "The Barr Effect. New Visualizations of Old Facts," *International Exhibition of Modern Art featuring Alfred Barr's Museum of Modern Art, New York*, ed. by Branislav Dimitrijevic, Dejan Sretenovic, Belgrade 2003, p. 49–59.

of the present back to the period of the historical avant-garde.

In addition, as an alternative to the grand narratives of the West, IRWIN develops the strategy of "Eastern Modernism," which the group formulated for the first time in 1990 in the context of the exhibition series *Kapital*.[10] In asserting the existence of an "Eastern Modernism," the group polemically attacks Barr's and Greenberg's modernism, which posits itself as being universally valid. By qualifying the concept in this way, IRWIN indirectly suggests that modernism is actually a "Western Modernism" that does *not*, after all, possess universal validity.

As a new "Eastern Modernism," this retro-avant-garde is pitted against Western particularity, which considers itself to be universal. The installation *Retroavantgarde* is both an independent work of art and a pragmatic, cartographic instrument. In this work, IRWIN transforms that which it was barred from for a long time—both locally, through the specific political situation, and beyond Eastern Europe, through the above-mentioned international discourse: its own independent art historical chronicle. By postulating the existence of a fictive Yugoslavian retro-avant-garde, IRWIN (re)constructs and posits a modernism intrinsic to Eastern Europe. This "Eastern Modernism," however, turns out to be just as construed, fictive, and artificial as its Western counterpart.

(Most of) the artists involved, however, prove to be real. The five-member IRWIN group, founded in 1983 in Ljubljana, has been part of the multi-media artists' collective Neue Slowenische Kunst since 1984.[11] Together with the band Laibach and the theatre collective Scipion Nasice it developed a kind of hyper-eclectic appropriation art dealing with the traumas of the 20th century—in (Central- and South-) Eastern Europe. One of the recurring motifs in IRWIN's art production, often taking the form of classical oil paintings, emerges in *Malevich Between Two Wars*, which depicts the historical avant-garde being crushed between two world wars, between the past and ultra-modernity (read: totalitarianism; i.e. Soviet Stalinism, Italian fascism, German national socialism).

Zagreb-based conceptual artist Mladen Stilinović focuses on language and its ideological effects. *The Geometry of Cakes* (1994) consists of simple aluminum plates and dishes covered with constructivist and suprematist patterns combined

10 IRWIN, *Kapital*, cat. Ljubljana 1991. The first exhibition of *Kapital* took place in December 1990 at Equrna galerija in Ljubljana.

11 Inke Arns, *Neue Slowenische Kunst (NSK) – eine Analyse ihrer künstlerischen Strategien im Kontext der 1980er Jahre in Jugoslawien*, Regensburg: Museum Ostdeutsche Galerie 2002; Inke Arns (ed.), *IRWIN: Retroprincip 1983–2003*, Revolver – Archiv für aktuelle Kunst, Frankfurt am Main 2003.

with various slogans like "Time is money", "A poor man has
no friends", "He who does not work shall not eat", and with
the single words "Smrt" ("Death") and "Bol" ("Pain"). Here,
Stilinović points directly to the fate of the historical avant-
garde. By "repeating"—although in an impoverished fashion—
the decorated pottery of the historical (Russian) avant-garde of

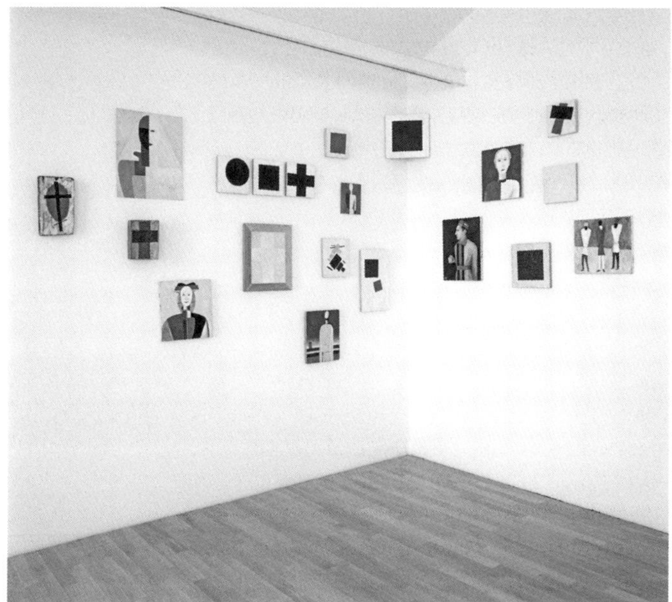

Kazimir Malevič / Malevich,
Zadnja futuristična
razstava / The Last Futurist
Exhibition, Beograd /
Belgrade, 1985-1986,
installation view of
exhibition The Present
and Presence, Museum
of Contemporary Art
Metelkova, Ljubljana,
2011-2012, photo by
Dejan Habicht, courtesy of
Moderna galerija, Ljubljana

the 1920s, Stilinović's pathetic plates transform into a devastating critique of the instrumentalization of the post-revolutionary
Russian avant-garde as well as of the political naiveté of parts
of the historical avant-garde itself. Stilinović's *Exploitation of
the Dead* (1984–1990) deals with the "DEAD OPTIMISM"
of the 20th century, which the artist localizes in the historical
avant-garde (constructivism, suprematism) as well as in the
grand narratives of Socialist industrialization, farming and
agriculture, physical discipline and sports, collectivism and
Socialist progress. For Stilinović, the signs or symbols of these
past (optim)isms have become completely dysfunctional and
obsolete (remember, we are in mid-1980s Socialist Yugoslavia)
and thus allow the artist to "conquer a language beyond the
reach of the terror of the past".[12] Finally, Stilinović's manifesto
Praise of Laziness (1993) is a case/work of late revenge on the
idealization of work (in Socialism), and is at the same time a

[12] Mladen Stilinović,
"Ein Gespräch mit Darko
Šimičić," *Zeichen im
Fluss*, Museum des 20.
Jahrhunderts, Vienna 1990,
p. 108.

shrewd rehabilitation of the exploited and expelled historical avant-garde.

From December 17, 1985 through January 19, 1986, a reconstruction of the *Last Futurist Exhibition 0.10* by Kazimir Malevich[13] took place in a small apartment in Belgrade, Yugoslavia, opening exactly seventy years after the exhibition in St. Petersburg of 1915/16. The installation consisted of a precise "re-enactment" of the only surviving photo of the renowned exhibition in St. Petersburg, which (photo) can be found in almost any serious publication on 20th century art. In addition to the reconstruction, one could see "the newest, neo-suprematist works" by Kazimir Malevich: suprematist figures on reliefs and sculptures from antiquity, as well as suprematist embroideries in kitschy golden frames.

First shown in Belgrade and Ljubljana in 1986, *The Last Futurist Exhibition 0.10,* together with the *International Exhibition of Modern Art* (a.k.a. The Armory Show, also shown in 1986 in Belgrade and Ljubljana) examines the relationship between original and copy, historicization and chronology, authorization and anonymity, center and periphery, as well as painting and conceptual art. This approach differs from American "appropriation art" through its radical anonymity and its conscious lack of authorship. While Sherrie Levine or Elaine Sturtevant may have made copies of artworks, they still signed them with their own names. In contrast, *The Last Futurist Exhibition 0.10* no longer allows such personal appropriations. This connects *The Last Futurist Exhibition 0.10* with other projects that are just as anonymous and obscure, such as the Salon de Fleurus in New York (since 1993), the Kunsthistorisches Mausoleum in Belgrade (since 2002), Alfred Barr's *Museum of Modern Art, New York, 1936,* and the Museum of American Art, established in Berlin in 2004.[14]

History transforms documents into monuments, wrote Michel Foucault.[15] Photography is not only a medium that allows society to build up extensive documentation; it also gives rise to (fictitious) memories and (hi)stories. Writing from Belgrade in 1986, Malevich remembers: "When I hung my suprematicist paintings here and there, I didn't even dream that the photo of this installation would become famous one day, and that it would be published in countless books and articles."[16] Projects like *The Last Futurist Exhibition 0,10*

[13] Earlier projects in this series (including *Short History of Art,* 1979/81; *Harbringers of Apocalypse,* 1981) can be ascribed to the authorship of Goran Djordjević, a visual artist originally trained as a nuclear physicist; but from 1985 onward his name disappears from the Yugoslav art context. Eda Čufer summarizes the rumors circulating around Đordjević as follows: "It is known that he left the country at the beginning of the 1990s after the fall of Yugoslavia, at the time when Serbia entered the war with other parts of the former country. After that stories began circulating about his reappearance in the United States, where it is said that he has worked for the last ten years as a doorman of the Salon de Fleurus, New York, a live re-enactment of Gertrude Stein's Paris salon from the early 20th century housing her collection of modern art. One heard, too, about Goran Djordjevic lecturing on the history of modern art on different occasions in the USA and Europe, presenting himself as a former artist and current second-hand (art) dealer. In the former Yugoslav and international art circles, however, Đordjević is remembered for a small number of highly enigmatic projects from the late 1970s and early 1980s, which introduced the philosophy of a very special branch of appropriation art and had a strong impact on the next generation of artists. His 1979 attempt to initiate an International Artist's Strike still occupies a special place in the dossier of the Neoist's Artists Strike history." (Eda Čufer, *In Search of Balkania,* p. 42)

repeat and adopt history, saving and preserving it by creating its simulacrum. In this process—and this is valid also for the *Retroavantgarde*—fiction and genealogy are no longer irreconcilable opposites, but become close accomplices.

[14] The exhibition *What is Modern Art? (Group Show)* gathered a series of art projects that have contributed to the development of a specific art practice based on anonymity and copying. Some of them, with roots in the (South-Eastern) European art scene of the 1970s-1980s, became a central point of inspiration for a younger generation of artists in Yugoslavia (i.e. Laibach, IRWIN) and elsewhere. *What is Modern Art (Group Show)* was the first exhibition to gather these projects in a comprehensive group exhibit in Berlin in 2006. See Inke Arns and Walter Benjamin (ed.), *What is Modern Art? (Group Show)*, 2 Vols. Revolver – Archiv für aktuelle Kunst, Frankfurt am Main 2006; Inke Arns, "Les trous de ver de l'histoire de l'art" ("Art History's Wormholes"), *Trouble*, 'Storytellers', Paris 2010, p. 131–149.

[15] Michel Foucault, *Archeology of Knowledge*, Routledge, New York/London 1972 [1969].

[16] Kazimir Malevich, "A Letter from Kazimir Malevich," *Art in America*, September (1986), p. 9.

"A Huge Amusement-Park Exhibition"[1] / *Vision in Motion* (1959)

Jan Ceuleers

Over and above the result of the calculation of space, time, and quantity, we must allow a certain percentage which boldness derives from the weakness of others, whenever it gains the mastery. It is therefore, virtually, a creative power.

Carl von Clausewitz, *On War*, I, 3 (1832)

In 1958 Belgium hosts the first post-war World's Fair. The enormous spectacle of progress is accompanied by large-scale works in and around the capital Brussels, which is quickly developing into a European business centre. Compared to this frenzy, Antwerp makes a hackneyed impression. The country's second largest city is an economic heavyweight as an international port, but its cityscape shows little evidence of this. New buildings, such as the Woonheid (Housing Unit) Kiel by architect Renaat Braem, who had worked with Le Corbusier, are located on the outskirts of town, as is the Middelheim Sculpture Park, where international works are presented every second year. Contemporary art is virtually invisible in Antwerp, apart from a few initiatives such as *Ad Libitum*, an international exhibition of lyrical abstract work organized by the future art dealer John Trouillard in 1956. Influenced by the new visual language conquering all of Europe, various young people are producing art of their time and in 1958, form a group under the name G58. They are not a movement with a program but an association of progressive artists urgently seeking opportunities to show their work. Mayor Craeybeckx is amongst the first of the local leaders to realize that the future will not bypass Antwerp and that it is high time for a (modest) catching-up with Brussels, where the Palais des Beaux-Arts runs an exhibition policy of high standard, which also includes contemporary art. G58 obtains access to the attic of the Hessenhuis [Hesse House], an abandoned 16th century warehouse in the harbor area, owned by the City of Antwerp. Paradoxically, from November 1958 until the spring of 1962 this sleepy metropolis tallies the largest amount of space given to contemporary art in Europe, more than 1000 m². The Centre for Contemporary Artistic Expression is initiated on

[1] Daniel Spoerri in a letter to Dieter Roth, February 1959, inviting him to participate in the exhibition known as *Vision in Motion—Motion in Vision*, Hessenhuis, Antwerp, March 21–May 3, 1959. Quoted from: *Roth Time*, The Museum of Modern Art, New York 2004, p. 85.

November 29, 1958 with a group exhibition, an eclectic ensemble of all varieties of abstract art. The opening is a great success, with 1,400 visitors, official speeches and a morning=after with lots of empty bottles. Until the spring of 1962 there is a busy program of exhibitions of new art from home and abroad, concluding with *Anti-peinture*, an international overview of kinetic art and assemblage.

The second major exhibition, *Vision in Motion—Motion in Vision*, in the spring of 1959, confronts the public with much newer art than the meanwhile marginally accepted *Nouvelle École de Paris*. An initiative to establish a "major international manifestation" around "The Movement" comes from Marc Callewaert, art critic and chairman of G58. For years Callewaert had defended the latest directions in art, also in the local right-wing conservative newspaper *Gazet van Antwerpen*, where he was a journalist. The first contacts he made date back to early January 1959. Paul Van Hoeydonck, the only G58 artist whose work fits the theme, is also involved in the organization. Letters from Van Hoeydonck to Agam and Schöffer[2] suggest that inspiration for the project comes from *Le Mouvement*, an exhibition at Denise René, the Paris gallery where kinetic art was launched in 1955. But when Pol Bury, who exhibits in the small space at the Hessenhuis in the winter of 1959, is asked to collaborate, the story takes a radically different turn. The initiative shifts to an informal network of experimental artists, with Jean Tinguely as the driving force. Communication lines run from Antwerp to La Louvière, an old industrial city 50 km south of Brussels, where Bury lives, then to Paris, and on to Düsseldorf, branching-off to Milan, Darmstadt and New York. In 1955 Bury had participated in *Le Mouvement* together with Soto and Tinguely, and Robert Breer presented a few short films in the associated film program. In the years that follow, Bury often visits Tinguely in Paris, in the Impasse Ronsin, where Yves Klein also has a studio. Since the end of 1958, Klein has been working on a huge wall decoration involving blue sponges, for the new theatre in Gelsenkirchen, 50 km from Düsseldorf. Tinguely comes to assist him in January 1959, and in March is himself commissioned to make two large mobile reliefs in the foyer of the same theatre. The exhibition *Concerto No.2* by Tinguely opens in Galerie Schmela in Düsseldorf on January 30, 1959, an animated occasion. Yves Klein—the gallery first began with

2 Letter from Paul Van Hoeydonck, Wijnegem (near Antwerp), to Nicolas Schöffer, January 3, 1959. Private collection.

his *Propositions monochromes* in 1957—delivers a speech about *"la collaboration entre artistes créateurs"* [the collaboration between creative artists], and Daniel Spoerri, who works as assistant director at the theatre in Darmstadt and publishes the journal *material,* containing concrete poetry, presents an *Autotheater* in which the same text is recited at different speeds by three persons. The after-party at Uecker's studio would last three days. Tinguely sees the project in Antwerp as a one-in-a-million chance to show experimental art on a large scale and puts together a dream-team. Naturally, Yves Klein takes part, as does Spoerri, who in turn invites Dieter Roth. He then ensures that the "sculptures" for which Roth sends sketches from New York are constructed and installed. Tinguely invites Mack and Piene, and later also Uecker, who together had not yet assumed the label "Zero." Bury brings along Soto and also Munari, a versatile artist-designer he had met in Milan a few years earlier. The arrival of Klein and Tinguely in the Ruhr region acts as a catalyst in an environment in which contemporary art is still largely "informal art". They bring with them extreme ideas and gestures, and are far more confident than the ever "aspiring" local artists. They have left Paris and now step into the international scene. In the new dynamics of the European art world circa 1960, they see the promotional opportunities quicker than most of their colleagues and realize that collective action has great advantages.

Apart from collaborations with artists in the margin, competition between dealers who clearly differ in their approach to new art also plays a role in the background. With geometric abstraction on the decline, Denise René must forfeit much territory to new galleries, such as Iris Clert, which is the-place-to-be in Paris in the spring of 1959. She makes much ado with unexpected presentations, exhibitions that are works in themselves, such as *Le Vide* (1958), when Yves Klein showed nothing but an empty gallery. In 1956 Tinguely left Denise René for Iris Clert, whose theatrical style better suited his work. In July 1958 he exhibited *Mes étoiles—concert pour sept peintures* and in November, together with Klein, the collaborative installation *Vitesse pure et stabilité monochrome.* Competition between Denise René and Iris Clert is not limited to Paris. At the beginning of February1959, Nicolas Schöffer, the constructor of spatio-dynamic works, let it be known to Van Hoeydonck that he

cannot participate because his pieces are too large and difficult
to transport, that during the upcoming season Denise René is
also planning a large exhibition on "movement in art," and that
she and Vasarely do not appreciate that Vasarely is not invited
to Antwerp.[3] Agam, like Schöffer, an artist of the Denise René
stable, replies that he cannot participate because the invitation
arrived too late.[4] As Tinguely hears about the obstruction he
reacts strongly with "*de toute façon le mot mouvement ne sera
pas utilize*" [anyway, the word "movement" will not be used].[5]
Antwerp will indeed not become a reissue of *Le Mouvement*.

The list of names on the poster—Breer, Bury, Klein, Mack,
Mari, Munari, Piene, Rot, Soto, Spoerri, Tinguely, Uecker,
Van Hoeydonck—better represents its weight than *Vision in
Motion—Motion in Vision*, the title of the catalogue text by
Callewaert in which he quotes from Moholy-Nagy's influential
book *Vision in Motion* (1947). The exhibition is the product
of a temporary alliance of like-minded artists who each had
their own agenda. They are almost all on the verge of breaking
through and want to exhibit as often as possible—like the G58
artists, but at a higher level. So they seize the unique chance
to freely avail themselves of a far larger space than that of the
studios or galleries where they had exhibited up until then. By
determining the selection themselves, they achieve a result that
is more coherent and creates more of an effect than the usual
eclectic group exhibitions. For the catalogue, too, the artists
provide the material themselves. The exhibition opens with a
hundred works characterized by virtual and real movement, but
that are more deregulating by design than the decorative *trompe
l'œil* of most kinetic art. Robert Breer recycles abstract art in
pre-cinema (mutoscopes) and "concrete" short films. In Pol
Bury's mobile reliefs, metal strips move back and forth or small
rods slowly and irregularly sweep a cloth forward. Yves Klein
does not present any work but realizes for the first time a "pure"
conceptual work. While present at the opening (where he quotes
Gaston Bachelard: "*D'abord il n'y a rien, ensuite il ya un rien
profond, puis une profondeur bleue*" [At first there is nothing,
after that there is nothing deep, and then a deep blue], he guar-
antees the effective existence of a *sensibilité picturale imma-
térielle* [immaterial pictorial sensibility], of which he has three
"zones" for sale, payable in pure gold. Mack shows *peintures
dynamiques* in resin and *reliefs lumière* in aluminum. In the

3 Letter from Nicolas
Schöffer, Paris, to Paul Van
Hoeydonck, February 6,
1959. Private collection.

4 Letter from J. Agam,
Paris, to "Chers amis",
March 12, 1959. Private
collection.

5 Letter from Tinguely
to Pol Bury, undated
(February 1959). Private
collection.

end, Mari does not participate. Munari projects ten slides of abstract motifs through a polarized filter, with constantly changing color effects. Piene presents white and yellow monochrome canvases. Roth has realized two projects: a metal hoop with hooks across which spectators can stretch a rope, and a structure with vertically mounted, rotating metal bands. Soto presents his latest work, metal wires and rods in front of a background of parallel lines. Spoerri exhibits in Antwerp for the first time as an artist: *Autotheater*, a construction with a revolving cylinder with three types of typed "instructions" against a background of vibrating metal plates mirroring the readers, and *Holzplastik*, an assemblage of wooden slats, including a saw, hammer and nails, that encourage the public to make changes. Three mobile reliefs with percussion bars, by Tinguely, together produce a "concert". Here to be seen for the first time is the work for which Uecker will become known, monochrome rectangular panels and a ball, covered with rows of nails. Van Hoeydonck presents long narrow panels, painted white-on-white with black or red stripes.

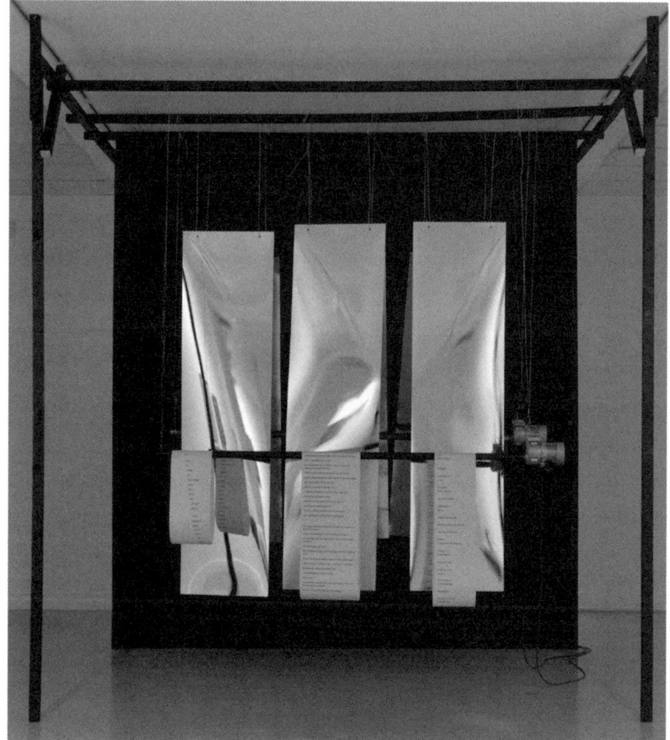

Daniel Spoerri, *Autotheater*, 1959, reconstructed with the artist, 2012, photo by M HKA

In the press release, Callewaert writes about the fusion of art and science and the necessity of new media in order to arrive at a more time-bound creation, and concludes on artists concerned with genuine renewal as follows: *Autant par le caractère spectaculaire de leurs œuvres que par le cadre où elles seront présentées, mais surtout par leur valeur de choc, leur venue en Belgique promet d'être un réel évènement artistique* [As much for the spectacular nature of their works as for the context in which they will be presented, but especially for their shock value, their arrival in Belgium promises to be a real artistic event]. On reading the comments in the press, the "*valeur de choc*" has done its work. For journalists, it is a reissue of Dada: the "exceptional stunt" by Yves Klein; the machines by Tinguely that mostly make noise... In this "salon of inventions" full of "amusement park attractions", the only positive elements of "balanced vision" are by Soto, Mack and Piene, and the "delicate" paintings by Van Hoeydonck. The references to Dada do not appear out of thin air. In the autumn of 1958, a major historical overview of Dada is held at the Stedelijk Museum in Amsterdam, which continues on to Düsseldorf. American critics are already using the label "Neo-Dada" for artwork by Johns, Rauschenberg and other artists who make assemblages or work with mixed media. At the same time, in revised histories of modern art, Duchamp is assigned a pioneering role, which only grows with the rise of Pop and *Nouveau Réalisme*.

The oft-told affray between Van Hoeydonck and Tinguely during the opening was certainly caused by a clash of personalities, but above all, by deep-seated differences. Opening in a smaller space next to *Vision in Motion* on the same evening, is an exhibition by Bert De Leeuw, painter and member of G58. Tinguely and his friends had dismissed abstract art, so they would definitely not be associated with it. When Tinguely demands that that outdated art disappear behind a locked door, the discussion turns into a dogfight with Van Hoeydonck. In a letter to the Polish Constructivist Henryk Berlewi, dated June 24, 1959,[6] Van Hoeydonck relays his views on the state of affairs, adopting the journalists' reactions: "Piene and Mack make neo-impressionist work that one can still defend, but the others—Tinguely, Bury, Spoerri, Rot—are simply neo-Dadaists, without the least originality." The conflict actually revolved around strategy. Artists such as Tinguely effectively assessed

6 Letter from Paul Van Hoeydonck to Henryk Berlewi, June 24, 1959. Private collection.

which experiments delivered usable material for the changing market and how brutally they could implant themselves without falling out of favor. Probably under the influence of the orthodox geometric abstract environment from which he comes, Van Hoeydonck wants to solidify his name as a "serious" artist. He sees the irony that characterizes so much Neo-avant-garde art as a threat to the "real" art that he makes and that he wants to show as efficiently as possible, without hindrance. As an illustration of these thoroughly different postures, here's a quote from a letter Spoerri writes to Roth in New York at the beginning of 1959: "On March 2nd there is a huge amusement-park exhibition of 2000 square meters in Antwerp where anybody who's interested in the movement in any form should, can and may contribute... you're invited too." [7]

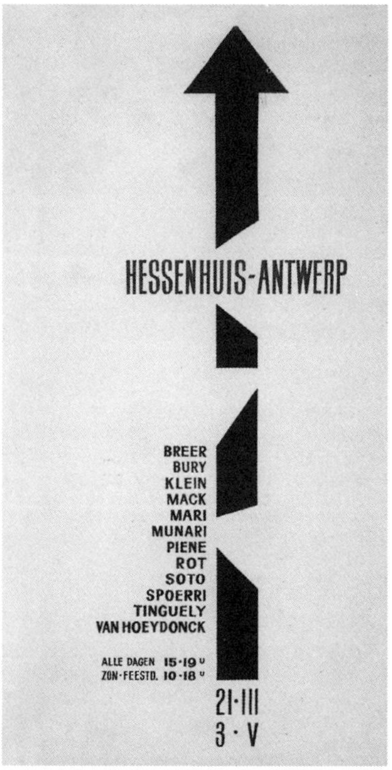

Poster *Vision in Motion
– Motion in Vision*,
Hessenhuis, Antwerp,
March 21 – May 3, 1959

[7] In: *Roth Time*. New York: The Museum of Modern Art, 2004, p. 85.

Vision in Motion is the missing link between *Le Mouvement* (1955) and *Bewogen beweging/Rörelse i konsten* at Stedelijk Museum in Amsterdam and Moderna Museet in Stockholm (1961–1962). These three exhibitions based on movement in art—whose participants partially overlap—reveal the growing dynamic of the art world. Not just in regard to the contact between the increasing numbers of mobile artists (and dealers, collectors, exhibition makers) but also at the level of the works themselves, which are becoming ever newer and faster—with the broken arrow in *Vision in Motion* as the dynamic, optimistic symbol par excellence. In Antwerp, the trends that will determine the new art of the next decade are evident. Behind the nostalgic patina of the works and the anecdotes of the phase preceding professionalization, the real interests of those involved often threaten to disappear. The story of that occurrence—the unique location, the good timing—is the story of a number of artists who become more acutely aware of their ambitions and who discover the resources they need in order to realize a career leap. Where *Le Mouvement* had been a gallery exhibition, *Vision in Motion* was managed by the artists themselves. *Bewogen beweging*, a larger scale version of *Vision in Motion*, organized by Spoerri, Tinguely and Pontus Hultén, marks the end of a number of artists' initiatives and rings-in the as-yet unclosed era of the curator. *Vision in Motion* is a dress rehearsal not only through the confrontational presentation announcing the grandest displays, but also through the altered character of the works that are no longer paintings or sculptures, but are more brutal, more intrusive than people were used to after ten years of lyrical and geometric abstraction. It is also the end of seriousness in art. The blending of high and low culture is not only visible in the imagery of Pop and the like, it also lies at the base of the theatrical presentation of art and causes artists to experiment with "strong" images until they discover a unique selling proposition. Up until the moment in which the artist himself becomes the artwork, as in the "performance" by Yves Klein—neo-dandy par excellence—that premiered in Antwerp in 1959. The journalists who labeled the latest artworks as "fairground attractions" have not yet realized that in a culture dominated by mass media, visual art has evolved into one product line among many others, and that art and the presentation of art will be judged on its entertainment value. Despite all invitations to participate, the "interactive" role of the public does not transcend that of consumers in supermarkets, which, at around the same time, also open their doors in Belgium. The viewer is tempted to surrender to a "fascinating" work of art that moves—at the touch of a button—or imitates motion on a "hypnotic" monochrome screen that evokes a sense of endless space. Light as an artistic "material" must enchant the eye, like comets or eclipses have done for centuries. Finally, as a modernized *l'art pour l'art*, the "new trends" befit the ultra-positive self-image of a triumphant economy. Barely ten years have gone by, but what a difference between the legendary photographs of Jackson Pollock making drip paintings and the well-known image of the happy screaming lady on Tinguely's meta-matic machines.

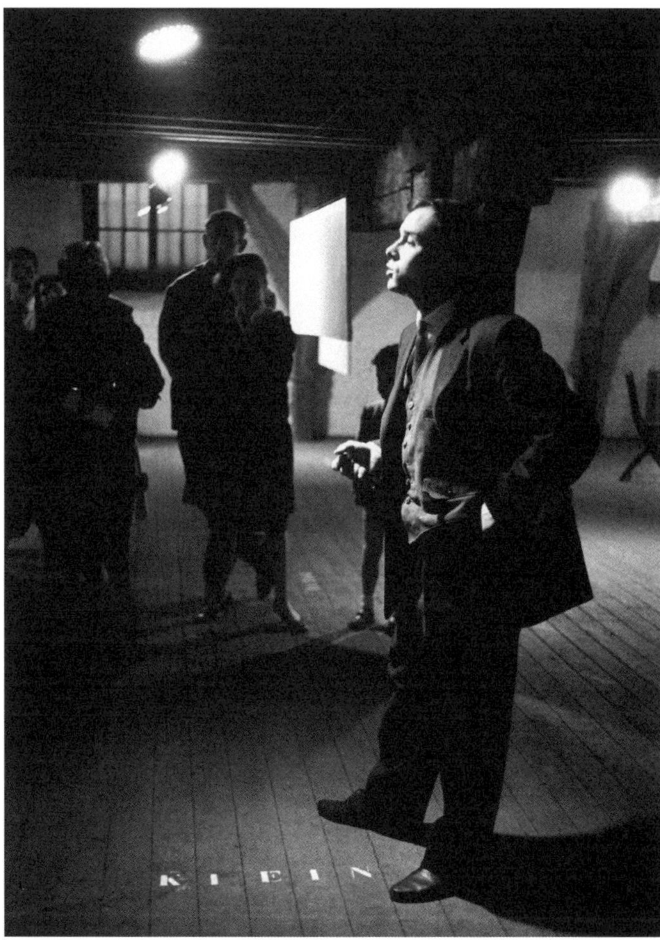

Yves Klein, proposing for sale, for the first time, *Zones of Immaterial Pictorial Sensibility*. Hessenhuis, Antwerp, March 21, 1959, photo by Frank Philippi

In the 1960s, together with a radical overhaul of the Belgian industrial apparatus, a changing of the guards also takes place in the ruling class. New captains of industry are adorning their

business doings in an up-to-date culture, from new architecture
to new art on the wall. New galleries respond to the growing
demand for contemporary art. John Trouillard establishes the
Ad Libitum gallery in Antwerp in 1961, with exhibitions by
nearly all of the participants of *Vision in Motion*. The cooperative nature of G58 is replaced by commerce, and all that
goes with it. With contracts and monopolies, Trouillard soon
occupies much territory: in the spring of 1962 he refuses to
allow Mack, Piene and Uecker to participate in *Anti-peinture*,
the last major G58 exhibition; in December 1962, under the
title *Dynamo* he organizes an exhibition with Mack, Piene and
Uecker at the Palais des Beaux Arts in Brussels; in the group
exhibition *Forum '62* in Ghent, he negotiates a separate "Zero"
section with works by the trio and by Bury, Fontana, Klein,
Soto, and Verheyen; in 1963 he advertises the new season with
Vision in Motion II.

At a local level, Galerie Ad Libitum illustrates the major
role that branding will play in the art world in the upcoming years. Critic/manager Pierre Restany launched the brand
Nouveau Réalisme in 1960, with Yves Klein, Spoerri, Tinguely,
and others. Mack, Piene and Uecker first exhibit under the
label *Dynamo* and then opt for *Zero* in order to safely secure
their market position. Until today, Zero is defended as a brand
and history is rewritten with the group in a unique pioneering
and leadership role. And, when necessary, an exhibition such
as *Vision in Motion* is hijacked *post festum*. Already in 1964,
Otto Piene writes: "Perhaps the most important Zero exhibition took place at the Hessenhuis in Antwerp in March 1959."[8]
Some forty years later, in a text about Yves Klein in Germany,
Marion Guibert states just as brutally: *"l'exposition 'Vision in
Motion – Motion in Vision', qui réunit pour la première fois les
protagonistes européens de Zero, comme Bury, Soto, Spoerri,
Tinguely, Munari, ou Hoeydonck"*.[9] Ever since the major exhibition *Zero International Antwerp* at the Antwerp Museum of
Fine Arts in 1980, certain authors have done their best to put
Antwerp on the map of new art circa 1960. And in one stroke,
the port of arrival in the Ruhr region also becomes an artistic
affiliate of Düsseldorf. For Jean Buyck, curator of the exhibition, initiatives such as *Vision in Motion* are moments in "the
international evolution of Zero-thought".[10] And it is almost
as if Fontana and Manzoni have only succeeded due to their

8 *The Times Literary
Supplement*, London,
September 3, 1964.

9 Marion Guibert, "Yves
Klein en Allemagne,
1957–1961," *Yves Klein.
Corps, couleur, immate-
rial*, Editions du Centre
Pompidou, Paris 2006.

10 Jean Buyck, "De jaren
'60 van Zero tot VAGA,"
Antwerpen. De jaren zestig,
Hadewych, Antwerp 1988,
p. 184.

"connections" with Zero. The German economic miracle obviously had a great impact via the Documenta exhibitions and the new museums and galleries, but without dominating the other artistic centers in Europe. The "New Figuration" that sets the tone around 1965 and shoves Zero and others to the background, does not, for example, depart from the German scene. The complex story of *Vision in Motion* breaches every monopolistic vision of the pivotal moment in the European art scene circa 1960. And of what came afterwards.

Translated from the Dutch by Jodie Hruby.

Overcoming Alienation / *New Tendencies* 1961–1973 Armin Medosch

On the August 3, 1961 the exhibition *nove tendencije / new tendencies* was opened at Galerija suvremene umjetnosti (Gallery of Contemporary Art) in Zagreb. This exhibition was the inaugural moment of an international art movement called New Tendencies (NT). This article presents, in brief, key aspects of NT, a project that subscribed to modernistic, socialist-humanist, utopian and emancipatory values. Giving consideration to NT means to gain a richer understanding of modernism at its peak, and a sense for the movement's unrealized potentials.

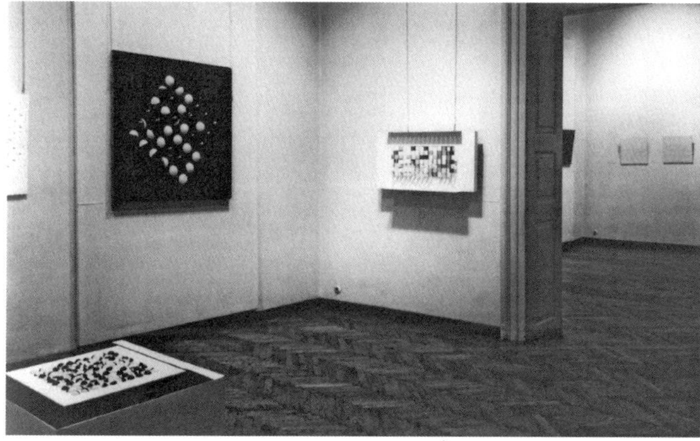

NT1, 1961, Exhibition view: *b 256 and k 36* by Paul Talman and Julio Le Parc, *Probability of Black Being Equal to White No. 4* (wall, right side), photo by MSU Zagreb

NT was held as a biennale in Zagreb in 1961, 1963 and 1965, and then again twice, in 1968/69 and in 1973. During its first phase, from 1961 to 1965, the biennale experienced rapid development driven by a decided opposition to abstract expressionism and informal painting. NT soon found itself included in major exhibitions in Venice, Paris, Kassel and New York. The exhibition *The Responsive Eye* (1965) in particular, at MoMA, New York, was seen by some as a crowning achievement; and by others as a "first class funeral"[1].

Following the MOMA show in New York, NT artists were subsumed under the label Op Art, which was specifically invented for *The Responsive Eye* and meant to signal a new trend that could rival Pop Art[2]. While a career-making

[1] Manfredo Massironi, "Kritike Primjedbe o Teoretskim Prilozima Unutar Nove Tendencije Od 1959 Do 1964 Godine," *Nova Tendencija 3 / New Tendency 3, New Tendencies Catalogues 3*, Galerija suvremene umjetnosti, Zagreb 1965, p. 23–33.

[2] "Op Art: Pictures That Attack the Eye," *Time*, October 23, 1964 <http://www.time.com/time/magazine/article/0,9171,897336-1,00.html> [30 August 2012].

exhibition for some, for others like Manfredo Massironi from the Padua-based Gruppo N it signified the "dangers that are characteristic of all kinds of intellectual work which takes place within a capitalistic society"[3]. NT's political concerns, which were closely intertwined with their formal innovations and the poetics and aesthetics of their works, were misinterpreted by the show's curator, William C. Seitz, who reassured catalogue readers, "these artists are not revolutionaries; they aspire to full cooperation with the modern world and are open to almost any application of their creativity"[4]. But what were the politics of a movement on which Italian curator Lea Vergine would look back, in the 1980s, as the "last avant-garde"[5]?

NT emerged from networks of artist-led initiatives that linked studios, storefront galleries and publications such as Azimut gallery and *Azimuth* magazine run by Enrico Castellani and Piero Manzoni in Milan, the groups N in Padua and T in Milan, Zero in Dusseldorf, Group d'Recherche d'Art Visuel (GRAV) in Paris and a number of former students of Ernst Geitlinger in Munich. In those networks around 1960 a flurry of activities preceded NT. In a manifesto written for one of those projects, the group exhibition *La Nuova Conzezione Artistica* (The New Concept of Art) (1960), the artists proclaimed that the new art was characterized by "a search and by research" and that it was transgressing "traditional aesthetics to defend an *ethics of collective life*"[6].

NT is not easy to pin down politically. If Matko Meštrović's text "The Ideology of New Tendencies"[7] serves as a point of orientation, then it did not adhere to any school of Marxist theory. Most participants would fall under the rubric "New Left," if that meant reading the young Marx. NT members were also contemporaries of the journal *Praxis*, run by a group of philosophers and sociologists from Zagreb and Belgrade, but there was not really much direct contact and the Praxis critics, influenced by the Frankfurt School, could not access the advanced neo-Constructivist positions of NT[8]. While some NT participants were not even Marxists, particular interpretations of Constructivism and Productivism[9] formed NT's core belief-system, along with a serious dose of the Bauhaus foundation course.

A significant role was played by Latin American artists who came to Paris after exhibitions by Max Bill in Brazil and

3 Massironi, 1965, n. p.

4 William Seitz and MoMA NYC, *The Responsive Eye* (exhib. cat. 1965–1966, Museum of Modern Art, New York, in collaboration with the City Art Museum of St. Louis et al.), Museum of Modern Art, New York 1965), p. 41.

5 L'ultima Avanguardia (exhib. cat., Palazzo Reale Di Milano), G. Mazzotta, Milano 1983.

6 Biasi, Castellani, Mack, Manzoni, Massironi (1960), quoted in Lucilla Meloni, "Geschichte / Geschichten Des Gruppo N (History / Stories of Gruppo N)," *Gruppo N – Oltre La Pittura, Oltre La Scultura, L'arte Programmata*, Collana Della Fondazione VAF, 9, VAF Fondazione and Silvana Editoriale, Frankfurt am Main and Cinisello Balsamo 2009, p. 41–76 (p. 45), my emphasis.

7 Matko Meštrović, "Untitled (The Ideology of the New Tendencies)," *Nove Tendencije 2 – New Tendencies 2, New Tendencies Catalogues 2, Galerija suvremene umjetnosti, Zagreb1963, no pagination.

8 Ljiljana Kolešnik, "A Decade of Freedom, Hope and Lost Illusions. Yugoslav Society in the 1960s as a Framework for New Tendencies," *Journal of The Institute of Art History Zagreb*, no. 34 (2010), p. 211–219.

9 This was hardly ever explicitly formulated but confirmed by a long letter from Matko Meštrović, Aug. 29, 1965, to the American curator Douglas MacAgy.

Argentina in 1950[10]; among them Almir Mavignier who, on a visit to Zagreb in 1960, had a serendipitous meeting with the Croatian art critic Matko Meštrović—NT's foundational moment. Mavignier and Meštrović connected the North-Italian, French, Dutch, German, Swiss and Austrian artists with the circle of artists and critics around the Gallery of Contemporary Art, Zagreb.

10 George Rickey, *Constructivism: Origins and Evolution*, G. Braziller, New York 1967, p. 62.

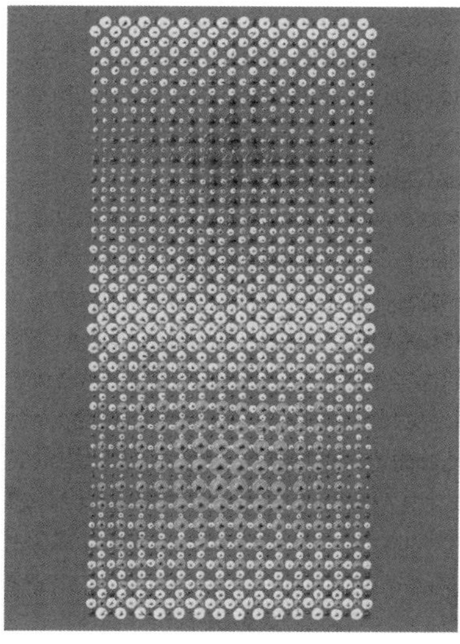

Almir Mavignier, *Rectangle*, 1961, MSU Zagreb Nr. 763

This circle consisted of former members of the group Exat 51 (Experimentalni atelje / Experimental Studio) like the graphic designer Ivan Picelj, the architect Vjenceslav Richter and the painter Alexander Srnec. Exat 51 had launched a discourse on Constructivist tendencies with their 1951 manifesto, which was published by reading it out at the annual plenum of the Croatian Association of Artists of Applied Arts[11]. Like many others involved in NT, Exat 51[12] saw "no difference between so-called pure and so-called applied art;" and assumed their task was to "enrich the sphere of visual communication in our country"[13].

The existence of NT was only possible because the Federal Socialist Republic of Yugoslavia was not part of the Soviet bloc. After the Yugoslav leader Tito had fallen out with Stalin in 1948, Yugoslavia was working to find its "own path to Socialism," which was based on notions of self-management and self-government[14]. The arts were liberated from the doctrine of Socialist Realism. Moreover, Zagreb had a specific

11 Ješa Denegri, "Inside or Outside 'Socialist Modernism', Radical Views on the Yugoslav Art Scene, 1950–1970," Dubravka Djuric and Misko Suvakovic (ed.), *Impossible Histories: Historical Avant-gardes, Neo-avant-gardes, and Post-avant-gardes in Yugoslavia, 1918–1991*, MIT Press, Cambridge, MA 2003, p. 170–208 (p. 178); WHW, "Modernism and Its Discontents: Croatian Avant-gardes of the 50s," *Id : Ideologija Dizajna = Ideology of Design : [zbornik tekstova/reader]*, Autonomedia, New York 2009, p. 211–219 (p. 211).

12 Members were the painter and designer Ivan Picelj, the painter and filmmaker Vlado Kristl, artist Aleksandar Srnec, and the architects Božidar Rašica, Vjenceslav Richter, Bernardo Bernardi, Zdravko Bregovac, Zvonimir Radić, and Vladimir Zarahovic.

13 Exat 51, "Manifesto Exat 51," *Impossible Histories*, p. 539.

pre-disposition towards Constructivism because of interwar avant-gardes such as *Zenith* magazine[15] and modernist architecture. At the time of the first NT exhibition in 1961, Yugoslavia was in a catch-up process of modernization, and trying to move from Soviet-style industrialization toward the production of consumer goods[16]. Because of this shift there heightened attention was given to improving the quality of product design and visual communication. Although Exat 51 initially experienced problems finding acceptance and had broken up as a group in 1955, its former members were strongly engaged in this modernization process—by designing and building pavilions and exhibition designs for world expositions and the like.

Others involved in NT were gallery director Bozo Bek and critic Radoslav Putar. Putar and Meštrović were both simultaneously members of Gorgona, a group of artists and theorists involved in "absurdist" practices who were important precursors of conceptual art[17]. The partial overlap between Gorgona and NT is evidence against any linear interpretation of art history, which slots NT in the "functionalist" box[18]. Neo-Dada and other non-functionalist influences were particularly strong in the first show, in which Piero Manzoni may have had a hand in curating the Italian contribution[19].

The result of the first Zagreb exhibition in 1961 allowed a new pattern of art making to emerge or become evident. *NT1* was dominated by works "that possessed none of the traditional characteristics of sculpture and had more the character of an object," argued Almir Mavignier, who accordingly arranged the exhibition, *"from painting to object"*[20]. Immediately after *NT1* in August 1961, the participants began to understand themselves as a movement.

Between 1961 and 1963 in a series of meetings in Paris and Zagreb the movement NT attempted to better define or refine its positions. NT rejected the notion of the artist as a genius who produces luxury commodities for the art market. The critique of the role of art in society guided NT to define art as visual research. The social structure most appropriate for this new definition was the group, which fostered collaboration and exchange—Gruppo N from Padua even signed their works collectively. NT also consciously worked with new materials and new media from mass production, which were cheap, such as punch cards, plastic ribbons, cardboard, and plywood[21].

[14] Dennison Rusinow, *The Yugoslav Experiment 1948–1974*, published for the Royal Institute of International Affairs London by the University of California Press, Berkeley 1977.

[15] Sonja Briski Uzelac, "Visual Arts in the Avant-gardes Between the Two Wars," *Impossible Histories*, p. 122–169.

[16] cf. Branislav Dimitrijević, "Consumerist Imaginary in SFR Yugoslavia (Case 3: Beba Lončar on a Lambretta Scooter)," *Id : Ideologija Dizajna = Ideology of Design : [zbornik tekstova/reader]*, p. 243–252.

[17] *Gorgona—Protocol of Submitting Thoughts*, ed. by Marija Gattin, MSU, Zagreb 2002.

[18] Jelena Stojanović brings forward such a critique in Jelena Stojanović, "Internationaleries: Collectivism, the Grotesque, and Cold War Functionalism," *Collectivism After Modernism: The Art of Social Imagination After 1945*, University Of Minnesota Press, Minneapolis 2007, p. 17–44.

[19] Ješa Denegri, *Constructive Approach Art: Exat 51 and New Tendencies*, Horetzky, Zagreb 2004, p. 264.

[20] Almir Mavignier, "A Surprising Coincidence," Margit Rosen (ed.), *A Little-Known Story about a Movement, a Magazine and the Computer's Arrival in Art: New Tendencies and Bit International, 1961–1973*, MIT Press,

Matko Meštrović wrote that the movement aimed at art becoming more like a science.[22] This idea (as expressed by Meštrović) can only be properly understood knowing that Meštrović simultaneously called for the "humanization of science"[23]. Science was understood holistically, as the sum of all forms of human knowledge, and not reduced to the natural and social sciences. Artists and critics involved in NT thought that art would benefit from scientific thinking; that they should formulate their methodologies in such a way that the process of making art would become transparent to others, and that this served the goal of the "final demystification of art"[24]. NT artists tried to objectify the creative process by inventing rules that governed the production of works[25]. The conceptualization of an artwork became separated from its actual production. This "move" coincided with the advances in industrial automation that so characterized the era.

NT emerged during the upswing of the post-war Fordist[26] economic expansion. The gestation period of NT in the late 1950s was a time of accelerated technological change, which in industrially advanced countries took the form of industrial automation. Automation can be described as an upgraded form of assembly-line production, which through sensors, cameras, and other means of electronic measurement adds an informational layer of "feedback" to the production system. Around 1960 the factory came to be imagined as a cybernetic hyper-organism. Norbert Wiener's *Cybernetics*[27] was a new meta-science of governance or control, which used feedback loops of information to create control cycles.

These new production systems and processes were first introduced in the U.S., where the social consequences of such too were first seen. Already in 1950 the sociologist C.W. Mills formulated the emergence of what he called "*White Collar* society"[28]. This new middle stratum of wage earners in the offices had made a relatively quiet entrance but significantly changed the demographic makeup of industrial societies. The old dichotomy of capital and labor, the latter understood as male factory workers, dissolved into a more fluid multiplicity of non-capital- owning salaried workers. The relative affluence of those middle layers allowed Daniel Bell to argue in his book *The End of Ideology*[29] that the time of social antagonism was over. In popular non-fiction works such as *Organization Man*[30]

Cambridge, MA 2010, p. 344–345 (p. 345).

21 Meloni, p. 41–76 (p. 55).

22 Meštrović, "Untitled (The Ideology of the New Tendencies)."

23 Matko Meštrović, "Scientifikacija Kajo Uvjet Humanizacje," *Od Pojedinačnog Općem*, Mladost, Zagreb 1967, p. 221–230.

24 Meštrović 1963/2010, op. cit.

25 François Morellet, "Pour un Peinture Expérimentale Programmée," *Groupe de Recherche d'Art Visuel Paris 1962* (exhibition catalogue: "L'instablité", Maison des Beaux-Arts, Paris, April 4–18, 1962), GRAV and Galerie Denise René, Paris 1962.

26 Following Antonio Gramsci's first use of the term in the 1930s, the French regulation school in economic theory adopted the term in the 1970s to describe a system of mass production and mass consumption first implemented in the U.S. and later copied around the world. Cf. Michel Aglietta, *A Theory of Capitalist Regulation: The US Experience*, NLB, London 1979.

27 Norbert Wiener, *Cybernetics or Control and Communication in the Animal and the Machine*, Technology Press, Cambridge, MA 1948.

28 Wright C. Mills, *White Collar: The American Middle Classes*, Oxford University Press, New York 1963.

the conformism demonstrated by this new type of subject was deplored. The new middle class became the target of advertisements that were aimed at overcoming hidden resistance in the sub- (or un-)conscious conscious of the prospective consumer [31]. The consequent bottom line, however, revealed that by the early 1960s "alienation" was one of the most common social ills.

Societies relying on advanced productive systems are necessarily dependent on a heightened division of labor. The number of knowledge- or skilled workers increases while the number of unskilled workers also increases, to the detriment of the subclass of skilled craftsmen. As Harry Braverman[32] has shown, this new stratum of intellectual workers was also subjected to managerial planning. Workers were subsumed under a fragmented system in which each had an overview of only a small part of the whole. The birds-eye-view was restricted to the upper echelons of management. Braverman argued that automation had profound implications for the politics of knowledge. Management wrested knowledge of the working process (away) from workers and implemented it in automated processes performed by machines. In the cybernetic imagery of the firm, the worker became a component in a control loop whose task was to add "information" to the system.

In his *Mechanization Takes Command*[33], Sigfried Giedion showed how automation in production affected nearly every aspect of the environment and thereby changed people's behavior, their posture, even their sense of comfort. Giedion argued that a new *dynamic equilibrium* between people and their environment had to be found. Similar ideas were expressed by the founder of the Chicago Bauhaus Laszlo Moholy-Nagy[34] and his colleague/collaborator György Kepes[35]. These artists and theorists were all connected with each other and were inspired by Norbert Wiener's cybernetics[36]. In the US, a technologically upgraded but politically softened version of Bauhaus ideas was developed. These ideas found their way to Europe via the HfG College of Design in Ulm, where NT co-founder Almir Mavignier had studied, and where Wiener and Kepes were guest lecturers; but also through Exat 51's Picelj and Richter's travels abroad, like their stay in Chicago in 1950 and their visit to the institute founded by Moholy-Nagy[37].

Today we can understand the art of NT as broadly in the service of restoring Giedion's "dynamic equilibrium" between

29 Daniel Bell, *The End of Ideology: On the Exhaustion of Political Ideas in the Fifties*, Harvard University Press, Cambridge/London 1988.

30 William H. Whyte, *The Organization Man*, Penguin Books, Harmondsworth 1967.

31 Vance Packard, *The Hidden Persuaders*, Penguin, London 1991.

32 Harry Braverman, *Labor and Monopoly Capital: The Degradation of Work in the Twentieth Century*, Monthly Review Press, New York 1974.

33 Sigfried Giedion, *Mechanization Takes Command: A Contribution to Anonymous History*, Oxford University Press, New York 1948.

34 Laszlo Moholy-Nagy, *The New Vision 1928, Fourth Revised Edition 1947, and Abstract of an Artist*, Wittenborn, New York 1947.

35 Gyorgy Kepes, *The New Landscape in Art and Science*, P. Theobald, Chicago 1956.

36 Reinhold Martin, *The Organizational Complex: Architecture, Media, and Corporate Space*, MIT Press, Cambridge/London 2005.

37 Denegri, p. 15.

humans' biological needs and the technologically transformed environment. Their art should both help to adapt to a rapidly changing world and to overcome its alienating effects. NT artists created fields of participatory relations between works and viewers. They exploited phenomena familiar from Gestalt psychology such as visual ambiguity, size and color constancy. NT were not interested in optical effects for their own sake but because a relationship with the viewer was established through them—the viewer was not just looking at but became part of the same space that the image/object inhabited. Sometimes the viewer, in order to enjoy such works, needed to move around in space. The works were created to produce dynamically changing visual impressions, to engage the viewer by making him/her move; by reacting to the work, the viewer became a co-creator of it. At a time when (a general sense/condition of) alienation had risen to new heights, the art of NT gave, according to Italian author Umberto Eco, people back their "lost autonomy at the level of both perception and intelligence"[38].

In 1962 Umberto Eco's seminal book *The Open Work* [39] was first published in Italian. Initially Eco had in mind works by informal painters and musical compositions; yet around 1961 he became acquainted with Gruppo N, Padua, and Gruppo T, Milan, who were involved in NT. Around the same time an exhibition project was launched where Italian and French groups and individuals involved in NT showed works sponsored by the Italian electronics and office equipment giant Olivetti. Eco's idea of what constituted an open artwork came to be increasingly shaped by NT. For the Olivetti exhibition, Eco wrote a piece under the title "Arte Programmata" (programmed art)[40]. The works in the Olivetti exhibition, which often used electrical motors, moving parts, light, plexiglass and other new materials, created a constantly shifting situation/relation between work and viewer, one that was partly pre-programmed and partly open to chance, and created "fields of possibilities"[41] through its interaction with viewers.

At about the same time a group of Marxists around the Turin-based magazine *Quaderni Rossi* recognized the danger automation posed for left-wing politics. The sociologist Romano Alquati infiltrated Olivetti to conduct *"con-ricerca"*, a new concept of militant activist research[42] and published his findings in *Quaderni Rossi*. In his analysis, Alquati described

38 Umberto Eco, The Open Work, Harvard University Press, Cambridge, MA 1989, p. 83.

39 Eco 1989.

40 Umberto Eco, "Arte Programmata, Programmed Art," *A Little-Known Story About a Movement, a Magazine and the Computer's Arrival in Art*, p. 98–101.

41 Eco 1989, p. 14–15.

42 Sergio Bologna, "Sergio Bologna Reviews Steve Wright," *Generation Online*, 2010 <http://www.generation-online.org/t/stormingheaven.htm> [August 30, 2012].

the future of labor relations in highly automated factories, where the myth of complete rational control through computers clashed with workers' self-organization[43]. Alquati's methodology and analysis influenced *Classe Operaio*, a magazine that continued the legacy of *Quaderni Rossi*, and was edited in Padua, home of Gruppo N. At some point, *Classe Operaio* used Gruppo N's studio as a meeting place. The work of Mario Tronti, Toni Negri and others connected with the magazine gave explicit rise to the Italian version of (the uprisings of) 1968, the "hot autumn of 1969" and became foundational for autonomous Marxism[44].

This interesting near miss between the developments and trajectories of political and art histories shows both the potentials and pitfalls of the art of NT. The "programmed artworks" of NT incorporated basic properties of the structure of interactions characteristic of environments shaped by automation and cybernation. For NT, the form their social engagement took in that context was not the dissemination of political messages but to intervene in the most common layer of the infrastructure of perception. NT artists believed that seeing was inextricably linked with knowing, with memory and interpretation[45]. NT's intervention implied the possibility of the creation of new relations and potentially new insights on the cognitive-visual level.

Paolo Virno links the creativity of the multitude[46] to the member of that multitude's capacity to partake in the commons of language. NT was working on the level of a *visual commons*, trying to establish, through experiment, new visual relations and constellations. Artists as visual researchers worked out proposals for new ways of seeing and interacting with the world and the environment.

However, the notion of *programmed art* suggested that the artist's role was to conceive of new algorithms for artworks whose execution could be carried out by non-artists. The artist became part of the planning department—metaphorically speaking—of the cybernetic society. While the trajectory of *Quaderni Rossi* moved in the direction of direct confrontation with capital, the indirect form of social engagement chosen by NT was prone to what the Situationists called recuperation.

The exhibition *NT3* in Zagreb of 1965 may have appeared to outsiders as the highlight of the movement. Influenced by Johan

43 Romano Alquati, *Klassenanalyse als Klassenkampf: Arbeiteruntersuchungen bei FIAT und Olivetti*, Athenaeum; Fischer Taschenbuch Verlag, Frankfurt am Main 1974.

44 Steve Wright, *Storming Heaven: Class Composition and Struggle in Italian Autonomist Marxism*, Pluto Press, London 2002.

45 They would have had access to earlier editions of works such as Richard L. Gregory, *Eye and Brain: The Psychology of Seeing*, 3rd ed., Weidenfeld and Nicolson, London 1977.

46 Antonio Negri and others, *Umherschweifende Produzenten: Immaterielle Arbeit und Subversion*, ID Verlag, Berlin 1998.

Huizinga's *Homo Ludens*[47], many of the participatory works appealed to the ludic instincts of viewers who happily engaged with this invitation to play. Catherine Millet has pointed out that the desire behind such works was, "to give us a glimpse of the kind of human relations that would be possible in a society that is spared alienation, separation and taboos"[48].

[47] Johan Huizinga, *Homo Ludens: A Study of the Play-Element in Culture*, Beacon Press, Boston 1955.

[48] Catherine Millet, *Contemporary Art in France*, Flammarion, Paris 2006, p. 46.

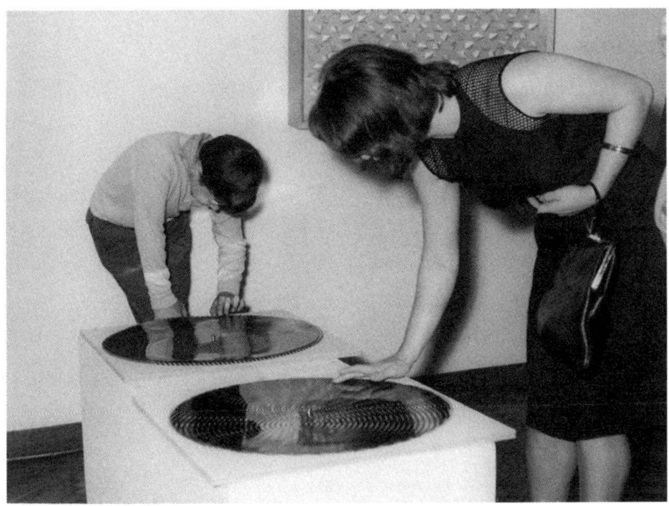

NT3, 1964-5, visitiors engage with Rudolf Kämmer's, *Rotary Graphic*, photo by MSU Zagreb

Yet while to outsiders it looked as if NT was conquering the art world, internal arguments had begun to dilute the sense of solidarity among groups and individuals since 1963. After *The Responsive Eye* (1965) many of the groups dissolved and NT as a movement fell apart. Some groups and artists still produced remarkable results. Members of the Milan-based Gruppo T developed a new type of interactive environment realized with electronically switched lights and projectors. At *NT3* Giovanni Anceschi and Davide Boriani presented *Ambiente sperimentale (Experimental Environment)* (1965), which, inspired by the ultra-rationalist discourse of the HfG College of Design in Ulm, was considered a tool for an experimental artistic research practice.

At the *Kunst-Licht-Kunst* exhibition at the Van Abbemuseum (1966) in Eindhoven many NT artists participated, among them GRAV, T, N, Zero, and the Russian group Divizenje. There, Gruppo T created an ensemble of four connected "programmed" light installations. "The "consumer" becomes conscious of himself at the center of an infinite, if illusory space, whose structure he explores through his own movement," wrote the show's curator Frank Popper. The "dematerializing effect" of the light enables visitors to experience space, duration and color in rooms that can become "inhabited psychologically"[49].

NT's hopes for the emergence of a new society, which would allow space for collectives of artists as visual researchers, became increasingly remote after 1965, as consumer society became steadily consolidated. NT's association with the terms kinetic and Op Art contributed to the sidelining of its political ambitions. NT was one of the first postwar art movements to make participation its central concern; it contributed to the formation of new subjectivities that led to the eruption(s) of 1968, but, ironically, did not come to be seen as the art of the revolution. From 1966 on, "New Art" practices began emerging in Yugoslavia, sometimes consciously defined in explicit opposition to NT[50].

NT initiated and developed important discourse about art's role in societies that employed advanced modes of production. In so doing, they represent a missing link between the 1920s Constructivist avant-gardes and the media art of the 1980s. Yet in contrast with much of today's media art, NT did not exist in a ghetto outside the art system, nor was their engagement with technology uncritical or naively techno-utopian. NT's unrealized potential lies in a constructive engagement with science and technology on the basis of an emancipatory and socialist-humanist agenda. Such an approach appears even more marginalized today than it was in the 1960s, based on the false dichotomy that a constructive engagement with science and technology would naturally, automatically imply being uncritical vis-à-vis socially dominant forces.

49 *Kunst-Licht-Kunst* (exhibition catalogue: Van Abbemuseum, Eindhoven, September 25 – December 4, 1966), Stedelijk van Abbemuseum, Eindhoven 1966.

50 Marijan Susovski (ed.), *The New Art Practice in Yugoslavia 1966–1978*, Documents 3-6, Galerija suvremene umjetnosti, Zagreb 1978.

The Furor of the Festival / *Los Encuentros* de Pamplona (1972)

José Díaz Cuyás

Los Encuentros de Pamplona, or Pamplona Meeting, in 1972, was the most significant and best-attended international avant-garde festival of any held in Spain after the civil war. In the form of the work of 350 artists, it brought together, in a country still under the sway of a military dictatorship, the latest trends of the national and international avant-garde. In particular, it included those trends that in the latter half of the 1960s chose to blur the boundaries between media, which tend to be classified loosely as conceptual. Shortly before the festival of Sanfermines, from June 26 to July 3, the public space of Pamplona, then a provincial town, was literally occupied by a full program of events and artistic interventions intended to celebrate the most radical trends of art that challenged its very limits and argued with an iconoclastic vehemence to dissolve the boundaries between art and life. The patriarchal presence of John Cage, with his influence on the anti-art trends of the previous decade, "whose spirit," the catalogue tells us, "is so present in many of the manifestations of these Encuentros," came to be seen as the symbol of that general propensity towards the act or event, towards the ephemeral, transitory poetics of art seen as mere happening.

Held in the early summer of 1972, the Encuentros marked the beginning of a cultural artistic tour that added the capital of Navarre to the route that included the Spoleto Festival, Documenta 5 in Kassel and the XXXVI Venice Biennale. It played a major role from the outset, as was only to be expected in a country where cultural tourism and the leisure industry were determinant factors in both the economic development policy of the previous decade and the correlative phenomenon of political opening-up.[1] Rather than a distinctive local feature, however, it was an element of international normalization at a time when, thanks to the development of communications, for the first time it was possible to speak of an intercontinental artistic debate.[2] This globalization of the art scene coincided, significantly, with the final phase of the avant-garde myth, characterized by the maximum radicalization of its postulates—due

1 "Tourism was our Marshall Plan [...] the great support that the Spanish economy received from developed countries [...] the most evident super factor in the development of the Spanish economy." Interview with Manuel Fraga Iribarne, Minister of Information and Tourism from 1962 to 1969, conducted in Santiago de Compostela on May 15, 2000, cited in Esther M. Sánchez Sánchez, "Turismo, desarrollo e integración internacional de la España franquista", *EBHA Annual Conference, Barcelona, September 16–18, 2004*, p. 1. The press of the time reported its value for tourism: see "Los 'Encuentros 72 de Pamplona'", *Diario de Navarra*, April 29, 1972, or Louis Dandrel's chronicle for *Le Monde* on July 9, 1972, in which he wrote: "Last week, the capital of Navarre left behind its traditions and welcomed its tourists with strange manifestations: the 'Encuentros'." For an introduction to action arts and Spanish experimental art in regard to tourism, see my articles "Popular el paraíso: la AAO en El Cabrito,"*Desacuerdos* 5, 2009, p. 115–128, http://www.macba.cat/PDFs/desacuerdos5_jose_cuyas_cas.pdf, and "La rarefacta fragancia del arte experimental español," *De la revuelta a la posmodernidad (1962–1982)*. MNCARS, Madrid 2011, p. 127–141.

to the objection to any limit, to the extent of totally negating art and culture—and its immediate depletion and consequent disempowerment.

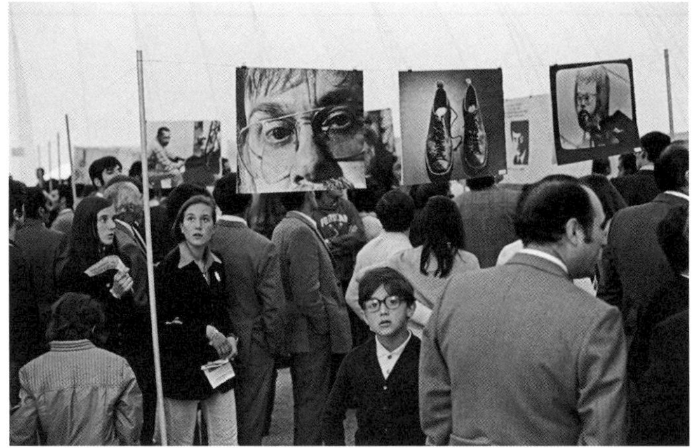

Proposals, experimental artistic practices and installations in the Pneumatic Domes. Los Encuentros de Pamplona, 1972, photo by Pío Guerendiáin. Courtesy of the Museo Nacional Centro de Arte Reina Sofía

What principally set it apart from other similar events were the peculiarities of its organizational structure, and the importance of the dialogue between art and music, and between the avant-garde and popular tradition. In terms of funding, it was almost entirely privately financed (Grupo Huarte) and managed by artists (Grupo Alea), more specifically a small team directed by the composer Luis de Pablo and the artist José Luis Alexanco. The peculiarities of its gestation, in that historic context, are indicative of its underlying paradoxical nature: firstly, under the dictatorship, only private initiatives could undertake an event of this kind; and secondly, it was precisely this disinterested, open-handed financing that marked it out as a public service, as a gift to the city that exploited the publicnature of these tendencies, offered to the city-people as an instructive, free, festive event.[3] The fact that it was a private initiative also gave the team of directors the freedom to make their decisions without the mediation of what they referred to rather contemptuously as "cultural intermediaries," turning their back proudly on the market and the art institution.[4]

Alongside foreign avant-garde movements and interacting with them, this was, then, a stage for the most experimental and therefore most minority trends of Spanish art. It showcased the latest manifestations of visual, sound and action poetry, coordinated by Ignacio Gómez de Liaño (featuring works by

[2] The Encuentros were marked by particular attention to media projection, and their impact was considerable in both the national and the international media. The press office was coordinated by Juan Manuel Bonet and Carlos Alcolea, and relations with the foreign press were conducted by Josephine Markovitz. Although the NODO, the official news service, ignored the Encuentros, two special chapters about the event made by the *Galería* television program have recently been recovered. The mediatic and touristic aspects of the event, which informed its entire nature, are indicative of a new age in festivals and art biennales.

[3] "Everything was free. Everywhere, people were rushing around, open, enthusiastic, spontaneous; students, of course, but then in the evenings there were lots of workers. For the first time in my life, a

Julien Blaine, Jean-François Bory, Augusto de Campos, Eugen Gomringer, Jiři Kolář, Décio Pignatari, Franz Mon, Paul de Vree, Herminio Molero, Pau Bertran, etc.) and public poetry by Liaño's own group, Alain Arias Misson and Carlos Ginzburg, as well as Lily Greenham's phonetic poetry performances .

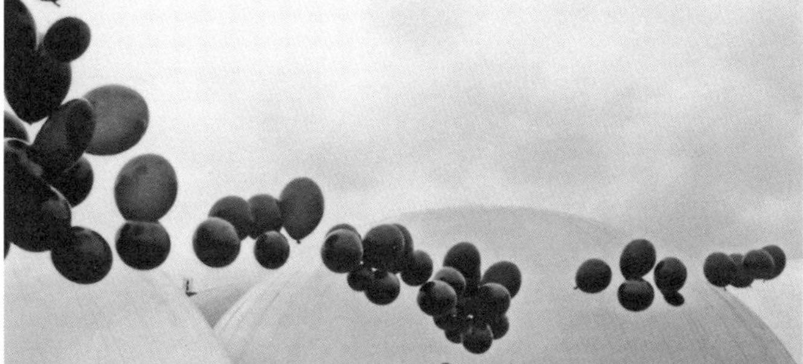

truly 'popular' public." Jack Gousseland, "Entre la fête et la crise: un succès inattendu,"*Combat: Le journal de Paris*, July, 1972.

Public poem by Gómez de Liaño, *Los Encuentros de Pamplona*, 1972. Courtesy of Muntadas

It offered conceptual art and what was referred to as proposals, creations and plastic montages, with works by Art & Language, Christian Boltanski, Victor Burgin, Christo, Walter De Maria, Al Hansen, Joseph Kosuth, Carl Andre, Artist Placement Group, Robert Smithson, Ben Vautier, Lawrence Weiner, etc.), with the presence of Bernar Venet, Leandro Katz and Ludwik Flaszen, a close collaborator of Jerzy Grotowski at the Laboratory Theatre, texts by Catherine Millet and Guy Debord, the exhibition of Systems Art, "Towards a Profile of Latin American Art," by the CAYC in Buenos Aires, the creation of a collective parangolé by Hélio Oiticica created for the occasion; and the participation of foremost Spanish figures such as Nacho Criado, Valcárcel Medina, Lugán, Julio Plaza, Equipo Crónica, José Miguel de Prada Poole, Alberto Corazón, Paz Muro, Gardy Artigas, Luis Muro, Robert Llimós, Jordi Benito, El Grupo de Gracia, Antoni Muntadas and Francesc Torres.

There was video art as well, marked by the attendance of Dennis Oppenheim and the cycle "This Is Your Roof," specially produced for Pamplona by Willoughby Sharp (with works, among others, by Vito Acconci, Mel Bochner, Nancy Holt and Gordon Matta-Clark); computer, plastic and musical art, with

[4] The Huartes were Navarrese builders who had connections with the regime, but they also featured strongly in the most ambitious and systematic project of modernization and cultural patronage under Francoism. As Luis de Pablo recalls, after the death of Félix Huarte Goñi, Vice President of the Diputación Foral regional council from 1963 until his death in 1971, his eldest son Jesús Huarte wanted to give the city a gift: "He wanted Pamplona to receive a very big gift." Interview with Luis de Pablo, February 23, 2004. With the exception of major funding for infrastructures and the contribution of engineers on the part of Pamplona Council, Grupo Huarte must have met all the expenses, managed production and applied for administrative permits, as well as undertaking responsibility for public order and security.

a large show coordinated by Mario Fernández Barberá in association with the Computer Centre of Madrid University (with artists such as Manuel Barbadillo, Iannis Xenakis, Soledad Sevilla, José María Yturralde, Robert Baker, Otto Beckmann, Gregorio Dujovny, etc.), including performances and talks given by the pioneer of computer music, Lejaren Hiller.

Then there was electronic, minimalist and action music, with concerts by, among others, John Cage and David Tudor; Steve Reich with Laura Dean's dance company; Zaj; Eduardo Polonio and Horacio Vaggione; Luis de Pablo in collaboration with José Luis Alexanco; Tomas Marco with Juan Giralt and Fernández Muro; Luc Ferrari and Jean-Serge Breton; Sylvano Bussotti, and pieces by Mauricio Kagel, Cruz de Castro, José Luis Isasa and Mestres Quadreny.

It also included experimental and historic avant-garde film, in collaboration with Henri Langlois, from Dziga Vertov to Stan Vanderbeek, Ian Breakwell, John Latham and Philippe Garrel, with showings produced personally by Martial Raysse, Shusaku Arakawa and Madeline Gins, Javier Aguirre, Rafael Ruiz Balerdi, Gonzalo Suárez and José Antonio Sistiaga.

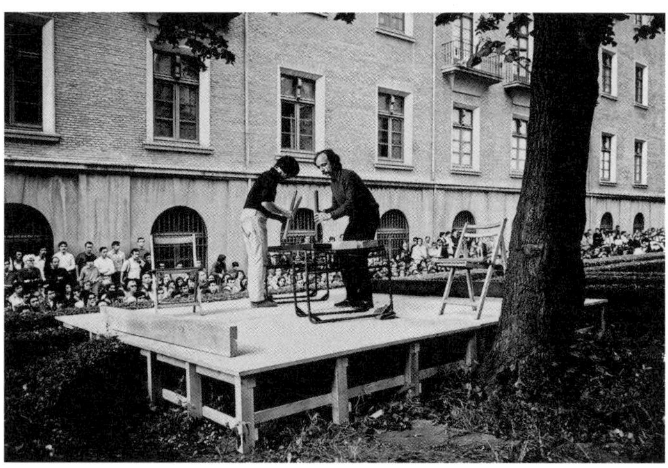

Performance by the Artze brothers on the *txalaparta* (Basque wooden percussion instrument) in the Museo de Bellas Artes at Pamplona. Los Encuentros de Pamplona, 1972, photo by José Luis Alexanco. Courtesy of the Museo Nacional Centro de Arte Reina Sofía

In addition to all of the aforementioned was the controversial "Contemporary Basque Art Show" curated by Santiago Amón, which, despite its general incongruence with the dominant poetics of the Encuentros, offered a comprehensive artistic panorama of recent decades in the Basque Country and Navarre. Completing the program was "Music of Other

Cultures," including concerts by Vietnamese Trân van Khê, Kathakali dance drama from Kerala, Basque *txalaparta* music by the Artze brothers, the flamenco of Diego del Gastor with the Morón gypsy group, and the Iranian trio of Hossein Malek.

This short list serves as an outline of the ambition and scope of the festival and how representative it was of the most active trends of the time. In an interview given in November 2009, Dennis Oppenheim remembered these Encuentros as one of the first occasions that brought together European and American artists who practiced a new kind of art: "I have to say," he commented in relation to the difficult reception of the final avant-garde manifestations, "that the people didn't understand a great deal of what we were doing at the time; only the artists themselves really understood that work." A state of uncertainty which also made it especially exciting for him, and which in the case of Pamplona contributed to the curiosity and excitement with which he received his invitation: "You can imagine the artists, we were all relatively young, being in an international exhibition, in a country that had a completely different political climate to our own and being considered important."[5] These declarations are quite indicative of the contradictions and conflicts, even the grotesque or carnival-like elements that came to dominate this festival, held in a political "climate" that was, in itself, exceptional and untimely.

It would seem that this art, which "only the artists themselves really understood," was characterized by the general desire to show reality quite literally: by the iconoclastic rejection of any figurative or metaphorical conception of the truth, and the desire—never satisfied—to *present* reality, to invoke it in the here and now.[6] What is both fascinating and terrible about that artistic situation could then be summed up as the "meeting"—or the collision—of the passionately snatched art of the *real* with Spanish social *reality* at its most critical moment. Hence the multiple outbursts that took place among the scheduled artistic proposals and the other events, festive or violent: two bombs and the manifestos against the festival by ETA; the semi-clandestine meetings and the press releases by a sector of artists in the orbit of the PCE (the Spanish Communist Party, the principal underground political organization, was opposed to the festival since, according to its viewpoint at the time, it offered other countries a distorted image of the

5 http://www.museoreinasofia.es/archivo/videos/2009/encuentros-pamplona/dennis-oppenheim. html

6 See "Literalismo y carnavalización en la última vanguardia", José Díaz Cuyás (ed.), *Encuentros de Pamplona 1972: Fin de fiesta del arte experimental*, MNCARS, Madrid 2010.

country); the various confrontations between the Basque artists that marked the end of the project that was the Basque School; the threats and pamphlets of extreme right-wing groups; the constant rumors of a shutdown and the ongoing police presence encouraged by a regime that regarded this public manifestation with suspicion; the anti-festival stances of the Basque Church and a sector of Catalan artists organized around Pere Portabella and Antoni Tàpies; and finally, the vandalism and the spontaneous outbursts of collective jubilation among much of the public. Many things, seemingly disparate, were happening at once, though all motivated by that artistic event.

The dysfunctionality between politics and society in the Spain of the time had reached an almost unsustainable level of tension. After the tragic travesty of the Burgos Trial, held the previous year, the regime had started to show evident signs of weakness, though it was another three long, hard years before the dictator's interminable televised death.[7] The general perception was that this was the end of an era, run through in equal measure by hope and uncertainty, most of all for a new generation that had grown up with development policies and been sustained by the trends of the new left and the counterculture of the late 1960s. There was a new but still precarious critical mass that identified with neither the overblown rhetoric of the regime nor the strict dogmatic style of the old culture of resistance offered by the "fellow travelers" of the PCE. Accordingly, calls for public action that partook of art-life trends, with their formal disobedience and their implicit content of bodily and ideological "liberation" found the ultimate sounding board in Pamplona. An individual artistic proposal could find itself overcome, contaminated or disguised, and at the Encuentros there were many examples, on the side of *life*. This was the case, for example, of Oiticica's parangolé, the piece embodying the most explicit carnivalesque substance featured in Pamplona. Its fabrics were "decarnivalized" and turned into festive or protest banners. Then there were the dummies of Equipo Crónica that imitated the "secret police" and were distributed among the audience at the concert given by Ferrari and Breton, ending in the "glorious orgiastic ritual"[8] of being tossed and destroyed, and which, in a comic twist, were saved from the mob thanks to the protection of the very police force they parodied. The same was true of the enthusiasm with which the audience danced

7 In early 1971, the Executive Committee of the PCE had issued what it intended as a definitive declaration: "After the Burgos Trial, the dictatorship of General Franco is potentially at an end." Gregorio Morán: *Miseria y grandeza del Partido Comunista de España 1939–1985*, Planeta, Barcelona 1986, p. 463.

8 Fernando Huici & Javier Ruiz, *La comedia del arte*, Editora Nacional, Madrid 1974, p. 160.

to and cheered Steve Reich's severe, mental minimalist piece, *Drumming*.[9] And also of the sarcastic misunderstanding of the artistic packets imitating bombs that Luis Muro planned to place in the streets and that had to be removed after ETA's first bomb, real in this case, went off at the monument to General Sanjurjo.

Amid the anxiety and uncertainty in the streets and at the various events, a contagious vandalistic joy reigned. Due to the way the public phenomenon took over that program of *public* works, the outcome was more like a boisterous, explosive carnival masquerade. Like a furious game of collective dressing-up in which any gesture, any thing, be it of an artistic or a political nature, could invert its meaning and end up "out of place". Like a multitudinous masquerade in which art, so eager for *life*, found itself, in a country already immersed in a grotesque reality, outdone by the contradictions and impulses of that *life* to which it so desperately aspired.

Translated from the Spanish by Elaine Fradley.

9 "Years later, Steve Reich himself told me that no public had danced to his music like the public in Pamplona." Llorenç Barber: "Música española de los años setenta," Mariano Navarro (ed.), *Los setenta: Una década multicolor*, Fundación Marcelino Botín, Santander 2001, p. 197.

The Avant-Garde, Sots-Art and the *Bullldozer* Exhibition of 1974
Vitaly Komar

1. The Avant-Garde and the Roots of Unofficial Art

The Russian avant-garde's revolutionary struggle with the traditions of the old culture led to the division of art into "official" and "unofficial." Prior to World War I, the first avant-garde opposed the academic salon art that was fashionable at the time. After World War II and Stalin's death, the second avant-garde opposed official Socialist Realism. However, by that time Soviet Russia's unofficial artists had shed the naïve nihilism of the early 20th century avant-garde. They were aware of the ancient Roman aphorism: "The new is only what has been well forgotten." They believed in the value of pluralism, in the gradual evolution of fashion, and certain traits of their art were reminiscent of late modernism.

An eclectic crowd was unified under the banner of opposition to the Soviet regime: it ranged from liberals and Trotskyites to religious nationalists and criminals. For unofficial artists, this conceptual eclecticism was an alternative to the tragic extremism of the revolutionary years, when the Russian avant-garde became the "official' art of the regime. Rather, it played the role of the "King of the Carnival," who was then sacrificed at the dawn of Stalinist culture. It is curious that Lenin, unlike Mussolini, didn't like the Futurists; however he used their anarchic energy to destroy a number of bourgeois traditions that hindered his pursuit of power. In the first years of the revolution, avant-gardists established a bureaucratic state system of support for art, and they enjoyed the privileges of the Soviet elite. The majority of old-fashioned realist artists were the unofficial non-conformists starving in the underground during the short-lived revolutionary carnival. True, they took their revenge. After staging a "palace coup' and seizing power, they put avant-garde artists on a diet of bread and water. We often forget today that the post-Revolutionary avant-garde and Soviet official realism were two sides of one coin, of one socialist utopia.

The "Soviet experiment" provides a lesson in paradox: during historical periods of avant-garde elitism, the role of the true avant-garde may actually be played by any vibrant irritant of elite taste, including tomorrow's "counter-avant-garde" of the art market.

In order to grasp the historical roots of Russian culture's division into official and unofficial, it should be recalled that the first Russian professional unions were established just after the February revolution in 1917. Artists of all styles and schools united under one Union of Cultural Workers. After the Bolsheviks disbanded the Constituent Assembly and forbade opposition parties and press, all the unions went on strike. A split took place: the avant-garde artists became "strikebreakers" and were given government positions and commissions. The recalcitrant leaders of several other unions, teachers and bakers, for example, were executed. As Lenin said, "world war has transformed into civil war."

The division of Soviet Russian art into official and unofficial was a latent continuation of the civil war and an echo of the great, forgotten strike. At the beginning of the 1930s, "Socialist Realism" won out. All artistic organizations were banned, and the avant-garde was exiled from Soviet museums into the underground. It was forbidden to exhibit, its works were not permitted reproduction in art magazines. Only the "conceptual branch" of the Russian avant-garde remained—but outside museum walls and exhibition halls. The red banners and slogans of Agitprop openly survived on the streets throughout the Stalinist period. Thus, official art was further divided into the art of the elite and the mass art of the people. For years, no one realized that in the 20th century USSR, within the framework of totalitarian Art Deco, there existed not only official "Socialist Realism," but "official conceptualism" as well. The latter wasn't acknowledged by art historians for decades, just as the street art of Western advertising was not recognized until the arrival of Pop art, which unified mass and elite art, placing popular images in a museum context.

Like all tyrants, Stalin was shortsighted. The dictator hadn't understood that in seizing half of Europe, he had actually let a Trojan horse in behind the iron curtain. After his death, "unofficial artists" gradually began to peek out from the underground. During Khrushchev's thaw, Yugoslavian, Polish, Hungarian, Czechoslovakian, Bulgarian, Rumanian, Albanian and German art books and magazines appeared in Moscow. They had no less an influence on my friends and me than the ideas of the Prague Spring had on Mikhail Gorbachev and other perestroika activists.

During my youth, artists of the second avant-garde, to which I belonged, were called "non-conformist" and even "dissident." Our art was termed underground and unofficial. Despite this, when I studied at the Stroganov Art Institute, the art works of a few unofficial artists began to appear in official exhibitions. This process came to an abrupt halt in 1962 at a huge exhibition in Moscow's Manège, when there was a confrontation between Khrushchev and the sculptor Ernst Neizvestny. After that, public poetry readings at the monument to Mayakovsky were forbidden as well.

2. Sots-art and the motivation of the unofficial artist

After Leonid Brezhnev came to power, Russian art entered a new stage. At the beginning of the 1970s "Sots-art" appeared—a conceptual movement that united unofficial and official art for the first time.[1] This method was apparent not only in Russian art, but later in Chinese art as well. Sots-art combined the conceptual branch of the Russian avant-garde— the banners and slogans of Agitprop—with a dangerous non-conformist gesture. It filled Socialist Realist form with the content of opposition. This unusual creative approach was an expression of the fundamental duality and conceptual eclecticism of our consciousness.

Sots-art was closer to conceptualism than Pop art. If Pop art resulted from the overproduction of goods and advertising, Sots-art emerged from the overproduction of Soviet ideology and its visual propaganda. Having lived in New York for many years now, I see Western advertising as "consumerist propaganda" and Soviet propaganda as "ideological advertising."

As one of the founders of Sots-art, I'd like to share my view of some of the psychological motives driving independent artistic creation when Soviet censorship reigned and there was a total absence of anything resembling a capitalist market. In this text the pronouns "I" and "we" are deliberately interchangeable—not only because at the time Alexander Melamid and I were co-artists, i.e. worked together as a single artist, but also because any artist's participation in a movement or style is always a form of unconscious collective authorship.

[1] Cf. Ian Chilvers, "Sots-art," *A Dictionary of Twentieth-Century Art*, Oxford University Press, Oxford 1998.

At the time, our criteria for gauging the success of our art had nothing to do with making a career no matter what the price. Most important to us was fulfilling our fantasies of freedom and independence. In trying to do this, we created our own curtain inside the Iron Curtain. It was an ephemeral curtain delineating a bohemian ghetto: a fragile model of the provincial eccentric's behavior in a totalitarian society. It was an attempt to preserve a mythological, almost perverse loyalty to our principles and image of self-worth. We were all attached to the old-fashioned, romantic notion of the "unacknowledged genius."

Inevitably, this drew us into a dangerous game with the "censor as a viewer" and with "the viewer as censor." Visual metaphors became protective masks as well as allegories. The "carnival' we created both mixed and juxtaposed form and content, parody and travesty, context and subtext. Our work was the development of our own artistic biography, and of our common historical context. At the same time, it was assumed that "historical value" would sooner or later become esthetic value. The artist's life was seen as a work of art, as the "novelization" of the artist's life. In 1973 Alex Melamid and I created two artists: their paintings, biographies, letters, documents concerning them, and so forth. One of them, Appeles Ziablov, was the first abstract painter. Ziablov was a serf who lived in the 18th century; in protest against the style of the official Academy of Arts that he was forced to conform to, he hung himself. The life of the second artist, Nikolai Buchumov, was no less dramatic. An argument with a left-wing avant-gardeist turned into a fistfight and the artist punched him, leaving him blind in his left eye. Buchumov then left Moscow and lived the life of a hermit; he painted landscapes, and as a true realist he faithfully depicted his nose on the left side of his paintings.

We saw our art as creating a conceptual history; our media consisted not only in photography, painting, text, installation and performance—but time itself. The contextual process of art's creation was more important in our evaluation of our work than the finished artwork itself. It seemed to me that the era of class struggle had mutated into an era of the struggle between contexts.

The Russian avant-garde called for Alexander Pushkin to be thrown off the ship of modernity. But I think that the following lines from Pushkin's own poetry actually shed light on the

avant-garde's most secret desire:
All that threatens us with peril,
An inexplicable pleasure does hold,
For the hearts of mortals.

As I already said, our art led to a dangerous opposition to totalitarian censorship. In effect, our art was a manifestation of the self-destructive impulse of the subconscious. The Russian characters in Sacher-Masoch's novels made it clear that there is no contradiction between hedonism and the desire for self-destruction. In this light, today we can see Van Gogh's suffering and suicide as a travesty of the "crucified artist". Both Christ and Van Gogh were recognized only by a narrow circle of followers during their lifetime. It is no coincidence that Van Gogh was a preacher in his youth. When he cut off his ear, he was subconsciously repeating the action of Saint Peter, who, according to the Gospel of John, cut off the ear of the high priest's guard in the garden of Gethsemane. The great Vincent thus saw himself as the guard and the apostle simultaneously. He was the self-destructive enemy and his own follower at the same time. And in this regard, I believe that one of the earliest analogies to unofficial art is the catacomb art culture of ancient Rome. Paradoxically, the mysterious "self-destructive instinct" is many-faceted: it can manifest itself as altruism, masochism, self-sacrifice in the name of ideas or children, as well as in alcoholism or drug addiction.

3. The Bulldozer exhibition and the Apogee of Unofficial Art

Apartment exhibitions were unique to the second Russian avant-garde. In the spring of 1974, at one of those "apartment exhibitions," during a Sots-art performance, everyone was arrested, including the veteran unofficial artist Oskar Rabin, and myself. We were interrogated all night. Unable to find anything criminal in our actions, the police released us the next morning. Much as they wanted to, the authorities could find nothing objectionable in the performance. The performance was noisy—Soviet marches were played, and my colleague Alex Melamid and I, playing Stalin and Lenin, shouted commands into a microphone to artists on a stage. Under our direction they created

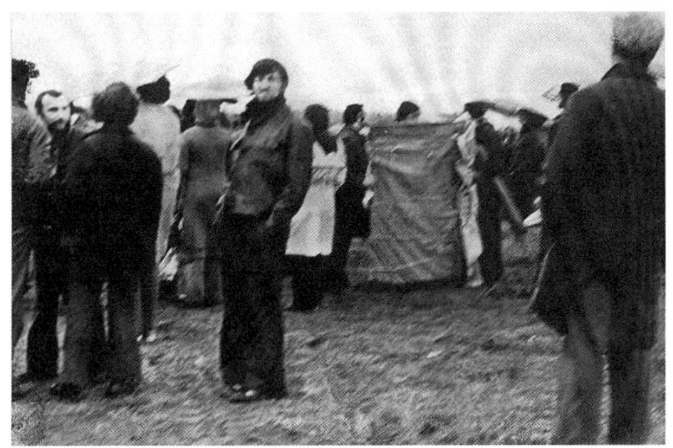

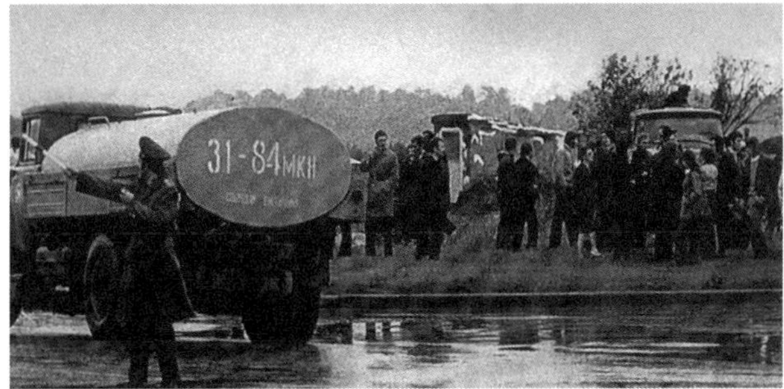

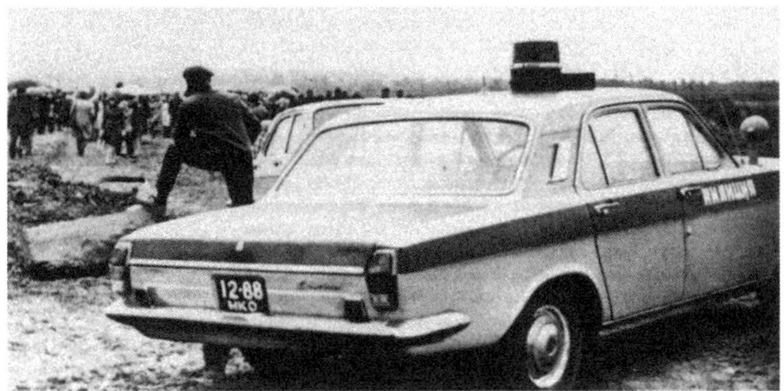

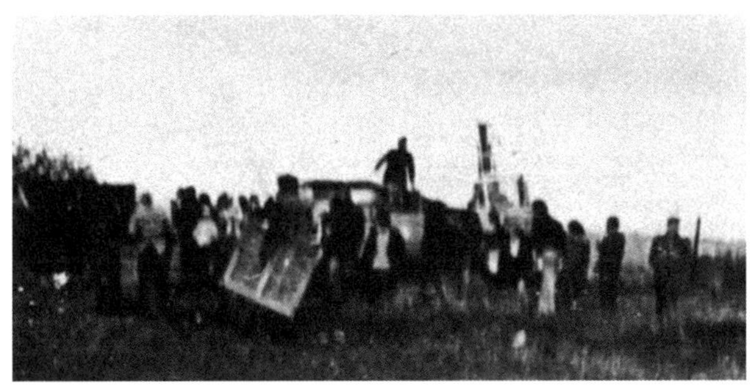

Scenes from the 1975
Bulldozer exhibition,
photo by Valentin Serov

a huge Socialist Realist canvas depicting the heroic labor of
Soviet workers. When there was an unexpected knock on the
door and the police appeared, the audience initially laughed—
people thought that this was part of the performance.

A few days after the arrests, Oskar called me and proposed
repeating the performance at the apartment of his friend,
the poet Alexander Glezer. This time the performance went
through without any brouhaha and we began to discuss new
ways of showing our art. We couldn't use the exhibition halls—
unofficial art was not allowed there. But the great outdoors
seemed possible. We believed that the authorities were changing their attitude toward artists. I even wrote a proposal for
the creation of a second, alternative artists union. Though this
project eventually came into being, there was dramatic public outcry just months after the performance. The "Bulldozer
Exhibition" became the apogee of unofficial art's history. On
September 15, 1974, in the Moscow park Belyaevo, the authorities destroyed art by many unofficial artists, among them
Oskar Rabin, Lidia Masterkova, Evgeny Rukhin, Vladimir
Nemukhin, and Alexander Melamid and me. Today, few people
can imagine the sensational flood of international press this
confrontation elicited. I'll never forget the words of the legendary BBC commentator Maksim Goldberg: "Many bureaucrats
in the West would love to send bulldozers out to destroy contemporary art, but the laws of the land don't allow them to."

When I saw the bulldozers heading our way, any illusions I
may have entertained regarding Soviet law disappeared instantly. I watched in a trance as people in plain clothes destroyed
our art and professionally beat and arrested whoever resisted
them. I froze. But when they knocked me down into the autumn
mud and grabbed my painting *Double Self-Portrait: Komar and
Melamid as Lenin and Stalin*, my fear vanished. A number of
our Sots-art pieces had already been mangled, but the "Self-
portrait" was particularly important to me. When one of them
stepped on the picture, intending to smash it, I suddenly imagined that it was a self-portrait of us not as Lenin or Stalin, but
as Tolstoy or Gandhi. I raised my head, and quietly, in a trust-
ing voice, said: "What are you doing? This is a masterpiece!"
Our eyes met and a different sort of contact arose inexplicably.
Perhaps on hearing the word "masterpiece" he remembered
something long forgotten. I don't know, but he didn't smash the

work, he simply tossed it into the back of a truck. A moment later, still lying in the mud, my eyes followed the garbage-filled truck as it drove off into history. I smiled. Was this my "finest hour"? Maybe every artist secretly dreams of his work being destroyed by the viewer?

As you can well imagine, I have no intention of excavating the 1970s layers of Moscow landfill to find it.

Like all avant-garde artists, we dreamed of breaking down the barrier between art and its audience, but the paradox was that at first we erected this barrier ourselves, by the very act of creating our works. At the Bulldozer Exhibition, as we advanced to meet them halfway, the audience (in this case the KGB) had literally broken down the barrier. It was the same form of collaboration as the destruction of Greek statuary by the Christians. Or Lenin and Stalin's destruction of Christian churches. Or the iconoclasm of Russian dissidents that wanted to destroy statues of Lenin.

The unbearable feeling of isolation made us leave the underground for the streets in search of an audience. Today many people have forgotten that the Soviet state owned everything: the army, the secret police, all the banks, offices, buildings and supermarkets. It also owned all the galleries, museums, exhibitions, art magazines, the entire press, all the film studios, all the radio stations and television channels. Therefore, unofficial artists could only work in the very rooms and cellars where they lived. In these living spaces we showed our art to a narrow circle of friends and acquaintances. We often drank all night, arguing about art and reciting poetry. Kitchen discussions substituted for the absence of freedom of speech and reviews by art critics. The idea of showing our art outdoors was born on one such evening at Oskar Rabin's apartment. Something that the West might see as a commercial gesture (an outdoor show) was an avant-garde gesture in Russia. For some time, I believed that the air wasn't the property of the bureaucracy.

Artists of varying styles participated in the Bulldozer Exhibition, but unfortunately not all our friends and colleagues supported us. For example, the artist Ilya Kabakov declined to participate a week before the exhibition. Speaking to Oskar, Ilya said that he'd been standing on all fours his entire life, and leaving the underground for the street was the gesture of a man who stood on two legs. Then he looked at Alex and me and added "or on two hands, like these young Dadaists." I cannot pass judgment on this "metaphorical cynicism." All of the publishing houses belonged to the state, and as a member of the official artists union Ilya earned his living by illustrating children's books. A kind of duplicity or dualism was typical of many of us, to varying degrees. Depending on our principles, we became "weekend" professional artists. For example, I gave drawing lessons and privately tutored students to take the entrance exams for the art institutes (in the USSR education was free, which meant the competition was fierce). Once I even designed a camp for the Young Pioneers. Such contradictions were manifested not only in our lifestyle but in our art as well.

Until the end of the 17th century, an original and colorful version of canonic Eastern Orthodox icon painting flourished in Russia. Subsequently, Peter the Great's reforms in the early 18th century brought Western Renaissance traditions to Russia, with their three-dimensional spatial perspective and realistic treatment of light and shade. But in folk art, the love of ancient Russian traditions remained: their two-dimensional treatment of color contrasted with the three-dimensional treatment of space. In some 19th century Russian cathedrals I have seen a unique dialectic of Eastern and Western styles: two-dimensional planes and three-dimensional depth. Faces and wrists are painted in a realistic academic manner, but the background and clothes are rendered in the style of medieval icons.

A similar conceptual eclecticism is apparent in some of the most original works of Soviet art in the period of "totalitarian art-deco," and during the transition from the avant-garde to Socialist Realism. Again, the faces and hands are painted realistically, while the background and clothes are rendered in a cubo-futuristic style.

The source of this dualism lies not only in Russia, which is located on the border of two continents, and the cultural traditions of Europe and Asia. Duality is universal. During the early Renaissance we see it in the art of Northern Europe, and in the south of Italy. It is a projection of humanity's basic duality, the division into male and female.

Many works of unofficial Russian art were ahead of their time, and were forerunners of what came to be called "postmodernism" and the "transavantgarde" in the 1980s. At the beginning of the 1970s, Oskar Rabin painted a portrait of his

Soviet passport: on a large canvas he combined conceptualism with expressionism. At the same time, another outstanding
unofficial artist, Oleg Vassiliev, began to combine geometric
abstraction with postimpressionism. In 1972, in Sots-art, we
(Komar and Melamid) combined two styles: "unofficial and
official," "private and public," "introvert and extravert," for the
first time, and also used a significantly larger number of "multifaceted" styles and concepts than had been done before. At that
time I realized that all individuals, in one way or another, become part of a collective historical style. We viewed the history
of art as a dictionary of intonations. In works such as *Heinrich
Böll's Meeting with Solzhenitsyn at Rostropovich's Dacha*, in
our installation *"Paradise,"* in the polyptych *Biography of a
Contemporary*, in our *"Post-Art"* project, and others, we reflected the multi-stylistic, conceptually eclectic consciousness
of the Soviet Union's second avant-garde.

Translated from the Russian by Jamey Gambrell.

Works and Words (1979) in the Shadow of I AM (1978)

Marga van Mechelen

The history of *Works and Words*, an international art event
that took place in Amsterdam in 1979, is the history of a semi-
failure, but an interesting failure nonetheless. *Works and Words*
was meant to be a continuation of another international show,
called *I AM*, held in Warsaw in 1978, and other smaller events
in "East-Central" Europe around the same time.[1] *I AM*, with
music, performances and lectures, had been a big success, and
Works and Words was intended to be equally productive if not
more so—but it was not. The source of the difference can be
traced back to the political situation of Europe at that time, and
to the suspicions amongst artists from "East-Central" Europe
about Western presentations of artists.

The concept of *I AM* was formulated by the artist Henryk
Gajewski, head of the Remont Gallery, affiliated with the
Socialist Union of Polish students of the Technical University
of Warsaw. His idea was quite simple: "I"—artist or critic—
want to introduce myself to you, artist, critic or student (note:
the general public was not admitted). Most of the artists and
critics invited—50 from abroad and 30 from Poland—were
known for their involvement in performance art. The artists represented several generations, with Krzystof Zarębski,
Alison Knowles and Peter Bartoš the eldest, while Tibor Hajas,
Petr Štembera and most of the Western European artists represented the next, younger generation, starting with performances in the early- to mid-1970s. The lecturers paid a lot of
attention to the generations or what they called "performance
models", making reference to other performance artists like
Miklós Erdély, Milan Knížák, Július Koller, KwieKulik and
Stano Filko.

International meetings of artists such as the *I AM* were common in Poland, though in the early years more emphasis was
placed on photography, conceptual art and contextual art. One
could, in 1978, still detect traces of its heritage in the polarized
discussions, but the contrast with earlier events—such as *Think
Communism* by Zygmunt Piotrowski and his Proagit Group
or the performances of Zofia Kulik and Przemysław Kwiek in

[1] I attended both the *I
AM* and *Works and Words*
events and reviewed both
for several Dutch maga-
zines and newspapers.
My text is based on those
publications and my book
*de Appel 1975–1983.
performances, installa-
tions, projects*, De Appel,
Amsterdam 2006. For this
publication I consulted several publications by Piotr
Piotrowski (*In the Shadow
of Yalta. Art and Avant-
garde in Eastern Europe,
1945-1989*) and Lukasz
Ronduda (*1,2,3..Avant-
Gardes. Film/Art between
Experiment and Archive*
and *Sztuka Polska Lat 70.
Awangarda*). Piotrowski
uses the expression
"East-Central" Europe, the
territory located between
the Iron Curtain and the
Soviet Union.

1972 commemorating the massacre in Gdansk in 1970—was, however, enormous.

Nevertheless, the discussions were strongly politically charged and motivated, and the theoretical reflection, even in performance art circles, was remarkable compared to what was going on in Western Europe. Poland's situation was distinctive, where ties with the regime were apparent—despite the artists' (perhaps equally apparent) criticism of the communist authorities. Poland was the only country (in the bloc) where artists were able, on occasion, to forget the Iron Curtain existed. The regime tolerated opposition to a certain extent and respected freedom of speech, which led to Poland's becoming a destination for Western artists—in order to meet artists from Hungary and Czechoslovakia and vice versa. To make connections with the West, one sometimes had to travel to the East. Poland was the only country in the Soviet bloc that could perform this role, paradoxically owing to the fact that it was safely hidden behind the Iron Curtain and still communist. However, the pressure on the communist regime from the *Solidarnosc* (Solidarity) movement at the time of the *I AM* meeting appeared somehow favorable.

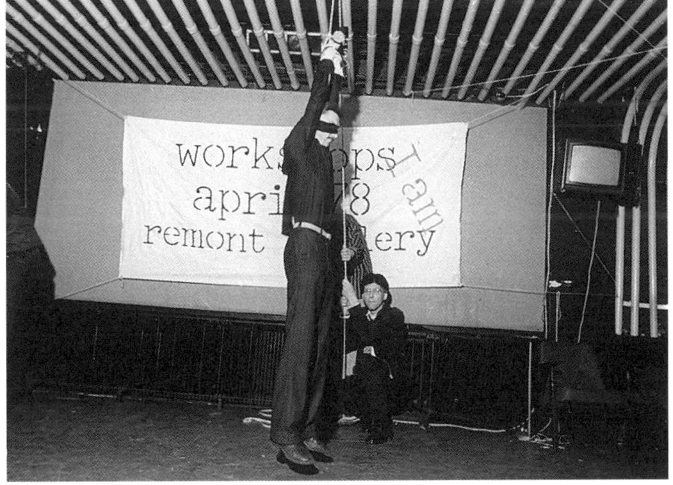

Tibor Hajas (1946-1980), *Dark Flash*, performance I AM, Galerie Remont Warsaw, 1978

The *I AM* enjoyed the support of the Polish officials in a number of ways. Artists like KwieKulik, who proclaimed their left-wing dissident credentials under the banner of Soc Art and New Red Art, were often commissioned by the state. It was a case of running the gauntlet with the risk of refusal of an exit visa as a

consequence—as KwieKulik experienced in 1977. During the
I AM, public political protest was no longer so popular; even
some resistance was seen directed at artists who still wanted to
be associated with these public happenings. Criticism appeared
in print, in theoretical reflections on the role and position of art,
as happened around Jan Swidzinski, who was influential among
young artists in Warsaw and Wroclaw. His conception of contextual art was similar to the engaged position of Joseph Kosuth
in his *The Artist as Anthropologist* (1975).

Meetings like the *I AM* were also possible in Yugoslavia,
but only for artists from the Eastern bloc who could afford it
and were allowed to travel. Artists from the GDR, Bulgaria,
Rumania, Albania and the USSR rarely, if ever, participated in
such meetings.

When the Amsterdam-based art centre de Appel began
its orientation trips to Eastern Europe to prepare for *Works
and Words*, it had no idea which artists from which countries
would take part. Soon after the trips began, however, it was
decided that they had to concentrate on Poland, Hungary,
Czechoslovakia and Yugoslavia, as the case had been at the *I
AM* and other meetings. During their trips the de Appel staff
discerned a palpable sensitivity arising from the political situation, in particular over the bad experiences of the 1977 Venice
Biennale, where artists were presented as being dissidents, and
over the irresponsibility of the Venice organizers that caused
artists from Czechoslovakia to be sent to prison. De Appel noticed the resistance was greatest in Hungary and Yugoslavia,
which was in turn later evident during the event itself. Most of
the invited artists were eager to come to a Western European
country for an international meeting, though some were apparently disappointed when they discovered that in this case "the
West" meant "only" the Netherlands.

During the event it became clear, yet again, how big the
differences were amongst Eastern bloc countries, even between
cities within the same country, as with Belgrade and Zagreb or
Bratislava and Prague. More than ten years before the breakup
of Czechoslovakia and the wars in the Balkans tensions were
already palpable. The artists, however, wanted to be judged
on the merit of their work and not on their geographical origin. "Eastern Europe" was a tainted word for them—they
preferred "Middle" or "Central Europe". And it should be

noted that some of them felt a greater affinity with Western European and American artists and their work than with the work of their own countrymen.

Similarly, organizers of exhibitions and events in the West were reproached for disregarding the work of individual artists from the East. Artists complained that whenever attention was devoted to them and their work it was always couched in terms of nationality or groupings, and never as individuals worthy of the same attention enjoyed somehow automatically or by default by Western artists. That perceived tendency would leave its mark on *Works and Words*, with both organizers and participants ultimately failing to dispel all such criticism and distrust.

Under the heading *Works and Words*, the aim was to focus attention on a common principle, in this case the relationship between action and reflection, which had also been a feature and focus of the *I AM* event. It was a way of pointing to the existence of a cross-border international avant-garde, in which the only differences lay in the fact that it had developed on either side of the political and social divide. Besides those involved in the *I AM*—amongst them Tomás Straus and Lóránd Hegyi—advisors such as Jaroslav Anděl from Czechoslovakia, László Beke from Hungary, Ješa Denegri and Marijan Susovski from Yugoslavia, and Józef Robakowski, Andrzej Kostolowski and Zofia Kulik from Poland were all approached by the organizers. *Works and Words* transformed into a ten-day event with lectures, discussions, performances, installations, videos, films (nearly one hundred by sixty artists), historical documentation, and conceptual photography featuring work by some forty artists. The gathering of artists took place between September 20 and 30, 1979, at several locations. The Holland Experimental Film Foundation, an initiative of Peter Rubin, took care of organizing film screenings in both the Stedelijk Museum and the Nederlands Filmmuseum in Amsterdam. The Fundatie Kunsthuis hosted the photography exhibition and Galerie A organized the exhibition *Gladness Drawings* by the Hungarian artist Endre Tót. A book about the event appeared a year later with photographic documentation and essays by authors from the four "East-Central" European countries, together with extensive chronologies detailing art-related developments and activities in those countries since the early 1960s.[2] Information was an important tool for understanding and exchange, but every effort was made to ensure personal contact was as vibrant and dynamic as possible—just as it had been during the *I AM*, by organizing communal dinners at de Appel in the evenings and by putting up the guests from abroad in the homes of people from the Dutch art world.

2 Josine van Droffelaar and Piotr Olszanski, *Works and Words. International Art Manifestation Amsterdam*, De Appel, Amsterdam 1980.

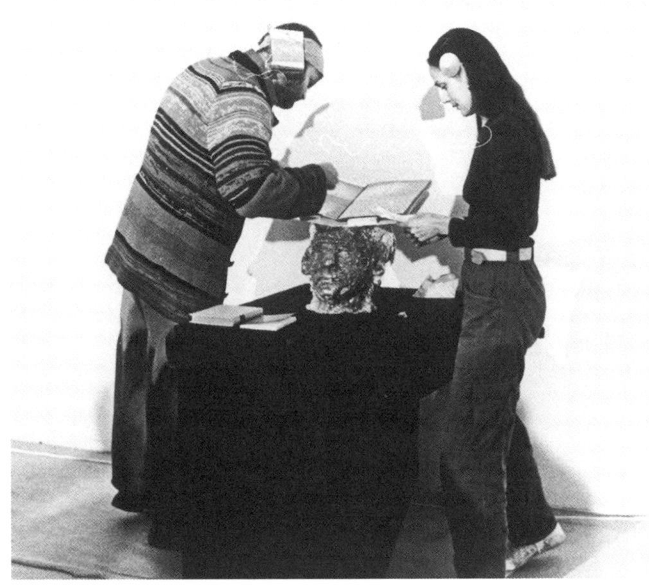

Kwiekulik (Przemyslaw Kwiek and Zofia Kulik), *The Light of the Dead Star*, Performance and installation comprising a sculpture and several hundred documentary photographs, Works and Words, Former House of Detention Amsterdam, 1979

Works and Words screened a great diversity of films by Hungarian artists like Dora Maurer, Agnes Hay, Zoltán Jeney, Gabor Body, Miklós Erdély, János Tóth, Peter Timar and Tibor Hajas. Hajas, a protégé of the Hungarian art historian László Beke and considered by Hegyi as a representative of a new type of heroic individualism (Miklós Erdély even made a tribute to him), like many others, could not be present. None of the Czechoslovak artists were granted permission to travel to Amsterdam. Only one, Jirí Kovanda, solved that problem by instructing others to make an installation for him. Photographs by him and other Czechoslovakian artists, including Michal Kern, Vladimír Havrilla, Jaroslav Anděl,

Július Koller, Karel Miler, Sandor Pinczehelyi, Jaroslav Richtr and Jirí Valoch, were shown in the conceptual photography exhibition. Their works, collectively, conveyed the impression that art and installation or performance art (usually known at the time as actionism) did not, as the Dutch seemed to understand, hail from nor arise from separate territories but rather were indeed often extensions of each other. For that reason, it seems, photographs documenting performances by Petr Štembera were shown in de Appel.

In the lead-up to the Prague Spring, artistic life in Czechoslovakia had been blossoming exceptionally, but the situation deteriorated markedly after the Soviet invasion of 1968 and well into the 1970s, particularly in Prague. Around 1979, Czech artists were living under highly repressive restrictions. Compared to their Slovakian colleagues, many Prague artists were less socially engaged and more focused on existential issues. Art historian Jaroslav Anděl refers to this development in his essay in the *Works and Words* publication, where artists often simply gave up making art owing to their dire financial/economic situation. The younger generation in particular no longer maintained fixed addresses and lived underground—and in fear.

The position of artists in Yugoslavia was quite different. They were strongly opposed to the concept of *Works and Words* and the way in which it was formulated and carried out. Under no circumstances would they deign to exhibit with artists from other Eastern European countries, because that would lead, or so they said, to political problems. Goran Đorđević was particularly critical of the aim of the event and described it as a ghetto. That such utterances came from a Yugoslav was perhaps remarkable in the first instance. Yugoslavia, after all, was a socialist country without a totalitarian regime, and its artists enjoyed relative freedom. However, artists in Belgrade were totally dependent on state institutions and student centers for getting their work shown, a situation some (of them) found particularly disturbing. Art critic Ješa Denegri made it clear in the *Works and Words* publication that he and the artists in his circle did not favor the Western commercial gallery scheme either; what they did want was to find ways of making contact with the Western art world and certainly, with like-minded Western artists.

The Yugoslav contribution to *Works and Words* consisted mostly of performances, films and lectures; with performances by Sanja Iveković, Dalibor Martinis, Mladen Stilinović and, particularly impressive, one by Raša Todosijević and Marinela Kozelj (*Vive la France/Vive la tyrannie*), alongside lectures by Goran Đorđević and films by Tomislav Gotovac.

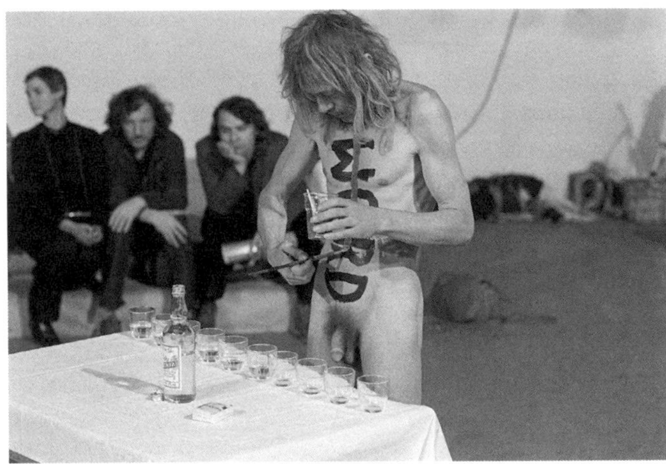

Jerzy Bereś, *Tractatus Philosophicus* Performance, Works and Words, Former House of Detention Amsterdam, 1979

The Polish artists, who were not subject to any travel restrictions, attended in large numbers. Highlights of the Polish contribution included a performance by Jerzy Bereś, a lecture by Andrzej Kostolowski and the films of Ryszard Wasko and Józef Robakowski. Bereś, already known in the Netherlands for work shown in the Stedelijk Museum, performed in the nude as a sort of philosopher, with the title of his performance taken from Wittgenstein's first major work, the *Tractatus Logico-Philosophicus*, and dealing specifically with the relationship between "word" and "work". Zofia Kulik and Przemysław Kwiek commented on the social function of art by juxtaposing the development of their autonomous practice with their commissioned work for the state. The contributions by the three performance artists clearly demonstrated that the distinction between artists on the one hand, and historians and critics on the other, was not so marked in Poland at that time. Some presented slide shows of work by like-minded artists as their own artistic activity, a method or procedure that followed naturally from the system of authors' galleries in Poland—centers led by one or more artists with a very personal stamp. The publication *Works and Words* included an essay by Grzegorz Dziamski entitled "Art in Poland in the Seventies".

But a problem did arise out of some tension between the conceptual artists and the performance artists, despite the fact that this discrepancy did not appear as particularly important during the I AM. The filmmakers formed a separate category from among those present; Józef Robakowski and his colleague Ryszard Wasko also taught at the flourishing film academy in Lodz, and had attained a prominent place in Poland's cultural life.

Despite the many conflicts among the visiting artists, however, all made a strong impression on the Dutch participants, indirectly pointing out substantial weaknesses in the way art functioned in the Netherlands, in particular the attendant bureaucracy. While this was never voiced outright, one got the clear impression, between the lines, that the Netherlands still had a lot to learn from these countries. Plainly, debate over the content and form in which art should operate commonly was and went a lot further in the four Eastern European countries represented. Despite all of the controversies and, for various reasons, the limited number of artist-participants, many felt that a great deal was achieved with *Works and Words*—if nothing else, it certainly served to encourage mutual communication between the artists of a greater Europe.

A European Institutional Effort / *Art in Europe after '68* (1980) and *Chambres d'Amis* (1986) Jan Hoet

Documenta IX in Kassel is the highlight of my career as an exhibition maker. But for me personally, the key exhibitions remain two previous projects intended to point out the relationship between art and society, as viewed from the position I occupied as director of the Museum of Contemporary Art in Ghent. In 1980, "Art in Europe after '68" aimed at bringing to the public an image of art grounded in the European avant-garde tradition; "Chambres d'Amis" (1986) intended to thematize the social nexus of art in the community, with the museum as reference but not as endpoint.

"Art in Europe after '68" was an exhibition of the kind of visual art that was not in vogue in previous years. Arte Povera, which was strongly represented, as well as figures such as Marcel Broodthaers, Panamarenko and Joseph Beuys, were already known by insiders since the 1960s, but they didn't determine the tone. Collectors travelled to America in adoration of minimal art and conceptual art, clear certainties that made unnecessary the more complex European thinking on art.

In those days, alongside these male and female collectors, I could easily surf to America, a continent that at that time cultivated the ideal image of innovation. One had the impression that in Europe we had washed up in a bottleneck. But America and the entire American art world were subject to the terror of politics, albeit unconsciously: "We are the land of artistic freedom."

In Europe we had to acrimoniously detach ourselves from that cliché-like pathos, from that American pretence, from that artistic theorizing.

My reaction was overt. At various symposia I declaimed: "In Europe there is a chain-reaction to important historical moments. You have the Prague Spring. The students want to work in seminars; they have a constant aversion to traditional research methods. They push the professor aside." This attitude was evident in the exhibition; also in the way I made the exhibition. An artist could choose another artist. I thus created solidarity among the artists. A scoop? Possibly. I also looked for another envelope. To strengthen the focus and surprise the public, I laid the emphasis on the emptiness of the space. But the surprise quickly turned into outrage, even anger. Peter Iden said: "Your exhibition is a complete void." I was very satisfied.

I had dared build that exhibition based on experiences gained in Romanesque churches as a fifteen or sixteen year-old. All you find there is an altarpiece. Yet another important aspect: when my father had our house repainted, only one work was hung back up in the renewed space; a week later, it was joined by a second picture.

I explicitly chose Europe because I wanted to revaluate the art of this continent. All the collectors bought American art. At a dinner, I remember the big collector, Dotremont, saying: "In ten years the price of a Brusselmans (which my mother had just bought, while he had sold his) will undoubtedly be double that which I have now received for it. And with the money that I now have in my wallet, I'm buying myself an Andy Warhol, and in the near future this will be worth a hundred times the price I'm currently paying." He was perhaps the first collector in Belgium to have an Andy Warhol in his house; moreover, it was paid for with the money he had received for a work by Belgian artist Jean Brusselmans.

In those years, the design world was increasingly intruding. Companies were cunningly seeking artists who answered to the taste of the collectors who, at that time, played a dominant role in the art market. Firms picked up these artists to design a new typewriter, a new phone, a new car. Think of Olivetti, Fiat ...

In deliberate contrast, I made a radical choice: I ignored the applause of the economy and the security of an *art sur place*. And I did not stand alone, in isolation with that idea. The artists who were my references also thought the same way. Merz and Beuys did not allow themselves to be swayed by economic interests either. Richard Long intuitively grasped the material that nature handed him.

Various artists wanted to integrate themselves in a broader world that you could call social and cosmic. They were also fascinated by the material history had handed them. Think about what Fabro did with the mirror in the Arnolfini portrait by Jan Van Eyck.

I am terribly fascinated by the early avant-garde in Europe. The artist was searching for a permanent position in society.

But that was no picnic. After the Second World War, Europe
was in tatters. The German tradition had marginalized the
Jewish one. The period that followed was not an easy one for
art. Behavior was provincial. The "nouveaux riches" were
greedy and imprisoned the avant-garde in a pernicious cult
of forms. I wanted to escape from this by letting my options
constantly evolve with regard to art. I loved the moving wave
that continuously rises and falls. I appreciated the sigh of the
searching artist as strongly as his bid for the elusive.

Initially, I wanted a "figure" in the museum. I long dreamed
of an exhibition of works by Rodin. And I would then say:
"Look, people, look—there's Balzac!" That idea kept running
through my head. Ah, that pedestal. Not as a decorative base,
but as a symbol. For me, that was the museum.

You can also see this in "*Over the Edges*" (2000), a subsequent exhibition in the extension of "Chambres d'Amis",
whereby the corners of the crossings functioned as pedestals.
That is something quite different than the filling of rotundas
with artistic events. Those are vanishing points, not "pedestals". I often thought of art within the 19th century cityscape.
Alongside its artistic value, a statue also had a functional
value. If you asked someone the way in a foreign city, they
would say: ".... up to that statue and then left." Art was a reference that structured the cityscape. It was effective. Now they
say: "... walk up to the traffic lights and then take the street on
your right."

The museum can serve as a reference for the mental cityscape. It must be that, too, if you take the avant-garde seriously, as well as its aspirations for a meaningful place for art
in society. And it should never be satisfied with itself. I've
always been connected with the museum and wanted to give
it a central place in society. Of course, you then have to ignore the Futurists who associated the museum with a grave, a
mausoleum.

The museum has a symbolic value: there, the whole of history is experienced as competitive. The best stands out. I like a
threshing floor. That's where one separates the wheat from the
chaff. And I've often wondered: does this idea correspond with
what I realized in "Chambres d'Amis"? In the mid-1980s art
imploded. It offered too little resistance to the economy. The
market managers forced their way inside. The break-in seemed

brutal. But "Chambres d'Amis" was once again the museum's
pedestal, but then "unfolded" into society. I increasingly
described the museum as a laboratory from which you pave
routes to the outside world. And the museum where I worked
is known as the Museum of the Ghent bourgeoisie. Brussels
bureaucracy did not create it; rather the best collectors laid the
foundations via an association bent on establishing a museum.

At the time "Chambres d'Amis" took place, I struggled with
the feeling that there was something changing, you had to try
to "negotiate". And on choosing the artists, I went on the experiences I had accumulated during visits to their studios. There
you experience an artistic climate and you try to take that with
you. Broodthaers exhibited in his own house, Spaletti's studio
resembles a kind of heaven—incredibly beautiful—and there
you see him walking around in a white suit. It's indescribable,
the atmosphere there with him, in that village near Pescara.
You come into Merz's studio, Zorio's studio, and you feel:
important artists are working here.

Their artistic proposal is immediately accessible, it hangs
in the air like a ghost, it is reflected in every little detail and
needs no explanation. And you immediately pose yourself
the question: how can you relay to the public what you absorb
sensorially at such a special moment?

In Bari, a major symposium on the city provided me with an
opening. American curators were also present. Thomas Messer
was the first speaker. He started with the fact that the old town
had almost become a ruin. And what do you then do with the
available space? So many square meters for administration,
so many for the museum and then you still have a surplus of
space for a cafeteria, a library... I made another proposal. "I do
not understand how one can opt for that kind of project in Bari,
such a fantastic city. Why not restore the old town and build
yourself a museum. Each year you invite five artists to transform a part of the ruins into an impressive work of art. After
a few years you have a beautiful museum. If you don't do that
here, I am going to try it in Ghent." Thus it happened and thus
"Chambres d'Amis" began to grow. That was in 1981. After
"Europe after '68".

With "Chambres d'Amis" I announced, for the first time,
an exhibition in which the dialectic with the "private public
"was the issue. Private has become public: in the early 1980s,

television, the Internet, and the computer had a clear impact on social events. With the creation of "Chambres d'Amis" I was aware of the fact that public space no longer imposed itself physically, but mentally. You experienced a kind of "dividedness," a community with countless individuals.

I often thought about a fusion of art and the city. The city becomes art. The museum is only a point from which everything grows. In Europe, art has always been a total experience. It was always something that evolved to completeness. With "Chambres d'Amis" I have tried to stay in the same vein.

I come from a collector's tradition, but my faith in the ever-renewing power of art has always prevailed. And at the time of "Chambres d'Amis" some artists were implementing a post-minimal climate. I'm thinking of Vercruysse and Kemps. Those were people who, in their way, tried to save the authentic spirit of art. The question remained: what is the function of art? For Jan Vercruysse it was almost tautological. He made a work at that time that even now you still experience as pivotal, a masterpiece. But Vercruysse got annoyed if you spoke about it in humorous terms. That should be possible. You have to put life in perspective. You also have to put art in perspective. That's taken for granted. If you saw a picture frame in Vercruysses's studio, he could not bear it if you said: "Does the artist know what more he has to create with that?" He was indignant. And he was right. With Vercruysse a creation existed via the frame.

In the 1970s art in Eastern Europe was in a delicate position: artists were called revolutionaries. That interested me. They had been prohibited from working. I'm thinking of Milan Knížák, Miklos Erdély, Tibor Hajas, Endre Tót… The underground. I remember a fascinating performance. The artist stood upside down, nearly naked, and ate Pravda. That could only happen in a small, closed circle.

I always have the tendency to associate those revolutionaries with someone like Ettore Spaletti, even if that sounds peculiar. He is revolutionary in his renouncing of everything. Give the void a material sensation! Provide a handhold for the esoteric. I call his art an alternative to the System. In the visual arts at present, we are in a state, an atmosphere, of crisis. In Germany you see collectors have become the reference. I've always fought to merge art with society. Now there is a

turnaround. Art is now central to society. But the managers
and collectors are seated on the throne. A Belgian collector
recently declared on television: "The era of Jan Hoet is over,
now we have the power. We, the collectors."

Translated from the Dutch by Jodie Hruby.

It is interesting to realize that, particularly in the 1960s and 1970s, the zones of contact between Latin America and Eastern Europe, as regards the circulation of artistic information and the success of collaborative efforts by artists, were far richer and more dynamic than they are today, despite the ease and extent of communication offered by the Internet and all attendant technologies.

This recent past reveals another synergy, which moved open platforms of interchange and moves one consider, by contrast, the sense and direction of actual networks.

Some contact zones from the period that emerged interconnected by the postal net will be addressed here. They are the collective exhibitions and the collaborative publications.[1]

Collective Exhibitions

Some exhibitions in Brazil are relevant to this narrative, particularly those organized by Walter Zanini during the 1960s and 1970s at the Museum of Contemporary Art of the University of São Paulo (MAC-USP). As a vanguard scholar, Professor Zanini integrated a generation of Brazilian idealist intellectuals who intended to see his country in close dialogue with the world, leaving behind perceptions of geographic and economic isolation. He was nominated director of the newly created Museum of Contemporary Art of the University of São Paulo in 1963.

Back then exhibitions were frequently organized through open calls, with invitations distributed throughout the net. The mail proved a great partner of MAC-USP, by enabling the participation of Brazilian artists in international exhibitions and allowing the museum to receive and show works from all over the world. This strategy was particularly useful at a time (the 1960s and 1970s) when Brazil, as well as a number of other countries in Latin America, were living under military rule.

At the time, Zanini was able to build a chain based on solidarity and trust, and sought to create a territory for freedom at the museum. By encouraging experimentation he suspended

[1] Cf. also Cristina Freire, *Poéticas do Processo. Arte Conceitual no Museu*, Iluminuras, São Paulo 1999; Cristina Freire, Ana Longoni (ed.), *Conceitualismos do Sul/ Sur*, Annablume; MAC-USP; AECID, São Paulo 2009.

those notions accepted and naturalized in the prevailing linear and exclusionary history of art, by interrogating the institutional places of creation and display.

As a public and university museum, far from the influence and demands of the market, the museum's program placed particular emphasis on communicating content and on the decentralized exchange of artistic information. The mail heralded not only a change in circulation channels, but also in the profiles of institutions such as the museum, particularly as regarded its task of preserving, storing and exhibiting artworks. Mail art made the museum closer to an archive, and these collective exhibitions became an active space of public participation. Moreover, international contacts, enhanced by exchange lists, boosted the international profile and internationalization of the collection, with works sent from all over the world sent not back to the artist but into the museum's growing collection.

A catalogue or some minimal record of the exhibition, sometimes just a list of names and images, would be sent back to every participant, fulfilling the net's motto: *"no juries, no fees, no returns and catalogues to all participants."*

These exhibitions served as the meeting point of an imaginary community that put together artists that never met personally but shared projects in common. This sort of exhibition marked an important moment in the public visibility of the net.

The artistic practices of Latin Americans, as well as Eastern Europeans (artists from countries such as Poland, Yugoslavia, Hungary and Czechoslovakia) kept in MAC-USP's collection today reveal the zones of contact of the time. Here it is possible to identify a common utopia launched in these points of connection, enabling, at least there, a society of free flows, despite the repressive conditions and circumstances of the time.

Some strategies and tactics are both similar and familiar. Use of the mail system to transmit or flow artistic information produced by easily accessible reproduction means is for example well known. New techniques and technologies of the time, like the photocopier, as fast and cheap means of reproduction aligned well with the comprehensiveness and universality of mail art which multiplied (itself) outside the closed system of galleries and museums.

The mail—and use of it—became an ideal device within this network, as it answered at least two urgent needs: first, it sidestepped the museum's lacking economic resources and expanded its international collection. Of course the demand for quality akin to the modern criteria was expunged from these exhibitions where the pluralism of propositions and nationalities involved became an expression of freedom.

Using the mail as both a tool and tactic for circulation and distribution sidestepped the mechanisms of censorship, making it possible for artists under dictatorships to make their works present, without the need (for them) to travel, which was often forbidden.

Mail Art and Exhibitions

Today, the ethics of mail art, which sought to integrate each member into a larger group, ultimately transcending the individual, may sound odd if not highly foreign to artists from younger, more recent generations.

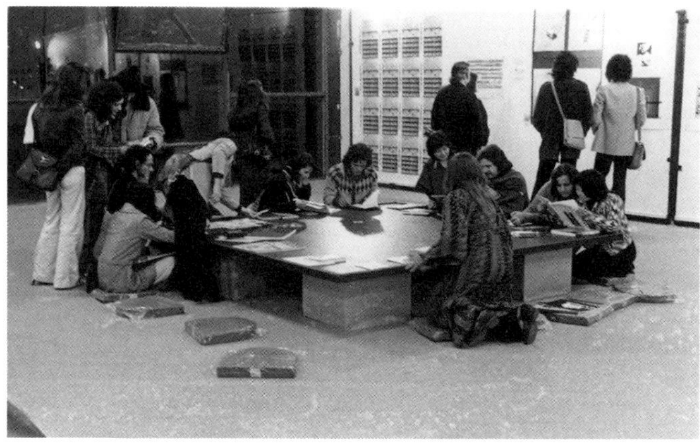

Prospectiva '74, 1974,
Exhibition view

The book *Grammar* (1973), by Jarosław Kozłowski, for example, was sent by mail to Brazil for an exhibition in 1974, and is an interesting example of the dynamics of this sort of exchange.[2]

The book is both testimony and a living example of the "SIEĆ/NET Manifesto," written in 1972 by Andrzej Kostołowski and Jarosław Kozłowski, and sent to hundreds of artists all over the world, proposing a more extensive and generous net of artistic exchanges outside and beyond the limitations imposed by political and/or economic restrictions: "NET

2 Jarosław Kozłowski, *Grammar (Gramatyka),* Galeria Akumulatory, Poznań 1973, 99 copies.

has no central point, nor any coordinates / NET points can be located anywhere / all NET points are in mutual contact and in concepts of exchange, proposals, projects and other forms of circulation (…)".[3]

In this manifest another cartography is announced, capable of drawing artists nearer (to each other) in distant, removed (in many ways) places, like Poland and Brazil, within a regime of artistic exchanges that found new territories via a proximity of purposes and a stake-holding in a kind of collective utopia.

These are artists that, in the words of Kozłowski, come together "on the fringes of the official scene, outside institutional circulation, in semi-shadow, there were other artists at work, artists who were not interested in careers, commercial success, popularity or recognition: artists who devoted more attention to the issue of their own artistic and therefore ethical stance than to their position in the rankings, whether the ranking in question was based on the highest listing on the market, or the highest level of approval from the authorities. These artists professed other values, and other goals led them onward, they were focused on art, conceived as the realm of cognitive freedom and creative discourse…"[4].

This definition clarifies both the (meaning of the) artistic practice and the personal ethics of many of the artists of that time. With such a project shared on the net, the artist is not defined by the kind of object he creates—which we call "a work of art"—but principally by the nature of the creative intervention he/she is capable of performing in society. The net as a principle of open exchange involves cultural dynamics, closes distances, redefines and redistributes roles. In this way, the solidarity of elective affinities becomes the principal operative beyond the privileged circles and social distinctions allowed by the system of art.

In the book *Grammar*, the verb "to be" is conjugated in all its variations. The many declensions of the verb suggest a reflection on the meaning one may give both to words and to actions. The simplicity in the making of this crafted book is revealing. Edited by the artist himself in Poznan, the quasi-utopian character of the edition of ninety-nine printed copies is evident. The conjugation of the verb "to be" extends throughout the sixty-eight pages of the book as the result of the decision of the artist to conjugate the verb "to be" over a three-month period in 1973.

[3] Andrzej Kostołowski and Jarosław Kozłowski, "NET Manifesto (1972), http://www.avantgarde-museum.com/en/museum/collection/4438-JARO-SLAV-KOZLOWSKI/

[4] Jarosław Kozłowski, "Art Between the Red and the Golden Frames," Liam Gillick and Maria Lind (ed.), *Curating with Light Luggage*, Revolver Books, Frankfurt am Main 2005, p. 44.

The action expresses, to the limit, the performative character of language. It becomes a gesture that is expanded within
the communication circuit of the mail art net and is completed
upon the reading of its addresses.

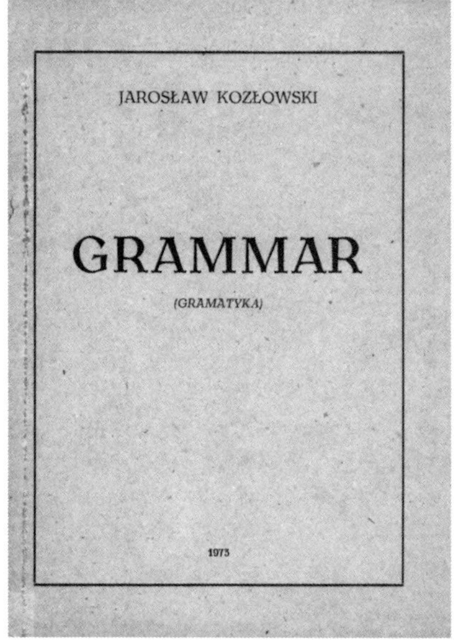

Jaroslaw Kozlowski,
Grammar, 1973

By being sent by the postal service to Brazil, the book
strengthens the efficiency of other more open, extra-institutional circulation channels for art, capable of welcoming, from
beyond the various economic or political imperatives, other
declensions of significance.

In the same year Kozłowski brought forth his enunciative
catalogue of the verb "to be," Brazilian artist Ângelo de Aquino
circulated his "Declaration" through the mail art net. The
postcard, signed by Aquino, reads (in English) "I am Jarosław
Kozłowski", together with the printed stamped that belies this
statement—"lie".

Naturally, when not in Polish or Portuguese, the language of
international exchange was English, which also introduced or
entailed a sort of false identity for the artist(s)—a language that
could make possible some kind of communication, but not identification. The internationalism expressed here was not ideological but had, instead, an instrumental function or purpose.

Perhaps, inspired by his exhibition organized by Kozłowski
that same year at the Akumulatory 2 gallery in Poland, Ângelo

de Aquino simultaneously organized some exhibitions in a shop
window in Rio de Janeiro.

The Akumulatory 2 gallery, created and run by Kozlowski,
was the result of a process on the net, meaning the possibility
of a relationship of exchange among artists outside the pre-es-
tablished axes and institutional structures. The precariousness
of the means, allied with the urgency of communicating beyond
the limited, exclusionary channels of the time and related to the
totalitarian political regimes, identifies many of the works that
circulated within this net.

Beyond the canonical narratives of art, these exchanges
mark or trace the path of artistic relations between Brazil and
Poland in those trying years, and express both the multiple and
most improbable manifestations of the verb "to be" in the field
of art.

The release of information in the 1970s related to the
atrocities committed by the military regimes moved the mail
network, eliciting strong public pressure and even the review
of lawsuits against artists prosecuted and persecuted by the
dictatorships. Information on the exile into which Chilean artist
Guillermo Deisler was forced under Pinochet's coup d'état, the
torture and imprisonment of the Uruguayans Jorge Caraballo
and Clemente Padín, as well as the disappearance of Palomo
Vigo (son of the Argentine artist Edgardo Antonio Vigo), to
name just a few circulated vigorously in the mail art network.

Some German artists, for example, enabled the publication of booklets by Latin American artists like the Uruguayan
Clemente Padín, which frequently denounced the situation
under the Uruguayan dictatorship (1973–1984). Therefore,
Instruments74 (1974), *Omaggio a Beuys* (1975) e *Sign(o)
Graphics* (1976) were all published in Olbenburg as a result of
contact with Klaus Groh through the IAC (International Artists
Cooperative). Klaus Staeck, from Edition Staeck in Heidelberg,
published the book *Instruments II* (1975). As such, various
de-centralized communities of artists where created apart from
the market and oblivious to the institutional imperatives—geographically removed yet united by communal survival tactics
in oppressive and oppressed environments. When his country
re-enters democracy Clemente Padín retrieves his passport,
which had been revoked by the military junta. In 1984, invited
by Dick Higgins, who was living there at the moment, Padín

traveled to Berlin, on which occasion he met artists from East
Germany like Joseph Huber, Ruth and Robert Rehfeldt, to name
but a few. On his return home to Montevideo, Padín organized
the exhibition "*El Arte Correo en La Republica Democrática
Alemana*" (Mail Art in the German Democratic Republic)
in 1986, at the Uruguayan National Library, with works by
56 East German artists. This relationship between the artists
from Eastern Europe and Latin America is worth mentioning
because it helps clarify the context of the period. This South-
East transversality establishes relations beyond or outside the
dominant political and ideological poles. Despite the different
characters or composition of the respective totalitarian regimes
(military dictatorships in Latin America and communism in
Eastern Europe) the mail art network functioned as a field for
shared poetic/political action. Similar utopias and communal
ideals of freedom, rather than the affirmation of local identities,
predicts or prefigures in the mail art network an exchange system, beyond national boundaries and in some way anticipating
a geopolitics of traffic and flow.

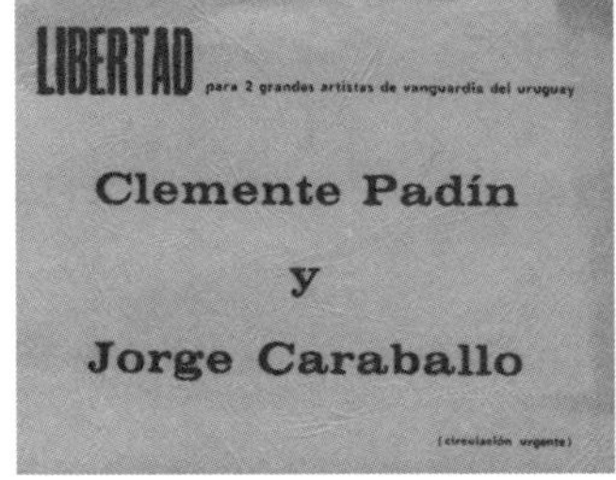

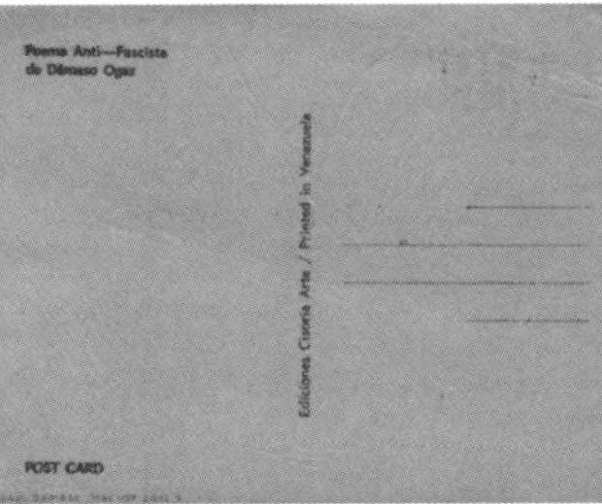

Damaso Ogaz, *Freedom
for two great avant-garde
artists from Uruguay*, 1977-
1985, front

Damaso Ogaz, *Freedom
for two great avant-garde
artists from Uruguay*,
1977-1985, back

Collaborative Publications

Beyond the exhibitions, collective and collaborative publications like assembly magazines also hold a central place in this
sort of subterranean network. They functioned as open, mobile
platforms of exchange. In this sort of collective publication the
emphasis moves from the magazine's contents to the ritual of
editing and distributing it throughout the network, having se-
cured democratic access to the means of (re)production. Today,
these publications comprise the fragmentary reports of and
from this subterranean history. Absolutely articulated by postal
circuits, the assembling of these magazines still serves today to

provide a snapshot of the network in a particular moment; that is
to say they reveal its connections as well as some aspects of the
work performed and contributed by each one of its members.

With these handmade publications, the precariousness of the
process and materials—an offset leaflet or a postcard—suggests the dynamism of the proposition rather than an "aura-
like" artistic value. The artists' intervention on a magazine
page or in a conventional newspaper, for example, was not
enough within this logic-scheme. What was necessary was to
somehow intervene in the media itself, opening up other channels to and for artistic circulation and distribution.

In the end, mail art and artists' publications mixed and
mingled, which spawned (naturally) many hybrid projects
that fused mail art with artist books. Upon assembling magazines, for instance, an artist-editor or a group of artists would
organize the publication. The print-run was determined by
the number of participants who would send their works in the
format and quantity previously agreed upon, in response to an
invitation-letter. Loose sheets in envelopes, plastic bags clipped
together or spiral-bound, all serve to illustrate the precarious
character of these publications. The Uruguayan artist Clemente
Padín is an important link in this network. He edited five experimental poetry magazines, which reached diverse parts of
the world through the mail service across difficult decades:
Los Huevos del Plata (1965–1969), *OVUM 10* (1969–1972) and
OVUM (1973–1976).

In Argentina, Edgardo Antonio Vigo published the magazines *Diagonal Cero* (1962–1968) and *Hexagono* (1971), which
were important vehicles for the dissemination of the so- called
"New Latin American Poetry". Guillermo Deisler in Chile
published *Ediciones Mimbre*, a periodical of graphic arts and
visual poetry and later, in exile, also presented the avant-garde
of Latin American artists with the publication of *UNI/vers*
(1987–1995).

The exile of many artists also stands as a possible explanation for the need, during those years, to search for other possibilities by which to create and circulate works. Physical displacement combined with proscription and a sort of consequent
marginalization only increased the desire—and search—for
alternative paths for communication. Against this background,
some artists used art as a means of communication, producing

projects as editors of artists' books, assembling archives out of
and generated by this network of exchanges, and creating alternative art galleries.

Ulises Carrión, a Mexican artist who lived several years
in Amsterdam, is one among several. He was also a librarian,
poet, editor, and a producer of both exhibitions and of his own
catalogues. He published several books (novels, short stories,
plays) before starting to work with the use of language outside
the literature/literary context. He also funded "*Other Books and
So*" (1975), which hosted an international network of idea exchange in the Netherlands, the sort of headquarters of an international network of postal exchange. On this mix of bookshop/
gallery/archive he offered: "Why should an artist open a gallery? Why should he keep an archive? Because I believe art as a
practice has been superseded by a more complex, more rigorous
and richer practice: culture. We've reached a privileged, historical moment when keeping an archive can be an artwork."[5]

The documental character of mail art also produced personal
archives of artists fed by the shifting, fluctuating network out of
which arose the dialectic between museum, library, home and
archive—public domains in private spaces where a significant
parcel of contemporary artistic memory resides.

Many of these works were not prepared for exhibition in
galleries and museums, but were intended for hand-to-hand
circulation in networks outside the official system. Here private
space touches public space and the personal and political sphere
intermingle. It was not by chance that this type of tactile, collective manifestation escaped the legitimating circuits—not in
a situation that was rapidly shifting and changing.

It is important to notice how the growing interest and the resulting rescue of many of these propositions have arisen in the
last decades. It emerges, from the point of view of the contemporary art memories, as a sort of return of the repressed. The
presence of such works at the museum represents the passage
from the autonomous object to processes. They are, therefore,
uprisings or rebellions against the hegemonic narrative and the
traditional museological procedures of documentation, conservation and exhibition. Thus it is not enough to preserve the
object in all its physical precariousness, but mainly, to provide
or open a view of the processes underlying its circulation that
goes beyond the standard predictable routes.

5 Ulisses Carrión,
"Bookworks Revisited,"
Print Collector's Newsletter,
vol. 11, n° 1, March–April,
1980.

The task of preserving these "other" works, frequently effected and produced with dubious, short-lived or short-term media involves the reconstruction of the intricate symbolic mesh that engenders them and in which they are inserted, and includes historical, political, cultural and social context. Thus, preserving means reconstructing these meanings, attributing significance and, finally, providing intelligibility.

The current attention afforded alternative strategies and tactics of production and distribution in the 1960s and 1970s compels us to consider what feeds such an interest today— when the concept of network is spread globally every day by technocratic cultural premises, tactics of artistic resistance are quickly assimilated by marketing strategies, and the potential critical component of artistic propositions is further neutralized by the market; and by cultural institutions converted into businesses guided by neoliberal policies.

This sort of mobilizing art that typifies those decades, a critique running strictly contrary to economic interests and removed from the hegemonic poles of exchange, may today bears witness to a utopia that throbbed; and might still throb, somewhere, in the subterranean.

From the International to the Cosmopolitan Piotr Piotrowski

The international is one of the main characteristics of modernist and avant-garde art. However, if we come closer to the issue, particularly in the case of East-Central European art of the second half of the 20th century, we can see how the situation was complicated, especially in the context of the so called inter/ or trans-national exchange; the process of nationalization of modern art is only too plain to see. In other words, the problem of the nationalization of modern art, i.e. the art of an international origin and in fact international character in the countries ruled by the communists, is the other side of the coin of the international understood as the main character of the avant-garde and modernist developments. This was possible due to the particular political situation in Eastern Europe, especially to its (to a different extent of course) isolation from the larger international art scene. While Western artists enjoyed international exchange without being labeled the "representatives" of particular nations, their Eastern counterparts were very often recognized as such.[1] However, there is no doubt that the year 1989 changed a lot, also in terms of international artistic exchange, and not only in Eastern Europe. The process of nationalization of modern and contemporary art from Eastern Europe seemed to disappear from the international art scene, and was followed by a different one, which I would call cosmopolitan. Before describing it, let me point out that the transformations in our part of the continent have been developing almost simultaneously alongside the fall of the authoritarian regimes in South America and South Africa, and as such have contributed to what I would call the rise of post-totalitarian or post-authoritarian studies (notably very different from the ever more popular post-colonial ones). In other words, it is an attempt to deal with something more general than the post-communist condition – a condition that could be provisionally called "post-authoritarian." Moreover, and this may be a crucial problem, the year 1989 very extensively remodeled perception of the world, from binary—operating with clear-cut oppositions—to pluralistic and multi-dimensional. What seems to me important now is how

[1] See: Piotr Piotrowski, "Nationalisierte Avantgarden. Osteuropäsche Modernismen und der Mangel an Internationalität," *springerin*, Winter 2011, p. 27–29, and Piotr Piotrowski, "Nationalizing Modernism. Czech, Slovak, and Hungarian Artists in Warsaw (1962, 1972)," Jérême Bazin, Pascal Dubourg-Glatigny, Piotr Piotrowski (ed.), *Internationalism in the Arts of Communist Europe* (in press).

much the model of the artistic inter-national and trans-national exchange has changed. Apparently, in our part (writing from Poland) of Europe the process of the nationalization of modern and postmodern art has come to an end, and a new situation has created frames, in this respect, for very different processes.

In general, there is no doubt that since 1989 categories such as Eastern Europe, the Eastern bloc, or even the politically more neutral Central Europe, have been dropped in reflections on or considerations of contemporary artistic culture. In other words, the eastern part of the continent has been deregionalized and geography has become much less important. In fact, apart from the problem(atics) of history, the present artistic initiatives seem to be shifting the emphasis from geography (thinking in terms of countries and regions) to topography (thinking in terms of places). Now we are more likely to speak about cities (Bratislava, Budapest, Bucharest, Prague, Warsaw, and Vilnius) than about Central or Eastern Europe. The latter term in particular is strongly determined by history and politics. This does not mean, however, that there are no projects out there based on or grounded in regionalism. Next to less successful political initiatives (like the Vyshehrad Group) as regards culture, various attempts have been made in the Balkans, where a sense of local artistic identity is experiencing dynamic revitalization, thanks to joint artistic and editorial events; also among the Baltic states, where such joint efforts are perhaps more modest and certainly less spectacular. Against the background of those two regional constructions, particularly the Balkans, Central Europe (as understood in traditional terms) maintains a very low profile, owing more to its local metropolitan centers than to any regional initiatives. The artistic legitimating of post-communist Central European identity must be specified not in geographical, but in topographic terms.

As a result of the shift in emphasis from geography to topography, the idea of the "transnational," so useful for the research on artistic culture of the recent past, has been losing relevance as well. At first glance, one might say that in this case the term "international" is more operative, which would mean a return to the idiom of modernism. After all, it was modernism that turned it into a cult of object(s), a sort of fetish of a new culture. Without making precise distinctions, one may, of course, casually argue that cultural exchange, when seen from a topographic perspective, is more international than transnational; however, such a claim is perhaps rather superficial. In fact, the name of the game is different now: it is cosmopolitanism. I understand this term in the original Greek sense as a combination of the city (polis) and the world (cosmos): cosmo-polis, a world city, a city-world, city-universe, one whose citizens are citizens of the world, for whom the proper space of the debate is both the municipal agora, and—shall we say—the space of the entire planet. A new culture, emerging from the general processes of globalization, is then literally cosmopolitan. The relations among particular cities or metropolitan centers should perhaps be called trans-cosmopolitan. Consequently, if the artistic geography, which was a comparative method of analyzing art of the communist period, implied transnational relations—and in fact resulting in the nationalization of modernism and the neo-avant-garde—the artistic topography, a method of analyzing culture of the post-communist era (though not exclusively), approached as part of the global structure of artistic exchange implies the concept of trans-cosmopolitanism.

In other words, since 1989, cities in (the former) Eastern Europe have become more important than countries. Certainly, the former have always had their own identities, which did not necessarily overlap (or specifically correspond) with the national ones. Still, in communist times, cities—particularly the capitals but sometimes also other, so-called provincial centers, such as Brno in Czechoslovakia, Zagreb in Yugoslavia, Leipzig in the GDR, Łódź, Kraków, and Wrocław in Poland, Leningrad in the USSR, and Cluj and Timişoara in Romania, functioned, as it were, as a *pars pro toto* of the national identity. Now it appears that along a general tendency towards the metropolization of culture on a global scale, the big cities of the (former) Eastern Europe have become far more specific, individual and autonomous, as well as independent of broader national identities. This trend has also been acknowledged in today's artistic discourse, for instance in *Leap into the City*, a book edited by Katrin Klingan and Ines Kappert, consisting of chapters focusing on particular post-communist cities—and not always metropolitan centers in the global sense, such as Ljubljana, Pristina, Sarajevo, Sofia, Warsaw, and Zagreb. What seems especially important in this book is that the cities have been approached from a number of different perspectives. It does not propose a uniform method of description or attempt to apprehend or express their uniqueness in the same way. Instead, it is a view composed of certain fragments, discussions, and partial analyses, far from essentialist generalizations. It is a genuine achievement on the part of the volume's authors and editors, since in this way the city can be rescued from the fate of sweeping nationalization to reveal, instead, its heterogeneous character.[2]

Most certainly, a very special city-place (cosmo-polis), quite difficult to compare with the other aforementioned cities, yet important for the debate around the (former) Central or Eastern Europe, is Berlin. We tend to take for granted the fact that East Berlin, the capital of the GDR, has been incorporated by the Federal Republic and by the Western part of the present-day capital. It may be worthwhile posing or addressing the question whether this genuine metropolis holds any significance in a discussion about the cosmopolitan character of this part of Europe. In other words, we should perhaps look for Eastern European traces in the German capital of today. One such trace was an exhibition called *Der Riss im Raum* (1994/95), organized by Matthias Flügge, showing the post-1945 art of the Czech Republic, East and West Germany, Poland, and Slovakia. Another was *Exchange and Transformation. Central-European Avant-Gardes* (2002), a show brought to Berlin from Los Angeles, focusing on the classic Central European avant-garde or, more precisely, the classic avant-gardes (in plural) of that part of the continent. Perhaps there are more. In this respect, one should also ask if such interests actually challenge the trans-national model in favor of the trans-cosmopolitan one. There are many examples that corroborate this intuitive claim, provided, among others, in the work of the Künstlerhaus Bethanien, run by Christoph Tannert, whose wide-ranging international program reveals numerous references to Eastern Europe. Surely, however, the case of Berlin is not a typical illustration of the cosmopolization of the former Eastern bloc. The cities examined in the Klingan-Kappert book provide better examples of this process. Certainly they are far smaller than the capital of the reunified Germany, and the local processes developing there are narrower in scope than those to be seen in Berlin. One of those processes is the development of art institutions of European (and sometimes even more general, broader)

2 See Katrin Klingan, Ines Kappert (ed.), *Leap into the City*, DuMont Literatur und Kunst Verlag, Cologne 2006.

significance, such as the Contemporary Art Center "Zamek Ujazdowski" in Warsaw, currently run by Italian director Fabio Cavallucci, likely the largest and most active public institution of its kind in post-communist Europe (excepting Berlin), and the private DOXa in Prague. Both organize big exhibitions of a cosmopolitan character. Another important factor that contributes to growing or spreading cosmopolitanism is migration, in particular that of both artists and curators. Increasingly often we see artists choosing—as has long been the case in the West—to live in a city or country where they were born or educated. Communist Europe did not know this phenomenon or, rather, experienced it on a far smaller scale. The movement or migration was largely one-way: Eastern European artists, intellectuals, managers of culture, dealers, and curators emigrated to Western Europe or the United States, never to return. Now, since 1989, not only have many of them come back, but they have started moving from one Eastern European city to another. What's more, some (though so far few) Western artists and curators have moved to the East (Fabio Cavalluci among them), and perhaps considerably more will be doing just that.

By the same token, however, what makes the metropolitan centers cosmopolitan in the first place are biennial exhibitions, the number of which, worldwide, now totals an alleged 146.[3] They are organized in Australia, Africa, the Americas, Asia, in China (both on the mainland and in Taiwan), as well as (the majority) in Europe, often by curators of international renown. Also the artists who take part in them often come from the highest or most celebrated strata of the global art(istic) culture. Frequently such shows are generously financed by both the private and public sectors, as local authorities look to publicize the various (cultural) attractions of their regions. For the local audiences, the biennales provide opportunities to become familiar with the current trends in art, while on the other hand they (the venue-cities) are transformed into cultural tourist traps, attracting the international public and media both. Some of the biennales are very open, while others concentrate on particular or problematic regions. These exhibitions are also organized also in the former Eastern Europe: in Bucharest, Iași, Prague (two competing events: one organized by *Flash Art* (Giancarlo Politi and Helena Kontova), the other by the National Gallery (Milan Knižak), and Mediations in Poznań, Poland. The latter

3 Irit Rogoff, "Geo-Cultures, Circuits of Arts and Globalizations," *Open. Cahier on Art and the Public Domain* (The Art Biennial as a Global Phenomenon. Strategies in Neo-Political Times), Vol. 8 (2009), No. 16, p. 114.

is actually rather special, since it has a double frame of reference—global and regional. It developed in the context of an
earlier exhibition, *Asia-Europe Mediation* (2007), prepared
by Tomasz Wendland (present biennale director), originally
intended to mediate between the two continents—a concept
adopted and continued by the current biennale. Initially, the
Asian component was central most, but its scope quickly expanded to the global. Interestingly, Eastern Europe has become
the focus of global perspective as a space of mediation between
and among various cultures. In 2008 the Poznań show arranged
by three curators—Lóránd Hegyi, Gu Zhenqing, and Yu Yean
Kim—attracted more than 200 artists from all over the world
and most every continent. At the same time, however, the
main focus centered on the Central European placement of the
"mediations"; not so much by virtue of the selection of artists
from that part of Europe (though this too was important), but
above all by creating, in the essays included in the catalogue,
their discursive context and interpretive frame.[4] The next biennale (2010) organized two years later, and curated by Ryszard
Kluszczyński and Tsutomu Mizusawa, was even bigger, and
was accompanied by other shows, including *Erased Walls,*
with a distinctly global character as well.[5] It is worth mentioning that in-between these biennales the *Mediators* exhibition
was shown, as organized by Tomasz Wendland (director of the
Poznań biennale) in the National Museum in Warsaw.[6] All of
them touched upon a number of interesting problems, the most
important of them a diagnosis of the state of global art, which
in this case was not at all critical, but aesthetically refined and
elegant. Thus, the exhibitions (both in Poznań and in Warsaw)
questioned and explored the identity of contemporary art in its
global capacity, invoking the question whether the idea of global art is identical to the larger, widely acknowledged concept
of contemporary art or perhaps reaches beyond it. By using the
term "contemporary art" back in the 1980s we meant or referred to a different problematic and aesthetic. What makes this
situation interesting is a sort of move of the institution (biennale) from one city to another, even if only at small scales and
short distances. Of course, the most famous biennales in (the
former) Eastern Europe are those of Moscow and Berlin. The
5th Berlin Biennale (2008), curated by Adam Szymczyk and
Elena Filipović, explicitly turned its attention toward the former

4 See Tomasz Wendland
(ed.), *Mediations Biennale*,
Centrum Kultury "Zamek,"
Poznań 2008.

5 Ryszard W.
Kluszczyński, Tsutomu
Mizusawa (ed.), *Beyond
Mediations*, Centrum
Kultury Zamek," Poznań
2010; Tomasz Wendland
et al. (ed.), *Erased Walls*,
Centrum Kultury "Zamek,"
Poznań 2010.

6 Tomasz Wendland (ed.),
Mediatorzy/Mediators,
Muzeum Narodowe,
Warsaw 2010.

East. And the 2012 edition (the 7th), curated by Polish artist Artur Zmijewski, had a decidedly political and thus in certain respects also cosmopolitan character.

The passing from artistic geography, in which specific countries and their trans-national relations was the subject, to topography, favoring or focused on cities, represents a highly interesting feature of contemporary culture. Consequently, one might assume that relations between cities will soon cease to be trans-national in character, instead becoming trans-cosmopolitan. The biennales—and analysis of them—is a good starting point for thinking in specific terms, in particular those as formulated by Boris Groys: that these events represent not only tourist attractions and opportunities for the promotion of international, global capital-driven interests, but also, and perhaps first and foremost, occasions to develop a global political forum, global *politeia*.[7] If we choose to adopt such a point of view, one could propose that the cosmopolitan cities, including those in (the former) Eastern Europe, together with their cosmopolitan cultural activity (like the biennales), will lead to the creation of a network of cosmopolitan intellectual exchange and trans-cosmopolitan relations, of which the topography of (the former) Eastern Europe will be a part.

The final problem that serves to reveal or demonstrate the cosmopolitan character of the particular place is intricately connected with the question of the museum—namely the question of the "museum of contemporary art." Contemporary art, observes Hans Belting, is global.[8] Not because it is globally distributed, but because it is global by definition, touching upon the problems important to the entire world, the global *politeia*. On the other hand, museums, including museums of contemporary art, are also local: they are located in particular places, they are related to the local history, social circumstances and similar. Consequently, what is local has become global. What we are increasingly dealing with is a different kind of art in terms of the particular making of artworks as well as communicating with the audience, both based on modern technology. A form to represent this development, rooted in the experience of global contemporary art as well as in the critique of modernism (the MoMA model), is exemplified by the "museum of contemporary art" (the MoCA). It is interested not only in presenting art to the spectator, but also in determining its varieties

7 Boris Groys, "From Medium to Message. The Art Exhibition as a Model of a New World Order," *Open. Cahier on Art and the Public Domain* (The Art Biennial as a Global Phenomenon. Strategies in Neo-Political Times), Vol. 8 (2009), No. 16, p. 64–65.

8 Hans Belting, "Contemporary Art and the Museum in the Global Age," Peter Weibel, Andrea Buddensieg (ed.), *Contemporary Art and the Museum. A Global Perspective.* Hatje Cantz, Ostfildern 2007, p. 16–38; Hans Belting, "Contemporary Art as Global Art: A Critical Estimate," Hans Belting, Andrea Buddensieg (ed.), *The Global Art World. Audiences, Markets, and Museums*, Hatje Cantz, Ostfildern 2009, p. 38–73.

and contributing to its critical mission. Evidently, this type of
museum is not (at all) free from the neo-liberal market game.
Quite the contrary, both the LA MoCA (Los Angeles Museum
of Contemporary Art) and the MassMoCA (in North Adams,
Massachusetts), to mention only the most familiar examples,
are deeply involved in this process. Yet this is not the point
since, as Belting observes, those museums have been opened
not to exhibit art history, but to show and exhibit the world in
the mirror of contemporary art.[9] Compared to the traditional
museum of modern art and its practices this is a major change.
What the MoCA is interested in is not art as such, but the world
that it represents—and this makes the local/global dialectics
possible.

9 Belting, "Contemporary
Art as Global Art: A Critical
Estimate," p. 48.

Naturally we have a couple of MoCA-model museums in
the (former) East, created after 1989. The newest or most recent
of them is perhaps MOCAK, Museum of Contemporary Art
Krakow—where we see the aforementioned local/global dialectics at work very clearly. The museum is situated in the former
Schindler factory, familiar from the famous Steven Spielberg
movie, standing side by side with the Historical Museum. The
latter tells the local story—the history of the Nazi occupation
of the city. However, since the Holocaust as such is a global
phenomenon, it constitutes a part of the world history narrative, only further globalized by Spielberg's movie *Schindler's
List* (1993), and immediately picked up by the tourist industry, the Historical Museum operates on two levels: the local
and the global. The MOCAK, located next door, had to deal
with this, so it is hardly a coincidence its first exhibition was
titled *History in Art,* curated by the museum's director Maria
Anna Potocka, which touched on the problems of historical
memory, including World War II, the Holocaust, contemporary
approaches to Nazi imagery in the arts etc.[10] The exhibition
is of course, international, and shows testifies to the fact that
Krakow is not only an historical tourist attraction (in fact the
most touristic Polish city), but also a center of contemporary
art. Similarly, the MOCAK was built on the "other" side of
the Vistula River, in the city's abandoned post-industrial area,
which is typically consistent with the neo-liberal process-
tendency in creating MoCA-model museums. Perhaps what is
in fact most interesting for consideration here is the fact that it,
this development, would place, posit Krakow on the global art

10 Maria Anna Potocka
(ed.), *History in Art,*
MOCAK, Kraków 2011.

map—and this not in connection with the notion of Poland, the (a) country, but rather with the (a) city. And further, this would serve to demonstrate the shift from geography to topography, the process, which began in and after 1989, and not at all in the (former) East alone.

Translated from Polish by Marek Wilczyński and Piotr Piotrowski.

Institutional Anxiety and the Politics of Naming

The humble personal pronoun, assumed blithely in speech
and passed over rapidly in writing, is fated to be the bearer of
resonant historical questions. While embarking on an inquiry
into the question of what constitutes "global" art, we must
first define the "we" in whose voice all of us, as theorists,
curators, art historians, artists and critics, address this question. Who are the "we" who are afflicted by the problem of
defining "global" art? Is this a Eurocentric "we," representing
interpretative bafflement at the diversity of artistic production
from beyond Europe's horizons? Or is this, more narrowly but
no less influentially, an institutional "we" speaking from the
embattled bastions of the academy and the museum? Or is this
the "we" who see the discipline of art history breaking down
or being made irrelevant by its supposed objects of inquiry?
Some hints as to the nature of this "we" may be gleaned from
a survey of recent endeavors within Europe-based art history
to align the classical mandates of the discipline with the unruly
and transgressive manifestations of contemporary art as these
emerge from diverse regions of the world.

Attending to this art-historical self-renovation, we are
struck by its tendency to map the paradigm shifts in our understanding of the global condition through exhibitional and discursive structures, rather than by reference to historical developments. For instance, it is not the emergence of postcolonial
societies into a position of confident self-assertion that attracts
the new art-historical eye, so much as the epiphenomenon of
"*Magiciens de la terre*". Likewise, art historians committed to
the transformation of their discipline seem content with the institutional response of imagining and scontext of the full range
of historical consequences that follow from the emergence of
post-Cold War blocs with new claims to self-definition. We are
only attending to the inner readjustments of art history when
we confine ourselves to considering changes within the academy, writing and pedagogy since the early 1990s.

Through his Global Art Museum project, Professor Hans
Belting has provided a critically attentive account of the term

"global" art, demonstrating how the valency of this term has changed through the course of the 20th century: originally, it signified an anthropological and archaeological interest in the traditional arts of societies outside Europe; now, it encodes an acceptance, however reluctant, of the multiple locations of contemporary artistic production across the planet. The former refusal of the imperial centers to accept that societies outside Euro-America could possess and perform a contemporary has, at length, given way to a realization that there are plural experiences and accounts of the contemporary. However, what remains undiscussed in an account such as Belting's, is the manner in which paradigm shifts in the understanding of what constitutes globality, globalism, globalization or the global contemporary have been attempted outside the West—that is, outside the conceptual space of Euro-American academia and strategic policy; outside the classical institutions of art history. I refer to such attempts as they have been staged in the global South: in the domain of a politics that mediated between culture and the postcolonial national space.

In the following I will, among other things, analyze such alternative starting points of a global consciousness—a globalism before globalism. Let me begin, so to speak, *in medias res*, with the critic John Berger's message to the first edition of Triennale India, which was organized by the Indian critic and novelist Mulk Raj Anand and opened in New Delhi in that fateful year of global upheaval and transition, 1968.[1]

Berger wrote: "I send my greetings to the first Triennale of Contemporary World Art to be held in India. It would suggest the possibility of escaping from or even overthrowing the hegemony of Europe and North America in these matters. This hegemony is disastrous because, whatever the personal feelings or ideas of individual artists or teachers may be, it is based upon the concept of a visual work of art as property. The historical usefulness of such a concert has long passed: it stands now as a barrier to further development. The ideology of modern European property is inseparable from imperialism. The fight against imperialism and all its agencies is thus closely connected with the struggle for a truly modern art. I wish you clear-sightedness, strength and courage in your struggle."[2]

1 For an account of the reception history of Triennale India (late-1960s and 1970s) and for an understanding of the differently nuanced positions on internationalism see Nancy Adajania, "Probing the Khojness of Khoj", Pooja Sood (ed.), *The Khoj Book 1997–2007: Contemporary Art Practice in India,* Harper Collins, Delhi 2010.

2 John Berger's message from London dated January 10, 1968, *Lalit Kala Contemporary-36,* Special issue on Triennale India, Lalit Kala Akademi, New Delhi 1990, p. 14.

The Alternative Beginnings of a Global Consciousness

Berger's message of 1968, despite the ringing tones of its 1960s Left rhetoric, reminds us that internationalism is not necessarily a monopoly of the industrially advanced societies and imperialist polities of West Europe and North America. The societies of the global South can equally stake their claim to articulate a vision of the world. The "will to globality,"[3] as Okwui Enwezor has observed, is not only reserved for those who can shuttle across the globe at will; it can, and is, also exercised by those whose mobility is either constrained or involuntary, those trapped in oppressive systems or those forced to migrate by adversity. And to such figures, the "will to globality" is a form of resistance, a form of self-articulation against all odds.

In the early phase of independence, the postcolonial societies of the global South had to confront a specific global structure of necessity, of economic and political asymmetry, because the process of colonization has already conscripted them into the world system of capital. At the same time, they could also draw on two sources of freedom, which promised new forms of globalist consciousness. First: members of the formerly colonized societies could subscribe to the same spectrum of Leftist internationalist thought and activity that was shaking the societies of Europe. Berger and Mulk Raj Anand, for instance, were united within this spectrum: Anand had been socialized within Fabian socialist and anarchist circles in London, and had fought on the anarchist side in the Spanish Civil War. And second: these societies could retrieve anterior histories of planet-wide coalitions and connections, in which they had participated in the pre-capitalist and pre-imperialist epoch. Globalism is not the outcome of a particular Western logic of economic and political expansion. Rather, it inheres in the transnational networks of the pre-capitalist epoch: the Mughal, Ching, Safahvid and Ottoman empires each had their world-circling networks of trade, pilgrimage and diplomacy; the Islamic world conceived of the planet as the space for the amplification of the *Ummah*, held together by the protocols of pilgrimage; the Buddhist world saw itself as a web spreading from a point of origin in northern India outward to diverse terrains. The Silk Route, the Spice Route, and the exchange networks of the Indian Ocean and the Mediterranean all offered

3 Okwui Enwezor, "The Black Box," *Documenta 11: Platform 5*, Hatje Cantz, Ostfildern-Ruit 2002, p. 42–55.

proposals for the envisioning and realization of world-wide social structures.

Thus, the ideological position of the 1968 Triennale India was clear. It was intended to demonstrate that a globalist consciousness, an internationalism, does not flow only from the former imperial centers to the former colonies. That is why I believe it is important to re-insert this neglected and even lost history into our discussion of present-day globalism. The narrative of globalization, with its driving momentum and many discontents, is all too often told from the vantage point of a West whose energies were triumphantly redeemed from the wastage of the Cold War and unleashed on the planet at large from the early 1990s onward. That narrative demands to be interrogated, dismantled, and opened out to accommodate other voices and other trajectories. My own concern in this debate is to emphasize the robust tradition of an internationalism articulated in and from the global South, a globalism from the South that was and is based on the shared perception—across borders and disciplines—of being caught up in the same historical predicament, confronting similar crises, looking for instruments and resolutions.

The Third Position in Cold War Politics

Triennale India was one of the cultural manifestations of the third position in the global politics of the Cold War period. In 1961, five visionary leaders of the post-World War II world—Nehru, Nasser, Sukarno, Kwame Nkrumah and Tito—founded the Non-Alignment Movement (NAM), to chalk out a position that was equidistant from the United States and the USSR, to demarcate the Third World as an alternative space for self-determination, despite the prevailing exigencies of the Cold War. The novelist, arts editor and cultural organizer Mulk Raj Anand, who proposed and founded Triennale India, embraced Nehru's internationalist position—which aspired to bypass the cartography of superpower-led geopolitics and remap the world, forging affinities between Asia and Latin America, Asia and Africa, Asia and East Europe. The dream that inspired these initiatives was that of a collegial and equitable multilateralism.

Nehru coined the term NAM in 1954 in Colombo, in a speech on the Sino-Indian relationship. The *panch-sheel* or "five principles" he stressed were: Mutual respect for each other's territorial integrity and sovereignty; mutual non-aggression; mutual non-interference in domestic affairs; equality and mutual benefit; and peaceful co-existence. The 1955 Bandung conference, held in Indonesia, was the most important platform for the enunciation of these ideals: it was dedicated to the very optimistic goals of promoting world peace and cooperation, and expressed these through a support for anti-colonial liberation movements across the globe.

The Non-Alignment Movement was a utopian project devoted to breaking the monopoly of the West over the definition and production of internationalism. As against this material and discursive domination of the West, NAM hoped to produce counter-models of political and cultural solidarity—these were to be based on perceived affinities, not on partisan investments on either side of the hegemonic binary of the US versus the USSR.

Normally, the genealogy of the term "globalism" is expressed as a continuous line from internationalism to globalism, from Cold War to post-Cold War politics, with the fall of the Berlin Wall and the economic liberalization of the 1990s taken as its paramount moments of transformation. What gets missed here are the points of rupture in this linear narrative. My take on present day globalism is informed by alternative starting points and anterior histories, such as those of NAM, cultural interventions such as Triennale India or the São Paulo Biennale.

I read globalism as the deliberate gesture of recovering the human potentialities of the lattices of globalization from the grip of neo-liberal policy. To the neo-liberal, globalism refers to a nation-state's policy of treating the entire world as a market and source of goods and services. For me, by contrast, the term has a completely different valency. We must not cede the power of words and ideas to the enemy. Globalism, to me, signifies a transcultural, collaborative, multi-participatory mode of performing ideas and conducting projects—with the emphasis on ethical responsibility and a transformative aesthetics. While neo-liberal globalism is an extension of the old imperialist and Cold War geo-politics, my perspective on globalism shifts the locus to the global South, and to acts of resistance.[4]

[4] See Nancy Adajania, "Time to Restage the World: Theorising a New and Complicated Sense of Solidarity," Miranda Wallace (ed.), *21st Century: Art in the First Decade*, Queensland Art Gallery/ GoMA, Brisbane 2011, p. 222–229.

The Nth Field

Since 2005, Ranjit Hoskote and I have been developing models
that deal with the transcultural condition in which we find ourselves today as cultural theorists and cultural practitioners. We
have over the last decade increasingly found post-colonial theory in its classical form (the early and undoubtedly seminal work
of Homi K. Bhabha, Gayatri C. Spivak and Edward W. Said) to
be no longer sufficient to the task of attending to our experiential and epistemological complexities. Classical post-colonial
theory was tremendously liberating and even formative for us,
during the 1980s and 1990s, but it is imperative for us to go beyond it now, through the mode of sympathetic critique. Indeed,
the foundational figures of postcolonial theory have themselves
explored further in the meanwhile, with Bhabha's account of
cultural citizenship in a post-national space, and Said's philosophy of engaged reconciliation in the Israel-Palestine context.
However, this still leaves us with the task of theorizing the
domain of transcultural exchanges, unbounded by prior historical confrontations, in a post-postcolonial space.

One of the first of our models was that of "critical transre-
gionality". Our interest was to remap the domains of global
cultural experience by setting aside what seemed to us to be
exhausted cartographies variously born out of the Cold War,
area studies, late colonial demarcations, the war against terror
or the supposed clash of civilizations. In place of these exhausted, even specious cartographies premised on the paradigm
of the "West against the Rest", we propose a new cartography
based on the mapping of continents of affinities, and a search
for commonalties based on jointly faced crises and shared predicaments—which produce intriguing entanglements among
regional histories staged in Asia, Africa Latin America and
Eastern Europe.

More recently, in refining this model, we have framed the
concept of the *nth field*.[5] The nth field signifies, to us, the un-
tagged and unnumbered zones of cultural and political possibility that arise from the unpredictable encounters among
diverse actors in the transverse spaces, which are opened up by
migration for dialogue and mutual curiosity. We draw this term
from the discipline of computer programming, where the nth
field stands for the as-yet-unspecified but foreseeable iteration

5 This section is based
on Nancy Adajania's and
Ranjit Hoskote's essay,
"The Nth Field: Horizon
Reloaded," Maria Hlavajova
et al (ed.), *On Horizons:
A Critical Reader In
Contemporary Art*, BAK,
Utrecht 2011, p. 16–32.

of a loop process (the "nth" representing an ordinal number). While it seems formally to be a repetition, its actual effects are amplificatory—and can only be experienced when, so to speak, one has arrived in the field. We have adopted the term for its expressive potential.

The nth field takes us beyond the default binaries of the post-colonial predicament. Whereas Homi K. Bhabha's "Third Space"[6] is often conceived of in terms of the colonial encounter and its various aftermaths—the contact zone, diaspora, the dissolution of the center/periphery binary, and the circulating mobility between former postcolonial hinterland and former imperial metropole—we have developed the concept of the nth field to mark a transitive engagement among individuals, ir- respective of a shared colonial history, which is no longer the only or the most important criterion for an intersection, en- counter, or exchange among dissimilar subjectivities. Thus we see the nth field as a site for the staging of a transitivity of ho- rizons, a space where different kinds of cultural imaginations may engage one another in dialogue.

Where the Third Space remains associated with the demar- cation of difference between Self and Other, or even selves and their others, arising from the specific historical crisis of the colonial encounter, the nth field is premised on the identifica- tion of affinities that form a ground for transcultural mutuality, to be explored through the extension of one's complicity in the crisis, but also the pleasure, of the Other; and through an ethi- cal responsiveness to the predicament of the Other. In the nth field, culture is produced through all forms of intersubjective encounters among heterogeneous actors—the crucial factor involved here is the unpredictability of circulation in the epoch of globalization. Today, cultural actors are developing nth fields for themselves, rather than simply finding themselves in contact zones by reason of inheritance or happenstance, or working their way through to a Third Space against the grain of inher- ited turbulence. Crucially, therefore, the nth field goes beyond Marie Louise Pratt's classical conceptualization of the contact zone, which she regards as the site of "spatial and temporal copresence of subjects previously separated... and whose trajec- tories now intersect."[7]

Instead, the nth field is a site for the active seeking out of engagement, exchange, and intersection through the modes of

6 Homi Bhabha, *The Location of Culture*, Routledge, London 1994, p. 37–39.

7 Marie Louise Pratt, *Imperial Eyes: Travel Writing and Transculturation* Routledge, London 1992, p. 6.

mutuality, collaboration, and emplacement, an experimental
poetics of belonging. The shift marked here is that from the
outcomes of structure to the choices of agency; from a scalar-
oriented vision of cultural actors acting out the consequences
of world-historical stagings of travel, colonial expansion and
imperial rule, to a vector-oriented account of cultural actors
shaping a way in and through a complicated world. In terms of
political spatiality, too, the nth field redistributes equity through
a lattice of newly formulated and negotiated relationships,
many of which begin in the awareness that the long-existing
constraints of asymmetry must be broken; indeed, such a resistance often overtly inspires and sustains the nth field's relationships of collaboration and synergy. The nth field is based on
confident encounter, on the understanding that Self and Other
need not be locked either in communion or antagonism, hostage
to fragmentation or subjugation, but that they can weave together a fabric of "adjacencies and distances,"[8] to adapt art historian
Miwon Kwon's memorable phrase for our purpose.

To our generation of cultural producers, location has long
ago liberated itself from geography. We map our location on
a transregional lattice of shifting nodes representing intense
occasions of collegiality, temporary platforms of convocation,
and transcultural collaborations. As we move along the shifting nodes of this lattice, we produce outcomes along a scale of
forms ranging across informal conversations, formal symposia,
self-renewing caucuses, periodic publications, anthologies,
traveling exhibitions, film festivals, biennials, residencies, and
research projects. This global system of cultural production
takes its cue from the laboratory—as in all laboratories, the
emphasis is on experiment and its precipitates. However, to the
extent that this system is relayed across a structure of global
circulations, it also possesses a dimension of theater: a rather
large proportion of its activity is in the nature of rehearsal and
restaging. We would like to address the dilemmas as well as
the potentialities of a mode of cultural production that is based
on global circulations yet is not merely circulatory; and a mode
of life that is based on transnational mobility but is not without
anchorage in regional predicaments.

Everywhere and increasingly—whether we are teaching at
a para-academic platform in Bombay, engaging in curatorial
discussions or conducting research in Berlin, co-curating a

[8] Miwon Kwon, *One Place
After Another: Site-specific
Art and Locational Identity*
MIT Press, Cambridge MA
2004, p. 166.

biennial in Gwangju, contributing to an international exhibition in Karlsruhe, responding with critical empathy to a triennial in Brisbane, or developing a research project in Utrecht—we find ourselves working with interlocutors and collaborators in what we think of as *nth fields*. All nth fields have similar structural, spatial and temporal characteristics. In structural terms, these are receptive and internally flexible institutions, rhizomatic and self-sustaining associations, or periodic platforms. In spatial terms, these are either programmatically nomadic in the way they manifest themselves, or extend themselves through often unpredictable transregional initiatives, or are geographically situated in sites to which none (or few) of their participants are affiliated by citizenship or residence. Temporally, the rhythm of these engagements is varied and can integrate multiple time lines for conception and production.

These nth fields certainly throw into high relief the vexed questions that haunt the global system of cultural production: Who is the audience for contemporary global art? How may we construe a local that hosts, or is held hostage by, the global? Can we evolve a contemporary discussion that does not merely re-visit the exhausted Euro-American debates of the late twentieth century by oblique means? Is it possible to translate the intellectual sources of a regional modernity into globally comprehensible terms? What forms of critical engagement should artistic labor improvise, as it chooses to become complicit with aspirational and developmentalist capital and its managers across the world? At the same time, these nth fields are optimal nodes for the staging of what the art theorist and curator Sarat Maharaj has described as "entanglements,"[9] the braided destinies that knot together selves accustomed to regard one another as binary opposites: colonizing aggressor and colonized victim; Euro-American citizen and denizen of the global South; Occidental and Oriental; and so forth. A history delineated under the sign of entanglement lays bare the ideological basis of all fixed identities, conjoins them in sometimes discomfiting but always epiphanic mutuality. When such identities are thus unmasked, de-naturalized and dissolved, we are free to work out new forms of dialogue and interaction across difference, a new and re-deeming solidarity. In these complex circumstances, the architecture of belonging can never be static. In our own practice as theorists and curators, we have drafted different versions of it in

[9] Sarat Maharaj, "Small Change of the Universal," unpublished keynote lecture, delivered at the 1st FORMER WEST Congress, organized by BAK, basis voor actuele kunst, Utrecht, November 5–7, 2009. A video recording of Maharaj's address may be viewed online at: http://www.former-west.org/ResearchCongresses/1stFORMERWESTCongress/SaratMaharajSmall-ChangeoftheUniversal

different places. We have drawn on various models of emotion-
ally and intellectually enriching locality, including the *mohalla*
(an Urdu/Hindi word meaning a web of relationships inscribed
within a grid of lanes, streets and houses), the *kiez* (a Germano-
Slavic, specifically Berlin word, meaning much the same thing,
and conferring on the resident the privilege of non-anxious
belonging), the *adda* (a Hindi/Bengali term meaning a venue for
friendly conversation and animated debate), and the *symposium*
(not the academic format but its original, a Greek word signifying a drinking party that was also a venue for philosophical
discussion). These traveling localities are the neighborhoods
and convocations where the nth field is manifested. [10]

And what might we discuss at these convocations? The power of infinitives, perhaps, to disclose the complicities between
an official contemporary and its unacknowledged cousins; to
celebrate the carnivalesque; to document the half-forgotten; to
allude to elusive historical realities; to annotate our encounters.
In the nth field, iterated freshly in every new and provisional
neighborhood and convocation, we could generate modes of
comprehending, critiquing, and resisting various hazards: the
incessancy of theoretical articulation and the riddle-like silence
of history; the volatile rhetoric of political elites and the absolute
secrecy of the strategic operations through which they exploit
the planet. The vibrancy of the nth field rescues us from being
conscripted in the cause of a single past or being mortgaged to a
single future. The nth field is a provocation to constantly destabilize and re-imagine ourselves beyond our provisional locations, to converse beyond our presuppositions about belonging
and alienation, and so to invite ourselves to the feast of hazard.

**Institutional Anxiety: "Containing" the Surplus
of Contemporary Art**

As is obvious from my account of the nth field, the emerging
forms of art practice across the globe will be distinguished by
a rich particularity, which arises from the specific textures of
particular sites, production systems, idioms of dialogue and
strategies of collaboration.

As such, this art will have to be gauged idiographically and
not in a nomothetic manner, instance by instance, and not along
the rubric of laid-down criteria. We cannot, *a priori*, enumerate

10 Some passages in this
section appeared previ-
ously in Nancy Adajania
and Ranjit Hoskote's text
entitled "Notes towards
a Lexicon of Urgencies,"
DISPATCH, the online
journal of Independent
Curators International
(October 2010), online at:
http://curatorsintl.org/jour-
nal/notes_towards_a_lexi-
con_of_urgencies

its features or themes; except to indicate that certain generic features may be predicated of art that circulates around the global production system of the biennale circuit or the residency circuit (such as portability, readability, scale, tendency to address planet-wide concerns or multi-specialist cooperation). But this enumeration scarcely exhausts the potentialities of forms that emerge in the nth field: forms that may not necessarily be portable or readily readable, and yet may exert a compelling effect on the viewer.

This turns the question "What is global art?" around on those who ask it. The real answers are: "Who's asking? And why?" What is the optic through which this question is being phrased—and does it perhaps, signal a profound institutional anxiety in the academy and the museum (as against the studio and the biennale). Perhaps it points to a widening divide between the practitioners of contemporary art and those who would wish to bear testimony to it from within the older institutions of art history.

There can no longer be a universalizing art history in the sense of an epistemological and discursive motor running the Euro-American centers and driving ancillary activity in various outposts and provinces of the empire. The demand that the artistic imagination situate itself in a universalizing production of meaning marks an unfortunate reversion to some notion of a transcendent aesthetic soaring above all the visceral struggles of particularity from which cultural production gathers propulsion. Rather, what we see is the generation of numerous regional histories, each faithful to the textures of its floating point of origin, that are nonetheless woven across each other, so that none may be fully understood without reference to the others with which it overlaps.

It is understandable that in an age of overproduction and excess, biennale fever and museum precarity, the art institutions are anxious about finding ways of "containing" the surplus of contemporary art activity. But this form of containment is only a reiteration of what Berger deplored way back in the 1960s—the tendency to treat art as "property". Those who wish to produce a global art museum or a global art history must attend to the hegemonic tendencies imminent within these projects.

Art in the age of globalization eludes neat classification—it is produced from transversal/crisscrossing relationships and

diverse subjectivities. These rich and unpredictable entanglements of practice and approach cannot be contained in a tem-
plate of global art.

We do not need a menu delineating the constitutive features
of global art, which is a reductive program. What we need, instead, is a greater, deeper and finer understanding of the particularities of practice, and the entanglements among practices. That
is why the nth field, as the model of the future, not only contains
the promise of Benjaminian "not-yet", but also proposes a model
of praxis that is achievable. The nth field is not produced out of
institutional or managerial desires, but from the desire of cultural practitioners to map new continents of affinities.

Coda

At a symposium held in Salzburg in Summer 2011, devoted to
the ongoing discussion on the problem of defining "global" art
and the role performed by art history in this context, various
resolutions were hinted at. We heard, for instance, of a possible
abnegation of Eurocentric narcissism that has underwritten discursive control over art history, and a corresponding receptivity
to the perspectives of other societies. We heard, also, of the
need to go beyond classical post-enlightenment aesthetics and
to engage with aesthetic philosophies of various societies.

Such efforts, even when they seem laudable, are susceptible
to basic problems. This could lead us either to arid compara-
tism or reinstate the kind of essentialism by which Indian art
would be judged by Indian aesthetics, Chinese art by Chinese
aesthetics—which is unproductive, since the contemporary
art produced in these societies eludes their classical aesthetics.
Meanwhile, would the art establishment admit the applicabil-
ity of these "aesthetics of the Others" beyond their designated
borders? Or will they continue with the United Nations approach to global art and global aesthetics, where every member
has their own locus, but there is no provision for their mingling,
dissolution, and re-emergence under the sign of radical transformation? Can the transgressiveness and fluidity that is the
most definitive feature of art submit itself to the legislations of
the canon, in however renovated a form?

Art history has committed itself to a self-defeating style
of thought: namely teleology. It assumes that art production,

circulation and reception will evolve through alternate phases of confusion and clarity, to arrive at a *telos* where artistic production and its aesthetic interpretation are unified in a state of clarity. But as in Plato's great dialogue, *Symposium*, art production and its interpretation are like two halves of the self always attempting to unite, but failing because one half eternally flees the other. That is the fate to which art history must reconcile itself. Art production will always elude, defy, mock and will mostly remain in advance of interpretation. It is not containable in categories and all our concepts and narratives are approximations, wagers and shifting pictures.

The nth field, on the other hand, marks a break with teleological thinking. It does not conscript artistic practice into *a priori* academic thinking ignoring complexities of the present. The nth field demands attentiveness to the present of the practice. It does not see artists as bearers of pre-existing culture, but as agents of volition. The nth field demands that the discipline of art history be broken and remade, re-imagined, to address the reality of changing art practice and not the other way round.[11]

[11] This essay is based on a paper I presented at the symposium "Global Art— Wish or Reality," at the NEW Auditorium, Juridical Faculty of Salzburg University, July 30, 2011. The symposium was organized by the AICA (Austrian and Swiss sections) and the Salzburg International Summer Academy of Fine Arts.

**Spirits of Internationalism, Van Abbemuseum (VAM), Eindhoven /
Museum van Hedendaagse Kunst Antwerpen (M HKA), Antwerpen**
Charles Esche, Steven ten Thije, Bart De Baere, Jan De Vree,
Anders Kreuger, curators

Introduction

Spirits of Internationalism takes place simultaneously at M
HKA in Antwerp and Van Abbemuseum in Eindhoven. The
exhibition covers the period 1956–1986, characterised by the
bipolarity of the Cold War and various reactions against it.
The point of departure is the Benelux region, which like all
of western Europe actively celebrated US domination—in the
arts and otherwise. This has tended to obscure the relations
that did exist between artists in all continents. The exhibition offers a cross-section of art and artist archives and shows
some unexpected resemblances between artists working in the
West, the East and elsewhere.

The exhibition is sub-divided into eight "spirits": "the
Concrete," "the Essential," "the Transcendental," "the
Subverted," "the (Dis)located," "the Universal," "the
Positioned," and "the Engaged". These tentative categories
invite viewers to explore new relationships between famous
and lesser-known artists and their works. The "spirits" reflect
"internationalism" in a double sense. On the one hand they
pull together artists living and working in different countries.
On the other hand they suggest how the works are suspended
between the specific and the general.

The exhibition is the last in a series entitled *1956–1986: Art
from the Decline of Modernism to the Rise of Globalisation*. It
was organised by the new network *l'Internationale* that connects six European collections—four museums and two artist
archives. Apart from M HKA and the Van Abbemuseum, the
partners are MACBA in Barcelona and Moderna Galerija in
Ljubljana, as well as the Július Koller Society in Bratislava
and the KwieKulik Archive in Warsaw. The first two exhibitions were *Museum of Parallel Narratives* at MACBA and
Museum of Affects at Moderna Galerija.

Spirits of Internationalism is made possible with the support of the Culture Programme of the European Union.

Close

The Concrete

The Concrete brings together "optical" and "kinetic" works created in the late 1950s and early 1960s. The works are based on tangible materials and structures and relate to our physical and sensorial existence. But they differ from the more familiar abstract art of Late Modernism—not least the American Abstract Expressionist painters (Jackson Pollock, Barnett Newman, Cy Twombly and others), for whom abstraction is often a form of "representation" of the unrepresentable. By contrast, the Concrete becomes a "tool" for intervening in the real (material, social, political) world by exposing and thereby changing its materiality.

Lucio Fontana (1899–1968, Argentina/Italy) regards art as part of the evolution of nature and its laws. Not surprisingly, perhaps, for him the whole of art history leads to his own *concetto spaziale* ("spatial concept"). At first Fontana tries to variously transform and transcend his selected media (oil on canvas, copper plates, ceramics), but later his trademark becomes the slashed painted canvas. This is his most consistent attempt to achieve a dimension different from the flat pictorial surface. He trades the illusion of space for its reality, pointing at the slashed canvas as formed matter and a container of energy. (M HKA)

Gego (Gertrud Goldschmidt, 1912–1994, Germany/ Venezuela) studies architecture and engineering before fleeing the Nazis in 1939. By the late 1950s she has become a leading artist in Latin America. Her drawings and small metal sculptures are reminiscent of architectural studies, but they are autonomous artworks uniting the spatial and the organic. She calls them "drawings in space". The *reticuláreas* or "networked areas" are room-sized versions of the earlier works. The "lines" are pieces of interlinked metal wire articulating a mental space by physical means. Gego said: "Each module is organised individually and breaks with the overall symmetry of the structure." (M HKA/ Van Abbemuseum)

Yves Klein (1928–1962, France) is the son of two painters who works in many techniques, among them sculpture, photography, film and performance. Yet he is best known for his monochrome paintings, the first of which he makes in 1949 while working for an art framer in London. Klein thinks

of them as landscapes of freedom, offering a space liberated
from depiction. The colour blue becomes his signature, together with his *Leap into the Void* (1960), a retouched photograph based on a performance during which Klein jumps from
the first floor of a Paris townhouse, spreading his arms like an
eagle. (M HKA)

Piero Manzoni (1933–1963, Italy) is a precocious painter
and writer of manifestos, notably *Per una pittura organica*
("Towards Organic Painting") in 1957. Inspired by Klein and
Fontana, Manzoni produces his first *achrome* (colourless
painting) in 1957, underlining the purity of the material. Yet
from around 1960, when he exhibits with the Zero Group, his
work addresses the material mostly through the intellectual.
Manzoni produces certificates of authenticity declaring a person an authentic artwork, the artist"s breath caught in a bal-
loon and his most legendary work, *Merda d"artista* ("Artist's
Shit"): small metal cans containing 30 grams of his own ex-
crement. (M HKA)

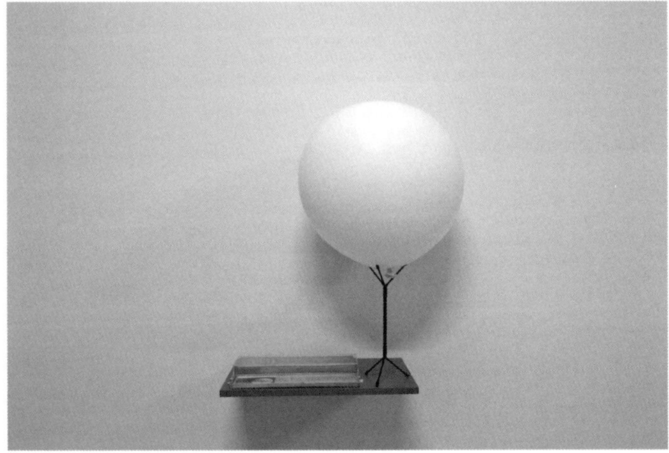

Piero Manzoni, *Body of Air*, 1959-1960, photo by M HKA

François Morellet (1926, France, lives in Paris) has chosen to follow a formal "objective grammar" for his paintings,
installations, and architectural interventions, basing them on
principles and systems established in advance of the execution rather than on a moment of subjective creativity. Morellet
joins the French *Groupe de recherche d'art visuel* ("Visual
Art Research Group") in 1960. His systemic approach, based
on optical effect, yields visually attractive and challenging

artworks. Viewers are intended to generate interpretations of their own, and Morellet is aware that he cannot always control them. Many of his works are designed for public spaces. (Van Abbemuseum)

The OHO Movement (1965–1968) and the OHO Group (1969–1971) are important for the development of neo-avant-garde art in Slovenia. OHO involves artists with different ideas and interests. Critique of consumerist society paves the way for research about "the thing" as distinguished from "the (consumer) object". The movement morphes into a group, whose initial members (Naško Križnar, Milenko Matanović, Marko Pogačnik, Andraž Šalamun) practise land art, body art, process art and conceptual art. Towards the end OHO is characterised as "transcendental conceptualism", striving to make the artwork "a medium for the detection of transcendental, esoteric and other spiritual content". (Van Abbemuseum)

Henk Peeters (1925, the Netherlands, lives in Hall) abandons a figurative, socially-engaged style of painting for an informal, material-based approach in the late 1950s, while remaining firmly anti-capitalist. In 1958 he is one of the founders of the Informal Group in the Netherlands, which maintains contacts with Piero Manzoni, Yves Klein and Lucio Fontana. In 1961 it transforms itself into the group *Nul*, connected to the German Group Zero and the French *Groupe de Recherche d'Art Visuel*. Thanks to these European connections Peeters is invited to participate in the second of the international *Nove tendencije* exhibitions in Zagreb in 1963. (Van Abbemuseum)

Tomaž Šalamun (1941, Slovenia, lives in Ljubljana) is considered the leading contemporary poet in Slovene, and he has been translated into many languages. He initiates the publishing of the first OHO book, EVA (1966), an anthology of concrete, experimental and visual poetry. Trained as an art historian, Šalamun works with OHO as a visual artist in 1968–1970, creating installations with natural materials. *Hay, Cornhusks, Bricks* (1969), now recreated for the Van Abbemuseum, is first created for the exhibition *Great-Grandfathers* in Zagreb. In 1970 Šalamun participates in the legendary *Information* exhibition at MoMA, as a member of OHO. (Van Abbemuseum)

Jan Schoonhoven (1914–1994, the Netherlands) starts as a draughtsman, inspired by Paul Klee's poetic expressionism.

From the mid-1950s he embarks on the project that will become associated with his name: the monochrome reliefs.
These are geometric figurations of non-hierarchical construction, usually colourless to focus all attention on the tones of
light falling on the white angular grids. The rectilinear order
is sometimes disturbed by Schoonhoven's own handwriting.
Striving for an impersonal and "objective" art, he becomes a
member of the Informal Group and a founder, with Armando,
Jan Hendrikse and Henk Peeters, of the group *Nul* in 1960. (M
HKA/Van Abbemuseum)

Paul Van Hoeydonck (1925, Belgium, lives in Antwerp)
co-founded the G58 group in Antwerp, which organises
a series of exhibitions at the Hessenhuis around 1960. A
frequent collaborator of the legendary French critic Pierre
Restany, he is always drawn to the utopian and the cosmic.
Van Hoeydonck is known for being the only artist whose work
is exhibited on the moon. One copy of his aluminium figure
Fallen Astronaut (1971) is surreptitiously placed there by the
Apollo 15 crew in 1971, commemorating the eight astronauts
and six cosmonauts who died in the Space Race between the
US and the USSR. (M HKA)

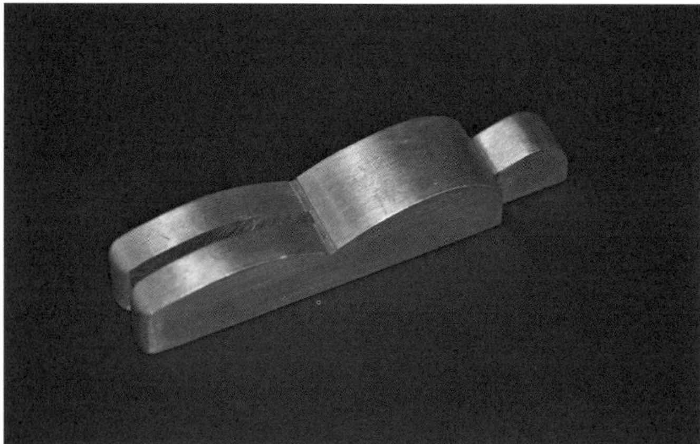

Paul Van Hoydonck, *Fallen Astronaut*, 1971, Collection M HKA, Antwerp

Victor Vasarely (1908–1997, Hungary/France) moves to
Paris in 1930 to work as a graphic designer and begins painting abstract geometric works after the war, at first inspired by
textures in nature. He is considered the founding father of Op
Art, a movement in art based on optically constructed patterns
and illusions and the sometimes disruptive effect they have on

our senses. In the 1950s his work is black-and-white; the gradual incorporation of colour takes place in the 1960s. Vasarely's geometrically based work helped formulates an "international grammar" for perceiving the Concrete. He executes many public art projects in various countries. (M HKA)

The Essential

The works selected for this category are clear and strong, both in their idea and their form. They are "essential" because they refuse to compromise their self-evidence, their presence as man-made objects in built space. They are sure of their value. "This is it; this is Art", seems to be their statement. The power of this statement is linked to the context where they were made, the US of the 1960s. The global dominance of the movements to which these works belong—Minimal Art, Conceptual Art—reflects the power of the Western world's dominant nation.

Carl Andre (1935, US, lives in New York) is an iconic representative of Minimal Art, a sculptor working with natural and industrially produced materials (timber, metal plates, bricks, hay bales). He showcases them "as they are", unadulterated and "merely" arranged in strict visual formations on the floor. Andre makes us experience the properties of matter, form, structure and place. A direct sensation of presence is the core value of his art. He says: "My sculptures are the result of physical operations in the material world." Andre has exhibited in Europe, not least in Belgium and the Netherlands, since the mid-1960s. (M HKA)

John Baldessari (1931, US, lives in Los Angeles) seeks to reconcile his city's surf-and-sex aesthetic with New York conceptualism. Joseph Kossuth famously dismisses his work as "'conceptual'" cartoons of actual conceptual art", and he answers with the now-classic video *John Baldessari Sings Sol LeWitt*. Baldessari typically tries out ideas in various permutations and makes them reappear at various stages in his œuvre. He has invested much energy into visualising the somehow self-evident but still inexplicable, almost mysterious mechanisms behind the Duchampian notion of "choosing": "I love the idea of doing just gratuitous things, in a world of things for use." (M HKA)

Dan Flavin (1933–1996, US) is a fundamental figure of
Minimal Art, famous for constellations of standard-issue neon
lamps, usually *Untitled* (but dedicated in brackets to artists,
critics or friends). Opulent and deliberately transitory, his light
pieces are now expensive commodities whose owners struggle
to prolong the lifespan of obsolete strips or bulbs. Flavin said:
"These "monuments" only survive as long as the light system
is useful, 2100 hours." The exhibited corner piece subtly sub-
verts our understanding of light, space and how they affect
each other, making a "new space" emerge and emphasising
how a predictable method can yield unpredictable results.
(M HKA)

Donald Judd (1928–1994, US) studies painting and philosophy and makes a great impact on post-war art as a sculptor,
printmaker and critic as a front figure and chief ideologue of
Minimal Art. In his essay *Specific Objects* from 1965 Judd describes the art of the 1960s as neither sculpture nor painting.
His later works, industrially manufactured box structures of
wood or metal, demonstrate the same tension between the two
art forms. He famously denies that his own work is composed
and analysable, claiming that it came to him "full-blown in the
middle of the night". A very essentialist position! (M HKA)

Robert Morris (1931, US, lives in New York) starts as a
painter with a strong interest in dance and improvisational
theatre. The performative and the participatory have remained
of essence in his mature work from the 1960s onwards,
which largely happens in the sphere of sculpture. Like many
of his peers and contemporaries, he takes inspiration from
Duchamp. Appearance and meaning, form and action are
pitched against each other in Morris's oeuvre, comprising
minimalist large-scale structures (often outdoor pieces), conceptual undertakings such as *Box with the Sound of Its Own
Making* and staged encounters between human performers and
sculptural objects. (M HKA)

Frank Stella (1936, US, lives in New York) studies painting and art history. The paintings from the seven years after
his graduation in 1958 have become canonical. They consist of
patterns of regular lines marked with unsteady penmanship,
at first restricted to white on black square canvases but gradually becoming more colourful and exploring other geometrical
forms. From the 1970s Stella makes reliefs in dynamic and

unpredictable combinations of colours, figures and textures. The later work is heterogeneous and overtly subjective, something Stella opposed in his early career and also made from more durable materials like metal and carbon fibres. (M HKA)

Lawrence Weiner (1942, US, lives in New York) is a very Transatlantic artist, who has lived in Amsterdam and worked all over Europe. He exhibited at M HKA last spring (with Liam Gillick). Unlike the visual poets, who start with language, Weiner bases his "tectonic" text pieces on sculpture and painting, as his most-quoted piece indicates. "1. THE ARTIST MAY CONSTRUCT THE PIECE; 2. THE PIECE MAY BE FABRICATED; 3. THE PIECE NEED NOT BE BUILT." Weiner's words are of the world, as concrete as things. Perhaps his greatest contribution to the Essential is to make the flesh become word. (M HKA)

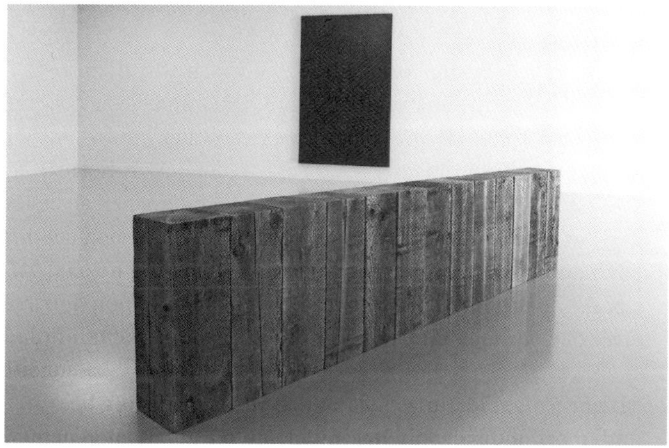

The Essential,
photo M HKA.I

The Transcendental

Crossovers between various levels of reality—dream, vision, utopia—fascinated many artists during the 1960s and "70s. Their work reveals an uneasiness with the self-assured and universalist position of what we choose to call "the Essential". Instead the artists of the Transcendental—many of whom belonged to the *arte povera* ("poor art") movement in Italy— created works open to interpretation and doubt and critique. These artists address issues that are relevant to humanity as a whole, but they often did so through individual, subjective,

even idiosyncratic gestures. Their ideological identification
was anti-authoritarian and deliberately open-ended.

Alighiero e Boetti (1940–1994, Italy) begins as a painter
and sculptor. His art gradually evolves to encompass the
fundamental concerns of human life, such as time and space,
sameness (identity) and otherness (alterity). Inserting the e
(Italian for "and") between his first name and his surname, he
suddenly becomes two individuals in one. Under this redou-
bled identity Alighiero e Boetti creates his most iconic work,
the map of all the world's countries and flags embroidered by
Afghan women in Kabul and Peshawar. The many versions
(1971–1994) reflect the changes caused by "artillery attacks,
air raids, and diplomatic negotiations". (M HKA)

Marinus Boezem (1934, the Netherlands, lives in
Middelburg) exhibits a stretch of polder as a ready-made in
1960. This is not untypical of his monumental-but-modest
œuvre, largely based on gesture and addressing the spiritual
through playful interventions in nature. In 1969 he "signs"
the sky with the exhaust fumes of an aircraft and appropriated "the weather" by exhibiting meteorological maps from
a newspaper. A recurrent theme in Boezem's work is the
Cathedral of Rheims, recreated in various materials (trees,
stone slabs, wine glasses). For his *Green Cathedral* at Almere
he plants 174 Italian poplars to form a gradually growing
cathedral.
(M HKA)

Marcel Broodthaers (1924–1976, Belgium) produces and
composes his work—objects, images, texts and installations—
to challenge the power of language over thinking. "Since 1967,
I have been using photosensitive fabric, film and slides to determine the relationship between the object and its image, as
well as the one that exists between the symbol and the meaning of an object; the written document." In 1968 Broodthaers
opens a museum in his Brussels home. *Musée d'Art Moderne,
Département des Aigles, section XIXe siècle* is an ironic and
subversive mirroring of the museum format, undermining the
mental and institutional organisation of meaning. (M HKA)

James Lee Byars (1932–1997, US) roams the world.
Long stays in Europe, Asia and Africa profoundly influence
his art, which becomes an idiosyncratic fusion of baroque
and Zen, the theatrical and the meditative. He elaborates

the non- doctrine TH FI TO IN PH (THe FIrst TOtally
INterrogative PHilosophy) in numerous works, such as the
installation in the Van Abbemuseum collection. Like some
colleagues (notably Carl Andre, Lawrence Weiner and Gordon
Matta-Clark) Byars has strong and sustained connections with
Belgium and the Netherlands. *Extraterrestrial*, a giant figurative textile piece in the M HKA collection, is made for a performance in Antwerp. (M HKA)

Jef Cornelis (1941, Belgium, lives in Antwerp) worked for
BRT, Belgian Radio and Television, from 1963 until 1998. He
first made documentaries about architecture and urban planning, but from the late 1960s he produces many programmes
about contemporary art, offering artists direct access to the
television medium. His critical documentaries of large-scale
exhibitions such as Harald Szeemann"s Documenta V (1972)
are both invaluable documentation and subjectively authored
statements. Cornelis also co-founds the A379089 art space in
Antwerp, co-ordinated by German curator Kaspar König in
1969–1970, where James Lee Byars, Marcel Broodthaers and
other internationally renowned artists stage significant projects. (M HKA)

Herman de Vries (1931, the Netherlands, lives in
Germany) studies horticulture before becoming an artist in the
early 1950s, starting with collages of found objects and gradually becoming more informal and abstract. In the 1960s he is
a co-publisher, with Armando and Henk Peeters, of the Dutch

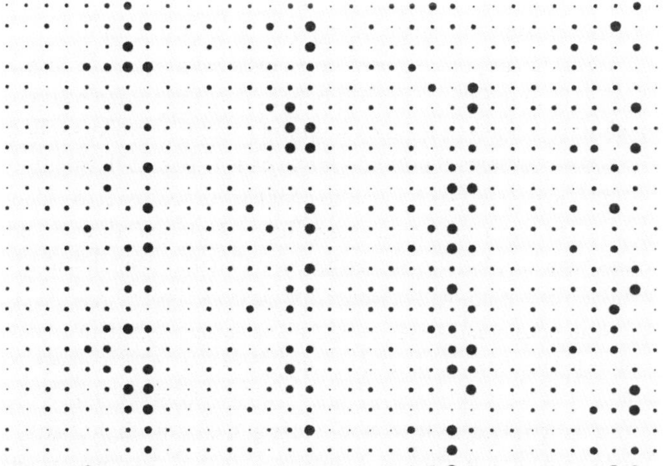

Herman de Vries, *V71-
63*, 1971, Collection Van
Abbemuseum, Eindhoven

journal *nul = 0*. He also produces paintings and drawings
with dots or stripes, some of them shown here. Later de Vries
reintegrates gardening in his art. His walled gardens from the
1990s are at the same time physical installations—with real
vegetation such as lavender or hops—and highly concentrated
poetic images. (M HKA)

Luciano Fabro (1936–2007, Italy) is a sculptor who "reasons with his senses" and one of the artists who defines *arte
povera* ("poor art") in Italy in the 1960s and 1970s. He uses
materials and figures grounded in long tradition, but in new and
stripped-down ways that enable him to create constellations
full of poetic meaning. At Sonsbeek in 1986 he installs a large
block of Carrara marble in a steel net. Such monumental gestures pointing at nature's bare essentials can also be found in
Fabro's more modestly scaled work, for instance his *Arcobaleno*
("Rainbow") made from multi-coloured cotton wads. (M HKA)

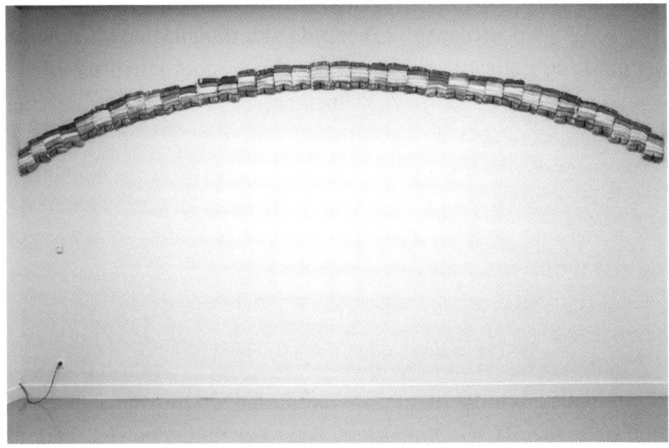

The Transcendental,
Luciano Fabro, *Arcobaleno*
[Rainbow], 1980,
photo M HKA

René Heyvaert (1929–1984, Belgium) trains as an architect
and practises architecture in Ghent and the US before becoming an independent artist in the late 1960s. His long-ignored
work is restrained and austere, but also subversive and un-
settling. It can be described as a fundamental formalism, or
even a formal fundamentalism. Contrary to first appearances,
Heyvaert's image–objects (drawings, small sculptures, everyday objects) are anything but a down- to-earth and unassum-
ing *Kleinkunst*. They respond to a very concrete and personal
need for meditation and almost seek to dictate the viewer's

response, as if they were theorems leaving no room for scepticism. (M HKA)

Guy Mees (1935–2003, Belgium) leaves behind a small but dense œuvre. His work is investigative, formally innovative and relentlessly precise. Mees has what musicians call *touch*—the ability to make tangible what usually remains unnoticed or hidden. *Lost Space* is a body of work from the 1960s, for which he uses machine-made lace and fluorescent bluish neon light. One of these pieces is shown here. Mees later explores pastels, coloured paper and low-key but intense painterly interventions in built space. He produces videos and photographs, in which he also works with variations on themes, as in musical composition. (M HKA)

Mario Merz (1925–2003, Italy) is a central figure in the *arte povera* movement of the 1960s. In the beginning of this decade Merz takes up sculpture, notably producing the characteristic "igloos". These images of a nomadic, boundary-less condition are composed of everyday materials: clay, stone, glass, jute, asphalt, branches from trees, metal, wax. They often carry neon inscriptions, such as this quote from the North Vietnamese general Vô Ngyên Giàp: "If the enemy concentrates he loses ground, if he scatters he loses strength." Yet Merz also continues as a painter, as we can see in this untitled work from 1984. (M HKA)

Michelangelo Pistoletto (1933, Italy, lives in Biella and Turin) has been associated with *arte povera*, defining a new kind of monumentality with his 1960s sculptures juxtaposing rags and other "worthless" materials with the forms of classical antiquity. From 1962 he has used mirrors and metals such as gold, silver or copper as reflective backgrounds for "cut-out" life-sized photographic human figures. These super-impositions fuse the present and the past into a single image, challenging the very idea of representation. In recent years the mirrors have often been shown without the added layer of figuration, and sometimes they have been deliberately smashed. (M HKA)

The Subverted

These different "spirits of internationalism" are rarely encountered in pure form. In the art of the 1960s and "70s there was constant traffic between lofty, utopian ambitions (for instance in Concretism, Minimalism and Conceptualism) and a fascination—or even obsession—with political, social and economic reality "such as it was" (a driving force behind Pop Art and politically-engaged art). Both these approaches, the inward-looking and the outward-looking, were used by artists to create distinctly personal, idiosyncratic agendas, which are almost by definition impure, subverted versions of the more dogmatic beliefs that fuel "movements" in art.

Anselm Kiefer (1945, Germany, lives in Paris) is a student of Joseph Beuys who becomes a painter and sculptor and occasionally makes large-scale installations. His work is characterised by broad and dark evocations of an unspecified mythologised past, with images of scenery referring to the Bible, the Third Reich or imaginary Germanic antiquity. *Märkische Heide* (1974) belongs to a series of images that entrust German nature with mystical powers with the help of unorthodox and expressive painting techniques. Kiefer's Wagnerian ambition comes to the surface in 2009, when he produces and designs an opera entitled *Am Anfang* ("In the Beginning"). (M HKA)

Bruce Nauman (1941, US, lives in New Mexico) studies mathematics and physics before becoming an artist. From the mid-1960s he has experimented with sculpture, performance and video. Building on Duchamp's ideas, he works from the conviction that everything happening in the studio can be art. This leads to a series of short films and videos based on repetitive gestures. In later works the scope broadens, but Nauman continues to explore and exploit the myths surrounding artistic creation. One example is an early neon work with spiralling text that states: "The true artist helps the world by revealing mystic truths." (M HKA)

Sigmar Polke (1941–2010, Germany) befriends Gerhard Richter in Düsseldorf in the early 1960s. Together with Konrad Lueg they coin the term "Capitalist Realism". Polke critiques consumerist society by incorporating images from popular culture in his paintings, drawings and prints and then superimposing a pattern of white, black or colourful dots. This device also problematizes the artist's "authentic" stance as an engaged, critical observer. In the series of paintings entitled *Höhere Wesen befehlen...* ("Higher Entities Command...") he redefines artistic creativity again, but in a more anecdotic and sceptical way, subtly ridiculing the artist's alleged connections with the powers that be. (M HKA)

Gerhard Richter (1932, Germany, lives in Cologne) is educated in East Germany as a mural painter in the style of Socialist Realism. He leaves in 1961 and co-organises actions in Düsseldorf under the provocative title "Capitalist Realism". Influenced by the banality of Pop Art, Richter bases his paintings on photographs, blurring the still wet image to create out-of-focus effects. Later he will make photo-realist and abstract paintings in parallel. This has continued until today. The content of the work may be political, as in his famous series on the German RAF terrorists, but it always also contains other, existential, dimensions. (M HKA)

Edward Ruscha (1937, US, lives in Los Angeles) is one of the leading painters of our times. He has a Catholic upbringing in Oklahoma and moves to California in the late 1950s. In his images, suspended between different modes of representation, the literal appears to dominate over the metaphoric, but you can never be sure. Ruscha's painted words, sometimes executed in the very substance signified by the word, have been interpreted as instances of trans-substantiation—the word become flesh. He is a quintessential West Coast artist, although he was "never really into television... but the print media, photography and books". (M HKA)

Andy Warhol (1928–1987, US) is probably the most famous 20th century artist. For him fame itself is an art form. Starting as a commercial illustrator, Warhol conquers the art world with consciously banal imagery, soon identified as Pop

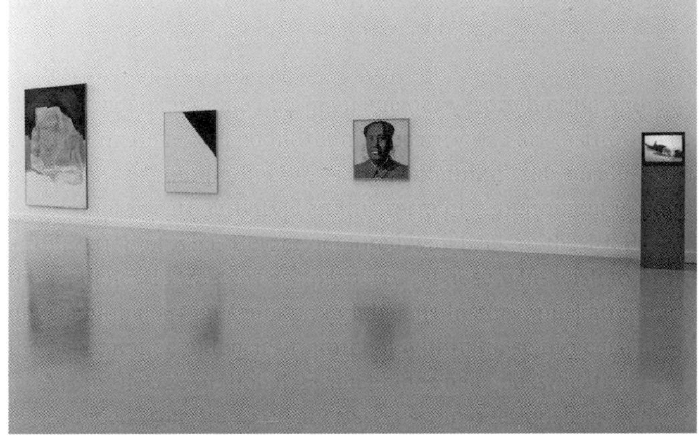

The Subverted,
photo M HKA

Art. Warhol is the antithesis of the Abstract Expressionists
who dominated the 1950s. Playing with serial production
and renaming his studio "the Factory," his art encapsulates
post-war consumerism. In his words: "If you want to know all
about Andy Warhol, just look at the surface of my paintings,
my films and me, and there I am. There is nothing behind it."
(M HKA)

The (Dis)located

Physical and mental space is almost always an active concern
for artists. Place and location, closeness and distance, belonging and alienation—these are realities that individuals are
still often unable to overcome, but during the Cold War period
artists experienced them more directly and physically than
in today's "globalized," inter-connected, networked world.
Distances, and the cost of overcoming them, were greater. The
(dis)located artists show a strong awareness of their located-
ness and let their direct surrounding become a central element
in their work, which they then used often to address more
general and universal issues.

Stanley Brouwn (1935, Suriname, lives in Amsterdam)
moves to the Netherlands in 1957. A representative earlier
work is the now famous this way Brouwn, a series of "drawings" made by passers-by asked for directions. Brouwn dedi-
cates himself to intense explorations of measurement. The
movement from a to b and the distance between them is of
central importance in his art, which makes tangible the tension between abstract measures (the metric scale) and embodied measures such as the "step". Size is essential to the work,
and photographic reproductions are not allowed. Brouwn is
exemplary in following his ideas logically and rigorously.
(M HKA)

André Cadere (1934–1978, Romania/France) is a strategically peripheral, and therefore influential, presence in the
Paris art scene of the 1970s. He "parasitically" installs his
round, painted wooden sticks in the exhibitions of other artists
and is a recognisable silhouette at gallery openings, carrying
a *barre de bois ronde* over his shoulder. These sticks consist
of painted individual units whose length equals their diameter.
The individual segments are arranged in a systematic logical

order in the eight colours of the light spectrum, black and
white. Cadere describes his works as "endless paintings" allowing him to comment on exclusion and inclusion. (M HKA)

Jef Geys (1934, Belgium, lives in Balen) is both intransi-
gent and enigmatic, but for more than 50 years he has consistently been putting his own (and Marcel Duchamp's) ideas
about art into practice in Kempen, the district where he used
to work as an art teacher. Following a correspondence course
in drawing, "to be able to impress my pupils with tricks of
perspective and illusion," Geys produces the series *ABC
Ecole de Paris* (1959–1961). Categories of form and modes
of production are as important to him as political content.
Observation and commentary are as important as instructions
for action. (Van Abbemuseum)

On Kawara (1933, Japan, lives in New York) has made
the registration of passing time his primary artistic form. His
series of *Date Paintings* started on 4 January 1966, making
one painting a day with the date in white lettering on black
background and storing them in boxes lined with newsprint.
There are more than 2000 such paintings. Kawara's three other series (*I Went, I Met, I Read*) follow a similar logic, while
other works have a more monumental form. *One Million Years
(Past)* (1969) is a book in several volumes that may also be
read aloud in public. (M HKA)

Július Koller (1939–2007, Slovakia) is focused on social
urban space and how individuals position themselves in it and
act together. *U.F.O.-naut J.K.* is a long series of photographic
documentations showing Koller in and around his house
with various domestic equipment or sports gear. U.F.O. may
be deciphered differently for different projects: as Universal
Futurological Orientation, for instance, or Universal–Cultural
Fantastic Ornament. In the manifesto *Anti- Happening
(System of Subjective Objectivity)* Koller describes his aesthetic interventions in everyday life as a cultural reshaping of
the subject. His works can be interpreted as anti-monuments
to movement and the freedom of speech. (Van Abbemuseum)

Zofia Kulik (1947, Poland, lives in Warsaw) and
Przemysław Kwiek (1945, Poland, lives in Warsaw) works to-
gether 1971–1987. Their politically-engaged collaboration as
KwieKulik is now considered an important chapter in post- war
Polish art history. It encompasses various public activities:

performances, outdoor actions, slide shows for children, students or other specially targeted audiences. KwieKulik experiment with film and photography, of which the series *Activities with Dobromierz* (1972–1974) is the prime example. Their little son is the central figure in these often surprising pictures taken in and outside their home and reflecting the realities of family life in Socialist Poland. (Van Abbemuseum)

Mladen Stilinović (1947, Yugoslavia, lives in Zagreb) questions the deep structures of society that determine the role of the artist as an agent (and captive) of language. He famously said: "An artist who doesn't speak English is not an artist." In collages and photographs based on the colours of the Croatian flag he challenges the authority of national symbols. His "taxonomical" installations use seemingly innocuous objects and paintings to critique socialist and neo-liberal ideology and expose the unequal and unstable relation between the individual and society. By juxtaposing dislocated signs Stilinović ironically visualises the constants of human powerlessness and suffering. (Van Abbemuseum)

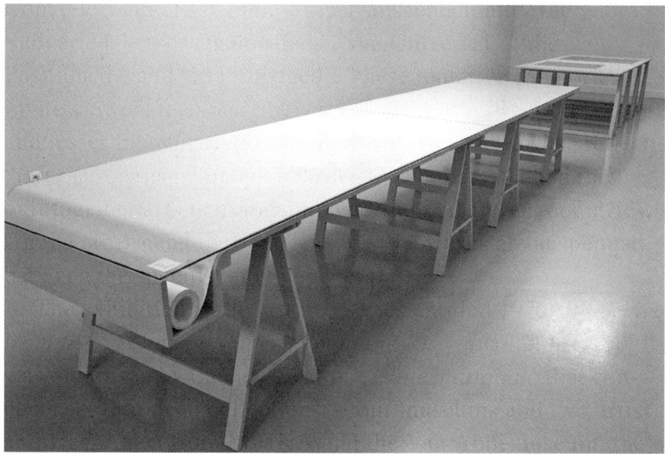

The (Dis)located, Stanley Brouwn, *This way Brouwn*, 1964, photo M HKA

The Universal

Who has the right to assume the position of speaking for all, of voicing universal concerns? In politics the Universal always seems to be in danger of degenerating into imperialism. Yet this does not prevent artists from productively using their

longing for universality, for solutions to problems that apply
equally to all, in all parts of the world. This tendency was
stronger during the Cold War period, when it also represented
a utopian wish to unite the First, Second and Third Worlds
(capitalist, communist and developing countries) of the unequal and violently imposed postwar order.

Luc Deleu (1944, Belgium, lives in Antwerp) works at the
intersection of art, architecture, urban thinking and politics.
A hybrid activism underpins his work, from the conversion
of the artist Panamarenko's townhouse in Antwerp in 1986
to the triumphal arches made from shipping containers in the
1990s. Deleu's outlandish "proposals" from the 1970s address
important societal needs: the environment (planting fruit trees
and growing vegetables in the cities), the social contract (introducing plastic money, completely de-regulating traffic and
television) or public memory (recycling monuments as social
housing, making Belgium a fully agrarian country). Four of
those proposals are presented here. (Van Abbemuseum)

Fina Miralles (1950, Spain, lives in Cadaqués) has created
performances, installations, videos, paintings, and photographs
focusing on landscapes and human dimensions of space. In the
video *Petjades* ("Footprints", 1976) she measures the city by
making footprints on the street. Her visualising of the body's
relationship to urban space becomes an act of socio-political
reflection. *Mar de Hierba* ("Sea of Grass", 1973) also exem-
plifies this subjective approach to land and politics. Miralles
creates an island and pulls it offshore as her personal territory.
A suitcase carries photographs of the island and the process of
shaping it from soil and dried grass. (Van Abbemuseum)

Pere Noguera (1941, Spain, lives in La Bisbal d'Empordà)
has worked with sculpture, installation and performance since
the 1970s, often incorporating the material that defines his
hometown. Raw or fired, clay becomes a "universal" symbol
of the earth. Noguera, whose work has often been associated
with *arte povera*, uses it in combination with other materials, everyday objects and geographical representations. *Mapa
d'Espanya* ("Map of Spain", 1979) and *Mapa d'Europa* ("Map
of Europe", 1979) inverse our understanding of the soil as
something that lies under political boundaries and divisions.
The drying dirt is crackling, indicating as yet unexplained
rifts between regions. (Van Abbemuseum)

Panamarenko (1940, Belgium, lives in West Flanders), the artist name of Henri Van Herwegen, is an abbreviation of PAN AMerican AiRlines and COmpany. Panamarenko's artistic universe is rooted in Cold War obsessions. He emerges in the mid-1960s as a builder of aircraft that don't fly and other utopian machines. Panamarenko shows the impossibility of separating art from non- art—or from society. The inside-outside divide ceases to exist in his art. The perfect demonstration of this is his townhouse in Antwerp, which he donated with all its contents to M HKA after retiring as an artist at the age of 65. (Van Abbemuseum)

The Positioned

Performance art was one of the new forces emerging in both the West, the East and the Third World (i.e. both in New York and elsewhere) during the period covered by the exhibition. The transition from the practice of "performance" to the more generalised and politicised notion of "performativity" began before the end of the Cold War. Female artists often led the way. They contradicted or made visible existing positions on how to communicate and present oneself. They are positioned in that they pose something explicitly and through this very act disrupt what is positioned.

Alain Arias-Misson (1936, Belgium, lives in Brussels, Paris, Venice and Panama City) is influenced by the happenings of the early 1960s when he returns to Brussels from the US in 1968. He is seen as the inventor of the public poem, an extension of visual poetry but distinct from the happening in that it is performed outside of any artistic or aesthetic context: in the streets or on the beach. Arias-Misson's public poems are both subversive and liberating, both provocative and playful. *The G D Public Poem* (1968), performed in central Brussels, substitutes the author for a possible letter O. (Van Abbemuseum)

Stuart Brisley (1933, England, lives in London and Istanbul) is very consciously invested in a direct and democratic relationship with his audience. Best known as a performance artist and community activist, he has also worked with painting, sculpture, installation, photography, film and other media to bring the marginalised, the useless and the excremental to the fore. In his performances from the late 1960s and onwards Brisley accentuates the perversity of consumerist society by letting things go to waste, decay or be meaninglessly repeated, degraded and debased in other ways. The film *Being and Doing* is produced together with Ken McMullen. (Van Abbemuseum)

Lili Dujourie (1941, Belgium, lives in Lovendegem) is an uncompromising, versatile artist who has been producing objects and images in various materials since the late 1960s. As a sculptor she has worked in steel, lead, marble, ceramics, velvet and *papier-mâché*, while her understanding of painting is best expressed in the black-and-white video works from 1972–1981, which she describes as grisailles of movement. In the earliest videos, *Hommage à... I–V*, she herself is both artist, model and viewer, striking nude poses from art history while following the action in real time on an (invisible) monitor behind the unmade bed. (Van Abbemuseum)

Esther Ferrer (1937, Spain, lives in Paris) is a leading artist of her generation in Spain, whose conceptual performance practice dates back to the Franco years. She is a member of the experimental music and performance group Grupo Zaj from 1967 until its dissolution in 1996. Ferrer creates performances and installations focusing on the human body—her own body—and almost always including a "measuring device" such as a chair. In *Íntimo y personal* ("Intimate and Personal", 1977), a work restaged many times, she covers her naked body with letters that spell out the title, reinforcing the exposure through language. (Van Abbemuseum)

Tomislav Gotovac (1937–2010, Yugoslavia/Croatia) emerges with Heads (1960), a series of close-up photographic self-portraits. He continues to produce photographs of himself performing activities that parody or problematize the desires of consumerist society or the manifestations of identity in mass culture, such as the series *Showing the Elle Magazine* (1962). Gotovac also produces collages, installations and experimental films, and he is famous for introducing performance art and happenings in Yugoslavia. In *Zagreb I Love You* (1981) he runs naked through the Croatian capital and kisses the ground—perhaps the ultimate embodiment of the irrepressible quest for artistic freedom that marked his career. (Van Abbemuseum)

Tibor Hajas (1946–1980, Hungary) explores the limits
of the body, life and death in performances often carried out
without an audience, for the camera. He will hang upside
down, blindfolded or in ropes, submitting himself to beating,
whipping or the insertion of syringes. Titles such as *Flesh
Painting, Coma, Dark Flash* and *Extinction* indicate the near-
death darkness he seeks to create. Hajas also produces objects,
films and theoretical texts. For *Self Fashion Show* (1976), he
films passers-by on a square in Budapest and adds a voice-
over that manipulates the perception of these people. Hajas
dies in a car accident. (Van Abbemuseum)

The Engaged

To some extent this is code for "politically or socially engaged
art". Political art does not have to follow a particular programme—it is usually recognisable anyway. Activism in art
sometimes involves physical activity to promote an alternative
view of the world, but also the subversive questioning of prevailing systems without a goal-orientated agenda for political,
social or economic change. As a term, the Engaged attempts
to capture an art that addresses power relations by making visible what is truly invisible—or simply hidden in the surface of
the images that occupy the public sphere.

Victor Burgin (1941, UK, lives in London and Paris)
has critiqued the overt and covert ideology of contemporary
western capitalist society in theoretically motivated works
since the 1960s. Combining texts that could be advertising
copy or extracts from scientific jargon with black and white
documentary-style photographic images, Burgin visualises
how everyday life is dominated by mediatised information
(even before the Internet). The best-known example of this
semiotic approach is the poster put up in Newcastle in 1976,
showing an couple in an intimate situation and stating: "What
does possession mean to you? 7% of our population own 84%
of our wealth." (M HKA)

Paul De Vree (1909–1982, Belgium) is a pioneer of
European concrete poetry and a visual artist. He founds literary journals such as *De Tafel Ronde* in Belgium (1953–1982)
and *Lotta poetica* (1971–1975) in collaboration with the Italian
poet Sarenco. De Vree's work successively covers typographic

compositions, audiovisual events, critique of the mass media and the poetic and political use of photographic images. With his Italian colleagues he elaborates *Poesia visiva*, a movement that activated both "the visual" and "the visionary". De Vree's works from his later period reflect his characteristic entanglement of the political and the erotic. (Van Abbemuseum)

Grup de Treball ("Work Group") is a group of Catalan artists who in 1973–1978 worked collectively as well as individually. Antoni Mercader, Pere Portabella and Carles Santos form the "ideological nucleus" of the variable collective, which sometimes also involves artists such as Francesc Abad, Jordi Benito, Antoni Muntadas and Francesc Torres. Their projects offer a discursive, research-based model for art production and interrogate the role of art and artists in society from a left-wing, anti-authoritarian perspective. In *Attraction Field. Document. Information Work on the Illegal Press of the Catalan Countries* (1975) Grup de Treball address the illegal press in Catalonia. (Van Abbemuseum)

Grupo de artistas de vanguardia is a 1960s avant-garde collective in Argentina. It gathers artists, journalists, and sociologists in Rosario and Buenos Aires who identify a gap between reality and politics and try to bridge it. Among the leading members are Graciela Carnevale, León Ferrari, Roberto Jacoby and Norberto Puzzolo. In their manifest for the action *Tucumán Arde* ("Tucumán Burning", 1968) the group states: "The collective work done is based on the present situation in Argentina, which becomes more radical in one of its poorest provinces, Tucumán, which has been subjected to a long tradition of underdevelopment and economic oppression." (M HKA)

Jenny Holzer (1950, US, lives in New York) visualises language as an instrument of political and psychological manipulation. Her use of language is inspired by commercial advertising and "political technology". Yet instead of enhancing the visibility of products or candidates for election, Holzer voices feminist concerns and addresses other moral or legal issues. Her messages appear in public space: projected onto walls, engraved on benches, printed on T-shirts. *Truisms* (1983) is composed of short statements—"truths" that are both revelatory and banal, designed to run on LED-displays in places like Times Square in New York or Piccadilly Circus in London. (M HKA)

Jörg Immendorff (1945–2007, Germany) studies under Joseph Beuys in Düsseldorf, where the social and political relevance of professional art is under scrutiny. In the late 1960s he stages several performances and political demonstrations based on the meaningless utterance of a baby named "Lidl". His fame, however, is made with paintings such as the *Café Deutschland* series or *Hört auf zu malen* that are both painterly and didactic, articulating self-doubt and critique of the painting medium as well as of Cold War-era politics in West Germany. The *Brechtzyklus* (1976) is a representative work from Immendorff's post-1968 decade. (M HKA)

Robert Indiana (1928, US, lives in Maine) is a painter, sculptor and printmaker, associated with Pop Art because of his attention to the rhetoric of the American dream as expressed, not least, through the road signs leading travellers through to the Open Frontier. Throughout his career Indiana creates assemblages of found objects entitled *Herms*, in reference to the signposts of Roman antiquity but actually commenting on the American Empire. His best-known works, paintings and sculptures of the word love, are good examples of this. The word itself symbolises profound human emotion, but as an image it becomes an empty signifier. (M HKA)

Cildo Meireles (1948, Brazil, lives in Rio de Janeiro) emerges early as artist, with a series of projects in 1969 that investigated the notion of lived physical and social space through the colour and texture of material, a theme that recurs in later three-dimensional works such as *Inmensa* (1982). The increasingly repressive military dictatorship in Brazil also prompts him to create politically engaged works. The "insertion" and "circulation" pieces are well-known: the anti-imperialist text printed onto Coca-Cola Bottles in *Inserçoes em circuitos ideológicos* ("Insertions into Ideological Circuits", 1970) or the *Zero Cent*, *Zero Centavo* and *Zero Dollar* pieces (1974–1984). (M HKA)

Antoni Muntadas (1942, Spain, lives in New York) has devoted his career to conceptualising and visualising the practice of communication, manifested as verbal, textual and audiovisual systems of information and representation. He is particularly interested in the mass media and how they condition our perception and understanding of the world. *Emission–Reception* (1976) consist of two parallel series of slides, juxtaposing images of television sets in bars and cafes with images of attentive audiences. Muntadas offers a visual behavioural analysis of collective spectatorship and how it might be manipulated. A later work contains this unambiguous statement: "Warning: perception requires involvement." (Van Abbemuseum)

Józef Robakowski (1939, Poland, lives in Łódź) is one of the pioneers of Polish independent filmmaking. A co-founder of Zero-61 and other groups in the 1960s experimenting with cinematic visuality, he also films the everyday as an object of behavioural analysis. *From My Window* (1978–1985) is composed of shots of a public square collected over a number of years, whereas *Market* (1970) compresses the moving image into a miniature of lived experience. Robakowski used only two frames every five seconds. "This condensed picture of reality was sufficient for many spectators to get the impression of a complete documentary registration." (Van Abbemuseum)

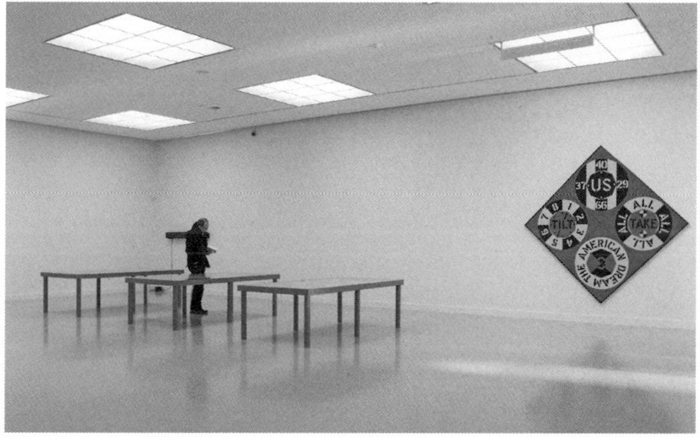

The Engaged,
photo M HKA

Martha Rosler (1943, US, lives in New York) combines conceptual art with social critique and political activism. In her installations, collages, videos, performances and other projects, she addresses many controversial topics: from equal rights for women and other excluded groups in society, social housing and segregation in the city and the shaping of male desire and women's role in the media to the forced participation of consumerist US citizens in the Vietnam or Second Gulf wars. "My main theme is the linking together of "place" and "body" (often woman's body) and its relation with the discourse of power and knowledge." (M HKA)

Nancy Spero (1926–2009, US) is a leading pioneer of feminist art and a member of the group Women Artists" Revolution. From the 1960s her mostly figurative work calls attention to the abuse of authority and supremacy, by the male gender or the western world, and seeks to identify alternatives. She finds inspiration in the writings of Antonin Artaud and his notion of a "theatre of cruelty". Spero creates numerous paintings, drawings and installations that speak to unfolding political events, such as the Vietnam War or the plight of Nicaragua's women, and reclaim feminine experience and thinking for "high art". (M HKA)

Toon Tersas (1924–1995, Belgium) is the artist name of the "self-taught" and "non-professional" Antoon Keersmakers, who supports a large family by working as a clerk for an electricity company and is now described as "grossly underestimated" during his lifetime. M HKA acquires a substantial amount of his works posthumously. Tersas's calligraphic re-drawn newsprint pages from the 1960s and 1970s, often in languages other than Dutch, offer a sharp, sensitive analysis of how the public is manipulated by political power and its frequent use of violence. *Portraits from the Cold War* are a good illustration of his subversive visual method. (Van Abbemuseum)

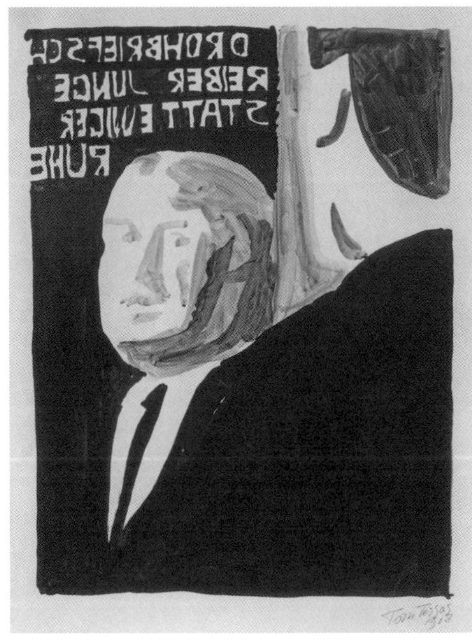

Toon Tersas, *Portrait from the Cold War*, 1968, Collection M HKA, Antwerp

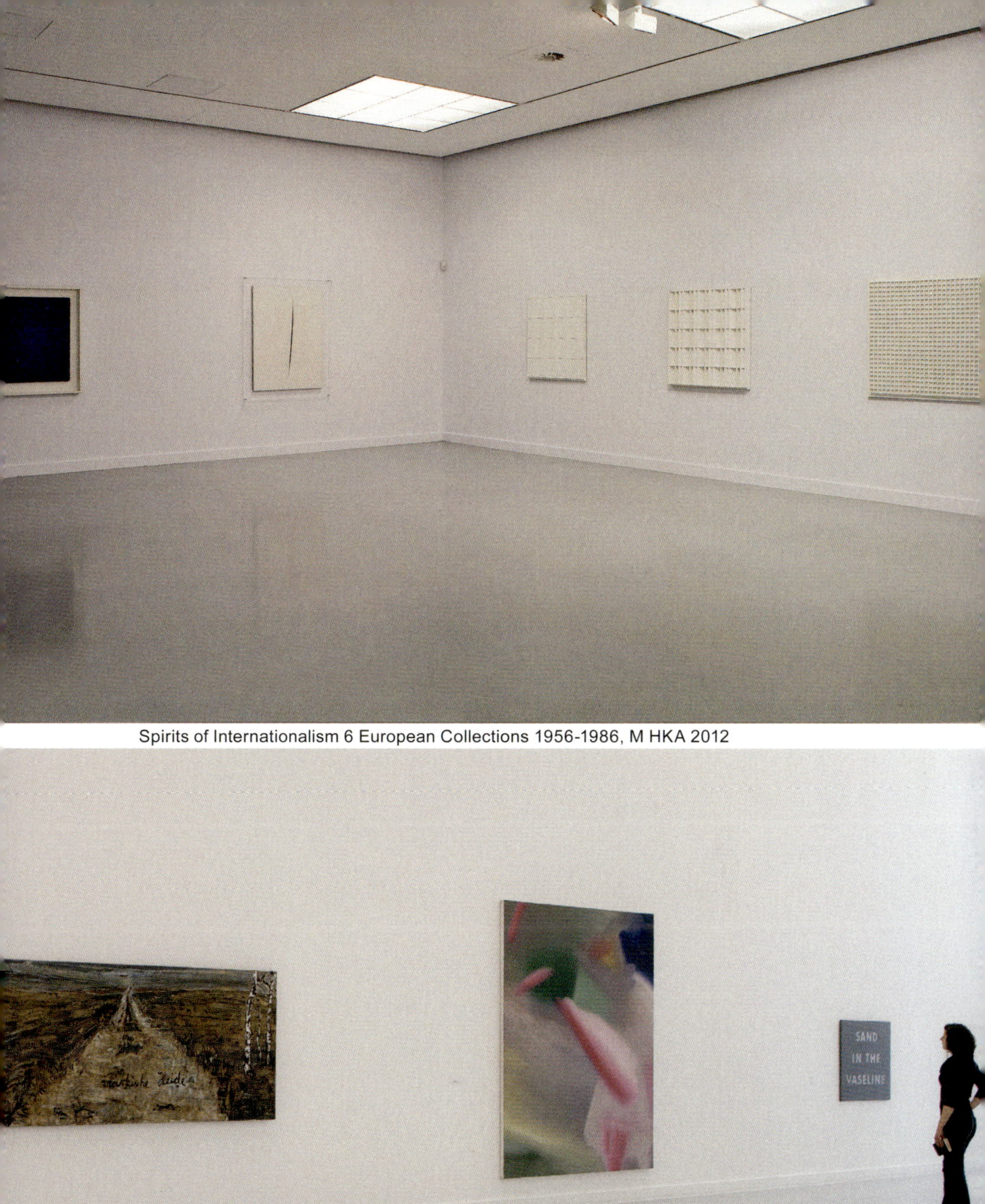

Spirits of Internationalism 6 European Collections 1956-1986, M HKA 2012

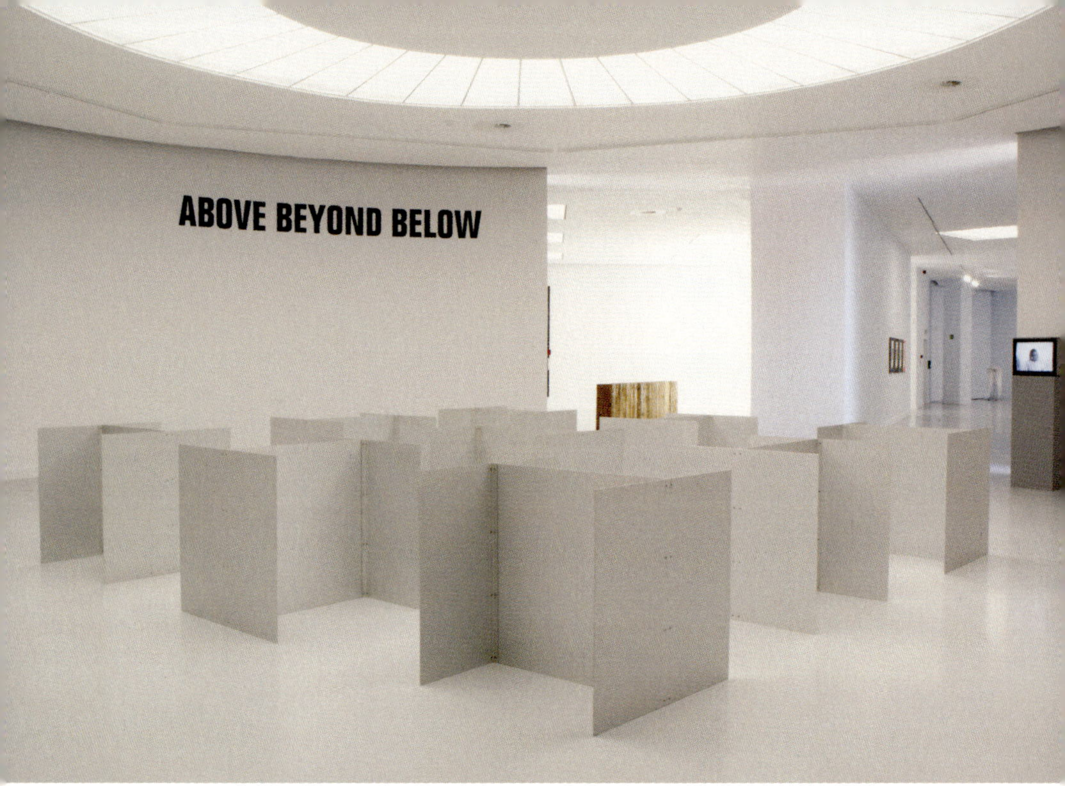

Spirits of Internationalism 6 European Collections 1956-1986, M HKA 2012

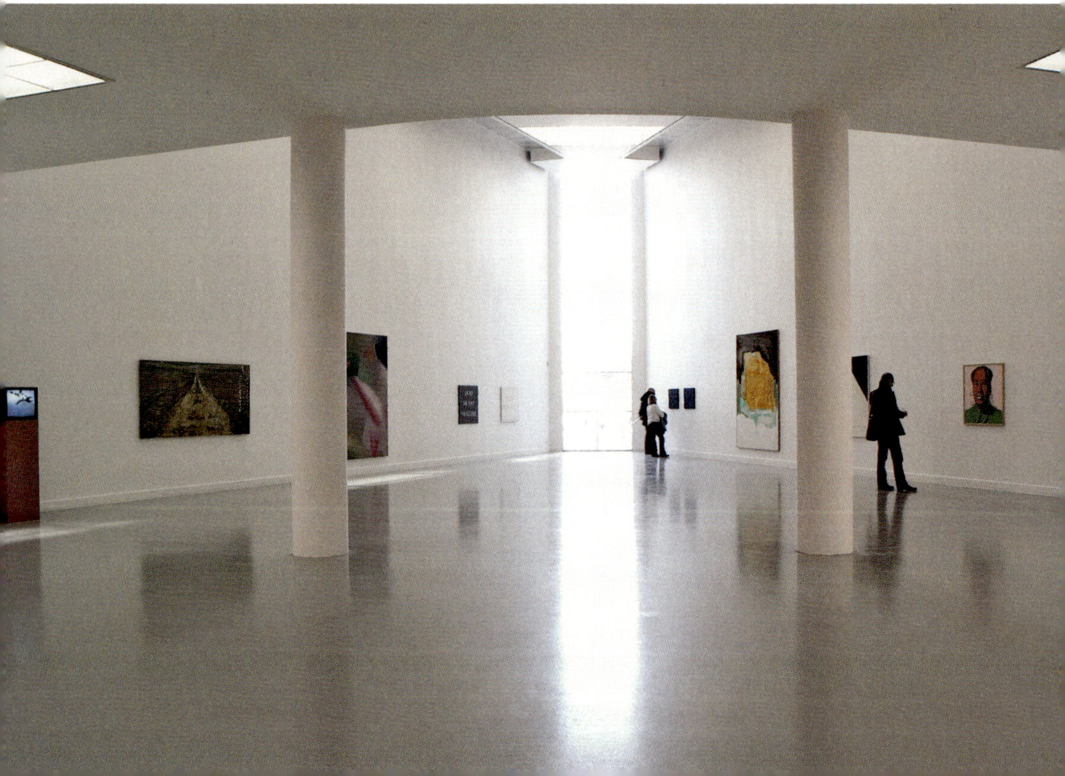

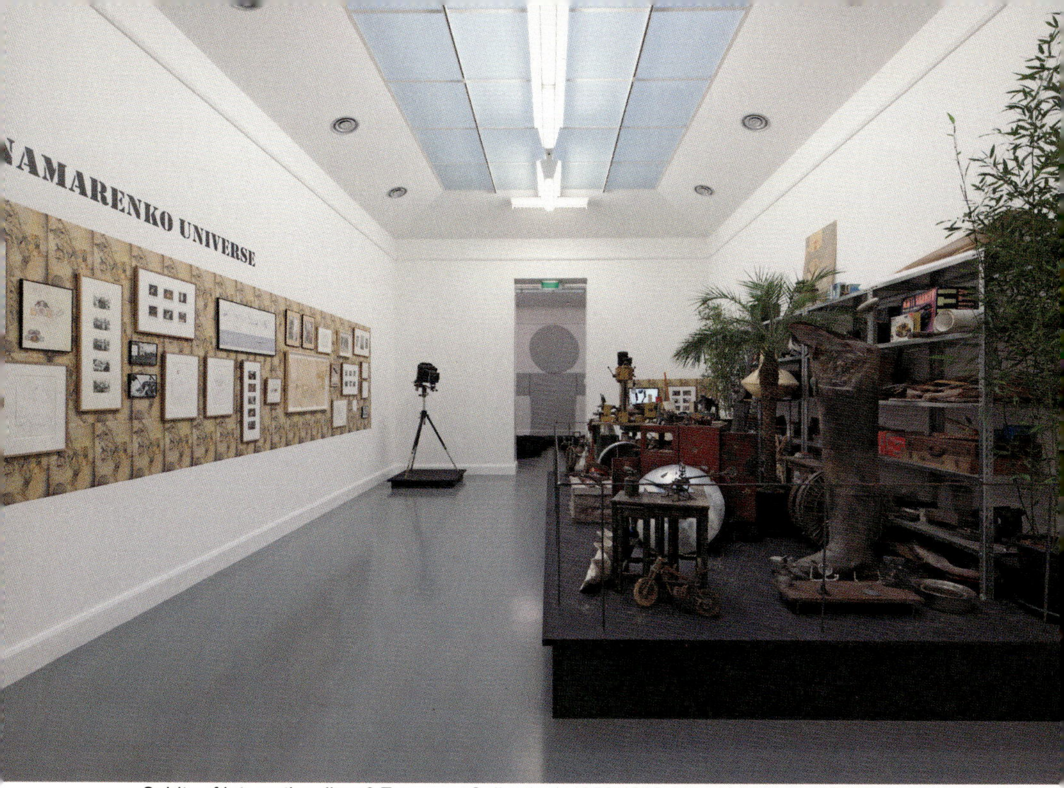

Spirits of Internationalism 6 European Collections 1956-1986, Vanabbemuseum 2012

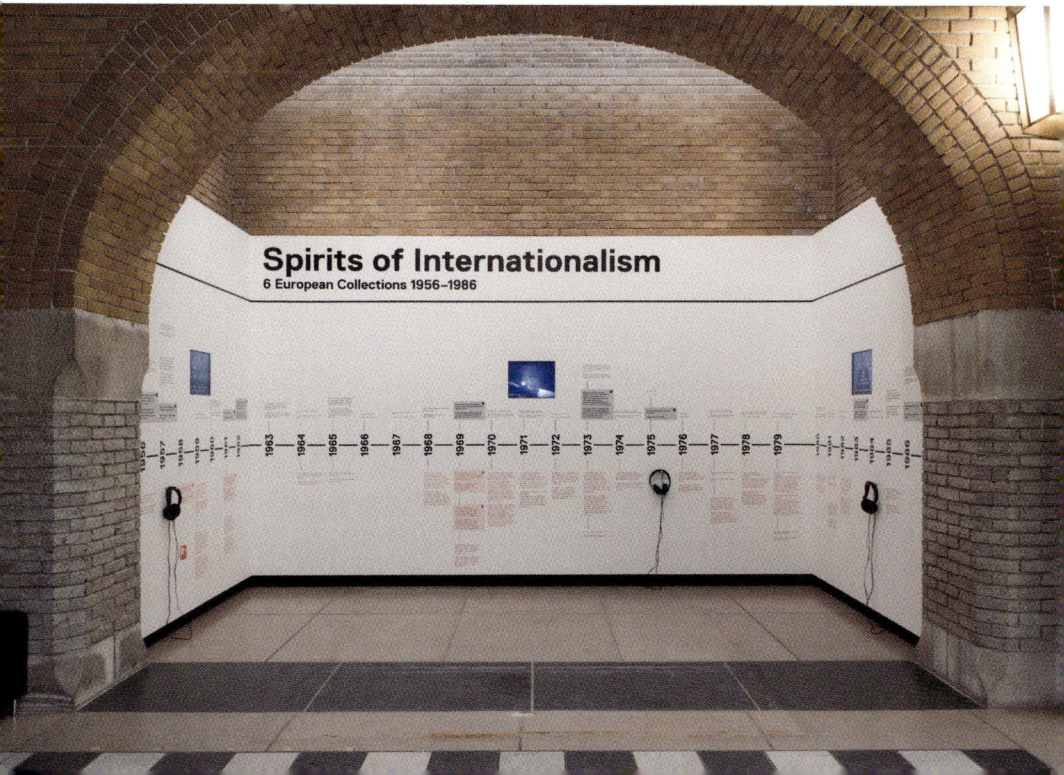

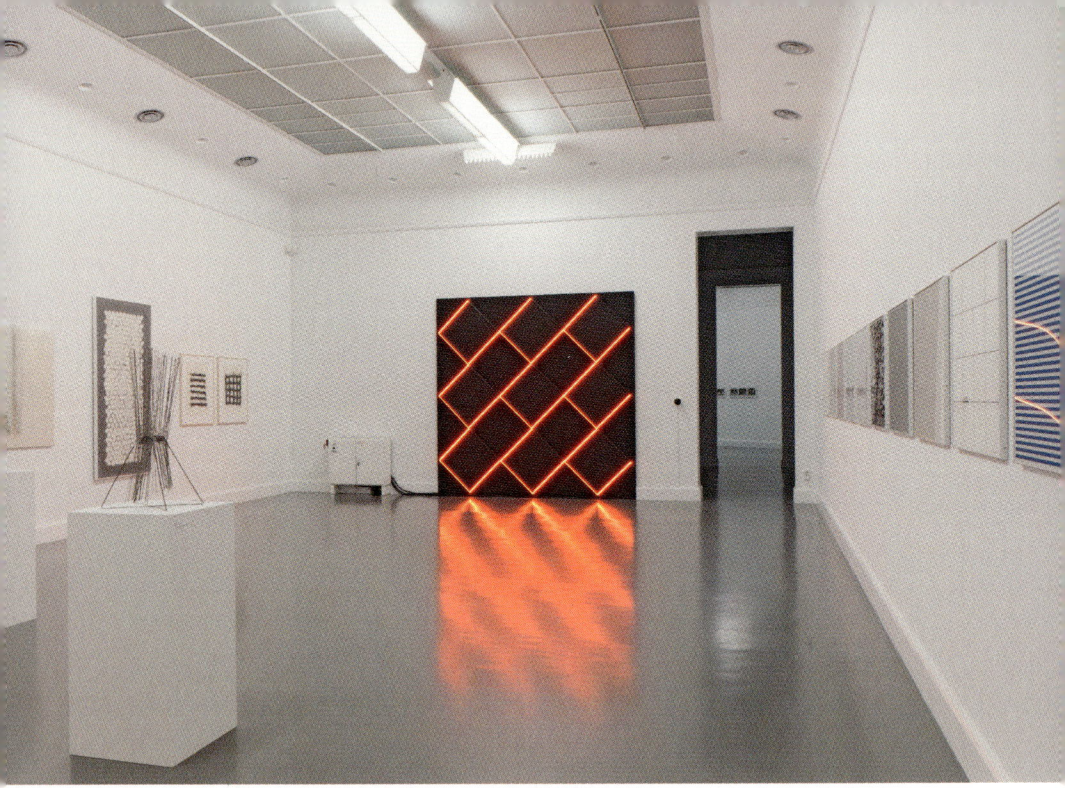

Spirits of Internationalism 6 European Collections 1956-1986, Vanabbemuseum 2012

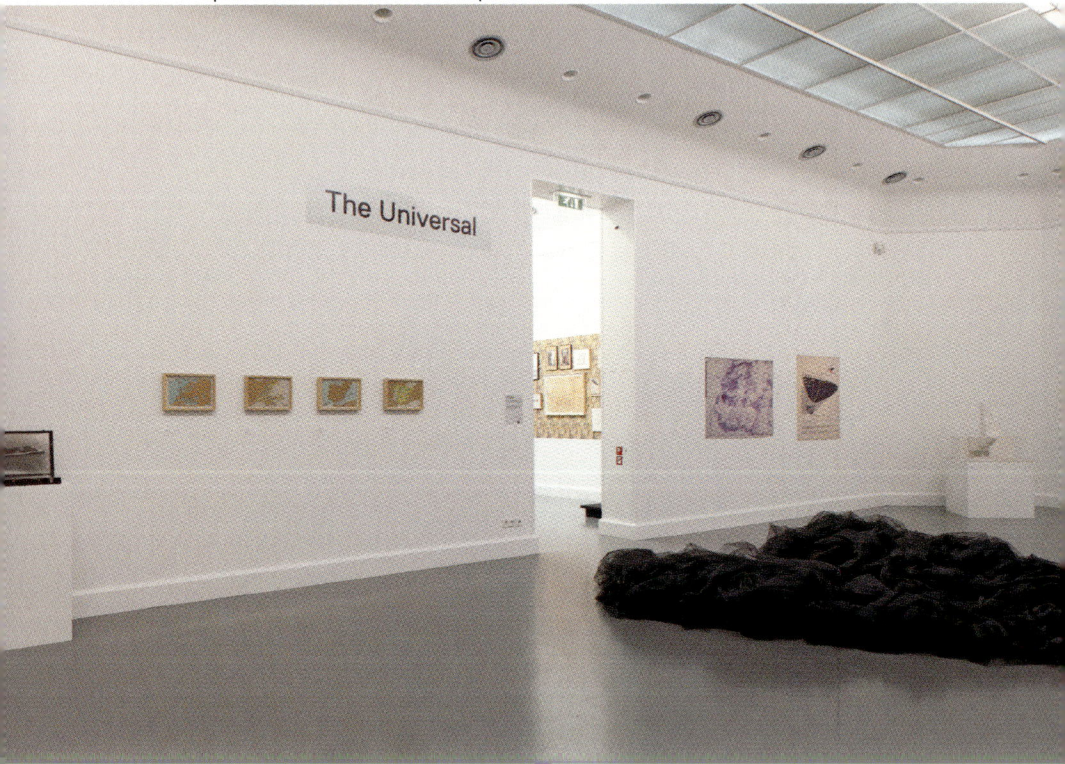

Contributors

Nancy Adajania is a cultural theorist and independent curator based in Bombay. She is co-artistic director of the 9th Gwangju Biennale, 2012. She has written and lectured extensively on transcultural art practices and the relationship between art and the public sphere at Documenta 11, Kassel; ZKM, Karlsruhe; Transmediale, Berlin; Kuenstlerhaus Vienna; Gulbenkian Foundation, Lisbon; and The Danish Contemporary Art Foundation, Copenhagen, among others. Adajania was Editor-in-Chief of *Art India* magazine and also edited the monograph *Shilpa Gupta* (Prestel, 2010). She is co-author, with Ranjit Hoskote, of "The Dialogues Series," an on-going series of conversations with contemporary Indian artists (Popular Prakashan/foundation b&g, 2011). She was research scholar at BAK basis voor aktuele kunst, Utrecht (2010–2011).

Inke Arns is curator and artistic director of Hartware MedienKunstVerein (www.hmkv.de) in Dortmund, Germany, since 2005. She has worked internationally as an independent curator, writer and theorist specializing in media art, net cultures, and Eastern Europe since 1993. She studied Russian literature, Eastern European studies, political science, and art history in Berlin and Amsterdam (1988–1996) and in 2004 obtained her PhD from the Humboldt University in Berlin. She has curated exhibitions at Moderna galerija, Ljubljana; Künstlerhaus Bethanien, Berlin; Karl Ernst Osthaus Museum, Hagen; Museum of Contemporary Art, Belgrade; KW Institute for Contemporary Art, Berlin; Videotage, Hong Kong; Museum of Contemporary Art Vojvodina, Novi Sad; Centre for Contemporary Art Zamek Ujazdowski, Warsaw; Centre for Contemporary Art "Znaki Czasu", Toruń; and Muzeum Sztuki, Łodz. She has been teaching at universities and art academies in Berlin, Leipzig, Zurich, and Rotterdam, and has lectured and published internationally. Her books include *Neue Slowenische Kunst (NSK) – eine Analyse ihrer künstlerischen Strategien im Kontext der 1980er Jahre in Jugoslawien* (2002), *Netzkulturen* (2002), *Objects in the mirror may be closer than they appear! Die Avantgarde im Rückspiegel* (2004). www.inkearns.de.

Zdenka Badovinac is a curator and writer, who has served since 1993 as Director of the Moderna galerija in Ljubljana, comprised since 2011 of two locations: the Museum of Modern Art and the Museum of Contemporary Art Metelkova. In her work, Badovinac highlights the difficult processes of redefining history alongside different avant-garde traditions within contemporary art. Badovinac's first exhibition to address these issues was *Body and the East—From the 1960s to the Present* (1998). She also initiated the first Eastern European art collection, Arteast 2000+. Since 2011, this collection has been permanently exhibited in the new Museum of Contemporary Art Metelkova. She has served as president of CIMAM since 2010.

Boris Buden is a writer and cultural critic living in Berlin. He studied philosophy in Zagreb (Croatia) and received his PhD in cultural theory from the Humboldt University, Berlin. In the 1990s he was editor of *Arkzin* magazine, Zagreb. His essays and articles cover topics related to philosophy, politics, and cultural and art criticism. Among his translations into Croatian are some of the most important works of Sigmund Freud. He is co-editor of several books and author of *Barikade*, Zagreb 1996/97, *Kaptolski Kolodvor*, Beograd 2001, *Der Schacht von Babel*, Berlin 2004, Übersetzung: Das Versprechen eines Begriffs (The Promise of a Concept), Vienna 2008, *Zone des Übergangs*, Frankfurt/Main 2009.

Jan Ceuleers (1952) spent his youth in Brussels, and has lived and worked in Antwerp since 1970. He is active as an antiquarian bookseller and an independent scholar in the field of the avant-garde. He is the author of, among others, the monographs *Georges Vantongerloo* (1996) and *René Magritte, Rue Esseghem 135, Jette-Brussels* (1999), portraits of George Wittenborn (2007) and Leo Dohmen (2009²), an essay on Grandville – *Un autre monde* (2011), and *Paul Van Hoeydonck – from abstract to white-on-white* (2011). He is the curator of *new art in antwerp 1958–1962*, a series of five exhibitions at M HKA, Antwerp, 2012–2013, and author of the accompanying book and brochures.

Eda Čufer is a drama advisor, curator and writer. In 1984 she co-founded the Ljubljana-based art collective NSK. In addition to her work with the NSK group she has also collaborated with the dance group En-Knap and with Marko Peljhan's "Project Atol". Recently, she co-authored a book on dance notation, *Chronotopographies of Dance* (Emanat, 2010). With the support of a grant from the Andy Warhol Foundation she is now completing a new book, *Art as Mousetrap*, which deals with the Shakespearean stratagem of "theater within theater," and its relevance for contemporary performative and activist art. Since 2005 she has been living in the USA, and teaching at the Maine College of Art.

Bart De Baere (b. 1960) is director of M HKA, the Antwerp Contemporary Art Museum. Previously he was curator of Documenta IX and at the Ghent Museum of Contemporary Art. He has been active as a writer and exhibition maker, realizing, among others, *This is the Show and the Show is many Things* in 1994, one of the exhibitions that initiated processual and relational practices in exhibition making. He assisted in the founding of the Johannesburg Biennial and is a co-founder of the Brussels Kunsthalle Wiels. He has also served as advisor to the Flemish Minister of Culture.

José Díaz Cuyás is a lecturer in Aesthetics at La Laguna University (Tenerife, Canary Islands). He curated *Los Encuentros de Pamplona 1972: fin de fiesta del arte experimental* (MNCARS, 2009) and *Ir y venir de Valcárcel Medina* (Fundació Antoni Tàpies, 2002). Since the 1980s, he has lectured and published articles in catalogues and the specialist press. He is director of Acto ediciones and the journal *Acto: revista de pensamiento artístico contemporáneo* (revista-acto.net).

Charles Esche is a curator and writer. He is Director of Van Abbemuseum, Eindhoven and co-director of Afterall Journal and Books based at Central Saint Martins, London. In the last years, he has focused on museum and exhibition histories and published on experimental institutionalism. He has (co-)curated international exhibitions including: *It doesn't always have to be beautiful, unless it's beautiful*, National Art Gallery of Kosovo, Prishtinë, 2012; *Strange and Close*, CAPC, Bordeaux, 2011, both with Galit Eilat; 5th U3 triennial, Ljubljana, 2010; 2nd and 3rd Riwaq Biennale, Ramallah, Palestine, 2007–2009 with Reem Fadda and Khalil Rabah; 9th Istanbul Biennial 2005 with Vasif Kortun, Esra Sarigedik Öktem and November Paynter; and 4th Gwangju Biennale, 2002 with Hou Hanru.

Cristina Freire is a curator and Associate Professor at the Museum of Contemporary Art, University of São Paulo. Among other exhibitions she served as curator for *Conceptual Art and Conceptualisms. The 1970's in the Museum of Contemporary Art*

Collection, São Paulo (2000); and *Experimental place for freedom: the Museum of Contemporary Art in the 1970s* (2002). During the years 2005–2006 she was co-curator of the 27th Bienal de São Paulo. She was also co-curator of *Subversive practices*, Kunstverein Stuttgart (2009) and *Clemente Padín: Word, Action and Risk*, Weserburg Museum, Bremen (2010), among others. Her books include: *Poéticas do Processo. Arte Conceitual no Museu* (*Poetics of the Process. Conceptual art in the Museum*), Ed. Iluminuras, S. Paulo 1999; *Arte Conceitual* (*Conceptual Art*), Jorge Zahar Editor, Rio de Janeiro 2006; *Paulo Bruscky. Arte, Arquivo e Utopia* (*Paulo Bruscky. Art, Archive and Utopia*), CEPE, Recife 2007]; *Conceitualismos do Sul/Sur* (*Conceptualisms from the South*), Annablume, São Paulo 2009). Cristina Freire is the Vice-Director of the Museum of Contemporary Art, University of São Paulo, Brazil (MAC USP)

Teresa Grandas studied History of Art, and is curator of temporary exhibitions at the Museu d'Art Contemporani de Barcelona (MACBA). She has curated a number of exhibitions, including: *Utopia is possible, ICSID. Eivissa, 1971*, 2012 (co-curator); *Ángels Ribé. In the Labyrinth, 1969–1984*, 2011; *Parallel Benet Rossell* (co-curator), 2010; *Palazuelo. Working Process* (co-curator), 2006–2008; and the collaborative research project *Desacuerdos. Sobre arte, políticas y esfera pública en el Estado español* (*Disagreements. On art, politics and the public sphere in Spain*) (co-curator), 2005.

Daniel Grúň (b. 1977, Piešťany, Slovak Republic) is an historian, curator and writer. He works as a lecturer at the Academy of Fine Arts and Design in Bratislava and as a researcher of the Július Koller Society. He is author of *Archeology of Art Criticism. Slovak Art of the 1960s and its Interpretations* (Slovart, 2009). In 2010 he won a working grant from the Igor Zabel Award for Culture and Theory. He was co-initiator of an exhibition and research platform dealing with non-institutionalized culture of the 1970s and 1980s in the former Eastern Europe. In 2012 he won a Fulbright scholarship at the City University of New York, and currently focuses on the relation between art institutions and artists' archives.

Ksenya Gurshtein received her Ph.D. in the History of Art from the University of Michigan in 2011 for her dissertation entitled *TransStates: Conceptual Art in Eastern Europe and the Limits of Utopia*. She has published articles on the work of the

OHO collective, as well as the Russian artists Vitaly Komar and Alexander Melamid, in English, Russian, and German. She is currently the Andrew W. Mellon Postdoctoral Curatorial Fellow at the National Gallery of Art in Washington, D.C., and has previously held a Getty Research Institute Predoctoral Fellowship, as well as internships at the Hirschorn and Hamburger Bahnhof museums.

Jan Hoet (b. 1936) was the first director of the Ghent Museum of Contemporary Art, MHK Gent, founded in 1975 (later SMAK, in 1999), where he stayed until 2003. After that he founded the MARTa Museum in Herford. Hoet is credited with changing the position of contemporary art in Belgium and giving it a broader public appeal. His exhibition *Art in Europe after '68* in 1980, positioning the museum "Chambres d'Amis" in 1986 with art works in private houses linking them to the museum, became the model for many route-exhibitions to follow. In 1992 he was director of Documenta IX.

Christian Höller is the editor of *springerin—Hefte für Gegenwartskunst* and has written extensively on art and cultural theory. Between 2002 and 2007 he was Visiting Professor at the École supérieure des beaux-arts in Geneva. He has curated the special programs *Pop Unlimited?* (2000), and *No Wave New York 1976–1984* (2010) at the International Short Film Festival Oberhausen; and in 2011 co-curated the exhibition *Hauntings – Ghost Box Media* (Medienturm Graz) as well as the accompanying concert series *Sonic Spectres*. In 2001, he edited the anthology *Pop Unlimited?* (Turia + Kant, Vienna); in 2005, the volume *Techno-Visionen* (Folio, Vienna/Bolzano; co-editor) and the catalogue *Hans Weigand* (Walther König, Cologne). His volume of interviews *Time Action Vision: Conversations in Cultural Studies, Theory, and Activism* was published by JRP | Ringier, Zürich / Les presses du réel, Dijon in 2010.

Vitaly Komar was born in 1943 in Moscow. In 1967 he graduated from Stroganov Art School in Moscow, Russia (former U.S.S.R). In the early 1970s, together with Alex Melamid, he founded the Sots-Art movement—conceptual pop art based on Soviet visual propaganda. Beginning in 1972 they began combining Sots-Art with conceptual eclecticism. In 1974 he participated in the scandalously famous "Bulldozer" outdoor art show where his works, together with works of other unofficial artists, were destroyed by the authorities. Since 1978 he resides and works in

New York. In 1982 he received the National Endowment for the Arts award. Before 2003 he worked in collaboration with Alex Melamid, as well as with Fluxus member Charlotte Moorman (1975–1976), with Andy Warhol (1979), with the elephant Renee (1994), with the chimpanzee Mikki (1998), and with the masses and public opinion polling companies. Selected exhibitions: Fruitmarket Gallery (Edinburgh, 1985–1986); Documenta 8 (Kassel, 1987); Venice Biennial (1997 and 1999); Moscow Biennale (2007); Ronald Feldman gallery (New York, 2009).

Lars Bang Larsen is an art historian and curator based in Frankfurt am Main and Copenhagen. His PhD, *A History of Irritated Material*, dealt with psychedelic concepts in neo-avant-garde art. His books include *The Model for a Qualitative Society 1968* (2010); he has co-curated exhibitions such as *Populism* (2005), *La insurrección invisible de un millón de mentes* (2005) and *A Society Without Qualities* (2013).

Bartomeu Marí (b. 1966, Eivissa) holds a degree in Philosophy from the Universitat de Barcelona and worked as a curator at the Fondation pour l'Architecture in Brussels (1989–1993). He was exhibition curator at IVAM-Centre Julio González in Valencia (1994–1995) and Director of Witte de With – Centre for contemporary art in Rotterdam (1996–2001). He served as Chief Curator at MACBA from 2004 until 2008, when he was appointed Director of the Museum. Bartomeu Marí has curated exhibitions by artists such as Raoul Hausmann, Lawrence Weiner, Rita McBride, Eulàlia Valldosera, Francis Picabia, Frederik Kiesler, Marcel Broodthaers, Michel François, and Francis Alÿs, among others. He has written numerous articles about contemporary art and is currently working on a volume of essays about the art of our time.

Marga van Mechelen (b. 1953) is Assistant Professor in Modern and Contemporary Art at the University of Amsterdam. She is a member of ASCA (Amsterdam School for Cultural Analysis) and currently a member of the board of AICA Nederland. She has published widely on conceptual, performance and installation art and on art historiographical, visual semiotic and psycho-semiotic subjects. She is the author of *De Appel. Performances, Installations, Video, Projects, 1975–1983* (2006). Her latest book, from 2011, is a monograph about the leading figure of the Dutch Zero (NUL) Movement, Henk Peeters (*Echt Peeters, realist—avant-gardist*). Forthcoming is: *Art at Large* (ArtEZ Press) on performance and installation art.

Armin Medosch has been working in media art and network
culture as a practitioner, curator and writer since the 1980s.
Living in Austria, Germany and the UK, he has been shaping the practice and discourse on art and technology as editor,
exhibition curator, conference organizer, critic and theorist. He
has initiated and co-curated the exhibitions *Waves* (Riga 2006,
Dortmund 2008) and is currently preparing the follow-up project
Fields (Riga 2014). In 2012 he was awarded a Ph.D. in Arts and
Computational Technology at Goldsmiths, University of London.

Viktor Misiano (b. 1957, Moscow) was a curator of contemporary art at the Pushkin National Museum of Fine Arts in Moscow, from 1980 to 1990. From 1992 to 1997 he served as director of the Center for Contemporary Art (CAC) in Moscow. He
curated the Russian participation at the Istanbul Biennale (1992),
the Venice Biennale (1995, 2003), the São Paulo Biennale (2002,
2004), and the Valencia Biennale (2001). He was on the curatorial team for the Manifesta I in Rotterdam in 1996. In 1993 he
co-founded the *Moscow Art Magazine* (Moscow) and has served
as editor-in-chief since. In 2003 he was a founder of the *Manifesta Journal: Journal of Contemporary Curatorship* (Amsterdam)
and has been an editor there since 2011. In 2005 he founded and
curated the first Central Asia Pavilion at the Venice Biennale.
In 2007 he realized the large-scale exhibition project *Progressive Nostalgia: Art from the Former USSR* in the Centro per
l'arte contemporanea, Prato (Italy), the Benaki Museum, Athens,
KUMU, Tallinn, and KIASMA, Helsinki. His latest exhibition
project is "*Impossible Community*" realized 2011 in the Moscow
Museum for Modern Art, which was awarded the national "Innovation" prize for "best exhibition of the year". From October
2010 he is Chairman of the International Foundation Manifesta.
He holds an honorary doctorate from the Helsinki University for
Art and Design. He lives in Moscow (Russia) and Ceglie Mes-
sapica (Italy).

Piotr Piotrowski is professor at the Art History Department,
Adam Mickiewicz University, Poznan, and its former chair
(1999–2000). He was also director of the National Museum in
Warsaw (2009–2010), and visiting professor at the Humboldt
University (2011–2012), Warsaw University (2011), Bard College,
USA (2001), Hebrew University in Jerusalem (2003), as well as
a fellow at CASVA, Washington D.C. (1989–1990), the Institute
for Advanced Study, Princeton (2000), Collegium Budapest

(2005–2006), and the Clark Art Institute (2009). He is the author of a dozen books including: *In the Shadow of Yalta* (2009), and *Art and Democracy in Post-Communist Europe* (2012).

Bojana Piškur is a writer and curator, and works in the Museum of Contemporary Art Metelkova (Museum of Modern Art in Ljubljana). Her main research topics deal with experimental art forms, concepts and context in relation to wider socio-political environments. Related exhibitions and projects include *Museum in the Street* (with Zdenka Badovinac), Moderna galerija Ljubljana, 2008; *This is All Film, Experimental Film in Yugoslavia 1951–1991* (with Ana Janevski, Jurij Meden and Stevan Vuković), Moderna galerija Ljubljana, 2010; *Museum of Affects* (with Bartomeu Mari, Bart de Baere, Teresa Grandas and Leen de Backer), Museum of Contemporary Art Metelkova 2010. In 2006 she initiated "Radical Education," a project whose aim was "to translate" radical pedagogy into the sphere of artistic production, with education being conceived not merely as a model but also as a field of political participation.

Georg Schöllhammer is a writer, editor and curator based in Vienna, Austria. He is the founder of the journal *springerin – Hefte für Gegenwartskunst*, is head of tranzit.at and chairman of The Július Koller Society (Bratislava). As Editor-in-chief of Documenta 12 in Kassel, Schöllhammer has conceived and directed documenta 12 magazines. Schöllhammer co-curated Manifesta 8 (2010) and directed Viennafair (2011). He is a member of the boards of Kontakt – The Art Collection of Erste Group, and steirischer herbst. Recent and forthcoming exhibitions and projects include: *Imagination of the Political Subject* (Vienna Festival 2013), *Sovjet Modern* (AZW, Vienna 2012), *Moments* (ZKM, 2012), *Sweet Sixties* (2011, ongoing), *KwieKulik* (BWA Wroclaw, PL, 2009), the 6th Gyumri International Biennial of Contemporary Art, (Gyumri, ARM, 2008) and *Void* (Tanzquartier Vienna 2008).

Branka Stipančić is a writer, editor and freelance curator living in Zagreb, Croatia, and graduated in art history and literature, Faculty of Philosophy, University of Zagreb. Former positions include curator at the Museum of Contemporary Art Zagreb 1983–1993, and director of Soros Center for Contemporary Art, Zagreb 1993–1996. Major shows include the Mladen Stilinović retrospective *Sing!*, Museum Ludwig, Budapest, 2011, *You are kindly invited to attend*, Kunstsaele, Berlin, 2010, and

Close

a Mangelos retrospective at Museu Serralves, Porto, 2003. Her books include *Mišljenje je forma energije* (Daf, Zagreb, 2007), *Vlado Martek – Poetry in Action* (DelVe, Zagreb, 2010), *Mladen Stilinović – Artist's Books* (Platform Garanti, Istanbul, Van Abbemuseum, Eindhoven, 2007), *Josip Vaništa – The Time of Gorgona and Post-Gorgona* (Kratis, Zagreb, 2007), *Mangelos nos. 1 to 9 ½* (Museu Serralves, Porto, 2003).

Steven ten Thije (b. 1980) studied art history and philosophy at the University of Amsterdam, and is a research curator working on a PhD on the genealogy of the exhibition curator at the University in Hildesheim, supported by the Van Abbemuseum in Eindhoven. He recently co-curated "Spirits of Internationalism" (2012), part of L'Internationale (http://internacionala.mg-lj.si), and was part of the organizing team for "Play Van Abbe" (2009–2011). He is also coordinator of "The Autonomy Project" (www.theautonomyproject.org) and has published various articles and reviews, among them *Exhibiting the New Art,* "Op Losse Schroeven" and "When Attitudes Become Form 1969" (2010).

Wim Van Mulders (Aalst, Belgium) graduated in art history at the University Ghent on a study of Paul Klee and his color theory. From 1972 to 2005 he as a lecturer in Modern and Contemporary Art at The Royal Academy of Fine Arts (KASK), School of Arts of University College Ghent; he also taught Art Philosophy at the same institution. His scholarship and art criticism writing has appeared in *Artforum, Art Press* (Paris), *+ - O* (Plus moins Zéro), *Journal d'Art Contemporain* (Genval/Brussels), *De Witte Raaf* (Brussels), *Kunst & Museumjournaal* (Amsterdam), *Streven: A Journal of Art and Culture* (Antwerp), *Kunst(H)Art* (Antwerp), *Kunst & Cultuuragenda* (Bozar, Brussels). He has published on Joseph Beuys, Marcel Broodthaers, James Lee Byars, Joseph Kosuth, Fluxus, Jef Geys, Gilbert & George, Bernd Lohaus, Mario Merz, A. R. Penck, Sigmar Polke, Ben Vautier, Jeff Wall and others.

Immanuel Wallerstein is Senior Research Scholar at Yale University. He is the author of *The Modern World-System*, and most recently, *European Universalism: The Rhetoric of Power*. He was the director of the Fernand Braudel Center (1976–2005), president of the International Sociological Association (1994–1998), and chair of the international Gulbenkian Commission for the Restructuring of the Social Sciences, which published a report entitled *Open the Social Sciences*.

L'Internationale – Post-War Avant-Gardes
Between 1957 and 1986

Published and Distributed by JRP|Ringier, Zurich

Edited by Christian Höller, for the L'Internationale
Project Network:
Moderna galerija Ljubljana, MACBA Barcelona,
Van Abbemuseum Eindhoven, M HKA Antwerp,
Július Koller Society Bratislava/Vienna

EDITOR
Christian Höller

COPY EDITOR
Jeff Bickert, ARK

PROJECT COORDINATOR
Ana Mizerit

DESIGN
New Collectivism

TYPEFACE
Times New Roman

PRINT AND BINDING
R-tisk

Special thanks to
Evi Bert, Mariana Camacho, Christine Clinckx,
Meritxell Colina, Daniël Dewaele, Clàudia Faus,
Jan Haerynck, Andreja Hribernik, Anders Kreuger,
Antoni Mercader, Ina Mertens, Ana Mizerit,
Nuria Monclús, Alexandra Obukhova, Gemma Planell,
Clara Plasencia, Pedro G. Romero, Daniel Spoerri,
Jan De Vree

Published and distributed by

JRP|Ringier
Limmatstrasse 270
CH-8005 Zurich
T +41 (0) 43 311 27 50
F +41 (0) 43 311 27 51
E info@jrp-ringier.com
www.jrp-ringier.com

ISBN 978-3-03764-311-2

JRP|Ringier publications are available internationally at selected bookstores and from the following distribution partners:

Switzerland
AVA Verlagsauslieferung AG, Centralweg 16, CH-8910 Affoltern a.A., verlagsservice@ava.ch, www.ava.ch

Germany and Austria
Vice Versa Vertrieb, Immanuelkirchstrasse 12, D-10405 Berlin, info@vice-versa-vertrieb.de
www.vice-versa-vertrieb.de

France
Les presses du réel, 35 rue Colson, F-21000 Dijon, info@lespressesdureel.com, www.lespressesdureel.com

UK and other European countries
Cornerhouse Publications, 70 Oxford Street, UK-Manchester M1 5NH, publications@cornerhouse.org
www.cornerhouse.org/books

USA, Canada, Asia, and Australia
ARTBOOK|D.A.P., 155 Sixth Avenue, 2nd Floor, USA-New York, NY 10013, dap@dapinc.com
www.artbook.com

For a list of our partner bookshops or for any general questions, please contact JRP|Ringier directly at info@jrp-ringier.com, or visit our homepage www.jrp-ringier.com for further information about our program.

This project is supported by:

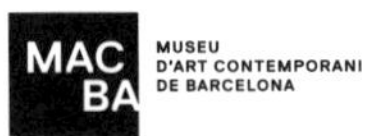

MUSEU
D'ART CONTEMPORANI
DE BARCELONA

MG+MSUM

M HKA

JÚLIUS   KOLLER

SOCIETY

vanabbemuseum

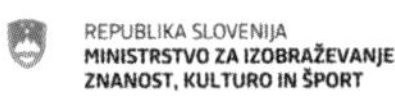

REPUBLIKA SLOVENIJA
MINISTRSTVO ZA IZOBRAŽEVANJE,
ZNANOST, KULTURO IN ŠPORT

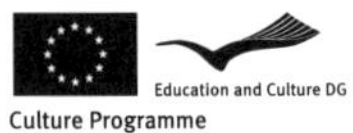

Education and Culture DG
Culture Programme